SUCCESSFUL INCLUSION

SUCCESSFUL INCLUSION

Practical Strategies for
a Shared Responsibility

Carol A. Kochhar
The George Washington University

Lynda L. West
The George Washington University

Juliana M. Taymans
The George Washington University

MERRILL,
an imprint of Prentice Hall

Upper Saddle River, New Jersey   *Columbus, Ohio*

Library of Congress Cataloging-in-Publication Data

Kochhar, Carol.
    Successful inclusion : practical strategies for a shared
responsibility / Carol A. Kochhar, Lynda L. West, Juliana M. Taymans.
        p. cm.
    Includes bibliographical references and index.
    ISBN 0-13-921172-1
    1. Inclusive education—United States—Handbooks, manuals, etc.
2. Handicapped children—Education—United States—Handbooks,
manuals, etc. I. West, Lynda L. II Taymans. Juliana M.
III. Kochhar, Carol. Handbook for successful inclusion. IV. Title.
LC1201.K63   2000   99-40336
371.9'046—dc21

Editor: Ann Castel Davis
Production Editor: Sheryl Glicker Langner
Production Coordination: Ann Mohan, WordCrafters Editorial Services, Inc.
Design Coordinator: Karrie Converse-Jones
Cover Designer: Dean Barrett
Cover Photo: Arthur Tilley/FPG International LLC
Production Manager: Laura Messerly
Electronic Text Management: Karen Bretz
Editorial Assistant: Pat Grogg
Director of Marketing: Kevin Flanagan
Marketing Manager: Meghan Shepherd
Marketing Coordinator: Krista Groshong

This book was set in Optima by Maryland Composition Company, Inc., and was printed and
bound by Victor Graphics. The cover was printed by Phoenix Color Corp.

© 2000 by Prentice-Hall, Inc.
Pearson Education
Upper Saddle River, New Jersey 07458

Printed in the United States of America

10 9 8 7 6 5 4 3 2 1

ISBN: 0-13-921172-1

Prentice-Hall International (UK) Limited, *London*
Prentice-Hall of Australia Pty. Limited, *Sydney*
Prentice-Hall of Canada, Inc., *Toronto*
Prentice-Hall Hispanoamericana, S.A., *Mexico*
Prentice-Hall of India Private Limited, *New Delhi*
Prentice-Hall of Japan, Inc., *Tokyo*
Prentice-Hall (Singapore) Pte. Ltd., *Singapore*
Editora Prentice-Hall do Brasil, Ltda., *Rio de Janeiro*

Preface

in·clude (in·klood). v. to have or regard or treat as part of a whole.

Inclusion of those who have been left outside is the first step in integration. The word derives from the Latin for shutting the door after someone has come into the house. Some people think that you can speak of integration without inclusion. This seems like nonsense to us. Integration begins only when each child belongs.

—O'Brien & Forest, 1989

Let no child be demeaned, nor have his wonder diminished, because of our ignorance or inactivity. Let no child be deprived of discovery, because we lack the resources to discover his problem. Let no child ever doubt himself or his mind because we are unsure of our commitment.

—Alan Martin, 1993

ADDRESSING THE TOUGH QUESTIONS: WHY THIS BOOK WAS WRITTEN. There are so many books, pamphlets, and reports on inclusion, what would motivate anyone to write another book on the subject? This book represents our efforts to clear a different path toward understanding inclusion. Over the past two decades we have struggled to initiate and implement inclusive practices in schools and community-based organizations. We have overcome our own doubts and fears, and we have helped our general and special education colleagues with the same struggles. Having developed and taught graduate level courses on inclusive practices over two decades; used countless textbooks, journal articles, and policy documents; and discussed textbook content needs with students and colleagues from a variety of disciplines, we have concluded that substantial improvements are needed in the organization and presentation of material on the subject. We have also concluded that there are several emerging issues and content areas that have not

been adequately addressed in the major texts on the subject.

First, the movement of children and youth into more inclusive classrooms and settings requires much more than cooperation between school and community agencies. Rather, a comprehensive overhaul of our educational and transition preparation systems is needed to better support youth with disabilities along their educational path and at each of the critical transition stages.

Second, in schools everywhere, growing populations of students with academic and social learning needs are adding to the challenge of teaching in the general education classroom and helping youth prepare for transition to responsible adulthood. Educators and support service personnel are concerned with the successful social development, educational progress, and transition of students with disabilities from preschool to postsecondary education and adult life. They generally agree that educators must end the dual tracks of special and regular education and create a unified system. Educators today are expected to develop educational programs that can serve diverse learners, including those with disabilities, those who are at risk for school failure, former school dropouts, students with limited English proficiency, teen parents, and many others. In some school systems today, these special populations represent a majority of the student population. Professionals who want to contribute to improved educational outcomes for students with disabilities must acquire a higher level of sensitivity to the needs of diverse ethnic and cultural groups and to the needs of various disability populations. They must achieve a greater understanding of how cultural orientation affects students' attitudes toward education, work, and careers. Daunting is the challenge of assisting the entire spectrum of diverse students in the passage through school and into responsible adult life.

Third, in a responsive and inclusive education and transition system, practitioners hold as the highest principle a belief in choices and in self-determination in life's pathways. Self-determined individuals should be actively engaged in the decision-making process, connecting present educational experiences with future goals and visions. The need to clearly link self-determination concepts, student rights and responsibilities, academic and career-vocational development, and individualized educational planning is sorely lacking in current texts.

Fourth, in implementing inclusive practices for special learners, general education teachers are moving to center stage. Although there are special education consultants, team teachers, and teacher aides, the responsibility for achievement and progress of students with disabilities is more clearly falling upon the shoulders of general education teachers. Teachers are called upon to restructure their classrooms to include students with more diverse needs and at the same time to reorient their teaching to meet new curriculum standards and to improve student performance on state standardized tests.

GENERAL EDUCATORS ARE ESSENTIAL TO THE PROCESS. General educators have recently indicated that they feel left out of the process of planning for and implementing inclusion in their schools, that they have not had a strong voice in shaping the inclusion debate (Putnam, 1993). General educators need answers to the following questions:

1. Does inclusion really work, and how is success defined?
2. How are the programs implemented?
3. Will I need more training?
4. Will I have adequate help to teach these students? Must I have different expectations for these students?
5. Will my other students need training or special preparation?
6. How can I enlist the expertise and help of the special educator?
7. What kinds of adaptations can I make?

In addition, general education teachers want answers to more difficult questions:

1. How do I teach children with diverse abilities when my education program did not prepare me to teach them?
2. What is appropriate placement?
3. How many students with disabilities should be placed into a regular class?
4. Will my school still provide a continuum of services for more needy students?
5. Will there be a negative effect on my other students, and will they be shortchanged?
6. Will I have the resources I need to make the accommodations required for students with disabilities?
7. Where will the money come from for extra materials, equipment, technology accommodations, or support staff?
8. Will my class composition or class size change if I take students with disabilities?
9. Do the benefits outweigh the costs?

The concerns of general education teachers should be squarely and honestly addressed if they are to be prepared to manage and teach in inclusive classrooms.

AN INCLUSION BILL OF RIGHTS. The new century is dawning, and the journey toward integration of all children and youth within their community schools has only just begun. The inclusion of children with disabilities into regular classes has accelerated in the past decade, and in many places it has occurred too quickly and without adequate planning for restructuring. There is a growing concern by teachers, special educators, and administrators that many ineffective inclusion policies are being implemented. These efforts are failing to provide the necessary supportive services that students with disabilities need when they are placed into regular classrooms. On the other hand, there are many models of very effective inclusion. It is these models of *effective* inclusion upon which this book will focus. The authors wish to provide the reader with an understanding of the possibilities and potential of inclusive philosophy and practices for the benefit of *all children.*

Many aspects of decision making about how inclusion will be implemented have not been adequately addressed in most texts or in the preparation of special or general educators. General education teachers have commonly been left out of site-based decisions about including students with disabilities in their classrooms. Therefore, there is a need to address their concerns about their ability to ensure success of students placed into inclusive classrooms. The rights of children with disabilities must be protected under law, but this protection also depends upon reconciling these needs with the clashing needs or rights of others, including parents, teachers, and administrators, in a manner that makes the promise and process of inclusion a rational and effective one. We take the position that the differing needs of students, teachers, parents, and administrators need not clash, but are complementary. We believe that considering the rights and needs of one group at the expense of another jeopardizes the inclusion process and its quality. All are essential to the process. (More details about the Inclusion Bill of Rights can be found on page 30).

WHAT WE BELIEVE ABOUT WHAT WE WRITE. Collectively, the authors have conducted research in the field of special education and transition services for a period of more than 25 years. Fortunately, during this period, the fields of general and special education have made their greatest advances in understanding the needs of children and youths with disabilities and in the movement toward inclusive education. The content of the chapters in this book has been shaped by our direct experiences in public schools, collaboration with a variety of community agencies, public lectures, and writing over the past two decades, as well as by the many questions posed by students and practitioners.

We believe that educators and researchers have an obligation to let you as the reader know the results of our work and help wed the practical knowledge with current research knowledge in order to assist you as an implementor of inclusion. Because the practice of inclusion is very new, many of the conclusions about existing research are often more speculative than those in more established fields of study, but there is a growing body of knowledge.

Inclusive practice, however, also draws its legitimacy and momentum from philosophy, civil rights history, sociology, and educational law. For this reason, we also believe that researchers are only one of the voices that you need to hear from. The story of continuous advances toward inclusive education is best told by those who are active participants in the process, those who are experiencing it as students, as teachers, and as parents. These individuals are living in these environments every day and are most capable of understanding and communicating the nuances of the emerging and developing inclusive classrooms. One way in which we present this perspective is through cases based on real-life experiences.

In this book, we present prevailing as well as contrary views on inclusion, emphasizing those held by the majority of researchers and practitioners. We then explicitly express our own research-based views and positions on inclusion, which are summarized here:

1. Like the civil rights victory in the fight for equal access for racial and ethnic minorities to public education, inclusion of individuals with disabilities represents a final frontier in the progress of human rights. It is not just another passing phase in the flow of educational reform.

2. As does a democracy, inclusion as a philosophy and set of practices embodies ideals and goals that are continually reached for, though possibly never perfectly achieved.

3. The implementation of inclusion in schools and classrooms must be guided by standards and principles, the first of which is to do no harm. Inclusive placements and practices must always be developed with the goal of effecting measurable progress in a range of academic, vocational, social, and life skills.

4. Inclusion is not a new program or an experiment confined to one or two classrooms or one or two schools within a school district. Rather, it is a transformation in the way we think about structuring educational environments for all children and youth in all classrooms and schools, and in how we think about empowering them to construct their own destinies.

5. Inclusion is not a new program, but a new way of thinking about educating all children. There are many tested processes and strategies that can make it work effectively, and these strategies must be part of preservice and in-service training for teachers, administrators, and related service personnel.

6. Inclusion is a shared responsibility between students, teachers, parents, and administrators, and the needs and concerns of each group must be addressed. All are essential to the process.

7. The principles of special education—assessing learning needs, providing individualized instruction, addressing the unique learning styles of students, and adapting materials and curriculum and teaching methods—are important considerations for *all students*.

According to recent research, educating students with disabilities in integrated settings requires, first and foremost, a change in attitude from the view that the education of students with disabilities is different or special and the education of nondisabled students is "normal and expected" (Stainback & Stainback, 1992). Students with disabilities can be full and productive members of their communities if efforts are made to include them. The goals of public education are most likely to be reached when all children are encouraged to study, play, and grow together, learning from each other as well as from teachers. Inclusion of students with disabilities into the whole spectrum of educational opportunities provided in the community school represents a final frontier in the progress of human rights. Like the concept of democracy, it is an ideal that we must continuously reach for; we are *never* finished.

While this book introduces readers to the range of perspectives on inclusion, it does so in the context of a firm emphasis on the positive power and potential of inclusion. Students of inclusion need to be guided by a compelling and consistent message about the possibilities and authority for inclusion, if they are to become leaders who are confident about implementing its practices and teaching others. The authors assert that inclusion leaders must understand and appreciate the basic legal and civil rights foundations for inclusion practices, including the implications of recent changes in laws related to students with disabilities.

WHAT MAKES THIS BOOK DIFFERENT? This book is for individuals who want a resource that gets to the point and answers the questions most asked about inclusion of students with disabilities in general education. It is for educators who have been searching for a resource that is balanced enough to address the greatest concerns of teachers about inclusion and its effects on teaching and learning for all students. We have assembled in this book the information most relevant for teachers. Several books discuss inclusion in 300 to 500 pages or more, but we have tried to present the information simply and concisely. The purpose of this book is to guide general and special educators and related professionals in schools and school-linked agencies in meeting the challenge to better serve special learners in inclusive settings. The book emphasizes inclusion practices that work, practical strategies that can lead to successful inclusion at both the classroom and school levels, and techniques for overcoming barriers to inclusion.

The book is written in a user-friendly, question-and-answer format centered on practical inclusion issues. It offers solid, practical help, as well as a useful perspective for those challenged to provide educational opportunities for all. At the end of Parts One and Two are cases highlighting various aspects of inclusion. These cases provide real-life examples that can be used to apply the information and concepts in each of those sections.

Along with teachers and related personnel, school administrators will also find this book useful as an introduction and overview to the inclusion concept and process for all educators. The content of each part can be divided into material for staff development sessions, in-service themes, and workshop sessions. Practical resources are distributed throughout that will be helpful to teachers in understanding and discussing the idea of inclusion.

HOW TO USE THIS BOOK. To develop inclusion initiatives in a school, you will need to select a small group of teachers to spearhead and guide the inclusion process. These individuals must be carefully selected for their ability to act as knowledge and attitude leaders and to exert a positive influence on this important journey for a school. The selection of those individuals is critical to the success of the inclusion process and to the individual success of students who are its beneficiaries.

It is necessary to select teacher-leaders who

- Are open to learning.
- Are not afraid of change.
- Have the interpersonal skills to constructively negotiate change.
- Can inspire others.
- Can share the spotlight and encourage everyone to own the effort.
- Can resolve conflicts in a positive manner.
- Can offer support and praise to teachers in their efforts.
- Understand the need for reward and renewal.

Once identified, the cadre of teacher-leaders for inclusion should become members of the inclusion planning and implementation team. This book provides the necessary tools to help you plan for, implement, or improve the inclusion efforts in your classroom and school.

TO THE COLLEGE OR UNIVERSITY INSTRUCTOR. This book is also written for university instructors who want to teach the collaborative approach to inclusion. It is particularly useful for the instructor who

- Has a mixed group of students in classes (e.g., special educators, general educators, administrators, related services professionals).

- Wants to present different inclusion models and information about their effectiveness.
- Wants to introduce students to the range of different perspectives on inclusion, but in the context of a clear author emphasis on the positive power and potential of inclusion.
- Wants practical tools that both help students examine their own attitudes and beliefs about inclusion and are useful for applying inclusion principles and strategies in teaching and professional practices internships.
- Wants students to benefit from a practical, step-by-step approach to implementing inclusion in a classroom or school, with self-assessments of readiness for inclusion.
- Desires to use case studies to illustrate principles and strategies and perspectives.
- Needs a practical text that emphasizes inclusion practices that work, practical strategies that can lead to successful inclusion at the classroom and individual school level, and techniques for overcoming barriers to inclusion.
- Considers it important that students understand and appreciate the basic legal and civil rights foundations for inclusion practices.
- Needs a course introduction to inclusion that reflects the most current laws related to students with disabilities.

This book combines versatility, practicality, and the power of its positive message. It can be used for in-service training, university training, and for student field-based internships. It would be useful with either homogenous or mixed groups of student participants (e.g., special educators, general educators, administrators, and related services professionals).

This book does not focus on the special educator as the key implementor of inclusion or agent of change. It moves beyond the notion of collaboration to placing the primary responsibility for successful inclusion on the general education teacher and school administrators. In implementing inclusion, the general education teacher is at center stage. Though there are special education consultants, team teachers, and teacher aides, the main responsibility for creating inclusive classrooms for students with disabilities falls on the general education teacher. This book reflects a belief that inclusion is good for *all students,* and bases its strategies on this belief.

ACKNOWLEDGMENTS We are most thankful to our reviewers from around the country who provided in-depth and constructive comments on various chapters: Marjorie A. Bock, University of Missouri, Kansas City; Christine Givner, California State University, Los Angeles; Maurice Miller, Indiana State University; Robert W. Ortiz, New Mexico State University; and Qaisar Sultana, Eastern Kentucky University.

At Merrill/Prentice Hall, we are very grateful to Ann Davis for her encouragement and confidence in this work; to Pat Grogg for her very patient support and assistance throughout the project, and to Carol Sykes for her skilled work with the photographs. We also extend our thanks to Ann Mohan at WordCrafters for her editorial talents in the production of this book under rigorous deadlines.

To Lin Ballard, we owe our gratitude for all her efforts with the original photography under very tight deadlines, gaining cooperation of school personnel and securing needed permissions as well. There are several school personnel who we must thank for their cooperation in allowing Lin to obtain photographs of students, teachers, and classrooms. At the Mount Vernon Elementary School, Alexandria Public Schools, we wish to thank Gail Smith, Principal; Ms. Meisner, Ms. Taylor, and Ms. Linehan, teachers; and the elementary students who welcomed the photographer. At the George Washington Middle School, we thank Mr. Murphy, Principal, for his assistance, and Ms. Baskin and Ms. Russell and the middle school students. At the Craddock Boat Building School (Alexandria Seaport Foundation), we are thankful to Joe Youcha, Director, and the students. We are also thankful for the assistance of Barbara Hunter, Director of Communications for the Alexandria Public Schools.

Finally, we thank those teachers, students, and colleagues who have used the previous book on which this one is based and have provided us with helpful feedback.

Contents

PART ONE

The Challenge of Inclusion

The ultimate rationale for inclusion is based not on law or regulations or teaching technology, but on values. What kinds of people are we and what kind of society do we wish to develop? What values do we honor?

—Gartner and Lipsky, 1992

CHAPTER 1

Why Inclusion?

Though we may never reach perfection, this nation remains relentless in its effort to achieve two parallel goals in education: (1) excellent teaching which results in student achievement, and (2) equal opportunity for all children. These two goals are at the root of fundamental changes occurring in education today.

AN AGE OF ANXIETY AND RESOLVE. In the United States today, the educational system as a whole stands at a crossroads—not only from an instructional perspective but also a moral, and social one. Many call this an "age of anxiety," because it is a time of tremendous change. Special education is also undergoing great change, particularly in where and how it is delivered to students. Furthermore, educators are seeking to achieve a new marriage of special and general education in order to move closer to the *goal of achieving equal educational opportunity for all children*. This trend toward merging special and general education shows that teachers and administrators have reached several important conclusions. First, they recognize clear benefits in special education practices and theories for many students who in the past have been in separate schools, segregated from their peers. Second, the benefits of special education practices can impact wider groups of students if they are integrated within the general education classroom. Third, the belief and practice of reducing class size for students with special learning needs is now even more relevant and appropriate for all students in today's diverse classroom.

THE FAILURE OF HAPHAZARD INCLUSION POLICIES. Just as "all means all" in regard to who should be served under special education laws, all also means all in regard to whom is doing the serving. In other words, the educational community as a whole must prepare all members of the educational community for a new kind of work. This requires all educators to depart from some old values and

practices. Teachers and administrators are asking questions: How can schools improve special education services for students who need them, and how can they develop reasonable policies for inclusion in general education classes? How can the schools appropriately support students with disabilities to ensure their success in the general education classroom? Lessons from past civil rights movements show that *physical access or placement alone* does not achieve integration or inclusion, nor does it guarantee better educational results for students. *The practice of inclusion must involve much more that a shifting of physical environments from a segregated class to the general education class. Instead it must address the needs of the student being included, as well as the impacts on the greater learning environment.*

AN INCLUSION BILL OF RIGHTS. There are many reasons for pursuing and sustaining the goals of inclusion. Children with disabilities have received an education that is not equal to that given other children. Yet the ultimate rationale for inclusion is based not on law or regulations or teaching technology, but on *values*. What kinds of people are we, and what kind of society do we wish to develop? What values do we honor (Gartner & Lipsky, 1992)? Even if our common values and beliefs are shared, agreement on how they should be implemented to create policies, practices, and programs usually differs widely among groups. Twenty years ago, it was thought that trying to implement inclusion in the schools was incredibly complex and ran "counter to the basic structure of the public education system," and that attempting to implement a "concept alien to the school itself was counter-productive" (Turnbull, 1991, p. 50). Much progress and change in attitudes has occurred since then, and the conditions for implementing inclusion in a rational way have begun to develop.

While many inclusion efforts today are failing to provide the supportive services that students with disabilities need in general education classrooms, many schools are realizing the possibilities and potential of inclusion to benefit all children. Such programs involve general education teachers in school-based decisions about including students with disabilities in their classrooms and address their concerns about their ability to ensure the success of students placed into inclusive classrooms. While the rights of children with disabilities must be protected under the Individuals with Disabilities Education Act (IDEA), this protection also depends upon reconciling the "rights" and responsibilities of parents, teachers, and administrators in a manner that makes the promise and process of inclusion a rational and effective one. All are essential to the process.

Many educational organizations believe that inclusion represents a major revolution in the way schools are organized and administered (Council of Chief State School Administrators, 1999; National Association of Secondary School Principals, 1997; National Association of State Boards of Education, 1992). As Walter Lippman said in 1922, "If a child fails in school and then fails in life, the schools cannot sit back and say: 'You see how accurately I predicted this?'" This prophetic comment anticipated the warning of experts today—that it is not special education but the total educational system that must change.

MORE EXPECTED OF TEACHERS TODAY. Today, teachers and other school personnel are expected to develop educational programs that serve a diversity of students, including those with disabilities, students at risk for failure, former school dropouts, students with limited English proficiency, teen parents, and many others. Each of these groups may be considered a special population of students that possess unique needs and require *specialized educational services*. Today, in some school systems, these special populations are the majority. Teachers are expected to work to improve the achievement and development of each of these groups of students. Many of the instructional and behavioral approaches once developed for students with disabilities, such as learning strategies, metacognitive strategies, or behavioral strategies (behavior contracts, token

economies), are now being applied in the general education classroom because they seem to work with these diverse groups of children and youth (Hughes-Booker, 1994; Putnam, 1993).

ALL MEANS ALL. Implementing successful inclusion means that all the people involved in an inclusion placement (student, family, teacher, principal) are fully informed about the placement. They must all anticipate and understand (1) what is expected for the student with a disability in the new placement and (2) the impact of that placement on the total classroom and the teaching process for all students. Special education laws require that all children must be served in free, appropriate public education programs, in the least restrictive environment. The educational community as a whole must prepare all members of the educational enterprise for a new kind of response to this mandate and responsibility. Educators must be guided by the belief that as a nation, we can develop a national policy that echoes to all the states, that prohibits discrimination and promotes equal opportunity and equal access to education for all.

All children must be served in free, appropriate public education programs in the least restrictive environment.

CHAPTER 2

What Is Inclusion?

DISABILITY IN PERSPECTIVE. Tracing the evolution of the term *inclusion* and the many facets of its definition is helped by first defining *disability* and *special education*. According to the Individuals with Disabilities Education Act (IDEA), (P. L. 105-17) "children with disabilities means children with mental retardation; hearing impairments, including deafness; speech or language impairments; visual impairments, including blindness; emotional disturbance; orthopedic impairments; autism; head injuries; other health impairments; specific learning disabilities; and others who need special education and related services."

WHAT IS SPECIAL EDUCATION? Since 1975, special education laws have promoted the practice of educating students with disabilities with their nondisabled peers to the extent that this is possible and reasonable. Schools are now required to assure that special classes, separate schooling, or other removal of children with disabilities from the regular educational environment occurs only if the student has such a severe disability that education in regular classes cannot be achieved even with the use of supplementary aids and services. Special education means specially designed instruction, at no cost to parents or guardians, to meet the unique needs of a child with a disability. The 1975 special education law, P. L. 94-142, defined a free, appropriate public education as special education and its related services which

    a. are provided at public expense, under public supervision and direction, and without charge;
    b. meet the standards of the state educational agency;
    c. include preschool, elementary school, or secondary school education;
    d. are provided in conformity with the individualized education program (IDEA, 1997, Section 602(25).

The 1997 Amendments to IDEA incorporated the former

definitions of "free and appropriate public education," but extended the definition to include out-of-school children: "*A free appropriate public education is available to all children with disabilities residing in the state between ages 3–21, inclusive, including children with disabilities who have been suspended or expelled from school* (IDEA, 1997, Section 612(a)(1))." This expanded definition greatly broadens the educational agency's responsibility to educate students in settings other than the home school, and to provide outreach to students who are of school age but are not in school. Special education can include classroom instruction and supplementary and related services, instruction in physical education, home instruction, and instruction in hospitals or institutions.

What Supplementary and Related Services Are Included in Special Education? *Supplementary and related services* are provided to enable students with disabilities to succeed within the general education setting and to be educated with nondisabled children to the maximum extent appropriate (IDEA, 1997, Section 602 (22)). Please see Chapter 19 for more information about these services. These services are provided in order to assist a student in benefiting from education in the general education setting.

Are Career-Related and Transition Services Considered Special Education? Transition services for students with disabilities are considered to be special education services (1) if they are provided as specially designed instruction or related services, and (2) if they are required to help a student with a disability benefit from special education. For many students, career vocational-technical education is an essential part of their transition plan, and the support services they need to participate are also considered to be special education services. Career vocational education programs are also required to provide the following assurances of full participation of all youth in transition services, particularly members of special populations:

- Provide equal access to recruitment, assessment, enrollment, and placement into the program.
- Provide equal access to the full range of school-to-work transition programs available to all students.
- Coordinate school-to-work transition programs with existing related career and transition programs for special populations.
- Provide information to students, and parents, or guardians about school-to-work programs at least 1 year prior to the age that such programs are generally available to students in the state.

SORTING OUT THE TERMS *DISABILITY, IMPAIRMENT,* AND *HANDICAP.* It is helpful to distinguish between three terms still used to refer to students with special education needs: impairment, disability, and handicap. Throughout this document the term *special educational needs* refers to many categories of children with disabilities, but also those with social and behavioral disadvantages and those who are at risk of developing more severe problems in the future. The term *children with disabilities* is used generally throughout instead of traditional terms such as *handicapped, retarded,* or *slow learner.* Educators in the U.S., as well as in other nations, are becoming dissatisfied with the term *handicapped* to refer to persons with physical, emotional, or intellectual impairments.

International Classification System. The World Health Organization presented a classification system that respects the consequences of disease or impairment. In that system there is a clear distinction between the terms *impairment, disability* and *handicap.* These terms help distinguish (1) a specific organic or bodily deficit, (2) the impact of that deficit on the child's ability to function in specific activities, and (3) the impact of these functional limitations on the ability to perform in broader social roles (e.g., student, worker, family member) (Lynch, 1995).

An *impairment* may be a consequence of congenital problems, birth trauma, brain damage, poor nutrition, disease, or injury. Impairments might include cognitive, physical, emotional, or psychomotor deficits. A child, however, can have an impairment without that impairment resulting in a limitation of the ability to function in daily activities (walking, dressing, eating, bathing, communicating). Such a functional limitation resulting from an impairment is referred to as a *disability.* In other words, disability refers to underdeveloped or lost ability to function in activities that are essential for daily living and essential for performing social roles, such as student or worker. Usually, disability is a consequence of an impairment and implies some deprivation which prevents the person from developing alternative ways of functioning. For example, an inability to read or communicate clearly may result from a head injury. The individual has a disability because he or she cannot perform the daily activi-

ties of reading or communicating with teachers. As a consequence, the child's ability to perform in the social role of student will be impeded unless the school and teacher can respond in a more flexible way to the disability.

A *handicap* is the result of social factors outside the person which interact with an impairment and disability and make the student less able to perform in an essential social role. Handicap is a distinctly *social concept* and includes factors in the environment, such as social discrimination, lack of physical accommodation, and inadequate educational and service responses. A focus only on impairments, because they are organic in origin, offers some degree of rationale for a medical model for providing help to students with disabilities, but it is not sufficient for the *contextual model* used in this handbook. The *sociological or contextual model* requires that in seeking *effective inclusion practices, equal attention should be given to the child's impairments and disabilities and the responses (interventions) of the teachers, administrators and school communities.* Table 2-1 compares the terms *impairment, disability,* and *handicap.* It is important to emphasize that impairments and disabilities do not necessarily result in handicaps if the necessary supportive services are available and the educational, social service, and health systems are designed to prevent and counteract the consequences of impairments.

MOST STUDENTS CAN BE ACCOMMODATED. If students with special educational needs are given the chance for small accommodations in the regular classroom, they can thrive in their local community schools. Because of their desire to compensate for their impairments, many are motivated to achieve highly when given opportunities to learn. *Most of these children are disadvantaged more by the failure of schools and teachers to support them in their formative years than they are by their disabilities.* Even children who have severe physical or mental impairments can be expected to achieve as much academically as many of their nondisabled peers. Because of impairments, some of them have lower levels of performance and have more difficulty than other children in applying new information and skills learned in classroom settings. Some may learn more slowly than their peers in all or a few curricular areas and may simply need more time than their peers to complete their work. Others may need to be given directions in very concrete terms, or with visual aids such as written notes or pictures. A few may need substantial special educational supports or accommodations to enable them to benefit from general education classes, while others may only require minimal adjustments in the classroom environment to succeed.

WHAT ARE THE MAJOR COMPONENTS OF INCLUSION? Special education and civil rights laws have promoted the practice of educating students with disabilities with their nondisabled peers, to the extent that this is possible and

TABLE 2-1. What's In a Name? Comparison of the Subtle Differences Between the Terms Impairment, Disability, and Handicap

Impairment	Disability	Handicap
Specific cognitive, physical, or emotional deficits that are consequences of congenital conditions, birth trauma, disease, or injury	Consequence of an impairment involving the loss of ability to perform daily activities or essential social roles	Social concept referring to environmental factors that interact with the impairment and often compound problems; includes social discrimination, lack of physical accommodations, and inadequate educational and service responses
Partial or total loss of vision	Inability to read in school	Inability to progress in school due to lack of special educational services for visually impaired and lack of physical accommodations
Partial or total loss of hearing	Inability to learn spoken language or perform in school	Inability to progress in school due to lack of special educational services for hearing impaired and discrimination by teachers and school peers
Paralysis of the legs as a result of infection	Inability to attend school or participate in family work or community activities	Inability to attend school due to lack of special transportation or lack of physical accessibility to the school building
Loss of cognitive abilities as a result of chronic illness or malnutrition	Inability to perform at grade level in writing and basic mathematics	Inability to progress in school due to lack of compensatory services for children with cognitive losses
Childhood phobias as a result of abuse, natural disaster, or war	Inability to attend school or participate in social events	Inability to progress in social development due to lack of counseling or support services to treat childhood phobia

reasonable. Schools are now required to assure that special classes, separate schooling, or other removal of children with disabilities from the regular educational environment occurs only if the student has such a severe disability that his or her education in regular classes cannot be achieved even with the use of supplementary aids and services. Sailor (1991) proposed six major components for inclusion of students with disabilities into general education classrooms.

Component 1: Home school placements. This means that students are educated in their community schools. No students are educated in separate special schools, or magnet schools, or enclaves with high concentrations of students with disabilities. Neighborhood schools provide opportunities for social inclusion at the school and in the community.

Component 2: Natural proportion at each school. Each school and each class contain the same proportion of students with disabilities found in the general community. For example, in a community with 10 percent disabilities among the population, an inclusive classroom would contain no more that 10 percent students with disabilities (or 2 to 3 for a 25 to 30 student classroom).

Component 3: A zero-reject philosophy. A zero-reject philosophy exists so that no student will be excluded on the basis of type or extent of disability. In other words, every school serves *all* children within its district. This philosophy helps develop a sense of community and fosters belongingness, interdependence, and relationships that value diversity.

Component 4: Age- and grade-appropriate placements. School and general education placements are age and grade appropriate so that no self-contained special education classes will exist. There is no cascade of services or

continuum of placements for students with differing needs.

Component 5: Cooperative learning and peer instructional methods. Cooperative learning and peer instruction are replacing traditional teaching as the preferred methods for inclusive classrooms.

Component 6: Special education in integrated environments. Special education supports exist within the general education class and in other integrated environments (Sailor, 1991, p. 116). This means that in the inclusive class, special education resources, such as personnel, supplies, and equipment, are redistributed for use by all students in the classroom. Also team teaching arrangements (a general education and a special education teacher) can be used to individualize instruction for students with disabilities (Sailor, 1991).

There remains a great deal of controversy among inclusion advocates about how to implement these components. Inclusion models are effective when they take into consideration (1) the expectations that the student can benefit from the educational program into which the student is being placed, (2) the conditions and resources needed to attain such benefits, and (3) the actual impacts of the placements on the total classroom. It is these models of effective inclusion which provide all educators with an understanding of the possibilities and potential of the inclusion movement.

WHAT INCLUSION IS AND IS NOT. There are many myths about inclusion and what it means in actual practice in the schools. Table 2-2 synthesizes and summarizes definitions of experts about what are believed to represent sound inclusion practices (what inclusion is) and unsound practices (what inclusion is not).

TABLE 2-2. What Inclusion Is and Is Not

Inclusion Is:	Inclusion Is Not:
All children learning together in the same schools and the same classrooms, with the services and supports necessary so that they can be successful there	"Dumping" all children with disabilities into general education classes without the supports and services they need to be successful there
All children having their unique needs met in the same setting they would attend if they had no disability	Trading of the quality of a child's education or the intensive support services the child may need for inclusion
All children participating in all facets of school life	Doing away with or cutting back on special education service
Children with and without disabilities having opportunities (and support when needed) to interact and develop friendships with each other	Ignoring each child's unique needs
	All children having to learn the same thing, at the same time, in the same way
Children who have disabilities attending their neighborhood school (the same school they would attend if they did not have a labeled disability)	Expecting regular education teachers to teach children who have disabilities without the support they need to teach all children effectively
A method of schooling which emphasizes collaboration by melding special and regular education resources (staff, materials, energy, etc.)	Sacrificing the education of typical children so that children with disabilities can be included
Supporting regular education teachers who have children with disabilities in their classrooms	Serving students with disabilities in separate schools or exclusively in self-contained classes, based solely upon their categorical label
Children learning side by side though they may have different educational goals	Scheduling students with disabilities for lunch and other activities at different time than students without disabilities are scheduled
Regular education teachers using innovative strategies for varied learning styles of children in the class	Placing students with disabilities into regular classes without the planning, supports, and services needed for successful and meaningful participation
Integrating related services (such as speech, physical therapy, occupational therapy, etc.) in the regular classroom	Limiting the opportunities for students with disabilities to participate in general education classes by doing all scheduling first for students with disabilities to participate only where space is available
Unconditional acceptance of all children as children	Providing separate staff development for regular teachers and special education teachers, thus reinforcing notions of separate systems
Unconditional commitment to providing as much support as the child needs to be successful in general education environments	Maintaining separate daily schedules for students with and without disabilities
A focus on the parents' dreams and goals for their child's future	Serving students with disabilities in age-inappropriate settings by placing older students in primary settings or younger students in secondary settings
Educators viewing themselves in new collaborative roles	Denying students with disabilities services in general education classrooms because the staff is not willing or hasn't been given direction in how to adapt instruction to meet the needs of diverse learners
A focus on what the child *can* rather than cannot do	
A team approach which includes parents as equal members and emphasizes creativity and a problem solving attitude	Referring to special education students in stigmatizing terms such as "the handicapped class" or "the retarded kids"
An understanding of the fact that students don't need to have the same educational goals in order to learn together in regular classes	Making precipitous placement decisions for students with disabilities without their prior preparation
Strong leadership by school principals and other administrators	Locating special education classes in separate wings at a school
Encouraging and implementing activities that promote the development of friendships and relationships between students with and without disabilities	Exposing students to unnecessary hazards or risks
	Ignoring parents' concerns
Providing the planning, support, and services necessary for meaningful and successful participation of students with disabilities in general education programs	Placing older students with disabilities in schools for younger children
	Requiring students or their parents to waive their legal rights under IDEA for the "privilege" of being placed into a general education classroom
Having a school and district mission that is comprehensive and sets high expectations for all students, including those with disabilities	
Providing professional development and support for all personnel regarding effective practices for inclusion of students with disabilities	
Scheduling classes for all school activities in a way that maximizes opportunities for participation by students with disabilities	
Assuring that all school and grade-level placements are age-appropriate	
Having all people on the staff understand and support the notion that students with disabilities can be served appropriately in general education classes and that this sometimes requires the staff to meet learning needs that differ from those of most students	
Using "person first" language ("students with disabilities" instead of "disabled students") and teaching all students to understand and value human differences	
Providing needed services within regular schools, regardless of the intensity or frequency	
Allowing students who are not able to fully participate in an activity to partially participate, rather than be excluded entirely. Arranging for students with disabilities to receive their job training in mainstream community environments	
Teaching all children to understand and accept individual differences	

Source: Courtesy of the Pisces Full Inclusion Project, Maryland State Department of Education

Inclusion means children learning side by side although they may have different educational goals.

CHAPTER 3

What Are the Legal Roots of Inclusion?

The Beginning. In 1973, four sets of parents found they had something in common. They all lived in the same community and they each had a child with a disability who was unable to attend the local community school with the neighborhood children.

Michael. Michael was 12 and was diagnosed with mental retardation. He had the intellectual level of a 6-year-old but had learned to dress and feed himself, and had begun to learn to read and write his name. He attended a special school for other children like him which was about an hour away, for which his parents paid high tuition. Michael wanted to be a carpenter like his father.

Sarah. Sarah, 10 years of age, was born with cerebral palsy and had limited use of her left leg and arm. She walked with great difficulty and used a cane. Fortunately she had the use of her right arm and hand and could write and perform many tasks at home. She also had a flare for painting and had produced works that revealed a real artistic talent. She had labored speech but was very bright, could read and write on the eight-grade level, and had an excellent vocabulary—beyond her peers'. She participated in physical therapy every week and attended, at her parents' expense, a school on the grounds of the hospital. Her mother took her to school every day, though Sarah wished she could go to the same school as the girls next door.

William. William was an active and bright boy of 13 who had attentional problems, hyperactivity, and a learning disability that prevented him from performing academically to his potential. He had difficulty reading and comprehending what he read, and yet, he showed signs of great aptitude for invention. He repaired most of the equipment that needed repair in the home and worked on developing an electrical door-opening device for his friend Marie, who uses a wheelchair.

William was tutored at home at his parents' expense because the local school had no program for someone with learning disabilities of his severity. William expressed a desire to be an engineer and design airplanes.

Marie. Marie was a very bright girl of 11 years. At age 4, she suffered a fall from a three-story window and suffered a severe neck injury, which left her paralyzed from the waist down. For mobility she relied upon a wheelchair and had no use of her legs and torso. She attended a separate school for children with physical disabilities, one which was barrier-free and designed to accommodate wheelchairs. Because it was in the next county, she rode in a special bus one and one half hours each way to the school. She was at the top of her class and wanted to be a lawyer when she grew up so that she can help others like herself. Marie, too, wished she could attend the neighborhood school around the corner.

A Common Dream. All of these children introduced above had a common dream—to attend their neighborhood schools with the other boys and girls who lived on their street. Their parents—they called themselves the parent-advocates—also had a common dream: to see their children playing, working, and riding the school bus with their peers and living like ordinary citizens. They were not so concerned that their children be in special classes within the schools, but only that they be able to attend the same school. The parents met every week and became ardent warriors fighting for the passage of a new piece of legislation being debated in Congress. *The Education for All Handicapped Children Act* (EHA) was passed as Public Law 94-142 in 1975 and later renamed Individuals with Disabilities Education Act (IDEA). They and their parents believed that, finally, access to their community schools might soon be possible.

Many educators, lawyers, and parents had been working for years for the passage of a national law which would guarantee the right of each child with a disability to attend community public school and receive, without private expense, the educational services that were appropriate for the child's individual needs. One phase of the long journey toward access to public education for all children had ended. However, the next important phase, implementing the law, had just begun.

HOW DOES INCLUSION RELATE TO THE CONSTITUTION? The inclusion movement is *not* another political fad, passing fashion, or social fancy. Rather it is another expression of a long-fought civil rights movement that has been in progress throughout this century in the United States. Two things have to occur to have a social movement. First, there has to be a fundamental change in thinking and beliefs about a social problem and what a society or community should do about it. Second, there have to be enough people believing the same way and willing to work hard to put the new ideas and beliefs into practice in order to change things. The civil rights "movers" believed that there should not be discrimination against people in America—neither against people of color, immigrants, senior citizens, people in poverty, nor people of different faiths. The American way of life meant protecting and strengthening the rights of all people, both citizens and newcomers, to share equally in the benefits and bounty, and responsibilities of a democratic society. The principles of the democratic society, written into our Constitution and the Bill of Rights, meant that our laws, policies, and social behavior should ensure each man, woman, and child an equal right to access the promise of equal opportunity. The inclusion movement is another extension of the widely accepted philosophy of equal protection under law, a principle that is grounded in the U.S. Constitution.

BEYOND PHYSICAL PLACEMENT. Though early special education leaders advocated for the right to basic physical access to all schools and public facilities, this demand reflected the challenge of the second goal—that society and the educational system had to change in a much more profound way. A vision of the world was constructed in which integration and acceptance of individuals and their differences is comprehensive and infused into all social responses of individuals and institutions. The first goal of physical access was much more easily accomplished. *The second goal, however, remains illusive.*

Historically, children with disabilities had been educated in separate settings in order to protect them from the stigma and rejection they might face with their nondisabled peers. The second purpose was to provide special teaching methods and materials appropriate for their special learning needs. It was believed that these children learn differently and that different psychological and educational theories and techniques were needed to educate them (Putnam, 1993, p. 10). For example, children with disabilities were thought to need more intensive instruction over longer periods of time. They were also thought to need environments with less stimuli and fewer students. The traditional general classroom was not appropriate for these students. But as early as the 1970s, educators argued against the belief that separate theories and psychological principles should be applied to students with disabilities (Sarason & Doris, 1978).

LEGAL FOUNDATIONS OF INCLUSION. The 1975 Education for All Handicapped Children Act (P.L. 94-142) and the most recent amendments in 1990 and 1997, (P.L. 101-476 and P.L. 105-17, respectively) were enacted to ensure that all students with disabilities under the age of 22 were guaranteed a free, appropriate public education. Before the law was passed, students with disabilities were either not provided an education at all, were educated in their homes, or were provided an inferior education in a separate setting, apart from their age-mates and separate from their community schools. Through this legislation, Congress declared that every child with a disability had an inalienable right to be schooled in the educational setting most appropriate for that child. The 1997 amendments to the Individuals with Disabilities Education Act (P.L. 105-17) incorporated the former definitions of "free and appropriate public education," but extended the definition to include out-of-school children: "A free appropriate public education is available to all children with disabilities residing in the state between ages 3–21, inclusive, including children with disabilities who have been suspended or expelled from school" (IDEA, 1997, Section 612(a)(1)). The law did not contain the word *inclusion,* but it defined the most appropriate setting as one that can be described as the "least restrictive environment." The expanded definition reflects the findings that many youth with disabilities are being expelled for violations of discipline policies, are dropping out of school at an early age, and are not being provided the supports they need in secondary education to prepare them for employment or transition to postsecondary education.

What Does Least Restrictive Environment (LRE) Mean?

Education in the least restrictive environment means that students should, to the extent possible, be educated with their nondisabled peers. The legislation requires the schools to assure that, to the maximum extent possible, children with disabilities in either public or private institutions, are educated with children who are not disabled, and that special classes, separate schooling, or other removal of children with disabilities from the general education environment occurs only when the nature or severity of the disabilities is such that education in regular classes with the use of supplementary aids and services cannot be achieved satisfactorily (Individuals with Disabilities Education Act, P.L. 101-476, 1990).

The term LRE has raised more questions than it has answered about integrating students with disabilities into mainstream settings.

THE MANY FACES OF CIVIL RIGHTS: EVOLUTION OF THE TERM INCLUSION. The term *inclusion* has a relatively long history in this nation. It is rooted in the civil rights movement that arose out of the struggle of people of color for their freedom in America in the 1800s and early 1900s. The following chart traces the evolution of the term *inclusion* and of the many terms that have been used to refer to the idea of integration of persons with disabilities into mainstream environments. Each successive term reflects a movement toward closer integration with nondisabled peers in ways that are both qualitative (approximating conditions similar to those of nondisabled peers) and quantitative (increasing the amount of time spent and number of types of settings with nondisabled peers) (see Figure 3-1). The last box reflects a trend toward focusing on inclusion benefits and outcomes. The last thoughts represent the authors' confidence that schools will continue to reexamine the quality and effectiveness of their inclusion practices. They will improve them to ensure maximum possible opportunity for inclusion of all students, but ensure that the environments in which children are educated do result in meaningful benefit.

New Expectations for Schools. The third phase in the struggle for integration began to emerge in the late 1970s and early 1980s. A group of educators, policymakers and parent advocates began to ask, why should we expect bright children with disabilities to settle for being educated *near* their peers, rather than *directly with them?* Shouldn't they be schooled in the *same classes* with their peers? If special education law assured equal access to free and appropriate public education for all, then why were separate classes needed under the same

1900s–1960s: *Normalization.* Philosophy imported from Scandinavia, based on belief that individuals with disabilities should be viewed as entitled to the same freedoms, life choices, circumstances, and opportunities as their nondisabled peers.

1950s–1960s: *Deinstitutionalization and community integration.* Two principles that gained wide acceptance after the Kennedy administration's leadership in promoting the movement of people with mental retardation out of large institutions and into families or smaller community facilities.

1970s: *Least restrictive environment (LRE).* A principle embodied in early special education laws and international human rights instruments requiring that all children be provided universal access to education and be educated in settings that were "least restrictive" of their freedom and interaction with nondisabled peers.

1980s: *Mainstreaming.* A term based on the LRE principle, which represented efforts to restructure school programs to permit students with disabilities to be served, to the extent possible, in classrooms with nondisabled peers.

Early 1990s: *Inclusion.* A term similar to mainstreaming, but which specifically refers to integration of students with a wide range of disabilities into regular academic classes with nondisabled peers.

Mid-1990s: *Full Inclusion.* Refers to the principle and practice of placing students into regular classrooms with nondisabled peers, regardless of the type or severity of their disability.

2000 and beyond: *Full participation and meaningful benefit?* Refers to the continuing efforts of schools to advance the principles of inclusion, but also to measure its benefits and outcomes for students. (Kochhar & West, 1996)

FIGURE 3-1. Evolution of the Term Inclusion

roof of the community school? These advocates argued, along with many legal advocates and educators, that we should take a close look at the individual disability and see who, with small accommodations, could be served directly in the general education classes. And in the effort, it should be determined which special education classes were really needed and which were not.

The third phase of the integration movement placed many high expectations on the schools—beyond those ever dreamed of by the parent-advocates of the 1970s. In the late 1980s the movement had accelerated for full integration of children with disabilities into classes with their nondisabled peers. This movement was spurred by a new philosophy which argued that in order to fulfill the promise of Public Law 94-142, special and general education had to be merged. The promise was made so that each child who could benefit from the general education curriculum was entitled to be served in the mainstream classroom with his or her nondisabled peers.

Emerging Definitions of "Appropriate Placement." In 1975, Congress passed the Education for All Handicapped Children Act (P.L. 94-142), which guaranteed children with disabilities a free and appropriate public education in the least restrictive setting. In 1982, the Supreme Court had the opportunity to further interpret the term "appropriate placement" (*Board of Education of Hendrick Hudson Central School District v. Rowley*, 1992). The following case provides an example of the court's role in defining "appropriate placement" and "least restrictive environment."

CASE EXAMPLE 3-1. Pivotal Case: The Supreme Court Interprets "Appropriate Placement"

This case involved a deaf student with excellent lip-reading skills, in the general education classroom. She was able to achieve average grades, but her parents believed she could attain a higher level of achievement (her maximum potential) if she had an interpreter in the classroom. This request was denied, and the case made its way to the Supreme Court. Chief Justice William Rehnquist, writing the majority opinion, stated that with regard to "the individualized educational plan. . . . If the child is being educated in the regular classroom of the public education system, it should be reasonably calculated to *enable the child to achieve passing marks and advance from grade to grade*" (102 S. Ct. 3049). The Court ruled that the sign language interpreter was not needed because the child was performing better than average and was receiving individualized instruction (*Board of Education V. Rowley*, 458 U.S. 176 [1982]).

This decision was important because it established a requirement that children with disabilities were entitled to a level of services sufficient for them to benefit from education and also required that special education services be provided in the least restrictive environment (LRE) (Friend & Bursuck, 1999; Hardman, Crew & Egan, 1999; Osborne, 1992).

A Revolution of Expectation. The Supreme Court's 1982 decision sparked major debate over expectations for students placed into mainstream classrooms—for the student, the academic program, and the teachers. Negative social attitudes about children with disabilities adversely affects expectations about what they can achieve academically. Often, these attitudes cause them to be

- Exempt from standards and assessments routinely applied to other students.
- Allowed grades that they have not earned.
- Excused from social and behavioral expectations set for other students.
- Exempt from making personal choices and decisions.
- Permitted special diplomas (Friend & Bursuck, 1999; Gartner & Lipsky, 1992; Halloran & Simon, 1994).

These watered-down expectations were thought to be in the best interests of the child (Gartner & Lipsky, 1992). However, today, students with disabilities included in general education classrooms are more likely expected to be held to the same standards and assessment measures as their nondisabled peers (McCoy, 1995; Smith, Polloway, Patton & Dowdy, 1995; Waldron, 1996). They are also expected to achieve the required Carnegie units needed for regular high school diplomas. The expectations expressed in early interpretations of P.L. 94-142—that the Individualized Education Program (IEP) should merely enable the child to "achieve passing marks and advance from grade to grade," is no longer acceptable for most students with mild to moderate disabilities.

Supreme Court Interpretations Hasten the Development of Inclusion. The 1982 Rowley ruling by the Supreme Court was criticized by advocates for people with disabilities for three reasons:

1. It did not provide a clear definition of "appropriate placement."
2. It was not consistent with what Congress had intended a school to provide.
3. It conveyed a message that students with disabilities should only be expected to receive a *minimal or basic floor of opportunity* rather than a higher level of services more similar to those of their peers.

After Rowley, lower court decisions supported the minimal education approaches, allowing schools to provide education that was of some benefit in providing students access to educational programs. Yet there was a lot of attention to the LRE doctrine. In putting together the minimal benefit and LRE principle, some lower courts interpreted appropriate placement to mean that students could be placed into mainstream settings for so-called social benefit, even at the expense of educational quality (*Bonnadonna v. Cooperman,* 1985). Court cases in the years that followed challenged the idea that IEPs need not provide substantial educational benefits. These cases were successfully argued on the grounds that Congress intended to provide children who have disabilities with an education that would confer *meaningful benefit* (Osborne, 1992). For example:

- North Carolina state standards exceeded Rowley standards, requiring that students with disabilities should be provided an opportunity to achieve their potential in a manner similar to opportunities provided to nondisabled students.
- Massachusetts standards required that an IEP, to be appropriate, should be designed to maximize the potential of a student with a disability (Osborne, 1992).
- Michigan's standards also required that IEPs be designed to develop the maximum potential of the child.

The term *maximum potential* did not mean utopian, or the best, education possible, but education had to be "meaningful." Today, the idea of "meaningful" for students is still unclear and is being debated in the states.

MANY DEFINITIONS OF INCLUSION. Today, inclusion is defined in many ways by many organizations and individuals. Terms such as *full inclusion, inclusive education, inclusive classrooms, progressive inclusion,* and *diverse classrooms,* have all evolved from the mainstreaming movement in the 1980s (Rothstein, 1995; Stainback & Stainback, 1992). These new terms that have replaced *mainstreaming* generally all refer to the *maximum integration of students with disabilities into general classrooms, or the increase in numbers and proportions of students who receive special services while attending general education classes* (Friend & Bursuck, 1999; McCoy, 1995; Putnam, 1993; Reynolds, Wang & Walberg, 1992; Sailor, 1991). These terms have replaced the word *mainstreaming* for an important reason. Mainstreaming emerged during the early implementation of special education law and was associated with the placement of children with disabilities into classrooms on the grounds of their community schools. But many were still being educated in separate classrooms and even separate buildings or trailers on the school grounds.

The Department of Education's Definition. According to the U.S. Department of Education, Office of Special Education, the *regular class* includes students who receive the majority of their educational program in the general education classroom and receive special education and related services outside the regular classroom for *less than 21 percent* of the school day. It includes children placed in a general education class and receiving special education within the regular class, as well as children placed in a general education class and receiving special education outside the regular class (*Eighteenth Annual Report to Congress on the Implementation of the Individuals with Disabilities Education Act,* 1996). The federal definition reflects a recognition that a continuum of services is needed and presumes that some students may not be able to benefit from full inclusion into a general education classroom.

Definition of Inclusion for Students with Severe Disabilities. Inclusion definitions are different for students with severe disabilities. Table 3-1 defines inclusion for such students. Students with severe disabilities are educated in integrated settings to promote a more "normalized" community participation by instructing them in the skills that are essential to their success in the social and environmental settings in which they will ultimately use these skills. *Meaningful educational benefit* for students with disabilities is being interpreted by many educators as maximum possible social integration with nondisabled peers and the provision of functional life skills. Functional life-skills training is best provided in a variety of settings which combine classroom, school, and community-based learning environments. *This view and these practices are very different from the "dumping" of students into general education classes, and is also very different from the segregated programs of the*

TABLE 3-1. Definition of Inclusion for Students with Severe and Multiple Disabilities

1. Placement	Classes placed in the general school building are the chronologically age-appropriate sites for the students.
2. Ratio	A balanced ratio, from 5–20% of such classes, is contained within a single school.
3. Interaction	Structured opportunities exist for regular and sustained interactions between students with severe disabilities and the nondisabled.
4. Nonacademic activities	Students with severe disabilities are provided opportunities for participation in all nonacademic activities of the school.
5. Curriculum	A functional life-skills curriculum is implemented for students with severe disabilities. The curriculum combines classroom, school, and community-based learning situations (Sailor et al., 1989).

past (Hehir & Latus, 1992; Janney et al., 1995; Sailor et al., 1989; West, 1991).

How the Professional Associations Define Inclusion. The 17 special education divisions of the International Council for Exceptional Children (CEC) believe in pre-serving flexibility in educational services for students with disabilities. They support the continuum of services and reject the notion that 100 percent placement into the general education classroom is the universal placement for *all children*. The following display provides examples of how several professional divisions of CEC define inclusion.

The Council for Exceptional Children Divisions Define Inclusion

Council for Exceptional Children General Statement

CEC believes that a continuum of services must be available for all children, youth, and young adults. CEC also believes that the concept of inclusion is a meaningful goal to be pursued in our schools and communities. In addition, CEC believes children, youth, and young adults with disabilities should be served whenever possible in general education classrooms in inclusive neighborhood schools and community settings. Such settings should be strengthened and supported by an infusion of especially trained personnel and other appropriate supportive practices according to the individual needs of the child (CEC, 1997; supplement to *Teaching Exceptional Children,* 1993).

Council for Learning Disabilities (Subdivision of CEC)

The Board of Trustees of the Council for Learning Disabilities (CLD) *supports* school reform efforts that enhance the education of all students, including those with learning disabilities (LD). The council *supports* the education of students with LD in general education classrooms when deemed appropriate by the Individual Education Program (IEP) team. Such inclusion efforts require the provision of needed support services in order to be successful. One policy that the Council *cannot support* is the indiscriminate full-time placement of *all* students with LD in the regular education classroom, a policy often referred to as "full inclusion." CLD has grave concerns about any placement policy that ignores a critical component of special education service delivery. Program placement of each student should be based on an evaluation of the student's individual needs. The Council *cannot support* any policy that minimizes or eliminates service options designed to enhance the education of students with LD that are guaranteed by the Individuals with Disabilities Education Act (*CLD, 1998; Learning Disability Quarterly,* 1993).

Council for Children with Behavior Disorders (CCBD) (Subdivision of CEC)

Consistent with IDEA, CCBD supports a full continuum of mental health and special education services for children and youth with emotional and behavioral disorders. Educational decisions depend on individual student needs. Consequently, in contrast to those individuals in groups who advocate for full inclusion, CCBD does not support the notion that all special education students, including those students with emotional and behavioral disorders, are always best served in general education classrooms. CCBD supports the concept of inclusive schools whereby public schools serve all children, and whereby all personnel demonstrate ownership of all children in their school (CCBD, 1998; *CCBD Newsletter,* 1993).

Division for Early Childhood (DEC) (Subdivision of CEC)

Inclusion, as a value, supports the right of all children, regardless of the diverse abilities, to participate actively in natural settings within their communities. A natural setting is one in which the child would spend time had he or she not had a disability. Such settings include but are not limited to home and family, play groups, child care, nursery schools, Head Start programs, kindergartens, and neighborhood school classrooms.

DEC believes in and supports full and successful access to health, social service education, and other supports and services for young children and their families that promote full participation in community life. DEC values the diversity of families and supports a family-guided process for determining services that are based on the needs and preferences of individual families and children (DEC, 1993, 1998).

Council of Administrators of Special Education, Inc. (CASE) (Subdivision of CEC)

CASE believes in and supports the evolving practice of inclusion for all students as an appropriate goal of our educational community. CASE believes that the decisions about an appropriate education for students must be made on an individual basis. While there are those exceptions for which full inclusion is not appropriate, we believe strongly in the goal of including all children with disabilities in their own school and community. This necessitates a shift in the focus of IEP teams from the place for a student to the intensity and scope of services that a student needs to be appropriately educated (CASE, 1993, 1998).

Source: Courtesy of The Council for Exceptional Children, Reston, Virginia.

CHAPTER 4

What Social Forces Led to the Rise of Inclusion?

There are many forces which have moved policymakers, educators, students, and parents to carefully consider the inclusion concept, although they have often disagreed on how it should be implemented. Overall, these forces have served to strengthen the inclusion movement and improve current practices.

CHANGING DEFINITION OF SPECIAL NEEDS. The term *special needs* populations once meant those who met the legal definition of disability. Now it includes other groups such as students who are at-risk of failure in the general education setting, disadvantaged youth, and incarcerated youth, as well as single parents. The sheer number of students who need special educational services has risen sharply over the past decade. These children are an average of 2 years behind their grade level in the 6th grade and 4 years behind by the 12th grade. About one third of American children are now considered to be at risk for school failure.

THE INCREASING NUMBER OF STUDENTS WITH DISABILITIES. The second population change affecting inclusion is the increasing number of students with disabilities being served in home schools and general education classrooms. Currently, at least 68 percent of students requiring special education services are attending inclusive classes for at least 40 percent or more of the day or all day (U.S. Department of Education, 1997). This increase in the numbers of students with disabilities served in general education classrooms is likely to continue to rise (Putnam, 1993).

RISE IN DROPOUT RATES. The third population change affecting inclusion is the alarming number of aged 15 to 18 students with disabilities who drop out of the school system each year. The school system is failing to meet the needs of students with disabilities in the schools and the general education classroom. As a result of increased re-

quirements for graduation, all students must meet higher standards for graduation from high school. These standards include additional state competency testing, increased academic requirements for all subjects, and increased Carnegie units. The Carnegie Unit is a measure of the number of hours a student has studied in separate subjects (e.g., 120 hours in Math, 4 to 5 times a week, for 40 to 60 minutes, for 36 to 40 weeks each year, earns the student one "unit" of high school credit) (Carnegie Foundation for The Advancement of Teaching, www.carnegiefoundation.org/history.html). Since more emphasis is being placed on academic requirements and improved academic outcomes, students with disabilities, their parents, and their teachers are faced with a dilemma. Given the increased number of academic units required for graduation, these students must enroll primarily in academic courses, which leaves little or no time for vocational education courses, career education, work experience, social skills training, or independent living classes. These are all areas of well-documented needs for students with disabilities (Halloran, 1991; Wagner, 1995).

RISE IN THE NUMBER OF MINORITY STUDENTS. A fourth population change affecting inclusion is the increasing number of students representing minority populations, including immigrants and migrant populations. Between 1980 and 1990, the White American population increased 8 percent, the African-American population grew 16 percent, the Asian population, 65 percent, and the Hispanic population, 44 percent (Hodgkinson, 1991). The concern for improving education and employment preparation outcomes for children and youth must embrace a broader range of individuals with diverse needs who must share the limited resources for special educational services. Educational practitioners and policymakers are coming to believe that educational resources should be directed at producing specific outcomes for students with disabilities in LREs and that teachers should be explicit about the outcomes toward which they are working, especially in regard to population groups that require a special focus (U.S. Department of Education, 1994b, Ysseldyke, 1994). An outcome focus on minority populations is viewed as vital to facilitating meaningful improvement in educational services for these groups and can provide the public with measures of the effectiveness of such change.

TOUGHER SCHOOL DISCIPLINE POLICIES IMPACT INCLUSION. A fifth population change affecting inclusion is the rise in violent and aggressive behavior among the general population of students and the increasingly strict discipline policies that are being implemented in schools. Many states have implemented "zero-tolerance" policies which reach far beyond the mandates of the recent Safe Schools legislation of 1998. These policies are often applied inconsistently and are resulting in some unreasonable judgments and precipitous actions against students, with little chance for due process (Kochhar, 1997). Students with disabilities are often at risk because they are not always aware nor do they understand the new discipline policies. As a result they are treated unfairly. Teachers and administrators are more likely to expect to have to discipline students with disabilities for infractions of such policies. The rise in violent behaviors among all students is a cause for concern for general education teachers.

THE EXPANDING ROLE OF HEALTH AND HUMAN SERVICES. Recent research and practice have confirmed the value of early intervention services in preparing infants, toddlers, and young children to benefit from therapeutic and educational services. In response to this new knowledge about disability intervention, legislation has expanded the role of health and human services in providing services to children in the early years, and requires preschools to include children with disabilities in mainstream settings. Inclusive early intervention services for young children with disabilities improves the likelihood that children will be successful in inclusive elementary classes.

NATIONAL NEED TO ACHIEVE BETTER RESULTS. In 1993 the U.S. Department of Education established national priorities for outcomes for children with disabilities (National Agenda for Achieving Better Results for Children with Disabilities), policies designed to advance *the goal of inclusive education and options to serve a more diverse population of children within a wider framework of educational services for all.* How schools implement inclusion should not be dominated by interest groups or politicians, but rather by what works and what improves student outcomes.

ECONOMIC FORCES THAT WEAKEN QUALITY INCLUSION PROGRAMS. When P.L. 94-142 was passed, the federal government promised to reimburse states at a rate of 40 percent of the per-pupil expenditure for each student with a disability served. The actual funding appropriated by Congress for special education never reached more than 12 percent and is now about 9 percent. States have had to make up the difference in order to serve an increasing number of students in a growing number of disability categories. Inclusion decisions, such as number of placement options, class sizes, number of trained personnel, and the number of available support services, are dependent upon available funds. Some districts have found that mainstreaming is consistent with cost-saving solutions, yet others admit that effective inclusion practices require more favorable student-teacher ratios, additional support staff, and a continuum of placement options (Kochhar & West, 1996; McCoy, 1995; Singer & Butler, 1987).

Budget reductions and changes in priorities in the states are likely to affect the quality of inclusive practices in the coming decade. In search for cost savings, local administrators often turn to cutting the major cost item in their control—personnel. Local educational agencies often respond to cost issues first by narrowing the population of students who are eligible for services, then reducing the amount of service. In addition, they may reduce the professional qualifications required of teachers and support personnel to provide the needed services (Singer & Butler, 1987). Particularly vulnerable are personnel who provide support services not specifically mandated by law. Reductions in special education personnel, vocational support team personnel, and related service personnel are occurring throughout the states today. In addition, severe cuts in career-vocational education programs and services in local educational agencies and school districts greatly limit opportunities for students to gain work-related skills and prepare for transition from school to adult life. These cuts are occurring despite evidence that vocational-technical education courses have been found to be effective in preparing for gainful employment many high school students with disabilities (U.S. Office of Vocational and Adult Education, 1994).

RISING ACADEMIC STANDARDS FOR ALL STUDENTS IMPACT INCLUSION. In 1983, the U.S. Department of Education released the *Nation at Risk* report, an examination of the conditions of education in the United States. This report has been criticized for its inability to prepare all learners for adult society. It has also been criticized for jeopardizing its leadership role in global economic and political arena. During the 1980s and 1990s, the federal government responded by establishing an ambitious set of national education goals. It also set in motion unprecedented attempts to restructure and improve public education and to improve both academic and social outcomes for all children at all grade levels. Academic standards and performance tests are being developed throughout the states in response to these mandates to improve standardized test scores for all students. Schools have been challenged to focus more on quality and excellence in education, and many school-reform proponents have argued that schools should not serve as cafeterias with a great menu of diverse special services (Cetron & Gale, 1991; American Federation of Teachers, 1997, Lieberman, 1992). Most teachers feel overwhelmed and overburdened with the new emphasis on achieving higher academic levels and view the goals of inclusion as at odds with this mandate (Hallahan & Kauffman, 1997).

Yet, most educators believe that three important goals of public education can be accomplished together: integration of special and regular education, reduction in the number of special classes serving small numbers of special education students, and the increased focus on academic excellence and basic education (*Nineteenth Annual Report to Congress on Implementation of IDEA,* 1997). The causes of equity, excellence, and economic efficiency can be unified and carried forward at the same time.

In the future, innovative combinations of funding sources will be needed to preserve the range of supportive services needed by students in general education classes.

ALTERNATIVE TEACHER CERTIFICATION THREATENS QUALITY INCLUSION EFFORTS. Some reform initiatives in general education have had a negative effect on the quality of inclusive practices. While there is movement toward professionalizing teaching, there is also widespread hiring of unqualified applicants for emergency certification and weakening of financial support for personnel training in special and general education (particularly in math and science areas and special education) (Darling-Hammond, 1994). Due to these critical shortages, "over the past few years virtually all states have changed their requirements" (Darling-Hammond, p. 5). *These conditions affect the ability of all teachers and related professionals to implement inclusive practices and school improvement activities.* In states in which alternative certification is in widespread use, leadership is needed to ensure continuing quality and updating of teacher, administrator, and related service professionals' knowledge and skills in creating inclusive schools. The achievement of quality education for all is a shared responsibility.

CHAPTER 5

What Is the Shared Responsibility for Inclusion?

Like the educational system in general, special education, as a component of the general system, has also been criticized for its failure to improve educational services to students with disabilities. After two decades of P.L. 94-142, (Amended in 1990 as P.L. 101-476 and renamed IDEA, the Individuals with Disabilities Education Act), parents, educators and policymakers have begun demanding sweeping reforms in the service delivery system and in the way special education has been organized and administered at the federal, state, and local levels. During the 1980s and early 1990s, special education policymakers were most concerned with ensuring that states and local educational agencies complied with the law (procedural compliance). More recently, educators and policymakers have become more concerned with improving the quality of special education services and measuring results for students.

Educators now believe that improvement in outcomes for all children requires a shared responsibility for educating all children. An initiative known as the *Regular Education Initiative* was developed by the U.S. Office of Special Education to convey the importance of the idea of inclusion as the nation crafted massive education reforms (Will, 1983). A broader, shared effort to improve outcomes for all school children means that the educational disciplines and agencies must work together in a different way. It means that schools and school-linked agencies must address the needs of children in a way that is holistic and integrated.

SHARING INFORMATION ABOUT WHAT WORKS. Many researchers have been trying to discover whether separate education and classes for students with disabilities help or hinder student progress. In general, over the last decade, researchers have not been able to clearly demonstrate that separate special education "pull-out" programs have had significant benefits for students (Friend & Bursuck, 1999; Hardman, Crew & Egan, 1999;

Hehir et al., 1994; Lipsky & Gardner, 1989, Skrtic, 1993). The cumulative effects of these changes, however, have divided educators into at least two camps:

1. Those who advocate for increased academic expectations, higher standards, and more standardized educational offerings.
2. Those who advocate for increased options in accommodating diverse student abilities, interests, and aspirations (Kochhar, 1995a; Kochhar & West, 1996).

A fundamental mission of all educators is to define a system that blends both. This mission requires a continued blending not only of general and special education, but also of many disciplines and service sectors.

TEACHERS FEEL UNPREPARED. Many general education teachers are fearful and feel unprepared to work with students with disabilities in the general education classroom. Teachers feel they have not had adequate training in how to adapt instruction, facilitate socialization, manage a diverse class, adapt technology to accommodate special learners, nor do they receive technical help when they need it (Putnam, 1993). The traditional practice of viewing special education teachers as those who teach special learners and general education teachers as those who teach "regular" children is being seriously questioned. Colleges and universities are also questioning the separate degree programs for special and regular educators and are experimenting with combined and integrated teacher training programs. Such a broader, shared effort can help support teachers in achieving national education goals for all children.

SERVING THE WHOLE PERSON: SHARING THE RESPONSIBILITY THROUGH COLLABORATION WITH SCHOOL-LINKED HUMAN SERVICE AGENCIES. Educators and human service personnel are now realizing that it is much more effective to serve the individual as a *whole person* and address his or her needs in a way that coordinates the services. Schools and community service systems are finding that shared approaches to addressing student needs bring the combined thinking, planning, and resources of many agencies to bear upon the problems of the individual student in a way that is not only more efficient, but works in improving the life of the child (Figure 5-1).

Human service agencies, however, respond to human needs in different ways. Traditionally, needs such as health, education, and employment have been addressed by separate agencies which work in isolation from one another and the schools. For example an individual who has multiple needs for health, remedial education, job training, and family counseling goes to the public health clinic, adult education center, employment services center, and the mental health center to obtain the different services needed. Each agency may serve the individual without communicating with the other agencies providing services to that same individual. Schools and school-linked agencies must collaborate more closely.

IT TAKES A WHOLE SCHOOL: WHO IS INVOLVED IN THE PROCESS OF INCLUSION? Some inclusion experts say that special educators are the most important professionals involved in inclusion. Others will say the general education teachers are most important. Actually, it takes a whole school to work toward successful inclusion. Everyone involved in the education of students within a school needs to be involved with inclusion. This in-

volves the parents, the students being included in general education classes, general education teachers, special education teachers and consultants, principals, librarians, physical education teachers, sports coaches, club leaders, and support service professionals. Inclusion is not confined to a single classroom or group of classrooms, or "pod," within a school. It is not a new program or experiment confined to one or two schools within a school district. Rather, it is a *transformation in the way we think about structuring educational environments for all the children in all of the activities and opportunities a school has to offer*. That means that the coach and the music teacher have to be just as committed to inclusion as the general education teacher and the administrator are to make it work. Table 5-1 shows the variety of people involved in a student's educational and developmental needs.

THE WHOLE SPECTRUM OF SCHOOL- AND COMMUNITY-BASED PERSONNEL MUST BE INVOLVED. There are many agencies and organizations that are essential to comprehensively planning and implementing inclusion. These groups may include parents, principals, social service personnel, public health service providers, community services personnel, corrections and juvenile services personnel, employers, employment and training personnel, postsecondary agency personnel, mental health professionals, guidance counselors, psychologists, resource center

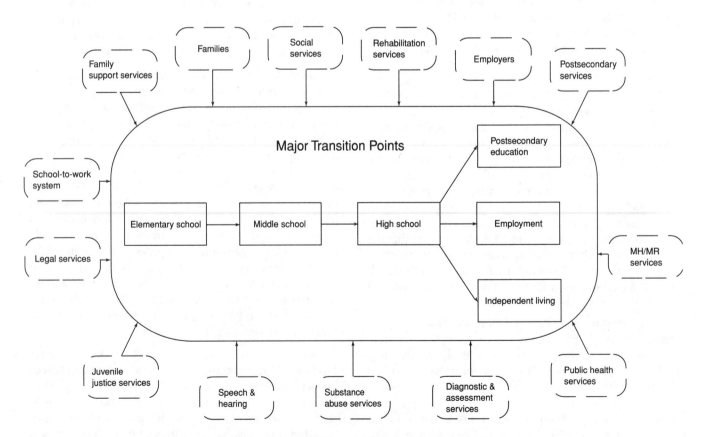

FIGURE 5-1. The Complex Service System That Shares the Responsibility for Youth Transition

TABLE 5-1 It Takes a Whole School

Educational Needs	Support Services Needs	Social, Physical, and Recreational Needs
• Student • General education teacher • Special education teacher • Parent or guardian	• Social and family services • Rehabilitation counselor • Counselor and case manager • Job coach • Job placement specialist • Work adjustment specialist • Occupational therapist • Physical therapist • Reading specialist • Speech/language therapist	• Classmates • Physical education teachers • Sports coaches • Personal assistant • Extracurricular activities and school club leaders • Theater, chorus, and music program teachers

personnel, and many others. There are a few strategies that can help in identifying "stakeholders," or related services and community personnel, who could be enlisted to support and plan for inclusion.

1. **Consider the range of service sectors and other significant community members who can support the inclusion initiative.**
   - Parents and advocates
   - Educators and administrators
   - Related support services staff
   - Business-industry personnel
   - Rehabilitation personnel
   - Adult and community-based services personnel
   - Public and private health services personnel
   - Postsecondary agency personnel
   - Employers, employment services, and private non-profit gency personnel
   - Job training program personnel
   - Social services personnel
   - Business-education liaisons
   - School board members
   - Key community decision makers
   - Probation and parole workers
   - Police
   - Advocacy agency workers and leaders
   - Recreation and leisure services providers
   - College and university personnel
   - Civic and religious group leaders
   - Local and state politicians concerned with the needs of children and youth

2. **Carefully consider the role of students, parents, and parent leaders. As you engage the school and community in the inclusion initiative, seek to enlist advisors and planners.** Parents should be included in planning activities. They are often opinion leaders in a school and community and sometimes the best champions for change or new initiatives—if they support the effort. Parent and advocacy organizations are an essential link between educational agencies and the community. They need to understand how the new initiative will benefit their children, the school, and future opportunities for their children. Parent groups may include
   - School alumni
   - Parent Association leaders
   - Parent school board members
   - PTA leaders
   - Parent volunteers and advocates

The strongest champions for inclusion can emerge from any sector of the community, once the value and benefits of the initiative are communicated. It takes the whole school working together—believing in inclusion, working to make inclusion decisions, and resolving inclusion problems—to make the process successful.

CHAPTER 6

What Are the Major Controversies Surrounding Inclusion?

ARE THERE DIFFERENT OPINIONS ABOUT INCLUSION? There are a wide range of beliefs about what are "best practices" in inclusive education. Some educators believe that all children, including students with severe disabilities, should be included in general education classrooms, regardless of their ability to benefit from the mainstream curriculum. This is termed *full inclusion,* and means that no student should be excluded from the general education classroom. For example, according to full inclusion advocates, the idea of accommodation means placing a 14-year-old student with a severe cognitive disabilities into a general ninth-grade class, but providing that student with an individualized educational program at a first-grade level. Advocates of this kind of full inclusion placement argue that it achieves social inclusion, but not academic inclusion.

Other inclusion experts believe that the full inclusion model is not successful and is promoting failure and backlash among students, teachers, and parents (American Federation of Teachers, 1994; Council of Chief State School Officers, 1998). They believe that the question of benefit should be considered and there should be varying levels of inclusion (Chalmers & Faliede, 1996; Friend & Bursuck, 1999; McLeskey & Waldron, 1996; Putnam, 1993). There are a set of conditions or standards (e.g., achieving a certain rate of academic progress, maintaining acceptable levels of behavior or conduct) that must be met before a placement into a general education class can be considered successful.

When students of inclusion are introduced to the broad evidence of the legal legitimacy, effectiveness, and potential of inclusion, it is important that they also be made aware of the range of perspectives that exist.

Students of inclusion must be guided by a compelling and consistent message about the benefits and authority for inclusion if they are to become leaders who are confident to implement its practices and teach others. As Friend and Bursuck (1999), in their discussion of inclusion perspectives, relate: "Ultimately, what is most clear is that federal, state and local educational agencies must continue to commit financial and other resources to ensure that students with disabilities receive a high quality education in the least restrictive environment (p. 17)."

HOW CAN WE APPLY THE LRE PRINCIPLE? Just how should the least restrictive environment principle be applied? Is there any need for separate schools or classes? What does *restrictive* mean, and what is *least?* For whom and how? In 1981, the American Association on Mental Deficiency convened a task force on LRE to help clarify the principle so that it might be better understood and applied by professionals and other policymakers (Turnbull, 1991). This task force addressed tough questions about definitions of LRE, and their discussions are still useful today. In the late 1970s and early 1980s, educators and policymakers were more concerned with how LRE applied to individuals in institutions who might be better served in their communities. Today, the application of LRE is more complex. Students with disabilities are largely being served in their community schools, in varying degrees of integration. Table 6-1 compares the problems with applying the LRE principle 20 years ago and today.

WHY MUST THE LEAST RESTRICTIVE ENVIRONMENT BE MANDATED? There are many reasons why the principle of least restrictive environment, formerly called the least

TABLE 6-1. Least Restrictive Environment: Yesterday and Today

What Issues Were Important in Applying the Principle of Least Restrictive Environment in the 1970s?	What Issues Are Important in Applying the Principle of Least Restrictive Environment in 2000 and Beyond?
The principle of LRE was relevant and useful	The principle of LRE is relevant and useful
1. To students in separate schools to address conditions in those schools.	1. To guide movement of students from special education to the general education class.
2. To advocates of deinstitutionalization.	2. To guide movement of elementary students from the general education class into special education class once they are assessed as having a disability.
3. For ensuring appropriate length of time of placement in the institution.	3. To determine the amount of time appropriate in general classrooms.
4. In supporting the right to refuse treatment.	4. To determine the amount of individualization appropriate for the student in the general classroom.
5. For developing guidelines related to the amount of supervision residents received and needed.	5. To support the accommodation of students with disabilities in the use of new technologies.
6. In addressing appropriate procedures with individuals with self-injurious behavior.	6. To determine the range and types of educational alternatives possible within schools and communities.

restrictive alternative, was written into special education law. These reasons include the following:

- The Supreme Court created the principle as a matter of constitutional law affecting individual rights, which are protected from infringements at national, state, or local levels.
- There is a long history of segregating students with disabilities from nondisabled students.
- There is ample evidence that many students with disabilities can be educated quite effectively in programs for students without disabilities.
- Students with disabilities should have the opportunity to associate with, and to learn from, their nondisabled peers.
- A separate special education system is unjustifiable if it does not benefit students.
- It is expensive to operate two educational systems—special and general education.
- Any kind of segregation in education simply violates the United States Constitution, which seeks to treat all people equally (Turnbull, 1994).

The Individuals with Disabilities Education Act of 1997 (IDEA) (P.L. 105-17) contains a *presumption in favor of educating students who have disabilities with nondisabled students.* Furthermore, a school may not remove a student from general education unless that student cannot be educated there successfully (with educational benefit), even after the school provides supplementary aides and support services for such. Recently, in their decisions the courts have taken into account social inclusion, as well as physical and academic inclusion (Halpern, 1994; Patton & Blalock, 1996; Turnbull et al., 1995).

THE CORE OF THE CONTROVERSY: AGE- AND GRADE-APPROPRIATE PLACEMENTS. Age- and grade-appropriate placement is the most controversial component of inclusion. Age- and grade-appropriate placement means

placing the student into a classroom with his or her age-peers, regardless of the actual academic level of the student. In other words, a 15-year-old student working at a first-grade level in reading and arithmetic would be placed, with his age peers, into the ninth grade. The component is most divisive because it is based on ideals, values, and goals that are not congruent with the realities of today's classrooms. Several issues at the core of the controversy are presented in Table 6-2, which gives a description of the controversy related to each issue and a summary of the opinions of the field.

Proponents of full inclusion believe that the general education classroom can and will be able to accommodate all students with disabilities, even students with severe and multiple disabilities. They believe that students with severe or multiple disabilities can achieve educational and social benefit from the placement. They also believe that, although methods of collaborative learning and group instruction are the preferred methods, the traditional classroom size and resources are adequate for the management and accommodation of many students with disabilities, without adversely impacting the total classroom.

In contrast, many special educators believe that while inclusion should be achieved to the extent possible in school activities (academic, social, physical education, technology, music and drama, service, and extracurricular) some students are unlikely to receive appropriate academic or functional academic education without placement into alternative instructional groups or alternative learning environments, such as part-time or full-time special classes (Kauffman & Hallahan, 1993; Lieberman, 1992).

During the 1980s the California Research Institute carried out major studies of long-term integration of students with severe and multiple disabilities. Researchers studied over 200 classes serving more

Table 6-2. Summary of Controversial Issues and Opinions on Inclusion

Issue	Controversy	Opinion in the Field
Issue 1: Should the continuum of placements be eliminated?	The continuum of placements refers to the provision of a spectrum of educational settings into which students can be placed, ranging from the alternative school to inclusion into the general education class. The continuum makes more restrictive placements legitimate and infringes on students' rights, is based on a readiness model, supports the dominance of professional decision making, and rejects the idea that specialized services can only be provided in separate settings (Taylor, 1988). There is an expectation that general education classrooms have the capacity to accommodate any and all students with disabilities.	There is little consensus and much diversity in opinion about eliminating the continuum of placements. It is not a federal requirement to reduce or eliminate the continuum of services. The U.S. Office of Special Education supports the continuum of services, as does The Council for Exceptional Children, the largest professional association of special educators in the U.S.
Issue 2: What should be the appropriate amount of time students with disabilities spend in the general classrooms?	The expectation is that spending all day in the general education classroom is appropriate for all students regardless of severity of disability.	In general, inclusion advocates do not insist on 100% placement into the general academic classroom for all students. The placement should be appropriate to the needs of the individual.
Issue 3: What extent or severity of disability *should be* accommodated in the general classroom to yield an educational benefit for the student?	The expectation is that placement into the general classroom can yield an academic and social benefit for almost all students with disabilities regardless of severity of disability.	Inclusion advocates do not uniformly insist that all students with all levels of disabilities should be placed into the regular academic classroom.
Issue 4. What extent or severity of disability *should be* accommodated in the general classroom without impacting negatively upon the majority of students in the classroom?	The expectation is that the placement would not have a negative impact on the total classroom.	Inclusion advocates do not uniformly insist that all students with all levels of disabilities should be placed into the regular academic classroom. The placement should be appropriate to the needs of the student.
Issue 5: What extent or severity of disability *can be* accommodated in the general classroom?	The expectation is that the accommodations required in the general class will be reasonable and affordable.	There is general agreement that placement should not harm the student. In other words, students should not be placed into a regular classroom if there is inadequate support or capacity to accommodate the student.
Issue 6: What is the appropriate rate at which children with disabilities should be transferred from more restrictive settings and placed into general classrooms?	The expectation is that the process of transferring students is harmful neither to the individual student being transferred, nor to the students in the receiving classroom.	There is a consensus among experts that the process of integrating students with disabilities into general education classes should not be harmful to the individual student being transferred, nor to the students in the receiving classes.

that 2,000 students with severe disabilities in 20 schools. They found some clear outcomes. Students' progress and achievements differed depending on the amount of in-class support they received from teachers, aides, and consultants. The National Education Association (NEA) also reviewed the direct experiences of many teachers in inclusive classrooms across the United States. Teachers saw significant progress with most special learners as long as the teachers themselves had the resources, administrative support, and adequate time for instructional planning and consultation (Dalheim, 1994; Hallahan & Kauffman, 1997).

CHAPTER 7

What Is the Conclusion About Inclusion?

HAVE WE REACHED CONSENSUS? As we approach the new millennium, there is still no general consensus on the definition of inclusion. As was true about integration of other populations of individuals into this nation in the early part of this century (e.g., African Americans; Italian, Irish, and Asian immigrants; and Hispanic populations), the dialogue about how they should be integrated has lasted for decades. However, out of such dialogue and debate has emerged renewed commitment to serving all children in the public school system throughout the nation. For students with disabilities, the range of positions and disagreements that many educators have about inclusion can be summarized as follows.

1. **Need to know more.** There is a lot we need to know about the effectiveness of inclusion and meaningful benefit of educational placements. Those in the field need to know more about the effectiveness of practices such as age- and grade-appropriate placement and are actively conducting research.
2. **No operational definition.** There is no specific operational definition of full inclusion that has been agreed upon in the field.
3. **Many benefits.** The benefits of inclusion outweigh the costs for students with and without disabilities.
4. **Full inclusion not generally demanded.** Inclusion advocates for the most part do not advocate 100 percent placement into the regular classroom; they do not uniformly insist that all students with all levels of disability should be placed into the general academic classroom.
5. **Appropriate placement benefits.** The courts agree that for students who are educated in general education classes, *appropriate educational placement* means receiving passing grades and advancing from grade to grade. For students with severe disabilities, progress toward greater self-sufficiency and functional skills would be more reasonable benefits (Osborne, 1992).
6. **Individualization a hallmark.** Most inclusion advocates agree that individualization of education is the

hallmark of special education and no single educational placement is always appropriate for meeting every student's academic, social, or career-vocational goals. There are no universal solutions or absolute answers for everyone.
7. **Do no harm.** There is general agreement that placement should not harm the student. In other words, students should not be placed into a general education classroom if there is inadequate support or capacity to accommodate the student. There is also a consensus among experts that the process of transitioning and integrating students with disabilities into general education classes should not be harmful to the individual student being transferred.
8. **Overall educational improvement needed.** There is general agreement that the effort to improve education for students with disabilities must be accomplished within a broader effort to improve education for all students. Advancing inclusive placements alone without restructuring the classroom, curriculum, and instruction will lead to the failure of inclusion (synthesized from the works of the following: Dalheim, 1994; Friend & Bursuck, 1999; Fuchs & Fuchs, 1994; Hallahan & Kauffman, 1997; Hardman, Drew & Egan, 1999; Janney et al., 1995; Kauffman & Hallahan, 1993; Lieberman, 1992; McCoy, 1995; Osborne, 1988; Sailor, 1991; Salisbury, Palombaro, & Hollowood, 1993; Reynolds, 1991; Taylor, 1988; Turnbull et al., 1995).

The central theme of IDEA is that there is no "one size fits all." All placement and programming decisions must be made on an *individualized* basis.

WHAT IS THE FEDERAL GOVERNMENT'S POSITION? The U.S. Department of Education's Office of Special Education reports annually on the progress that the states are making in implementing IDEA. Each year, they synthesize what has been learned from a range of research studies related to the progress of students with disabilities in

The central theme of IDEA is that there is no "one-size-fits-all" approach. Placement and program decisions must be made on an *individualized* basis.

general education and special education classes, and in making a successful transition from schooling to employment, postsecondary education, and adult independence. The following summarizes the facts and conclusions about the movement toward more inclusive education, gleaned from these extensive reports over the past several years.

1. Unfortunately, there is no single answer to the question "what works?" because of the tremendous and growing diversity of students attending schools today. Cultural and language diversity in the classroom, for example, means that no single mode of teacher-student relating and no single pedagogical (teaching) style is likely to be effective for all children in that classroom. Among students with disabilities, too, the great variation in their abilities and disabilities underscores the critical importance of the individualized programs that are one of the hallmarks of special education, as required by law (U.S. Office of Special Education, *Thirteenth Annual Report to Congress,* 1992, p. 102).

2. Time in regular education and vocational classes for secondary education students was associated with positive school results, according to the National Longitudinal Transition Study of Special Education Students (NLTS). For example, secondary education students who succeeded in regular education had higher employment, independent living, and community participation rates (U.S. Office of Special Education, *Eighteenth Annual Report to Congress,* 1996, p. 19).

3. Data for students with disabilities, ages 6 to 21, show that during the past several years, the percentage of students with disabilities served in regular classes has increased, while the percentage of students in resource rooms has decreased. Other placement percentages have remained stable (U.S. Office of Special Education, *Eighteenth Annual Report to Congress,* 1996, p. 20).

4. Placement patterns vary by disability. The majority of students with speech and language impairments are served in regular classes. Students with learning disabilities, orthopedic impairments, emotional disturbance, and traumatic brain injury are generally placed in the regular school buildings, but are then spread in placements across regular classes, resource rooms, and separate classes. Separate classroom placements are most prevalent for students with mental retardation, autism, and multiple disabilities. However, resource room placements are also commonly used to serve students with mental retardation and multiple disabilities.

5. The Office of Special Education has determined that the requirements with the strongest links to results include (a) access to the full range of programs and services within a school, with proper supports as determined through an individualized education program (IEP) available to nondisabled children; (b) statements of needed transition services for students with disabilities no later than age 14 (also see Section 23 on School-To-Career Transition Services); and (c) education in the least restrictive environment (LRE).

6. Quality education and proper supports are essential components of successful school experiences. There is no single special education policy that benefits all students. A range of options tailored to meet the individual needs of all students continues to be the most effective approach (U.S. Office of Special Education, *Eighteenth Annual Report to Congress,* 1996, p. 19).

NOT JUST ANOTHER EDUCATIONAL REFORM: SUMMING UP. Inclusion is not just another educational reform or fad that is based on shifting curriculum priorities, instructional beliefs, political values, or diminishing educational budgets. The movement toward more inclusive education for individuals with disabilities represents a final frontier in the progress of human rights. As with the fight for the right to equal access to public education by racial and ethnic minorities in this century, the inclusion debate is another expression of and necessary stage in the civil rights movement. Inclusion embodies the ideals and goals of a democracy that are continuously reached for, though possibly never perfectly achieved.

Implementing inclusion in schools and classrooms has to be guided by rational standards and principles, the first of which is to ensure that no harm comes to the student as a result. Second, inclusive placements and practices must be developed with the goal of effecting measurable progress, not just in the academic domain, but in a range of developmental areas, including career-vocational, social and life-skills development, physical development, and creative development. Inclusion is not a new program or experiment confined to one or two classrooms or one or two schools within a school district, but it is a transformation in how we think about structuring educational environments for all children and youth in all classrooms and schools. It is a change in how we help to empower children and youth to imagine and construct their own destinies.

CHAPTER 8

With All the Controversy, How Do We Develop a Rational Approach to Inclusion?

THE NEED FOR BALANCE IN DEFINING INCLUSION AND THE LEAST RESTRICTIVE ENVIRONMENT. Special education law was passed in order to establish a right for all children and youth to benefit from an education that was appropriate to their needs. It was also passed to ensure that individuals were not subject to excessive restrictions and to protect their right to have lives as close as possible to the normal lives of nondisabled peers. *The concepts of benefit, individual liberty, and freedom from restriction* are central to the principle of least restrictive environment (LRE), a pivotal concept in the law. The LRE doctrine is linked to the democratic principles of freedom and individual liberty. Yet none of us is entirely free; we are constrained in our behavior socially, legally, economically, morally, and ethically (Turnbull, 1981). Most of us recognize that freedom is relative and the freedoms of the individual must be balanced against the freedoms of others in society.

PERSPECTIVE ON INDIVIDUAL FREEDOM AND RESPONSIBILITY. In education, individual freedom is restricted for social and moral reasons. For example, children are required by law to go to school. Students are not permitted to carry radios, beepers, or weapons to school. They are not allowed to keep medicines or drugs in their possession or in lockers, and they are restricted to some extent in their dress. These restrictions are imposed because society believes that they provide benefits to students as individuals and groups. These restrictions protect students from inappropriate and unsupervised use of medicines, potential injuries from weapons, and the distractions from learning that radios and beepers present.

Behavior of students and their choices in educational programs and services are also limited by costs, since schools cannot afford to make all possible program options available to everyone. Choices are also limited by the decisions of governments. Governments and courts can set forth two kinds of rules to govern human behavior and mediate among competing individual rights.

1. Firm or absolute rules on behalf of a whole group of individuals.
2. Broad guidelines, or "preferred" choices, which have some flexibility and that are highly subject to interpretation.

FIRM RULES, GUIDELINES, AND LRE. Firm rules often are established for minor children and adolescents (e.g., no minor may purchase alcohol). More flexible guidelines, which can be bent if adequate circumstances exist, are also used by policymakers to control behavior and conduct. For example, traffic laws that require the general public to stop at red lights may be routinely adjusted by emergency vehicles attempting to reach an accident scene as quickly as possible.

The LRE principle is a tool for guiding *decisions* about students with disabilities. It falls into the category of broad guideline or preferred choice, for which there is flexibility and which is highly subject to interpretation. The practice of inclusion has evolved from the doctrine of LRE to include an accepted array of placements depending upon the needs of the individuals (e.g., general education class, resource room, separate special education class). The least restrictive, or more inclusive, setting is considered the preferred choice because it leans in favor of the student's greater liberty. Leaning in favor of a student's greater liberty is, therefore, the preferred choice in general, unless there is a need to accomplish a greater purpose or valid reason for not granting the more inclusive choice. The greater purpose may be to protect the safety and well-being of other students. For example, if a student is self-destructive, violent, has a communicable disease, or has uncontrollable behavior, then the general classroom as the least restrictive alterative would not be appropriate. So some restriction is justifiable.

Suppose the greater purpose is not for safety, but to meet the educational needs of the student who is performing academically far below age peers (for example the student who is age 15 but performing at a first-grade level in reading and arithmetic). The least restrictive placement would be considered the ninth-grade classroom with age peers, but such a placement may not be of benefit to the student. Therefore, the *preferred choice of placement may not always be the least restrictive placement.*

TOWARD A SENSIBLE FRAMEWORK FOR INCLUSION. Many inclusion advocates highlight the difference between inclusion and the principle of least restrictive environment. They argue that the LRE principle and the U.S. Department of Education's Regular Education Initiative sought to restructure general education so that it could improve access to and better accommodate the needs of students with disabilities in general education classrooms (Turnbull et al., 1995). Inclusion, on the other hand, is seen as a

> value that is expressed in the way we plan, promote and conceptualize the development of children. In inclusive programs, the diverse needs of all children are accommodated to the maximum extent possible within the general education curriculum. . . . Driven by a vision of schools as a place where all children learn well what we want them to learn, schools become creative and successful environments for adults and the children they serve. (Salisbury et al., 1993)

Framework for Rational Inclusion. Based on the discussion above, inclusion, according to contemporary educators, differs from least restrictive environment because it is a *broader and more comprehensive reform effort.* Yet the LRE principle and concept of inclusion share the common assumption that all children should "learn well." This means that there is an established right for all children and youth to benefit from an education that is appropriate to their needs. It also means that individuals should not be subject to excessive restrictions, and they have protected rights to live lives as close as possible to the normal lives of their nondisabled peers. Rational inclusion, therefore, is defined as inclusive practices which are consistent with these assumptions of appropriateness and protection from excessive restriction. Rational inclusion is defined in terms of practices consistent with five basic principles.

Principle 1: Right to Benefit from an Education Appropriate to Individual Needs. Special education law was passed in order to establish a right for all children and youth to benefit from an *education* that is appropri-ate to their needs. In a democracy, ensuring that all children have access to appropriate educational opportunities is a social responsibility.

Principle 2: Right to Be Educated to the Extent Possible with Nondisabled Peers. The 1975 Education for All Handicapped Children Act (P.L. 94-142) required that placements be "based on the child's individualized education program in which appropriate services are described. To the maximum extent appropriate, children with disabilities must be educated with children who are not disabled, and special classes, separate schooling, or other removal of children with disabilities from regular educational environments occurs only when the nature or severity of the disability is such that education in regular classes with the use of supplementary aids and services cannot be achieved satisfactorily."

Principle 3: Right to Least Restrictive Environment. The restrictiveness of the placement, therefore, is integrally linked to the potential of the placement to benefit or provide appropriate education. These two cannot be separated and must be considered and weighed together in placement decisions.

Principle 4: Increase in the Number of Less Restrictive Alternatives. A placement should not be any more restrictive than is necessary to achieve educational benefit. As schools implement the LRE principle, the focus of effort should be on creating less restrictive alternatives, rather than only on reducing overly restrictive choices (Turnbull, 1991). This means that while school personnel may be working to reduce the number of separate classes and resource rooms (more restrictive placements), they should simultaneously be increasing inclusive placements in general education classrooms having adequate supports. They should also be seeking to provide inclusive opportunities in a wide range of school curricular and extracurricular activities. The experience of freedom and greater control over one's life is a prerequisite for growth and development.

Principle 5: Ensure Both Social and Educational Benefits. Social benefits are related to, but are not synonymous with, educational benefits. As such, a least restrictive alternative for some students may not be the general education classroom. Some children who differ greatly from the norm (e.g., the 12-year-old with a very superior IQ who is ready for college material) would find the typical seventh-grade class very restrictive. Similarly, children with severe cognitive, behavioral, and emotional disabilities need curriculum modification and differentiated educational services, goals, and standards. Some children with more severe disabilities may need differentiated services delivered in settings that provide a reduced teacher–student ratio and other modifications to the environment that cannot be provided in a regular classroom. These decisions must be driven by individual student needs. To be in accordance with the intent of the

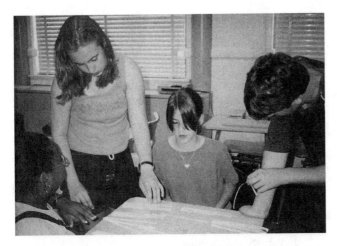

Placements in the general education class yield social as well as educational benefits.

law, less restrictive placements, cannot be made without regard to educational benefit.

BALANCED DECISION MAKING FOR INCLUSION. Many considerations are necessary to make decisions about an appropriate match between the student's needs and the capacity of the classroom to accommodate the student. If inclusion planners apply the principles for rational inclusion outlined above, they are more likely to achieve a balanced approach to implementing inclusion, one that integrates the ideas and requirements of educational benefit, individual liberty, and least restrictive alterative. These elements define the success of inclusion.

Two additional principles must be considered in implementing inclusion. The first addresses *the placement decision,* and the second, the *impact of the decision on the classroom* (Figure 8-1).

Implementation Principle 1. Placement and Accommodations Are Based on Student Need and Expectation of Benefit. The first and primary principle on which the placement decision is based is on the assessed individ-

APPROPRIATE
EDUCATION

- Individualized education
- Individual evaluation
- Least restrictive placement
- Expectation of educational benefit

- Impact of placement on the student
- Impact of placement on the classroom
- Resources and support
- Accommodations and resources in the environment

Successful inclusion

FIGURE 8-1. Decisions about least restrictive placement, resources, and supports must be made with consideration of the impact of the placement on the student and the classroom environment.

ual needs of the student and expectation of benefit for that student (appropriate placement first). Questions that decision makers should ask when considering a placement of a student into the general education class include the following:

- With support and accommodation, can the student be expected to participate in and benefit from the curriculum being delivered in the regular classroom?
- With support and accommodation, can the student benefit from the support of the teacher or cooperating team of teachers during class or in after-school help sessions?
- With support and accommodation, can the student maintain an achievement level comparable to that in the self-contained class or previous placement?
- With support and accommodation, can the student be expected to display appropriate social behavior for the grade level and to interact positively with others?
- With support and accommodation, can the student participate in the classroom assessments used for all other children in the classroom?

Implementation Principle 2. The Impact on the Classroom Is Assessed and Needed Resources Identified. *If principle 1 is met,* then the second decision relates to the response on the part of the teacher and the student's peers as to the new student's placement. This principle requires that the teacher assess the impact that placement is likely to have on the learning environment for other students. The teacher does not assess impact *in order to argue against the placement,* since principle 1 has been met. Rather, the teacher does so in order to determine how the class and program can best accommodate the student, what resources are needed to appropriately support and sustain that student, and how other students in the class should be prepared for the changes that will occur in the classroom. The questions decision makers should ask when considering such a placement include the following:

- How can the classroom and curriculum be reasonably modified to accommodate the student and ensure levels of achievement equivalent to others'?
- What resources are needed to make the accommodations to the classroom and curriculum?
- How can the student's peers be best prepared for the participation of the new student?
- How can the assessment process be reasonably modified to accurately assess the student's progress relative to that of peers?
- What resources are needed to modify the assessment process to accurately assess the student's progress and performance?
- How can the student with a disability receive academic support from students in the general education class?
- How can the student with a disability be helped to feel comfortable as a participating member of the class?
- What environmental accommodations will be needed (e.g., access modifications for use of technology, rearranged seating, enlarged print on displays), and how will these be introduced to the class?

Once principle 1 has been met, principle 2 requires that the responsibility for making an accommodation for the student lies with the parent (guardian), school principal, and classroom teacher(s), including consulting or team teachers. Part 2 of this handbook provides illustrations of how these principles are applied in real classroom situations.

TOWARD AN INCLUSION BILL OF RIGHTS. The inclusion of children into the regular classes has accelerated quickly in the past decade and in many places has occurred too fast and without adequate planning for restructuring or teacher reeducation. There is a growing concern by teachers, special educators, and administrators that many poor inclusion policies are being implemented. Such poor inclusion efforts are failing to provide the necessary supportive services that students with disabilities need when they are placed into regular classrooms.

In schools everywhere, students with greater academic and social learning problems are adding to the challenge of teaching. Teachers are expected to develop educational programs that can serve a diversity of special needs students, including those with disabilities, students at risk for failure, former school dropouts, students with limited English proficiency, teen parents, and many others. Today these special populations represent a majority of students in some school systems. At the same time, teachers today are being asked to accept greater responsibility for the performance and achievement of their students. As teachers restructure their classrooms to include students with disabilities, the success of each student is the product of what happens there. Teachers are being subject to pay-for-performance incentive programs and merit pay plans, yet are uncertain that their hard work in serving students with disabilities in inclusive classess will be considered in their performance evaluations.

Many aspects of decision making about how inclusion will be implemented have not been adequately addressed in the training of preservice or inservice special or general educators. General education teachers have commonly been left out of site-based decisions about including students with disabilities in their classrooms. Therefore, there is a need to address their concerns about their ability to ensure success of students placed into inclusive classrooms. To reiterate a previous point, the rights of children with disabilities must be protected under law, but successful inclusion also depends upon reconciling the needs and concerns of all who are involved, including parents, teachers, and administrators, in a manner that makes the promise and process of inclusion a rational and effective one. The authors, in their development of an Inclusion Bill of Rights, take the position that the differing needs of students, teachers, parents, and administrators need not clash, but are complementary. We believe that considering the rights and needs of one group at the expense of another jeopardizes

the inclusion process and its quality. All are essential to the process. As Putnam (1993) put it, it only seems fair that teachers who are asked to educate students with differing abilities receive adequate preparation, special supports and services, the commitment of administration, and opportunities to engage in positive team approaches.

Why an Inclusion Bill of Rights? Because general education teachers have generally been left out of decisions about implementing inclusion. Our *Inclusion Bill of Rights* addresses their role as key implementors by addressing and reconciling the concerns and responsibilities of

1. Consumer-students
2. Parents and guardians
3. Teachers and support personnel
4. Principals and administrators

These sets of concerns, described in Tables 8-1, 8-2, and 8-3, are complementary and form a coherent and coordinated set of responsibilities for inclusion for each of the key participants. Each of these groups is responsible for the success or failure of inclusion. Considering the concerns and needs of one group at the expense of another is to jeopardize the inclusion process and its quality. All are essential to the process.

GENERAL EDUCATION TEACHERS AND ADMINISTRATORS ARE KEY PLAYERS FOR SUCCESSFUL SYSTEM CHANGE AND INCLUSION SUCCESS. Experts and advocates for inclusion generally agree on the need to end the dual tracks of special and regular education and create a unified system. Most concur that general education teachers and administrators and their attitudes toward inclusion are the key ingredients to success in its implementation. School principals and other administrators provide the leadership that leads either to success in implementing inclusion or to increased barriers. They have considerable control over the distribution of funds, development of school policies, and use of personnel resources and can make the difference in the quality of the implementation effort. The early development of special education has led to the creation of a parallel system but one that is disconnected from the general education system. This dual structure continues to create organizational problems within schools and prevent program coordination essential for the *embedding* of specialized educational services into the general education framework. The American Society for Curriculum Development's review of change initiatives (1990) identified 8 barriers to innovation effectiveness that were common to four large-scale change projects:

a. An inadequate theory of implementation, including too little time for teachers to plan for and learn new skills and practices.
b. District tendencies toward faddism and quick-fix solutions.
c. Lack of sustained central office support and follow-through

(List continues on page 35.)

TABLE 8-1. Inclusion Bill of Rights for Students

In participating in inclusive classrooms, students have the following rights:

Right	Explanation
1. Right to participate in a range of school programs and activities	The right to accommodation of persons with disabilities in the full range of general and special educational programs available to all students, including academic, vocational education, transition services, and job training programs and placement opportunities and articulated school-college programs.
2. Right to needed related and supplementary services in general education class	The right to access a range of student support services in general education classrooms, including guidance and counseling, career counseling, peer support, assistance with application to colleges or postsecondary placement, health and medication services and counseling, and other support.
3. Right to participate in school extracurricular activities	The right to accommodation of persons with disabilities into the full range of extracurricular opportunities generally available, including student clubs, sports (as appropriate), drama and theatrical productions, chorus, debate teams, trade-related clubs, student governance organizations, booster clubs, student fund-raising activities, and others.
4. Right to participate in technology-related opportunities	The right to accommodation of persons with disabilities into the full range of technology-related opportunities generally available, including access to libraries, information centers, technology laboratories, and school-based weather stations, as well as accommodations in such centers and adaptations to equipment as may be necessary for use of the technology and participation in student group activities using technology.
5. Right to participate in your own IEP	The right to participate in the development of your IEP/ITP (Individualized Transition Plan) to the extent possible, and the right to be present and participate in your IEP/ITP placement meeting prior to placement to discuss and assess needs and available accommodations.
6. Right to advanced notice	The right to an informed placement, which means you have the right to know at least several days in advance of a change of placement.
7. Right to know about your disability	The right to know about your disability and its implications for your educational program. If you have a physical, medical, emotional, or behavioral problem that might result in the need for you to take an emergency action, you also have the right to know whether there is a written school emergency policy and that the teacher is trained in and knowledgeable about the emergency procedures.
8. Right to know about emergency procedures	The right to know that there are clearly defined emergency management policies and procedures for the school, to guide teachers and other personnel in the event of a behavioral, medical, or natural emergency.
9. Right to know reasons for placement	The right to information in advance about the Interdisciplinary Team (IDT) rationale for a decision to place you into an inclusive classroom, as well as a statement of the expectations of the IDT for the benefits of the placement and expected progress in the classroom within a specified period of time.
10. Right to receive an evaluation of your educational needs and to receive supplemental supports in the classroom	The right to supplemental materials, equipment, or personnel deemed necessary by the IDT for your benefit from the educational and social program in the classroom, including, but not limited to physical assistive devices or equipment, technology adaptations (computer adaptations), physical adaptations to the classroom, personal or classroom aides, instructional materials, interpreters, recording devices, or other equipment.
11. Right to advanced knowledge about classroom accommodations	The right to be informed in advance about the availability of such supplemental materials and equipment and to have an introduction to or training, if necessary, in the use of such equipment and materials in advance of or, minimally, at the time of your placement into the classroom.
12. Right to access your IEP	The right to access and review your IEP/ITP at any time after your placement into the classroom.

TABLE 8-1. *(continued)*

Right	Explanation
13. Right to communicate problems	The right to a fair and accessible process in which you as the student may raise issues or concerns at any time about your placement and your progress and may request consultation or assistance in problem solving or seeking additional support.
14. Right to have trained personnel	The right to have teachers and support personnel adequately trained in the education and support of students included into regular classrooms.
15. Right to vocational assessment	The right to receive a comprehensive vocational assessment as part of the transitional services required under IDEA.
16. Right to trained personnel in career-vocational education	The right to adequate numbers of and proper preparation of direct support service and instructional staff to ensure access to the range of educational, career-vocational, technical and technology-related, and transition services.
17. Right to participate in school-to-work opportunities	The right to participate in coherent career-vocational and school-to-work opportunities that directly address the needs of students with your special needs and explicitly describe services and provide activities and resources to support your participation in these opportunities.
18. Right to inclusion in school-reform opportunities	The right to participate in GOALS 2000 (National Educational Goals initiatives; see Chapter 10 for more information) and other school-reform activities and to have your special needs addressed in such reforms or restructuring.
19. Right to reasonable inclusion in national standards	The right to have special needs such as yours addressed and assessed in relation to your preparation to meet local, state, and national standards for academic achievement, work preparation, and job training.

TABLE 8-2. Inclusion Bill of Rights for Parents

In participating in inclusive classrooms, parents have the following rights:

Right	Explanation
1. Right to have your child participate in range of school programs and activities	The right to accommodation of your child in the full range of general and special education programs available to all students, including early intervention, academic, vocational education, transition services, job training and placement opportunities, and articulated school-college programs.
2. Right of your child to have related and supplementary services in general education class	The right to accommodation of your child in the range of student support services in general education classrooms, including guidance and counseling, career counseling, peer support, assistance with application to colleges or postsecondary placement, health services, medical and counseling, and others.
3. Right of your child to participate in school extracurricular activities	The right to accommodation of your child in the full range of extracurricular opportunities generally available, including student clubs, sports (as appropriate), drama and theatrical productions, chorus, debate teams, trade-related clubs, student governance organizations, booster clubs, student fund-raising activities, and others.
4. Right of your child to participate in technology-related opportunities	The right to accommodation of your child into the full range of technology-related opportunities generally available, including access to libraries, information centers, technology laboratories, and school-based weather stations, as well as accommodations in such centers, and adaptations to equipment as may be necessary for use of the technology and participation in student group activities using technology.
5. Right to participate in your child's IEP	The right to assist your child in participating in the development of his or her IEP (to the extent possible for students with severe cognitive disabilities) and the right to be present and participate in the IEP placement meeting prior to placement to discuss and assess needs and available accommodations.
6. Right to advanced notice about your child's placement	The right to be informed in advance about your child's placement and to participate in an IEP meeting to discuss the change.

TABLE 8-2. *(continued)*

Right	Explanation
7. Right to know about your child's disability	The right to know if your child has been determined to have a physical, medical, emotional, or behavioral problem that might result in the need to take an emergency action by teachers or other school personnel, that there is a written school policy on emergency procedures, and that the teacher is trained and knowledgeable about the emergency procedures or action that may be needed.
8. Right to know about emergency procedures for your child	The right to know that there are clearly defined emergency management policies and procedures for the school, to guide teachers and other school personnel in the event of a behavioral, medical, or natural emergency involving your child.
9. Right to know the reasons for placement decisions about your child	The right to information in advance about the IDT rationale for a decision to place your child into an inclusive classroom, as well as a statement of the expectations of the IDT for the benefits of the placement and expected progress in the classroom within a specified period of time.
10. Right to know the outcomes of the evaluation of your child and the needed supplemental supports in the classroom	The right to supplemental materials, equipment, or personnel deemed necessary by the IDT to ensure that your child benefits from the educational and social programs in the classroom, including, but not limited to physical assistive devices or equipment, technology adaptations (computer adaptations), physical adaptations to the classroom, personal or classroom aides, instructional materials, interpreters, recording devices, or other equipment.
11. Right to advanced knowledge about classroom accommodations for your child	The right to be informed in advance about the availability of such supplemental materials and equipment so that you as the parent may support or augment your child's orientation or training on the use of needed equipment and materials in advance of or, minimally, at the time of your child's placement into the classroom.
12. Right to access your child's IEP	The right to access and review the IEP/ITP of your child and the right to frequent communication with teachers and administrators about the progress of your child or about changes in the curriculum or program for your child that may be related to adjustment to the inclusive classroom.
13. Right to communicate problems about your child to teachers and administrators	The right to a fair and accessible process in which you as the parent may raise issues or concerns at any time about your child's placement and progress and may request consultation or assistance in problem solving or seeking additional support or suggestions on how the home environment may support the problem-solving process.
14. Right to have trained personnel in your child's classroom	The right to have your child taught by teachers and support personnel who are adequately trained for educating children in inclusive classrooms.
15. Right to vocational assessment for your child	The right to have a comprehensive vocational assessment as part of the transitional services required under IDEA, and to have an interpretation of the meaning of the results in terms of your child's future program, services, or home enrichment.
16. Right to have trained personnel in the career-vocational education classes of your child	The right to adequate numbers of and proper preparation of direct support service and instructional staff to ensure access to the range of educational, career-vocational, technical and technology-related, and transition services.
17. Right of your child to participate in school-to-work opportunities	The right to have the needs of children such as yours addressed in a coherent school-based plan for career-vocational services and school-to-work opportunities, a plan that explicitly describes services, activities, and resources to support your child's participation in these opportunities.
18. Right of your child to be included in school-reform opportunities	The right to have your child's needs addressed in a school's improvement or reform plan.
19. Right of your child to be included in state and local assessments and curriculum reforms	The right to have your child's needs assessed in relation to academic achievement, work preparation, and job training.

TABLE 8-3. Inclusion Bill of Rights for Teachers and Support Personnel

In participating in inclusive classrooms, teachers and support personnel have the following rights:

Right	Explanation
1. Right to know about expected success	The right to know the expectations for students placed into general education classes from the pool of students with disabilities.
2. Right to technical assistance and support services	The right to technical assistance and support services in accommodating students with disabilities in (a) the full range of general and special education programs available to all students, including academic, vocational education, transition services, job training placement opportunities, and articulated school-college programs; (b) the full range of extracurricular opportunities generally available, including student clubs, sports (as appropriate), drama and theatrical productions, chorus, debate teams, trade-related clubs, student governance organizations, booster clubs, student fund-raising activities, and other extracurricular opportunities; and (c) the full range of technology-related opportunities generally available, including access to libraries, information centers, technology laboratories, and school-based weather stations, as well as accommodations in such centers, and adaptations to equipment as may be necessary for use of the technology and participation in student group activities using technology.
3. Right to needed supplementary services in the general education class	The right to be informed about and have access to the range of available student support services in general education classrooms, including guidance and counseling, career counseling, peer support, assistance with application to colleges or postsecondary placement, health and medication services and counseling, and other supportive services.
4. Right to participate in your students' IEP meetings	The right to participate in the development of your students' IEPs and the right to be present and participate in the IEP placement meeting prior to placement to discuss and assess needs and available accommodations.
5. Right to advanced notice about placement	The right to be informed in advance about a student's placement and to participate in an IEP meeting to discuss the change.
6. Right to know about extent of disabilities	The right to an *informed placement*, which means you have the right to know if a student placed into your classroom has a physical, medical, emotional, or behavioral problem that might result in the need for you to take an emergency action, and the right to know what type of emergency procedures or action you may need to take. IDEA promotes the inclusion of children with chronic health impairments and those dependent on medical technology into the regular classroom.
7. Right to know about and be trained in emergency procedures	The right to have clearly defined emergency management policies and procedures for the school and to be trained in such procedures, in order to safely guide yourself and others in the event of a behavioral, medical, or natural emergency.
8. Right to know reasons for placement	The right to information in advance about the administrative and IDT rationale for a decision to place a student into your classroom and a statement of the expectations of the IDT regarding the benefits of the classroom placement and expected progress of the child within a specified period of time.
9. Right to related services and supplemental resources in the classroom	The right to supplemental materials, equipment, or personnel that are deemed necessary by the IDT for the student to benefit from the educational and social program in the classroom, including, but not limited to, physical assistive devices or equipment, technology adaptations (computer adaptations), physical adaptations to the classroom, personal or classroom aides, instructional materials, interpreters, recording devices, or other equipment.
10. Right to advanced knowledge about classroom accommodations	The right to be informed in advance about such supplemental materials or assistive technology or equipment and to be trained in the use of such equipment and materials in advance of, or minimally at the time of the student's placement into the classroom.

TABLE 8-3. *(continued)*

Right	Explanation
11. Right to access the IEP	The right to be present and participate in a student's IEP placement meeting prior to placement to learn about the child and the child's needs and accommodations and the right to access and review the IEP of the child placed into the classroom.
12. Right to constructive problem solving	The right to a fair and accessible process in which the teacher may raise issues or concerns at any time about a placement of a student, the student's progress, or the student's behavior and may request a consultation or assistance in problem solving or seeking additional support.
13. Right to receive needed training on inclusion	The right to have the in-service training needs of regular educators, special educators, career-vocational educators, and related services personnel addressed in the local and state personnel development plans, and to receive needed training for inclusion.
14. Right to have planning time	For team teachers, the right to have common planning time each week and time to develop agreed upon goals for joint students.
15. Right to inclusion support for school-to-work	The right to have the needs of students with disabilities and teacher supports addressed in a coherent, school-based plan for career-vocational services and school-to-work opportunities, a plan that explicitly describes services, activities, and resources to support students' participation in these opportunities.
16. Right to inclusion support in school reform	The right to have the needs of students with disabilities and teacher supports addressed in the school's improvement plan.
17. Right to inclusion in national standards	The right to have the needs of students with disabilities and of teacher supports addressed and assessed in relation to their preparation for academic achievement, work preparation, and job training.

d. Underfunding of the project and trying to do too much with too little support.

e. Attempting to manage projects from the central district office instead of developing school leadership and building-level capacity.

f. Lack of technical assistance and other forms of intensive staff development.

g. Lack of awareness of the limitations of teacher and school administrator knowledge about how to implement reforms, particularly inclusion.

h. Failure to understand and take into account site-specific differences among schools. (p. 7)

In implementing inclusion, the general education teacher is also at center stage. Though there are special education consultants, team teachers, and teacher aides, the main responsibility for creating inclusive classrooms for students with disabilities falls on the general education teacher.

SOME TELLING STORIES: CONVERSATIONS WITH SCHOOL DISTRICT LEADERS IN SPECIAL AND GENERAL EDUCATION. There is a great deal of confusion in the field about the goals and strategies for providing inclusive services to all youth and young adults. Examples of actual problems being faced by educational leaders in six states in the process of school improvement are revealed below from personal communications with state and local leaders.

- "The principal told us we are now an 'inclusion school'; we have not had any training, the regular education teachers are scared and angry and we have no time to plan together. Kids and teachers are frustrated. No one is learning."
- "New language arts curriculum is not being shared with special education staff in our county, but at the same time, we are giving lip service to inclusion and then developing separate regular and special education teams!"
- "We have a team of 25 teachers who are selected as an instructional support team which goes into schools and provides professional development, works with individual teachers, and facilitates reform efforts; these teachers form three clusters, who serve all schools that feed into an area high school, including elementary and middle. But these teams do not include special educators."
- "I had to get really aggressive to be placed onto our State School-To-Work Planning Committee as the only special populations representative. They wouldn't call me back, so I contacted State legislators and finally got myself included."
- "Our students cannot get into the Tech Prep programs to participate in the new career/technology training; they are told that they have to take at least two unrelated courses of custodial services before they can qualify to get in."

- "There is only one special education representative (the same person) on the development teams for curriculum development and vocational-technical education development."
- Our regular education teachers, especially vocational education instructors, are not given time to attend IEP/ITP meetings. In fact, they often aren't invited and can't get copies of students' IEPs."

Clearly new leadership is needed to ensure the participation of everyone in *inclusive* learning systems and to develop schools that promote full participation of all youth. Leaders need skills that enable them to promote comprehensive, flexible approaches to learning and development that link education and community and that embrace academic development, social development, physical education, career development, and preparation for life roles.

CHAPTER 9

What Are the Benefits and Outcomes of Inclusion?

The benefits of inclusion far outweigh the difficulties for students with and without disabilities, for families, and for the community. The following sections summarize the many benefits of inclusive schools and classrooms for students, teachers, parents, and the wider community.

Benefits for Students with Disabilities

- Facilitates more appropriate social behavior because of higher expectations in the general education class.
- Fosters higher self-esteem as a result of direct and frequent interaction with nondisabled peers.
- Promotes higher sense of personal success from inclusion in the general education classroom.
- Improves ability to keep up with the everyday pace of instruction.
- Creates enjoyment of working with learning teams and being viewed as contributing members of the class.
- Improves ability of students and teachers to adapt to different teaching and learning styles.
- Provides opportunity to be evaluated according to the same criteria applied to all students.
- Promotes achievement at levels higher or at least as high as levels achieved in self-contained classes.
- Heightens enjoyment of social interaction in the larger classes.
- Provides for the development of an individualized education plan.
- Increases opportunity for personal decision making and setting of personal goals and plans.
- Provides opportunities for participation in career-vocational and school-to-work transition activities with nondisabled peers.
- Offers a wider circle of support, including social support that includes nondisabled classmates.
- Provides opportunities with classmates to take risks and learn from successes and mistakes.
- Improves the quality of life with more satisfying and meaningful experiences.
- Offers a greater opportunity to complete Carnegie units

(specific number of hours spent during the year in a specific subject, which leads to the completion of a high school "unit" or course) required to receive a regular high school diploma.

- Provides opportunities to receive specialized support in the general education environment.
- Increases skills in self-determination and self-advocacy for youth with disabilities through peer teams and learning groups.

Benefits for Nondisabled Peers

- Facilitates greater acceptance of students with disabilities both in the classroom and on learning teams.
- Promotes better understanding of the similarities among students with and without disabilities.
- Facilitates understanding that classmates who have disabilities are not always easily identified.
- Provides opportunities to be group team leaders.
- Offers the advantage of having an extra teacher or aid to help them with the development of their own skills.
- Provides opportunities to mentor, tutor, or guide a classmate with a disability.
- Increases learning about the range of different types of disabilities and the abilities of such students to adapt and cope with general education classes and classwork.

Benefits for Schools and Teachers

- Improves school atmosphere of acceptance for diversity.
- Provides greater student awareness of each other and tolerance for difference.
- Provides greater teacher awareness of the needs of students with disabilities.
- Provides teachers with knowledge about individualization of education.
- Provides teachers with knowledge about how to apply specialized educational strategies to other students who are not disabled but need extra help.
- Provides teachers who are learning more about support services available in the community for students and families.

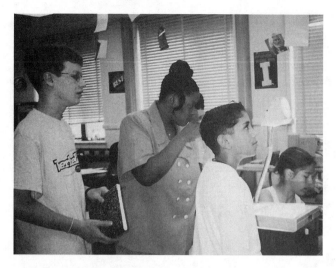

Inclusion provides opportunities to take risks and learn from successes and mistakes along with classmates.

Benefits for Parents or Guardians of Students with Disabilities

- Provides parents with a broader support network through linkages with parents of nondisabled students.
- Involves parents as equal partners in the educational planning process.
- Links parents with teachers, counselors, and administrators and improves ongoing communication.
- Includes parents in student exhibitions and demonstrations of student performance.
- Includes parents in the individualized education and school-to-work transition planning process.
- Better prepares professionals to help parents strengthen personal decision making, goal setting, and self-advocacy in their children.

Benefits for At-Risk and Dropout Youth with Disabilities

- Creates strategies to locate and motivate dropout students with disabilities to return to school to complete their degrees and learn skills they need to live and work in their communities.
- Develops strategies to identify, recruit, train, and place youth with disabilities who have dropped out of school.
- Provides services to diverse populations of students by developing integrated academic-vocational-technical education that meets industry-based performance standards.
- Provides intensive support to students who return to school to complete their education.
- Creates innovative, alternative performance assessments (exhibitions and demonstrations) of achievement and outcomes in vocational-technical areas.
- Promotes the sharing of resources among inclusive schools and other community agencies, to develop career-vocational education, work experiences, and school-to-careers transition supports for all students.
- Promotes the development of business-education partnerships to (1) enable educators to expand the learning environment to include both the school and community, (2) increase the relevance of education to adult life, and (3) establish bridges between schools and community resources, to facilitate transition.
- Provides methods for earlier intervention by means of early identification and assessment of at-risk youth and dropouts.

Impact on Teacher Knowledge and Understanding and Local Knowledge Sharing

- Encourages teachers to demonstrate methods and strategies that promote cooperative learning among students with and without disabilities.
- Helps teachers understand the support needs of students in various transitions between classroom settings.
- Introduces general education teachers to the individualized education program process and the role of the student in that process.
- Helps teachers understand that the IEP process requires that learning not be separated from *deciding to learn* and the expectation that students can and should envision and direct the planning for their own future.
- Produces tangible products that can be shared with other local schools also trying to implement inclusion:
  1. Teacher strategy manuals describing the implementation process and policies that support inclusion.
  2. Principal's records describing the planning process, problems, and solutions worked out.
  3. In-service training and orientation manuals that prepare new teachers and staff.
  4. Handbooks for parent involvement in full inclusion.
  5. Curriculum manuals describing adaptations and team collaboration.
  6. Inclusion evaluation reports.
- Provides a "living laboratory" in which to operationalize and evaluate new assessment approaches and the IEP decision-making process and its impacts upon students.
- Helps teachers learn and integrate strategies beneficial for all students, such as
  1. Student progress assessment methods and strategies, including student-developed portfolios and exhibitions.
  2. Performance-based assessment strategies, including situational, community-training-based, and employment-based.
  3. A student-centered and student-directed educational planning process that promotes self-determination and decision making.
  4. Implementation of the interdisciplinary team process.
  5. Development of an ongoing classroom evaluation process.
  6. Integration of technology into instruction.
  7. Involvement of families as integral partners in the student's decision-making process.

Benefits to the "Marriage" of Special and Regular Education

- Increases the number of students with disabilities who are appropriately placed into general education classes and who are able to benefit from the regular curriculum.

- Includes the needs of students with disabilities in annual school goals and assessments of resource needs.
- Provides joint orientation and training to general and special educators.
- Promotes partnerships between schools and rehabilitation agencies.
- Increases the supply of teachers in a district who are skilled in interdisciplinary planning, curriculum adaptations, and team consultation.

Benefits for Student Assessment and Empowerment in the Learning Process

- Promotes student goal setting and cooperative learning.
- Encourages students to engage in self-assessment of their own performance and progress.
- Promotes more alternative assessment strategies and more authentic assessment of student performance.
- Develops strategies that engage the student in self-assessment of his or her own performance and products.
- Encourages students and teachers to keep portfolios of student work and to use multiple forms of assessment.
- Builds on youths' natural attraction to applied work experiences and use of innovative technology.

Benefits for Creating a Positive Climate for Learning

- Reinforces a holistic (whole-child) view of the student learner and his or her needs.
- Reinforces the holistic (whole-classroom) view of the teaching and learning environment in which student diversity is celebrated and built upon to enrich the educational process.
- Creates an atmosphere conducive to successful curriculum integration across subject areas.
- Creates multimedia environments through use of hands-on activities, computers, and a variety of teaching strategies.
- Promotes cooperative learning in student teams.
- Shifts the role of teacher as isolated subject matter specialist to that of collaborator and promotes the formation of subject matter teams.
- Promotes regular teacher in-service training and learning sessions.
- Allows for orientation of students to "the rules of engagement," such as making responsible choices, working cooperatively, seeking and giving help, setting goals, using computers and equipment correctly, and keeping records.
- Promotes advanced peer training in team building and conflict resolution.

Benefits for Cost Sharing Among Schools and Community Agencies

- Promotes interagency collaboration for support services to children and youth.
- Stimulates sharing of resources among schools and support service agencies.
- Promotes collaboration among schools and social services agencies.

Benefits to Businesses and Community Agencies

- Promotes innovative linkages with the business community to provide career-vocational and school-to-work transition services.
- Shifts the locus of vocational support services to real-world work environments.
- Transforms the role of the business and community agency partners from that of donor or philanthropist to active partner in the school restructuring and career-vocational educational development process.
- Combines the resources of employers and community agencies, improving student outcomes through these interagency linkages.
- Promotes teacher opportunities to update, upgrade, or maintain their skills or to acquire more in-depth knowledge about the labor market, community industries and businesses, community service agencies, and the requirements and opportunities of the workplace.
- Provides educators with firsthand knowledge and experience of the expectations of the business community, knowledge of effective curricula and methods of instruction based on workplace requirements and experience, and preparation to guide students regarding their options and opportunities.

Benefits to Schools Partnering with Local Colleges or Universities

- Promotes long-term partnerships between schools and universities who prepare general and special educators for area schools.

Cooperative learning and hands-on activities benefit students with disabilities in the general education setting.

- Promotes long-term partnerships for in-service training between general and special education personnel.
- Provides resources for in-service training in the integration of academic and vocational-technical education and school restructuring.
- Provides skilled student interns to promote inclusion efforts and goals.
- Provides teachers-in-training with internship experiences directly related to the inclusion efforts of area schools and teachers.
- Promotes opportunities for teachers-in-training to participate in the development and evaluation of school inclusion initiatives.
- Improves the rate of employment for teachers-in-training in area schools.
- Strengthens focus of university teacher-training programs to respond to the needs of area schools.

Note: This information was developed with some material synthesized from the works of several authors and organizations: Biklen, D., 1985; Bruno, Johnson & Gillilard, 1994; Cornett, 1995; Council for Exceptional Children, 1993; Dalheim, 1994; Evans et al., 1993; Friend & Bursuck, 1999; Fuchs & Fuchs, 1994; Hardman, Drew & Egan, 1999; Janney et al., 1995; Kochhar, 1998; Kochhar & West, 1996; Leconte, 1994; Lenni, 1994; Lipsky & Gardner, 1989; MacMillan, 1991; McCoy, K. M., 1995; McLaughlin & Warren, 1992; National Alliance of Business, 1987; National Council on Disability, 1993; National Information Center for Children and Youth with Disabilities, 1993; Putnam, J., 1993; Rusch et al., 1992; Sailor, 1991; Sherer, M., 1994; Sitlington, 1992; Turnbull, 1994; Turnbull, Turnbull, Shank, & Leal, 1995; U.S. Department of Education, Office of Vocational and Adult Education, 1994; U.S. Department of Education, Office of Special Education, 1997; Wagner et al., 1991; West, 1991; Ysseldyke & Thurlaw, 1993.

CHAPTER 10

How Does Inclusion Relate to National Educational Reform?

Since the early 1980s and the release of the *Nation at Risk* report by the National Commission on Excellence in Education (U.S. Department of Education, 1983), a wave of reform has created considerable change in the nation's schools. After that report, many traditional practices in education were questioned and restructuring of schools became a general mandate throughout the states. The specific practices which were questioned include the following:

- **Tracking or ability grouping.** Refers to the practice of placing students into different tracks, or homogeneous groups, to receive instruction. Research has shown that tracking and ability grouping has a negative impact on the potential, expectations, and performance of children (Oakes & Lipton, 1992; Putnam, 1993). In addition, the practice of pulling students out of general classes, or educating them in separate classes, narrows their opportunities for social interaction and development with nondisabled peers. Separate education only perpetuates social deficits, which then compound the academic learning deficits (Resnick, 1990). Tracking and ability grouping create barriers to inclusion by forcing students with disabilities into separate classrooms.
- **Alternative diplomas.** Refers to the practice of offering a variety of alternative graduation certificates for individuals with disabilities, including IEP diplomas, special certificates, and other alternatives. Research has shown that for a majority of students with disabilities, the alternative diploma closes off many employment and postsecondary opportunities that would be available to them if they attained a standard high school degree (Halloran & Simon, 1995). Alternative diplomas can also serve as barriers to inclusion by making it easier for schools to systematically lower expectations for students with disabilities and provide less demanding graduation requirements.

- **Minimum competency testing.** Refers to the practice of establishing minimum standards in academic subject areas. Students at specific grade levels would be expected to meet these standards in order to move to intermediate school, to high school, or to graduate. Minimum competency testing has influenced inclusion by raising expectations for students placed into general education classroom.
- **Nine months of schooling.** Refers to the need for a longer school year or all-year schooling being examined by many educators who are concerned that the U.S. provides fewer instructional days than most other Western nations (Sizer, 1992). The impacts of the 9-month year on students with disabilities are similar to those for all students. Three-month vacations for students with disabilities often lead to lack of preparation for the next school year and a decline of motivation for learning.
- **Traditional instructional methods.** Refers to the teacher practice of lecturing to students while standing in the front of class and delivering information to the students, with little interaction or active learning. In addition, for students who are failing in traditional classrooms, alternative learning environments are being experimented with, including work-based learning, apprenticeships, community-based service internships, integrated academic and occupational instruction, and cooperative learning. Teacher's reliance on traditional instructional methods has not helped to promote socialization and cooperative learning among students in inclusive classrooms.
- **Compartmentalized curriculum.** Refers to the traditional practice of rigidly separating the curriculum into separate disciplines or subjects and teaching them in isolation of each other. Research shows that a curriculum that integrates learning between subject areas leads to better learning and better student outcomes

(Kaufman & Hallahan, 1993). Compartmentalized curriculum has affected inclusion by creating barriers for team teaching among special educators and general educators of various disciplines.

- **Delay of transition services.** Refers to the practice of waiting until the student is ready to graduate before providing preparation for transition from school to work or college. Research shows that early preparation for transition improves outcomes for youth, particularly those who have needed special educational services during their high school years (U.S. Department of Education, 1993; U.S. General Accounting Office, 1994b; Ward, 1995). Late attention to transition planning affects all students, including those in inclusive classrooms. It fails to provide transition opportunities and adequately prepare students for integration into the social and economic mainstream.

Case Example 10-1 provides an analysis of a placement conflict and its implications for school inclusion initiatives.

Expectations of achievement for all children are increasing. Educators are also demanding that students with disabilities be included in new performance measurement and reporting systems for all schools and districts. However, how we define educational benefit for the mainstreamed student with disabilities and how schools provide accommodations to achieve such benefits represent the central challenges to the inclusion movement.

WHY WERE STUDENTS WITH DISABILITIES EXCLUDED FROM EDUCATIONAL REFORM INITIATIVES? Until recently, students with disabilities were excluded when educators and policymakers developed new standards and requirements for education. Though the *National at Risk* report (1983) made extensive recommendations for improving education (e.g., emphasizing science, mathematics, and language arts; challenging homework assignments; and a longer school year) it made no mention of students with disabilities. In 1993, the U.S. General Accounting Office

CASE EXAMPLE 10-1. The Florence County School District v. Carter: Implications for School Restructuring for Inclusion

Summary:

This case involved the education of Shannon Carter, who is now 22 years of age. She attended her first-grade home school, Timmonsville Elementary School of Florence County, South Carolina, School District. She attended a nearby private school through grade six and reentered the public school system for seventh grade during the 1982–1983 school year. She performed poorly in school during seventh grade and was tested twice in early 1983 for learning disabilities, but the school determined that Shannon was not learning disabled. After Shannon performed poorly during the first semester of the ninth grade, her parents prompted the school district to conduct additional tests in April of 1985. Based on these tests, the school psychologist concluded that Shannon was indeed learning disabled under criteria set forth by the South Carolina State Department of Education. The disability had gone unnoticed by the school district for almost 3 years, and the district court found that the disability was comparatively severe.

Following the April 1985 evaluation, the school district proposed an IEP in which Shannon would remain in the general education classes but would spend at least two periods a day in the resource room. Shannon's parents objected, believing that it would be inappropriate to place Shannon alongside students with emotional illness and mental retardation. Instead her parents requested a learning disabilities itinerant program in which Shannon would receive individual attention from special education teachers. The itinerant program placed Shannon for three periods a week of individualized instruction, with the remainder of the week in general education classes. The IEP set a goal of

4 months' progress in 1 year for reading and mathematics. Dissatisfied with the IEP, Shannon's parents requested a due process hearing to challenge the appropriateness of the school's educational program. Both the local educational agency (LEA)* hearing officer and the state educational agency (SEA)** hearing officer rejected the argument of Shannon's parents and concluded that the IEP was appropriate and provided Shannon with a free, appropriate public education.

Because of their dissatisfaction with the IEP, Shannon's parents placed her for the 1985–1986 school year at the Trident Academy, where she remained until graduation in 1988. Trident, a private school that enrolls only children with learning disabilities, specializes in the education of children with severe learning disabilities, and is accredited by the Southern Association of Colleges and Schools. In this case, approval of Shannon's placement at Trident had never been sought from the State Department of Education. Yet on previous occasions, Trident's enrollment included students sent there by the public schools under the aegis of the Act (IDEA). There was no evidence that the State Department of Education had ever disapproved Trident for placements under the Act.

---

* LEA is the basic unit of administration of schools. The local school district encompasses a small geographic area and operates the schools within a specific community (e.g., county, township, city). Every public school is part of a local school district (Lunenburg & Orntein, 1991).

** SEA operates the system of education implemented throughout the state. The SEA is comprised of the state Board of Education chief state school officer, and state department of education (Lunenburg & Ornstein, 1991).

Important Facts and Points for Discussion:

1. The court found that Shannon's need for an appropriate individualized education takes precedence over the fact that a school is or is not state approved. The school may not have state approval for reasons that are irrelevant to Shannon's specific needs for specialized education.

2. The parents and the court determined that the IEP program goal of 4 months of progress in 1 year was unacceptable and failed to satisfy the requirement of IDEA that the IEP provide more than minimal or trivial progress. The court concluded that the IEP must be reasonably calculated to enable the child to receive educational benefits. In particular, "when the handicapped child is being educated in the general education classrooms of a public school system, the achievement of passing marks and advancement from grade to grade will be one important factor in determining educational benefit." In Shannon's case, the district court did not err in finding that a goal of 4 months over a period of 1 year was modest for this student and was unlikely to permit her to make passing marks and advance from grade to grade.

3. The school district suggested that the Act's preference for mainstreaming students with disabilities justified the IEP proposed and made the public school placement superior to Trident Academy, which educates only children with disabilities. The court did not concur, concluding that the preference of IDEA for mainstreaming students with disabilities did not justify an IEP for the learning disabled 10th grader and did not make the public school placement superior to the private school placement with only children with disabilities. The court stated that *"where necessary for educational reasons, mainstreaming assumed a subordinate role in formulating educational programs."*

4. Shannon's parents rejection of the school district's proposed resource room placement in favor of the less intensive itinerant program did not relieve the school district of liability for failing to provide an appropriate individualized education program, since there was no finding that the proposed resource room placement would have provided appropriate education and may have been less appropriate than the itinerant program.

5. IDEA permitted reimbursement to the parents. In a unilateral decision, they placed Shannon into a private school that had not been approved by the state. The private school succeeded in providing an appropriate education.

6. When public schools default in their obligations under IDEA to provide appropriate education, then private school placement is "proper under the Act" if the education provided by the private school is reasonably calculated to enable the child to receive educational benefits.

Outcome

The Supreme Court Ruling. The Supreme Court held that parents who believe that the education offered by the public school is inappropriate may unilaterally place their child in a private school and are entitled to reimbursement from the state for tuition and expenses if it is subsequently determined that the public school system has failed to comply with its statutory duties and that the private school provided an appropriate education. The question is whether reimbursement under the Act is barred when parents have enrolled their disabled child in a private school that has not been approved by the state for the child's placement under the Act. The circuit judge held that placement in a private school not approved by the state is not a bar to reimbursement under the Act and, therefore, affirmed the judgment of the district court ordering reimbursement.

Analysis. First, the outcome of the challenge resulted in a segregated placement in which Shannon was removed from a least restrictive environment of the general education classroom and placed into a school which only educated children with disabilities. Unfortunately, the court decision supported such segregated placement. The school district may have been right in saying that the public school placement was superior if the IEP goals had been "reasonably calculated" to enable Shannon to receive educational benefits. The school rightly argued that the IDEA has a preference for mainstreaming and deems placement in public school general education class is superior to segregated private school placement. However, it appears that the student could have been maintained in the general education classes in the public school if the school district has modified the IEP and utilized the itinerant program to provide more intensive services so as to bring Shannon's progress up more than 4 months. In essence the itinerant program was an intensive individualized special tutoring program which provided extra support while maintaining the student in the least restrictive environment. The fact that the relatively severe learning disability had gone unnoticed by the school district for almost 3 years was also a factor in the court's decision to uphold the parents' decision.

Implications for the Inclusion Movement. The important implication for the inclusion movement is that the court concluded that the Act's mainstreaming policy was of no avail to the school district. Under the Act, mainstreaming is a policy to be pursued so long as it is consistent with the Act's primary goal of providing disabled students with an appropriate education. The court held that the appropriateness of the education to address the educational needs of the students was of greater interest to the state than its efforts to mainstream. In other words, the general goals of inclusion are of lesser importance than ensuring an appropriate individual educational program. In addition, the school district presented no evidence that the policy was meant to restrict parental options when the public school fails to comply with the requirements of the Act. When the parent exercises such an option, then the school is not relieved of its liabil-

continues

CASE EXAMPLE 10-1. *(continued)*

ity. The parents were not rejecting an appropriate IEP, but an inappropriate one.

The school district also argued that the Act does not permit reimbursement when parents unilaterally withdraw their child from the public school system for enrollment in a school not approved by the state. However, the Act does direct a court to "grant such relief as it determines as appropriate." This remedial provision is intended to allow a court to order reimbursement when the court concludes that a public school has failed to provide a free, appropriate public education. The parents are faced with the choice of (1) going along with an IEP to the detriment of the child, or (2) paying for what they consider an appropriate placement. If the parent had to pay for an alternative educational program when the IEP was inappropriate, then IDEA would not be protecting a child's right to free, appropriate public education.

On the issue of state approval of the private school, state approval had never been sought, so the school had never been disapproved. This is an important distinction. IDEA actually allows for the private placement of children for special education if they are placed in or referred to such schools by the state or a local educational agency (LEA) as the means of carrying out the requirements of the Act. The Act imposes no requirement that a private school be approved by the state in parent placement-reimbursement cases.

Broader Implications for School Restructuring for Inclusion. This case presents issues that are significant for the school reform and inclusion initiatives that are emerging at national, state and local levels. The national special education leadership is developing an agenda that communicates clear messages, one reinforcing the IDEA statutes' preference for mainstreaming children into general education classes, and the other, that the merger of special and general education must be accelerated. State and local educational agencies are accelerating their initiatives to place more special education children into the general education classroom, oftentimes precipitously, before adequate time is allowed to inform students and parents, and before teachers and administrators are prepared to receive them. This trend toward massive shifts of special education students into general education classes means that there are more likely to be challenges to the schools to ensure the provision of free, appropriate public education.

Growing Reaction of Parents. There is a growing reaction on the part of many parents. Those of children with disabilities are afraid that appropriate education will not be provided in the larger general education classes, and parents of nondisabled students believe that more attention will have to be given to the students with greater needs—diminishing the time the teacher has to spend on direct instruction to the class as a whole. These are legitimate concerns about the conditions of the general education classrooms in many schools. There are many qualitative issues for teaching and learning environments for all students. As school improvement plans address these quality issues, they have implications for students with disabilities entering general education classes.

The Central Questions of the Case. An IEP must be *"reasonably calculated to enable the child to receive educational benefits, and . . . when the handicapped child is being educated in the general education classrooms of a public school system, the achievement of passing marks and advancement from grade to grade will be one important factor in determining educational benefit."*

The central questions for mainstreamed students placed into least restrictive environments are

1. Can the school provide appropriate education at the same time?
2. Are the IEPs developed "reasonably calculated" to enable the student to receive educational benefit.

Least restrictive, therefore, becomes defined more specifically. It does not merely mean in the general education setting, but is defined as the environment in which the student is most likely to receive educational benefits and achieve passing marks and advance from grade to grade. This interpretation has implications for students with severe disabilities who are placed into general education classes where they cannot be reasonably expected to receive passing marks relative to the level of the general class or be advanced to the next grade unless being evaluated against a fully individualized alternative curriculum. It also has implications for students with mild disabilities for whom IEPs must provide for intensive enough support as to help the student make sufficient educational progress to achieve passing marks and advance to the next grade. Grade retention, attendance, and drop-out rates are becoming very important measures of the success or failure of regular and special education. The definition of educational benefit also becomes central, particularly as expectations for all children in general education classes are rising, and educational outcomes are more heavily focused upon.

released the report *Systemwide Education Reform* (April, 1993), which discussed the importance of linking student learning goals to systemwide education reform. The report states that if all elements of the educational system are linked together and all school personnel are encouraged to work together, then student progress is more likely to improve. Adoption of educational standards, curriculum goals, and assessments clearly linked to those standards and curricula allows meaningful measures of progress toward those goals. *Adequate instructional materials and professional development are the key tools that teachers and principals need to help all students succeed, particularly those placed into inclusive classrooms.* Systematic reforms in expectations of students, and in outcome measurement, instruction, and administration are occurring. In addition, there is a clear trend toward more decentralized decision making and teacher involvement, both in school management and in instructional changes. The needs of students with disabilities must be considered in these reforms.

STATE AND LOCAL AGENCIES EXPERIMENT WITH REFORM. In recent years, at state and local levels, education and community agencies have experimented with restructuring both educational and vocational programs. Examples of such innovations include the following:

- Increased graduation requirements
- Statewide minimum competency testing
- Expanded school year or all-year schooling
- Employer certification
- Apprenticeships
- More stringent teacher certification standards
- Integrated academic vocational-technical curricula
- Business mentorships
- Secondary/postsecondary articulation programs

Many of these reforms are aimed at improving outcomes for students with diverse needs.

NATIONAL EDUCATIONAL GOALS EMERGE. With the passage of the Goals 2000: Educate America Act of 1993 (P.L. 103–227), the nation wrote into law eight challenging educational goals for state and local educational agencies to achieve over the balance of this decade.

These goals generated new national standards for teaching and learning, and they have since been adjusted to include provisions for students with disabilities. They have affected the inclusion movement by raising expectations for all students in general education classes, including students with disabilities.

SCHOOL-TO-WORK TRANSITION SERVICES FOR ALL YOUTH. The national educational goals also included school-to-work transition services for all secondary youth preparing for employment or postsecondary training. Since the 1990 Amendments to IDEA, transition services for youth with disabilities must be implemented in each public school throughout the nation. Goals 2, 5, and 7 are particularly relevant for the expansion of school-to-work transition services for special needs populations. Goal 2 requires innovative drop-out prevention strategies, as well as outreach to students who have dropped out of school. It also encourages transition support strategies to ensure that all students get the support they need to make a smooth transition to postsecondary education, employment, and adult life. Goal 5 specifically addresses strengthening the connection between education and work. Furthermore, it challenges educational institutions to ensure literacy for all workers and provide them with the knowledge and skills (basic and technical) needed to adapt to modern technology and work methods. Goal 8 challenges schools to increase parental involvement in the education of their children and to re-

Goals 2000: Educate America Act

By the year 2000:

1. All children in America will start school ready to learn.
2. The high school graduation rate will increase to at least 90%.
3. All students will leave grades 4, 8, and 12 having demonstrated competency over challenging subject matter, and every school will ensure that all students learn to use their minds well so they may be prepared for responsible citizenship, further learning, and productive employment in our nation's modern economy.
4. U.S. students will be first in the world in mathematics and science achievement.
5. Every adult in America will be literate and will possess the knowledge and skills necessary to compete in a global economy and exercise the rights and responsibilities of citizenship.
6. Every school in the U.S. will be free of drugs, violence, and the unauthorized possession of firearms and alcohol and will offer a disciplined environment conducive to learning.
7. (Goals 7 and 8 were added in mid-1994.) The nation's teaching force will have access to programs for the continued improvement of their professional skills and the opportunity to acquire the knowledge and skills needed to instruct and prepare all American students for the next century.
8. Every school will promote partnerships that will increase parental involvement and participation in promoting the social, emotional, and academic growth of children.

spond to actively engage parents and families in shared educational decision making (U.S. Department of Education, 1993a).

WHY IS INCLUSION ESSENTIAL TO ACHIEVING THE NATIONAL EDUCATIONAL GOALS? Goodlad (1992) offered a few broad guidelines that reflect current beliefs about effective schooling for all children and youth in inclusive environments.

1. The community must understand and support the schools in the spirit of shared responsibility for the futures of all learners.
2. We should not underestimate the ability and trustworthiness of most learners.
3. Schools must be safe, engaging, inviting, and joyful.
4. Learning should be driven by specific goals in the form of "exhibitions," through which learners can display their grasp and use of important ideas and skills in a variety of intellectual domains.
5. Incentives are at the heart of serious learning; adolescents as well as adults learn only what they want to learn—what they are convinced is important and what

TABLE 10-1. Why Inclusion Is Essential to Achieving the National Educational Goals

Issue	Why a Greater Focus on Inclusion Is Needed
1. Identification and placement of students with disabilities	• The number of students classified as having a disability has increased steadily during the 1990s. • In the U.S., males are disproportionately identified as having disabilities. • African-American youth are disproportionately identified as having disabilities (24% of youth with disabilities are African-American). • Thirty percent of students with disabilities have been placed in separate classrooms or schools.
2. Student performance	• Students with disabilities spend a majority of their instructional time in general education programs; one third of them failed one or more courses; 12.7% failed six or more courses in secondary school programs (National Longitudinal Transition Study, 1992; Wagner, 1994).
3. School completion	• More than 20% of all American youth do not complete high school, 25% for African Americans, and 35% for Hispanics. • Only *45%* of students with disabilities graduate from high school with a diploma. • Youth with disabilities who have dropped out of school are 50% less likely than other youth to earn a GED certificate or return to school.
4. Transition to post-secondary education, work, and independent living	• In 1991 64% of Whites, 46% of African Americans and 57% of Hispanic graduates enrolled in college; only 14% of students with disabilities reported attending postsecondary institutions 2 years after high school. • Employment rate for youth with disabilities has increased from 46–57% (National Longitudinal Transition Study, 1992). • Within 2 years of completing school, 37% of youth with disabilities live independently compared with 60% for the general population.
5. Increased expectations	• The national educational goals set standards for improvement in eight areas. • Many states have increased the number and difficulty level of courses and employ minimum competency exams to assess student mastery. • Changes in the workplace require that students gain greater proficiency in math, science, reading and writing, problem solving, logical reasoning, and decision making. • Performance of minority children, individuals with disabilities, and children from disadvantaged backgrounds must be significantly raised.
6. Changing standards of accountability	• The general public and state legislatures are holding schools accountable for meeting higher expectations and producing improved outcomes for students, including those with disabilities. • Schools are accountable for outcomes in a wide range of areas, including student performance on subject matter tests, student attendance, school completion, enrollment in advanced classes, and successful transition to work and college. • Some states are using accountability formulas (for example, California's School Performance Report) in which contextual and demographic factors of schools and students are considered in comparing schools. • Both general and special educators are increasingly responsible for outcomes of students with disabilities.
7. The quality and quantity of teachers	• To meet higher expectations, teachers will be required to teach more to more students, and more efficiently. This will require major revisions of curricula, instruction strategies, school organization, and the relationships between teachers and students. • Educators, administrators, and related service personnel are not adequately prepared to educate diverse student populations in inclusive settings. • Increased demands for interagency collaboration between schools and community services require new skills for teachers and cross-disciplinary training for individuals working with youth and their families. • General education teachers are not specifically trained nor experienced in working with students with disabilities, even though more and more students with disabilities are assigned to general education classrooms for all or part of the day. • Not enough general or special educators are prepared to work with children with medical conditions such as pediatric AIDS and those caused by prenatal drug exposure. • Schools face a continuing shortage of special education teachers and related service personnel.

TABLE 10-1. *(continued)*

Issue	Why a Greater Focus on Inclusion Is Needed
8. Technology in the schools	• There is an increasing gap between the technological haves and have nots. Some schools and districts have a wealth of computers, while others do not expose their students to this technology. The same holds true for students' access to computers at home.
	• The high cost of assistive technology, much of which is customized to the needs of individuals, raises questions of access and equity. Access to these devices and financial support for purchasing them are lacking for many individuals with disabilities.
9. Funding	• Although state and local funding doubled for public schools in the 1980s, several economic and political forces have begun to erode the funding base for education. In fiscal year 1992, 10 states suffered "negative growth"; a total of 35 states made mid year budget cuts totalling $4.5 billion.
	• In the last decade, federal per-pupil funding declined substantially, resulting in increased burdens on state and local governments.
	• There are questions about the appropriateness of current funding levels for special education, as well as other categorical programs.
	• The traditional funding methods for special education—based on the identification and labeling of students—are also being questioned, as more students are served in general education classrooms, and special educators press for full inclusion of students with disabilities.

inspires them. Coercion and humiliation are poor incentives to serious learning.

6. Effective and productive education must be coherent in two ways: There should be a sensible sequence of activity for each learner over a number of years, and the academic and vocational/technical demands should be clear and connected.

7. Serious learning in school is hard work which requires involvement, intensity, and loyalty on the part of the learner; the learner must develop the habit of using knowledge and employing it in new settings.

Table 10-1 provides a summary of the reasons why inclusive schools are essential for achieving the national educational goals.

INCLUDING ALL STUDENTS IN REFORM GOALS. Special education laws were written to promote equal opportunities for students with disabilities so they could function in mainstream society. In order to achieve such integration, these students, to the extent possible, need access to the range of opportunities that schools make available to all students. A core curriculum, theater and arts education, extracurricular activities and school clubs, sports, enrichment activities, vocational-technical or occupational training opportunities, community service learning opportunities, student government opportunities, and any other new opportunities provided under school reform initiatives must be made available to all students within a school.

CHAPTER 11

What Is the Philosophical Basis for Inclusion?

In recent years, there has been a great deal of discussion about changing philosophies and new paradigms in education and human services. To understand how schools can improve inclusion practices, it is helpful to examine changing philosophies about learners with disabilities and the kinds of environments they need to grow and develop their potential. These shifts in philosophy have shaped the inclusion movement over the past few decades.

Great transformations or revolutions in philosophy, beliefs, or assumptions about science, society, or social problems is referred to as a *paradigm shift*. The term was first introduced by Thomas Kuhn in his book, the *Structure of Scientific Revolutions* (1962). A *paradigm* is a framework, model, or set of assumptions that can guide what we think we know about a social problem and how we design a solution to that problem. These paradigm shifts, brought about by new research on teaching and learning, have provided new sets of assumptions or beliefs about how students learn, what they need to progress, which teaching strategies can accelerate learning, and what outcomes should be expected from students with all levels of disability. With new knowledge comes skepticism about old practices and ways of thinking.

New assumptions and beliefs about students with disabilities and their potential have raised new questions about the most appropriate kinds of settings and supports. Questions are being raised about how school and community agencies should work together to provide supportive services to students with special needs. The most important question for those who wish to build inclusive schools and classrooms is this: Are we seeking to "fix" the student, the family, the teachers and schools, our own agencies, or the community at large? In other words, the question might be unpacked into the following subquestions:

- Whom or what should be the focus of change or intervention—should it be the individual student and his or her problems (individual deficit orientation)?
- Should the focus be on fixing the environment of the student or facilitating new responses in the environment to accommodate differences among children and youth (the environment-deficit orientation)?
- Should the focus be on both of the above (the interactionist orientation)?

How a school community answers this question—fix the student, the family, the school, or the whole service system—makes a great difference in the kinds of inclusive practices it will use.

WHAT HISTORICAL AND PHILOSOPHICAL FORCES HAVE SHAPED INCLUSION? Several changes in the philosophy about integrating people with differences into mainstream society have accelerated the inclusion movement for children and youth with disabilities. Over the past few decades, service models have focused less on fixing problems within the individual and more on *seeking ways to change or improve the individual's environment in order to accept the individual into mainstream settings and to improve the learning and growth process*. Table 11-1 summarizes the differences between the traditional and more recent educational and human service philosophies. Such new philosophies of service and new practices are more likely today to focus on *changing the structure of services to accommodate and maximize abilities of the student and to integrate them into mainstream environments*.

WHAT ARE THE NEW ASSUMPTIONS ABOUT LEARNERS WITH DISABILITIES? It is important that teachers understand the assumptions that underlie recent educational approaches for students with special learning needs. A clearer understanding can assist them in their inclusion efforts.

TABLE 11-1. Recent Shifts in the Philosophies of Services

Traditional Services	Recent Service Philosophy
• Educational and developmental services for children with special needs begin in elementary school.	• Early intervention and early childhood education programs begin in the first year of life.
• Young children enter segregated "special child" preschool programs.	• Young children are integrated into preschool programs with nondisabled peers.
• Children with special needs are offered pull-out programs in segregated settings.	• Children are provided resource supports and assistance within the general education classroom.
• Preparation of youth for employment and careers involves simulated work experiences.	• Preparation for employment involves real world work experiences in community-based settings.
• Social, family, and health services are offered in separate centers.	• Services are cooperatively located within the community and, more often, services are provided in the home.
• Large institutional facilities are utilized for children and youth with severe disabilities.	• Small residential programs are utilized for disabled children and adults with severe disabilities.
• Students with disabilities are denied admission into postsecondary education and job training programs.	• Students with disabilities are provided with support services in community colleges, universities, and job training programs.

In many current efforts to improve educational services for all students, professionals are beginning to apply a *different set of assumptions from those used in the past,* emphasizing that it may not be effective to focus simply on individual deficits or environmental deficits alone. Solutions to human problems require that we look at all aspects of the problem—the individual, the environment, and in the *interactions* between them. Table 11-2 explains three theories reflecting these three perspectives on human deficits and learning. Two examples of the interactionist view of disability follow Table 11-2.

WHAT PHILOSOPHICAL IDEAS SHAPED THE INCLUSION MOVEMENT? Six major systems of ideas that have shaped the inclusion movement include the following:

- The human potential movement
- General system theory
- Normalization philosophy and community integration
- Philosophy of individual liberty
- Self-determination movement
- Management theory and principles

The Human Potential Movement. Over the past century a *human potential movement* has emerged and often referred to by many theorists in the field of psychology (e.g., Fromm, Rogers, Erickson, May). This movement represents a philosophy founded upon the belief that all individuals have a basic desire to grow and to develop in positive ways. The human potential movement has been called a philosophical revolution in psychology and human services for persons with disabilities and disadvantages. Programs which embrace the human potential ideology subscribe to the following principles and beliefs:

- Society must defend the basic rights of all citizens to "life, liberty and the pursuit of happiness," which includes equal educational and social service opportunities for all.
- Our social policies should be based on the conviction that society has a responsibility to provide extra support

to some to enable them to compensate for past and present disadvantages (Rawls, 1971).
- All children can learn and have a right to education and support services appropriate to their developmental level.
- All citizens have an inalienable right to resources and environments that support positive growth and development in children, youth, and adults whether they are disabled, ill, or disadvantaged.

The movement is actually a mix of several emerging new philosophies which are driving many practical reforms in education and human services.

General System Theory. Educators referred to as "system thinkers" examine the needs of the individual student as a whole person in order to develop responses that are integrated rather than fragmented. The teacher-pioneer looks for connections between different disciplines or agencies that can lead to collaborative relationships. General system theory (Bertalanffy, 1968; Sutherland, 1973) provides some basic principles that may be helpful to teachers and administrators seeking a broader, interdisciplinary perspective on student needs.

The general system thinker searches for theories and ideas that have applications across many disciplines and that have been successfully used in solving problems that practitioners recognize as shared. *General system theory offers a framework for understanding complex relationships among organizations or social systems and offers a unique, integrated set of principles that can be broadly applied in many disciplines.* General system theory promotes interdisciplinary interchange and increased communication between teachers and other specialists from different fields. Teachers can benefit from applying general system principles that challenge them to look at complex service system relationships in a different light.

In general system theory, individuals are viewed as wholes greater than the sum of their parts. This means that understanding human growth, development, or behavior cannot be accomplished by reducing behavior

TABLE 11-2. Comparisons of Three Theories About Human Deficits and Learning

Theory/Paradigm	Assumptions and Strategies
Individual-deficit orientation (medical model)	The cause of individual deficits or failure rests within the individual and his or her physical body (Golby & Gulliver, 1985). Individuals do not progress satisfactorily in services because of inadequate cognitive, behavioral, sensory, motor, linguistic, medical, and physical characteristics (Salvia & Ysseldyke, 1988). In the same way that a disease is understood as being "owned" by the infected individual, learning problems also are thought of as the exclusive property of the individual or student (Fedoruk, 1989). Intervention strategies under the individual-deficit orientation involve assessing individual attributes and include such strategies as correcting conduct disorders and remediating sensory deficits.
Environment-deficit orientation (behavioral model)	While internal factors may make an individual more or less responsive to the environment, these internal factors are not the chief cause of poor outcomes. Since behavior is learned, individuals fail to progress in services because of inappropriate or inadequate environmental circumstances in which they develop or learn. Within the environment-deficit orientation, typical intervention strategies include evaluating the learning environment, matching the characteristics of teachers and related service providers to individual student characteristics, evaluating student–teacher ratios, and facilitating family involvement.
Interactionist orientation (contextual or sociological model)	Learning and behavior deficits are not a result of individual deficits or environmental inadequacies, but are a *product of inappropriate individual to environment interactions.* Approaches to remediating deficits in learning, development, or physical health are shifted away from the search for causes within the individual and *toward specifying the conditions under which different individuals can and will learn and progress* (Wixson & Lipson, 1986). Intervention strategies involve assessing individual and environment interaction and include measures of professional-client interaction, peer interaction, and family support for service participation.
	The interactionist or sociological model is most useful for examining inclusion because it considers the individual, the environment, and the interaction between the two. It also shifts the focus of efforts to intervene in human problems away from the search for causes of problems in individuals and their environments and toward defining the conditions that will lead to individual progress. Under a sociological model, service strategies require the shared responsibility of the total community. Many community sectors provide different but complementary kinds of services or interventions that are essential for helping the individual maximize his or her potential.

Source: Kochhar, C. (1995) *Training Modules in Interdisciplinary, Interagency Service Coordination.* Des Moines, IA: Mt. Plains Regional Resource Center and the Iowa State Department of Education.

into parts and analyzing these parts in isolation of each other. The individual's behaviors and experiences must be viewed as a dynamic, whole system interacting within a unique environment. Teachers and support personnel who view students from a general system perspective seek to understand the environment in which the students live and the impact of that environment upon their behavior and experience. In other words, if a student has many more needs that other students typically have, then we cannot look at each need in isolation of the others nor can we attend to the different needs in isolation of one another. Human needs intersect each other, and intervening to change one will result in change in others.

Normalization, Community Integration, and Early Civil Rights. The concept or principle of *normalization* has resulted in a major shift in what society believes about the potential abilities and rights of individuals with disabilities. Normalization is defined as letting the individual with a disability obtain an existence as close to the normal as possible (Bank-Mikkelson, 1969). The principle of normalization originated in Scandinavia and gained popularity in North America through the 1970s (Bank-Mikkelson, 1969; Nirje, 1976; Wolfensberger, 1972, 1980). It formed the early foundations of a civil rights movement for persons with special needs and is closely related to the principle of individual rights and

Example 1: The Interactionist View

Factors in the individual and in the individual's environment interact in different ways for each person. For example, having a physical disability may not necessarily create problems in learning, but the disability, in combination with other environmental factors, may contribute to the individual's inability to perform necessary social roles. One of the most important social roles for school children is that of student. Social and cultural factors in the environment may intersect with the disability to create problems with access to schools or classrooms. These factors will ultimately have an effect on learning. For example, providing accommodations to enable an individual to be mobile will solve one aspect of a problem that lies within the individual. The second part of the problem—the interaction between the individual and the environment—requires a change in the school's response to the individual. The solution requires helping the school respond to the individual differently, by providing additional accommodations.

Example 2: The Interactionist View

An important social role for the individual is that of parent or family member. A chronic health problem combined with the stresses of being a parent and having to care for others may create substantial problems for the family as a whole. Intervening to solve the health problem may address one aspect of the problem—that which lies within the individual. The second part of the problem is the family's response to the parent with a health problem. Therefore, an interactionist solution would combine treatment for the health problem with family intervention and support to help the family cope with the impact of the single member.

freedoms in a democracy. Normalization has many implications for the education of individuals with disabilities and other special learners. Wolf Wolfensberger brought the concept of normalization to the United States and defined it as "the use of culturally normative means to offer persons life conditions at least as good as those of average citizens, and as much as possible, to enhance or support their behavior, appearances, experiences, status and reputation" (Wolfensberger, 1972, p.8).

Society's Response to People's Differences Changes. The idea of normalization reflects a shift in society's response to persons who are different. The attitude shifts from viewing people with disabilities as deviants who should be banished and segregated, to making an effort to restore, rehabilitate, and reintegrate individuals into mainstream society. Today there are numerous signs that the general public is accepting people with disabilities, as evidenced in television productions, movies, theater, sports, advertising, and other arenas. The normalization principle can be applied to any type of profession, to any type of agency, and to any type individual consumer or student. McWorter (1986) stated that *ideology is more comprehensive than law* and extends into day-to-day educational practices and relationships among people. Normalization is the only developed and articulated value system which is

- Consistent with ideals upon which Western democracies legal structures are based.
- Readily disseminated and applied through established training and evaluation methods.
- Well known in the field and routinely included in the curricula of manpower development programs across North America.
- Relevant to human services in general (Wolfensberger and Thomas, 1983).

Community Integration. Community integration practices have resulted directly from the influence of the principle of normalization. The *community integration philosophy* incorporates the concepts of civil liberty, least restrictive environment, right to treatment and to refuse treatment, care versus cure, quality of life, engaging natural helpers, and coordination of the system. Interagency service coordination is also rooted in the normalization principle. Normalization of service environments, social integration, and advocacy for the individual have become hallmarks of the self-determination or 'social enabling' philosophy.

Philosophy of Individual Liberty. Over the past 50 years, American philosophy about freedom and autonomy, learning, and the potential to improve the mental, physical, and emotional capacities of individuals with disabilities has changed dramatically. These changes have effected the integration of persons with special needs into mainstream schools and society. For schools, questions such as how much help should be given; how much should professionals intervene in the life of the individual student; and how much individual decision making is prudent become very important questions. Through this century, the progressive tradition in education and human services has reflected a strong belief in *individuality and individual freedoms* and the belief that social support systems should facilitate the development of individual personality and skills. Table 11-3 expresses in terms of progressive stages the passage toward increasing personal freedom and achieving maximum independence and self-determination for persons with disabilities.

TABLE 11-3. **Philosophical Path Toward Individual Liberty and Full Citizenship for Persons with Disabilities**

Stage 1 Dependence (1900–1950s)	1. Devalued status; neglect
	2. Social concern; benevolence
	3. Physical intervention; medical treatment
	4. Educational and psychological intervention
Stage 2 Partial integration (1950s–1990s)	5. Access to special education
	6. Access to mainstreamed classes
	7. Access to vocational education and rehabilitation services
	8. Access to employment preparation
	9. Access to transportation and communication
Stage 3 Individual liberty and full citizenship (1990s and into the 21st century)	10. General public facility access
	11. Access to paid community-based work
	12. Access to medical and life insurance
	13. Access to career advancement opportunities
	14. Access to postsecondary and higher education
	15. Access to political power (state and national government legislative and executive positions)
	16. Access to private business enterprise and control

Most communities in the United States remain in Stage 2. However, there are lively efforts in many communities to lead education and human service agencies into Stage 3. The drift toward integration of individuals with disabilities into mainstream school and community settings has been occurring over the past several decades, in parallel with the civil rights movement.

The Self-Determination Movement. Another major challenge for teachers and support personnel is how to empower and enable students and families to make decisions about services and to determine the course of their future (*self-determination*). Many communities are making efforts to transfer decision-making authority for educational services from large organizational units and professionals to individual schools and to students and families. Self-determination includes characteristics such as assertiveness, creativity, flexibility, as well as decision making, self-esteem and self-advocacy. Students with disabilities do not automatically practice self-determination upon reaching age 21. These skills are gained in developmental stages that begin in early childhood and continue throughout adult life.

To accomplish this, educational processes for children and youth must shift from being strictly *student-centered* to being *student-driven* (with appropriate levels of support). In such as system, the student assumes more control and learns to manage his or her educational or personal development program. Explicit training for self-determination and self-advocacy is essential if students and families are to have greater control over their lives and their futures. Some critics of this new thinking warn that this signals an attempt to reduce the government's responsibility in the social service arena and that the possibility of regression exists. However, self-determination advocates should resist such negative thinking and "seize the many positive opportunities this new thinking offers us to empower people and create inclusive communities" (*Word From Washington,* 1991, p. 21).

There are five basic themes that are useful in promoting self-determination in students with disabilities in inclusive settings.

1. *Empowerment and leadership:* National, state, and local policies are calling for strong student and family involvement in planning of services and in decision making for early intervention, K–12 education, and transition to postsecondary education and work.
2. *Flexibility and individualization:* Students with disabilities need flexible and individualized programs based on their assessed needs and those of their families.
3. *Support at home:* Creative approaches to family supports should be based on the belief that students' families should have a major voice in designing and evaluating family-oriented services that support students' educational programs.
4. *Full community participation:* Students with disabilities and other special needs will advance beyond mere physical presence in schools and communities to enjoying all that the community has to offer through participation in the range of services and civic activities—community, recreation, and leisure.
5. *Positive public education:* The public's perception of and attitudes concerning people with special needs will improve as people gain better understanding of and more exposure to this special population.

Management Theory and Principles. Management theory and its principles of "total quality management" have affected not only the business community, but education and human services as well. These effects have increased emphasis on accountability for teachers and human service professionals to perform more efficiently and show positive outcomes for the students they serve. Principles of management deal with topics such as authority, efficiency, communication, productivity, outcomes, quality standards, and organizational change. There is an increasing trend for educational and human service policies to demand greater accountability and responsibility for improved outcomes of services, to efficiently utilize funds and resources, and to promote collaboration among agencies in order to facilitate inclusion.

CHAPTER 12

What Public Policies Promote Inclusion?

Before 1975, more that half the children with disabilities in the U.S. were either institutionalized or did not receive appropriate educational services (Lance, 1976; Rothstein, 1995). Congress then recognized that education, health, and employment outcomes for all children with disabilities remained a great concern throughout the United States. As a result, several laws were passed to expand state and local coordination efforts to ensure equal access to educational programs and services and to develop supports for students to be integrated into schools and community programs (Figure 12-1). These laws have required that schools ensure, to the extent possible, that students with diverse needs are served with their nondisabled peers.

INCLUSION AND THE GOALS 2000: EDUCATE AMERICA ACT. With the Goals 2000: Educate America Act of 1993 (P.L. 103-227) the nation has written into law eight challenging educational goals which state and local educational agencies are expected to attempt to achieve over the balance of this decade (also see Chapter 10—How Does Inclusion Relate to National Educational Reform?).

THE INDIVIDUALS WITH DISABILITIES EDUCATION ACT (IDEA), 1997 AMENDMENTS. The Individuals with Disabilities Education Act of 1990 (IDEA, P.L. 101-476) and of 1997 (P.L. 105-17) requires that students be placed into the least restrictive environment, and provides due process protection, free and appropriate public education, individualized educational programs, early intervention services, and transition services for youth exiting the schools. When IDEA was reauthorized in 1997, it strengthened (1) inclusion requirements for schools; (2) transition services requirements for secondary students, (3) the role of parents and guardians in the educational programming for students, (4) the role of the student in his or her own educational planning, and (5) the responsibility of community agencies for sharing resources to

provide related services. It also expanded the definition of free appropriate public education to include children and youth who have been suspended or expelled from school, a requirement that greatly expands the responsibility of state and local educational agencies to continue to educate students appropriately, even if they are placed into alternative settings other than the home school. Furthermore, the following additions and requirements impacting inclusion have been added to IDEA 1997:

- Definition of "orientation and mobility services."
- Definition of "related services" under "transition services."
- Clarification of the roles of legal guardians and surrogate parents.
- Requirement that supplementary aids, services, and supports be provided in the regular classroom or other education-related settings.
- Expanded definitions of developmental delay to include an option for LEAs to serve children aged 6 to 9.
- Deletion of "serious" from the term "serious emotional disturbance."
- Cross-references to the Higher Education Act and the Improving American's Schools Act definitions to ensure coordination of special education with school reform initiatives and postsecondary programs in institutions of higher education.
- Requirement that each state have in effect a Comprehensive System of Personnel Development (CSPD) to ensure an adequate supply of qualified personnel (including those with expertise in the provision of transition services) and procedures for acquiring and disseminating significant knowledge derived from educational research and for adopting promising practices.
- Requirement that states establish performance goals for children with disabilities and develop indicators to judge children's progress.
- Requirement that states identify, locate, and evaluate children and youth with disabilities, regardless of the

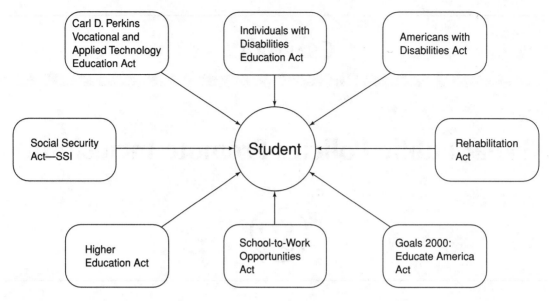

FIGURE 12-1. Major Laws Promoting Inclusion

severity of the disabilities, including those in private schools.

- Requirements that states establish a *voluntary* mediation system (which does not deny or delay right to due process), provide mediation by qualified and impartial individuals who would set forth agreements in writing, and set limits on attorney's fees by prohibiting fees for IEP meetings (except if convened as a result of an administrative proceeding or judicial action).
- Requirement that schools address cultural and linguistic diversity by notifying and providing information to parents in their native language, reporting data by race and ethnicity, prohibiting placing children into special education based only on their lack of instruction in reading or math or limited English proficiency, and requiring greater coordination between special educators and general educators, particularly LEP teachers and administrators.

NEW REQUIREMENTS FOR THE INDIVIDUALIZED EDUCATION PROGRAM (IEP). Since the passage of P.L. 94-142, the expectations for student involvement in their own educational planning have grown (Kupper, 1997). Toward this end, several new transition requirements were added in the 1997 amendments. The first is that the IEP, beginning when the student is *aged 14 and every year thereafter,* must include a statement of the transition service needs for the student's courses of study. The purpose of the requirement is to focus attention on how the student's educational program can be planned for successful transition to the student's life goals after secondary school. By drawing attention to the need to begin transition at age 14, Congress was not intending to simply move back the requirements for 16-year-olds, but rather to seek strategies that are relevant to the developmental levels of 14-year-olds. The intent is to build on those activities so that the services at age 16 are more

meaningful and allow the student time to develop the skills for self-advocacy (Cashman, 1998).

The second new IEP requirement relates to the *age of majority,* or the age when the student under state law is considered an adult rather than a minor. The 1997 IDEA amendments outlined a procedure for the transfer of parental rights to the student reaching that age. Public agencies must now notify both the parents and the students about the students' rights upon reaching the age of majority. Under this provision, 1 year before the student reaches the age of majority under state law, the IEP must include a statement that the student has been informed of the rights, if any, that transfer to him or her upon reaching the age of majority. This provision is important because the postsecondary, adult service, and rehabilitation systems deal directly with individuals and not their parents (Cashman, 1998). The rehabilitation system is very alert and cautious when someone else wants to intervene in the decision of the individual. This transfer of rights is an enormous step toward empowering students as adults and encouraging them to become much more involved in their education and future planning (Kupper, 1997).

Several modifications were made to the definition of transition services, changes that strengthen the requirement that states and local educational agencies provide such services to all youth with disabilities. The Individuals with Disabilities Education Act, 1997 Amendments, redefined transition services as:

- A coordinated set of activities aimed at a specific student outcome (e.g., employment, referral to rehabilitation services, enrollment in college).
- Activities which promote the movement of a student from school to post-school activities, which may include postsecondary education, vocational training, in-

tegrated employment (including supported employment), continuing and adult education, adult services, independent living, or community participation.

- A coordinated set of activities (above) that must be (1) based on the individual student's needs, (2) take into account the student's preferences and interests, and (3) include needed activities in the areas of instruction, community experiences, the development of employment and other post-school adult living objectives, and, if appropriate, daily living skills and functional vocational evaluation (Section 614(d)(1)(A)(vii)).

The words "based on the student's needs, preferences and interests" were added in the 1997 amendments and did not appear in the 1990 definition. This addition was made because research showed widespread evidence that many IEPs contained transition goals and objectives written without consideration of students' interests and needs (Baer, Simmons & Flexer, 1997; Clark & Kolstoe, 1991; Cobb & Johnson, 1997; Eighteenth Annual Report to Congress on IDEA, 1996; Fabian, Lueking & Tilson, 1995; Field, Martin, Miller, Ward & Wehmeyer, 1998; West, Taymans, Corbey & Dodge, 1994).

THE REHABILITATION ACT SUPPORTS INCLUSION. The Rehabilitation Amendments (P.L. 102-569), now part of The Workforce Investment Act of 1998, provided grants and incentives to encourage greater participation in employment by youths (e.g., transition services) and individuals with severe disabilities (e.g., supported employment). Rehabilitation services have been cross-referenced in IDEA and school improvement laws that require local educational agencies to describe in their local school improvement plans their coordination of school improvement efforts with Vocational Rehabilitation Service agencies, Social and Human Service agencies, Health Service agencies, and other agencies responsible for coordinating services to children and youth.

The Rehabilitation Act requires cooperation among agencies responsible for transition of students from school to employment or postsecondary settings. Interagency agreements are system-change strategies which operationalize shared interest and shared responsibility. The State Unit must create and annually update a plan which "transfers responsibility for transitioning students . . . from the local education agency . . . to the local agency providing vocational rehabilitation services." This provision links the IEP and the Individual Written Rehabilitation Plan (IWRP) in accomplishing rehabilitation goals prior to high school graduation.

The 1992 and 1997 Amendments to the Rehabilitation Act addressed the individual's opportunity to make informed choices in the selection of services and providers. Informed choice provisions address quality issues in the delivery of services. These provisions target the performance of providers in creating relevant services that are valued by consumers. Under this provision, every consumer would receive information concerning the range of service options available and the performance history of the providers considered to deliver them.

Several provisions of the Rehabilitation Act advance the delivery of transition services as a coherent system. The State Rehabilitation Agency is required to collect data on the allocation of transition responsibilities among job roles in vocational rehabilitation, including the preparation of vocational rehabilitation professionals in institutions of higher learning. These provisions are to assure a current and future supply of rehabilitation professionals who have the interdisciplinary transition training required to perform the collaborative functions the law requires.

AN INCLUSIVE EMPLOYMENT POLICY: THE WORKFORCE INVEST-MENT ACT OF 1998. The Workforce Investment Act (P.L. 105-220) establishes a state workforce investment board that will assist each governor in developing the state's 5-year strategic plan for providing state job training services for all youth and young adults. This law also establishes local workforce investment boards responsible for setting training policy at the local level, in conjunction with the state plan. The law requires that a one-stop delivery system be established locally, to include postsecondary educational institutions; employment services agencies; private, non-profit agencies; or a government agency. The one-stop delivery system is to provide core services such as outreach and intake, initial assessment of skill levels, job-search and placement assistance, career counseling, assessment of skills necessary for jobs, case management services, short-term prevocational services, and information about available training services. The law also authorizes Individual Training Accounts (vouchers) through which participants choose and pay for training from providers. This law encourages coordination among multiple service sectors. States may submit unified plans to ensure the coordination of (and avoidance of duplication of) workforce development activities for adults and youth, adult education, secondary and postsecondary vocational education, vocational rehabilitation, and others.

THE INCLUSIVE MANDATE OF THE AMERICANS WITH DISABILITIES ACT OF 1990. The ADA (P.L. 101-336) mandated civil rights for people with disabilities and barred discrimination in the areas of employment, transportation, public accommodations, state and local governments, and telecommunications. The ADA promotes nondiscrimination on the basis of disability in any private entity (including colleges and universities, postsecondary vocational-technical schools, employer-based training programs, and other private training programs). The law promotes collaboration among general, special, vocational, and postsecondary personnel to assist young adults to exercise their rights to access postsecondary programs. The promise of equal opportunity and full participation for *all youth* cannot be realized without assurances that students with disabilities have access to the range of opportunities in the secondary and postsecondary systems and to improvements in the learning environment. This also includes ensuring participation of youths with disabilities in local school improvement plans at both the secondary and postsecondary levels. Local plans must describe how they will provide students with comprehensive academic and career guidance, vocational counseling, and placement into postsecondary education.

According to regulations of the ADA, "reasonable accommodations" include modifications made to a postsecondary education admission procedure enable an individual to be considered for admission, as well as modifications in classrooms, test taking, and instruction that would help the student participate in and learn in the college setting. Under the ADA, transition activities can include preparation for college interviews, knowledge about reasonable accommodations provided in the programs, and assistance with applications and supporting documentation. The ADA promotes the participation of professionals with disabilities in higher education through its antidiscrimination provisions. In other words, colleges, universities and postsecondary institutions are required to fairly consider applicants with disabilities in their recruitment of teachers, professors, and support personnel.

INCLUDING ALL YOUTH IN PREPARATION FOR WORK: THE SCHOOL-TO-WORK OPPORTUNITIES ACT. The School-to-Work Opportunities Act (STW) (P.L. 103-239, 1994) was designed to provide transition services for all students with all kinds of learning needs, including students with disabilities. The law was developed because lawmakers recognized the growing number of youth exiting the schools who failed to successfully make the transition to postsecondary education and employment. In the 1980s, the U.S. Government Accounting Office (GAO) evaluations of education, vocational education, job training programs, and youth transition programs revealed a lack of coordination among education and training agencies to help youth with transition (GAO, 1992, 1993, 1994b, 1994c). A more aggressive effort, therefore, had to be made to prepare teachers and community personnel to address the continued poor outcomes for youth. This realization led to the passing of the School-to-Work Opportunities Act in 1993, extending to all youth the promise of transition support to help improve postschool outcomes. The Act moved earlier education reform efforts further and provided a framework for including all students in programs that prepare them for constructive contribution to their communities—and to define themselves, their role in the work world, and in continued learning. School-to-work transition outcomes are a national priority and a chief measure of the success of all that we invest in specialized instruction and supports. One of the chief purposes of the Act is to

> (a) offer opportunities for all students to participate in a performance-based education and training program; (b) to promote all youths, including youths with disabilities, to stay in or return to school and strive to succeed; (c) to promote the formation of local partnerships that are dedicated to linking worlds of school and work, parents, community-based organization and human service agencies; and (d) create a universal high-quality STW transition system that enables youths to identify and navigate paths to productive and progressively more rewarding roles in the workplace. (Title I)

STW programs include several elements, the first being a *school-based learning component,* which promotes awareness of the variety of careers that exist, assistance in the selection of a career, support for developing a program of study consistent with career goals and interests, integration of academic and vocational learning, regular evaluations of student performance, and assistance with entry into postsecondary education. STW programs also include a *work-based learning component* that involves work experience relevant to the student's career choice, work-place mentoring, and academic instruction in the work setting. Third, STW programs include *connecting activities* designed to match students with work experiences and employers, provide a link between school and employer, collect data on program outcomes for students, and provide outreach to employers to engage them directly in program development.

To promote full participation in school- and work-based programs and services, state plans under the STW must contain language that is at least as explicit as that found in other statutes addressing the education and employment preparation of individuals with disabilities. Access to mainstream employment and economic self-sufficiency, as promoted by the Americans with Disabilities Act, cannot benefit individuals with disabilities unless the means and opportunities for access and full participation are provided for youth, through appropriate career-preparation and transition services. STW programs must be a vehicle for such.

IDEA requires schools to coordinate with other system-change and reform initiatives such programs under the Goals 2000: Educate America Act or STW. For example, the definition of "transition services" is closely aligned with the definition of school-to-work activities under the STW. Under STW State Development Activities, funds are available to the SEA to coordinate with many agencies including businesses, vocational education programs, and activities that promote joint planning and coordination with programs carried out under the Higher Education Act of 1965 (20 U.S.C. 1001 *et seq.*). These can include activities related to developing and providing leadership, supervision, and resources for comprehensive career guidance, vocational counseling, and placement programs.

ENSURING FULL PARTICIPATION IN VOCATIONAL EDUCATION: THE CARL D. PERKINS VOCATIONAL AND TECHNICAL EDUCATION ACT AMENDMENTS OF 1998. Over the past two decades, vocational education legislation has increased the emphasis on serving youth with special needs in schooling and employment. In 1985 and again in 1990, special provisions were included in the law to ensure equal access to vocational services by all youth, including those with disabilities. These adjustments in the law were made because policymakers and the general public realized that (1) special needs learners and disadvantaged youth and adults have experienced enduring patterns of discrimination in education and the work place, and (2) they have not received adequate help from education and training institutions to ensure access and supportive services to successfully participate in programs and services. The continued support for vocational education legislation reveals that the nation is committed to developing a coherent system of career and work preparation that addresses the needs of all people, including those who may not be able to enter or graduate from college (Hansen, 1993).

The 1990 and 1998 amendments to the Carl D. Perkins Vocation and Technical Education Act (P.L. 101-392 and P.L. 105-332, respectively) required states to ensure equal access to vocational education for youths with disabilities, and they dedicated approximately half of available funds for the purpose of serving special populations of individuals. Special populations includes individuals with disabilities, educationally and economically disadvantaged individuals (including foster children), individuals with limited English proficiency, individuals who participate in programs designed to eliminate gender bias, and individuals in correctional institutions. In 1990, the Act mandated that students with disabilities have equal access to recruitment, enrollment, and placement activities in the full range of vocational education programs in the public schools, including tech-prep programs. The Carl D. Perkins Vocational and Applied Technology Education Act, 1990 and 1998 Amendment, contained language (assurances) promoting the inclusion of students with disabilities into general vocational education classes. The term *inclusion* is not actually used, but instead the term *full participation* is defined. The Act requires each recipient to use Perkins funds to improve vocational education programs with "full participation of individuals who are members of special populations." In the regulations, the U.S. Department of Education interprets full participation to mean that programs must provide "the supplementary and other services necessary for them to succeed in vocational education." Under the 1998 Amendments, states receiving federal funds under the Act are still expected to provide assurances that

- members of special populations will be provided equal access to recruitment, enrollment, and placement activities and to the full range of vocational education programs;
- individuals with disabilities will be provided services in the least restrictive environment and will be afforded certain rights and protection;
- vocational education planning for individuals with disabilities will be coordinated with special education and rehabilitation agencies;
- the provisions of vocational education will be monitored to determine if that education is consistent with the IEP for each student and ensure that disadvantaged students and students with limited English proficiency have access in the most integrated setting possible.

Secondly, the Act requires each organization or agency receiving funds to provide assurances that it will

- assist students who are members of special populations to enter vocational education programs, and with respect to students with disabilities, assist in providing certain transitional services;
- assess the special needs of students participating in programs using Perkins funds, with respect to their successful completion of vocational education programs in the most integrated setting possible;
- provide certain supplementary services to students who are special populations members, including individuals with disabilities;
- provide certain guidance, counseling, and career development activities;
- provide counseling and instructional services designed to facilitate the transition from school to post-school employment and career opportunities. (Sections 118 & 235) (P.L. 105-332, Section 122(c)(131).

This definition helps protect and promote the inclusion of students with disabilities into regular vocational-technical education opportunities, as well as activities in which students work in their communities.

Recent reports such as the National Longitudinal Transition Study (Wagner, 1994) and several GAO reports (1989, 1994a, 1994b, 1994c) have provided substantial evidence that special needs students are benefiting from vocational education programs. The vocational education system has been and continues to be a nationally supported program that is vital for assisting youth and young adults to prepare for and make successful transitions to postsecondary education, employment, and independent adult life.

ENSURING FAIRNESS IN THE WORK PLACE: THE FAIR LABOR STANDARDS ACT (FLSA). The key provision of the Fair Labor Standards Act (P.L. 99-486) is the "right to fair wages" for all workers, and provision of overtime compensation to workers for more than 40 hours of work per week. The Act covers private and state and local public employees, and also addresses special categories of workers, such as youths and young adults with disabilities. For youth and adults with disabilities, the severe restrictions on earnings have been removed and special alternative wage structures have been established to allow for work internships or employment training programs. The FLSA also addresses work-related issues such as the following:

- Minimum wage.
- Labor standards protection for prison inmates.
- Strengthening of child labor law.
- Status of "model garment" seamstresses and industrial home workers.
- Labor standards for blind workers and workers with disabilities.
- Overtime pay revisions to allow for more flexibility.
- An amendment to allow employers to benefit from services of a volunteer through a 6-month period without wages.

The FLSA has many provisions that allow for training and work internships at modified wage structures. Many youths with disabilities participate in work-based training using such special wage arrangements with businesses.

ENSURING FULL PARTICIPATION IN JOB PREPARATION: THE JOB TRAINING PARTNERSHIP ACT OF 1982 AND JOB TRAINING REFORM ACT OF 1993 (P.L. 97-30, P.L. 102-367). The forerunner to the Job Training Partnership Act (JTPA) was the Comprehensive Employment and Training Act (CETA) of 1973 (P.L. 93-203, and the Amendments of 1978, P.L. 95-524, which began federal involvement in job training to target economically disadvantaged youth and adults and which required that persons with disabilities be addressed in planning and application for funds. The CETA program was reauthorized in 1982 and renamed the Job Training Partnership Act. This law reformed CETA by improving the efficiency and performance of the program. It also established procedures to involve private business and industry in partnerships with the public sector to provide programs and services to assist young people in preparing for and entering employment. The Act targeted disadvantaged youth and adults, which included individuals with disabilities. The JTPA also established Job Corps centers for disadvantaged youths who need additional education, vocational and job skills training, and other support services in order to make a successful transition into employment.

ENSURING EQUAL ACCESS AND INCLUSION IN POSTSECONDARY EDUCATION: THE HIGHER EDUCATION ACT. The Higher Education Act is divided into several major sections, each of which has a specific purpose. Several of these are particularly relevant for students with disabilities. Title I of the Higher Education Act (HEA) (P.L. 89-329) encourages partnerships between institutions of higher education and secondary schools serving low-income and disadvantaged students, including students with dis-

abilities. Such partnerships may include collaboration among businesses, labor organizations, community-based organizations, and other public or private organizations. Title IV is aimed at increasing college retention and graduation rates for low-income students and first-generation students with disabilities. A high priority is placed on serving students with disabilities who are also from low-income situations. This priority challenges colleges and universities to collaborate with schools and other community agencies for outreach and support of such students.

Title IV allows for grants for experimentation and development of model programs that provide counseling for students about college opportunities, financial aid, and student support services. It also encourages creative collaborations among colleges, universities, financial aid organizations, and support service agencies. Title V is intended to provide assistance to the teaching force to improve professional skills, address the nation's teacher shortage, and support recruitment of underrepresented populations into the teaching force. This includes special instruction for college and university teachers, to introduce them to the needs of students with disabilities.

Title XI provides incentives to vocational-technical schools, colleges, and universities to encourage them to work with private and civic organizations to (1) address problems of accessibility for students with disabilities in regard to institutions of higher education and (2) to reduce attitudinal barriers that prevent full inclusion of individuals with disabilities within their academic communities, including the social and cultural community of the campus. Such activities can include encouraging student visits to postsecondary settings, providing information about student support services on campus, holding special teacher and administrator seminars about student accommodation needs, and providing accommodations in the classrooms and on campus.

INCLUSIVE PROVISIONS OF THE NATIONAL SERVICE TRUST ACT OF 1994. The National Service Trust Act (P.L. 103-82, 1994) has the potential to revolutionize secondary education for youth in this country. The legislation creates a voluntary national service program which provides community service in exchange for scholarships for college. This is not viewed as a jobs program nor an educational program, but rather, according to the White House Office of National Service, a "way station" for serving the community. This service corps program encourages the participation of all students in the program.

INCLUSION IS HERE TO STAY! Many major public laws are crafted in such a way that a durable framework is formed that weaves together the constitutional rights of access and inclusion. This framework sets an expectation of shared responsibility for including individuals with special needs in the full range of educational programs and services available in classrooms and schools.

Together these philosophical forces and public policies that embody them provide compelling evidence that inclusion is a movement that is here to stay. But inclusion, as a major integration initiative, is not easy to implement. It is, however, part of an expanding vision and a goal that is linked to a greater effort to advance a democratic and civilized society. But, we are *never* finished. The commitment and effort of all the key players—students, teachers, parents, principals, administrators, and community agency leaders—must be strong and sustained as we enter the next century.

As schools share successes with inclusion, it is a time for necessary debate, experimentation, and creative collaboration among the many professionals and organizations. Such experimentation, however, carries both *promises and pitfalls*. As schools undergo change to expand educational services to all students, we must *pay the price of vigilance* to ensure that students with disabilities are not excluded from these reforms. Educators and administrators—all pioneers—must develop a renewed commitment and become part of the work of creative redesign, and the search for what works best.

CHAPTER 13

Where Are We Headed with Inclusion in the 21st Century? A Revolution of Expectations

INTERNATIONAL COVENANTS PROTECT THE EDUCATIONAL RIGHTS OF CHILDREN. Several international covenants supporting educational rights of all children, particularly those with disabilities, have established the following principles or values for state responsibility for children:

1. Basic education should be provided to all children, on the basis of equal opportunity.
2. Education should be free at the elementary and fundamental stages, and shall be compulsory (United Nations Center for Human Rights, 1988).
3. Children should be given an education that will promote their general culture, and enable them, to develop their individual judgment, and their sense of moral and social responsibility, and to become useful members of society (United Nations, 1960);
4. The child who is physically, mentally or socially handicapped shall be given the special treatment, education and care required by his particular condition (United Nations Center for Human Rights, 1988).
5. Children with impairments have the right to enjoy a full and decent life and the state has an obligation to provide for their special needs (World Bank Report, 1995).
6. An active commitment must be made to removing educational disparities.
7. Underserved groups (the poor, street and working children, rural and remote populations) should not suffer any discrimination in access to learning opportunities.
8. The education of persons with impairments, as far as possible, should take place in the general school system. Responsibility for their education should be placed upon the educational authorities, and laws regarding compulsory education should include children with all ranges of disabilities, including the most severely disabled (World Bank Report, 1995).

In order to achieve the goals outlined in these international documents, there is a need to better understand the meaning of success or failure of inclusion, and the need for improved

- Planning and support.
- Preparation for interdisciplinary and team teaching.
- Curriculum integration.
- Understanding of the integration of technology into instruction.
- Individualization of instruction for all students.
- Community-based instruction.
- Acceptance of diverse classrooms.
- Staff development.
- Availability of teacher incentives.
- Strategies for improving parental involvement.
- Professional and paraprofessional training.
- Preparation of students for school-to-work transition.

BROAD GOALS OF THE INCLUSION MOVEMENT. Although inclusion may have begun in many schools as a way to integrate students physically into general education classes, the strategies have helped teachers, students, and parents to develop enduring and caring relationships among all students. As we continue along the path of increased teacher collaboration, as well as interdisciplinary and interagency relationships, the inclusion movement will focus its efforts on 10 broad goals.

1. Develop a Unified System for Education. New organizational approaches are needed to reduce the fragmented approach to educating students who are not learning effectively, who are "falling through the cracks." The dual system of separate administrative arrangements for special programs is being eliminated. If a separate special education system is maintained, education will continue to operate on the assumptions that students with and without disabilities require two sets of services that must be delivered apart, funded separately, and administered separately. While many students with disabilities do need extra and specialized support services, most of those services can be delivered within the general education setting. The inclusive schools of tomorrow will assume that designs that integrate both students with disabilities and those without will benefit all students (Reynolds, Wang & Walberg, 1992, Wang, 1993). Such a concept requires a fundamental change in the way teachers and others think about differences among people and how we view the purpose of education (Gartner & Lipsky, 1992). It also requires that teachers and administrators remain committed to providing the needed supportive services that can enable students with disabilities to successfully participate in inclusive classrooms and activities. The results of school reform must benefit all students. To better integrate diverse students into general education classes, a greater emphasis must be placed on collaborative team teaching and learning. Instructional methods such as these combine the support of the teacher and structure the social relationships for inclusion.

2. Preserve the Rights of Full Participation in Restructured Schools. As the pace of education restructuring quickens and budget reallocations begin to have a greater impact on students and their families, the inclusion rights movement will intensify. Advocates for the students with mild to moderate needs for specialized educational services will become more vigorous advocates for inclusion in the general education classroom and school activities. Such a movement will be fueled by a growing public expectation that (1) all children and youth need a greater role in decision making and self-determination in their education, careers, and futures, and (2) all children and youth can benefit from participation in mainstream education, and career preparation in school-based and community-based training. In the future, students with disabilities will tutor other students with and without disabilities.

The philosophical principles of inclusion are reflected in many of the laws and policies that govern the education of students with disabilities. State and local guidelines on inclusion are written to interpret and remain consistent with federal special education law and to provide guidance to schools in the implementation of inclusion at the school level. Since 1975, national, state, and local regulations and guidelines have been aimed at

- Improving the quality of services.
- Increasing the participation of special populations in the full range of programs and services available, but preserving intensive services for those with the greatest need.
- Ensuring coordination and collaboration among service sectors to improve access to and efficient delivery of services.

3. Create a Revolution of Expectations. Social attitudes about children with disabilities adversely affects expectations about what they can achieve academically and

vocationally. These attitudes have caused and continue to cause them to be

- Exempt from standards and tests routinely applied to other students.
- Allowed grades that they have not earned.
- Excused from social and behavioral expectations set for other students.
- Exempt from making personal choices and decisions.
- Permitted special diplomas. (Cornett, 1995; Friend & Bursuck, 1999; Halloran & Simon, 1994; Gartner & Lipsky, 1992)

These watered-down expectations have been believed to be in the best interests of the child (Gartner & Lipsky, 1992). Students with disabilities included in general education classrooms are being expected to be held to the same standards and assessment measures as their nondisabled peers. They will, more and more, also be expected to acquire the required Carnegie units needed for regular high school diplomas. The expectations expressed in early interpretations of P.L. 94-142—that the IEP should merely enable the child to "achieve passing marks and advance from grade to grade," will not be acceptable for most students with mild to moderate disabilities.

4. Achieve Educational Rights Without Labels. The stigmatization of continued low expectations of success for students with disabilities is not acceptable in any educational system that promotes the growth of the individual student. There will be increased questions about the validity of the learning disability category (percentages of special education students labeled with learning disabilities vary widely among the 50 states and among 30 large cities) (Gartner & Lipsky, 1992). In the coming decade, students with learning disabilities are likely to be fully included in general educational classrooms. This means that teachers and administrators must find a way to provide the needed services for students, without the damaging effects of classification and labeling (Gartner & Lipsky, 1992).

5. Improve Placement and Support Processes. Policymakers are already proposing alternative methods of funding special educational services for students, and such proposals include capping of the number of students who can be provided special education (Council for Exceptional Children, 1994). While capping may solve economic problems of eroding educational resources in some states and localities, it does not address the educational support needs of many students. The nature of placement decisions must no longer be adversarial. Inclusive schools will increase the effectiveness of how students are identified and placed into classrooms.

6. Improve Family Partnerships. Schools and related support services agencies will make heightened efforts to engage the families of children, youth, and adults as partners in the education, development, and progress of their sons and daughters. There will be efforts to increase federal and state funding and policy incentives to support innovations in parent linkages.

7. Improve School and Community Coordination and Transition to Adulthood.

Schools and related support service agencies need assistance to coordinate their services to improve early intervention and early childhood development services to ensure that children have a beginning in life that is physically, cognitively, and emotionally healthy. Furthermore, school and community agency personnel must continue their efforts to work together to ensure that the K–12 gains made by children and youth are not lost in the transition to employment, postsecondary training, and independent living. Several new issues related to school-to-work transition now challenge educators and related services personnel who implement the Individuals with Disabilities Education Act (IDEA) as it was newly reauthorized in 1997. These will require a continued commitment to investing national resources to provide free and appropriate education and transition services, with appropriate support services for students with disabilities. These issues include the following:

- **Empowerment and meaningful involvement of parents, students, and the community in the transition process:** lowers the required age for receiving transition services to age 14, allowing for teachers to intervene earlier with students at risk either of dropping out or of placement in alternative educational settings. This also allows more time to implement student-directed IEP planning.
- **Increased recruitment and training of all personnel involved in the transition process:** will require initiatives to prepare teachers to provide transition services and to participate in interagency coordination among special and general education, rehabilitation, and community services.
- **Increased cooperation and collaboration among agencies and personnel involved in the transition process:** will require (1) the removal of barriers to interagency collaboration; (2) requirements for closer collaboration among agencies that provide vocational education, job training services, juvenile services, and youth services; and (3) a commitment to referring students in inclusive classrooms for needed related and support services, including vocational and transition services.
- **Clarification of the definition of transition:** will require (1) expanding the definition of transition to include emphasis on transition planning within general secondary educational programming, as well as postschool activities, (2) providing all youth some form of transition assistance appropriate to their needs, and (3) including transition-service outreach to out-of-school youth.
- **Clarification of responsibilities of key players in the transition process:** will require incentives for interagency resource sharing for transition, particularly in the postgraduation transition phase.

- **Improved monitoring of local and regional labor markets:** will require that local educational agencies (LEAs) collect labor market information and utilize such information when developing transition plans.
- **Development of a service delivery continuum in which student graduation, outreach to school dropouts, participation in innovative 2 + 2 programs, and transition support are complementary, not mutually exclusive:** will require an amendment to IDEA to allow students continued eligibility for free and appropriate public education (FAPE) if they are within the age range for services within their state, regardless of whether they have received a high school diploma.
- **Protection for students placed into alternative school programs:** educators will be required to ensure legal protection to students placed into alternative settings. There is evidence that students who are outplaced into "alternative placements" (classes and schools) are not being assessed for special educational needs, nor receiving services. The dropout rate, as well as the increasing rate of outplacement of youth with disabilities to alternative educational programs and schools, indicates a need for earlier implementation of transition services and supports.
- **Increased support for innovative transition service models:** will require increased state and local funding for secondary and transition services, particularly to expand the replication of innovative secondary programs in LEAs, which integrate academic, vocational-technical, functional, and community-based programming.
- **Consistent information from multiple local-level agencies:** will require that LEAs collect data on students who are placed into alternative settings.

8. Implement System Change Through a New Generation of Teachers and Support Personnel.

With the great transformations that are occurring in the way children and youths are educated and prepared for careers, there is a need to prepare a new generation of creative teachers and support personnel. These new leadership personnel and change agents must be prepared to respond to changing life roles that youth face as their families and communities change. They must have the knowledge to collaborate on and build inclusive services that embrace academic development, social-psychological development, career development, and preparation for work and broader life roles. College and university training must prepare general and special educators for such collaboration and model such collaboration through team teaching that integrates course work, assignments, and practical experiences.

9. Place New Emphasis on Reducing Youth Violence.

Continued poor outcomes for many populations of youth are likely to continue to stimulate new approaches to improving educational and developmental conditions for all youth. New educational, employment preparation, and transition support services are emerging under the Violent Crime Control Act and the School-to-Work Opportunities Act. Educators and job training experts realize the need to respond to changing life roles that youth face along with deteriorating school, home, and community conditions. New community approaches similar to those used in the 1960s and 1970s under the Community Development Block Grant initiatives seek to address environmental problems for youth, such as poor supervision in the home, economic deterioration in communities, and lack of work preparation and employment opportunities. These conditions are believed to be associated with problematic youth outcomes such as teen pregnancy, violent and aggressive behavior, substance abuse, and lack of responsible citizenship. Use of such community approaches can promote inclusive violence prevention services for all youth.

10. Explore New Roles for the Business Community.

The business community has been concerned with academic preparation but is equally concerned with preparation of youth for contemporary work environments. Business and industry are ready for a greater involvement in new initiatives for linking education and work environments. The business community supports competition among schools to encourage weak schools to perform better, increased private investment in educa-

tion, and business involvement in educational policy. They also want a strong focus on outcomes and accountability for education and work preparation programs (Asche, 1993; Rigden, 1992;). School programs that can demonstrate success in occupational skills training programs that integrate relevant academic skills with functional and social skills are likely to gain the support of the business community (Kochhar & Erickson, 1993). Programs that serve mixed populations of students with and without special needs, and that involve wider community resources, will be of particular interest to the business community.

The new decade in the 21st century will be one of experimentation with shared resources and new community partnerships among the many agencies concerned with the educational and social development of children and youth. It is a time for debate, experimentation, and creative collaboration among the many agencies involved. Such experimentation, however, carries both promises and pitfalls. As school and work-based programs are restructured to expand educational and transition services to all students, we must pay the price of vigilance to ensure inclusion for all special populations in these reforms.

PART TWO

Successful Strategies for Implementing Inclusion

Part Two is designed to provide strategies to help general and special education teachers and related professionals in their challenge to better serve special learners in inclusive settings. It emphasizes inclusion practices that work, practical strategies that can lead to successful inclusion at the classroom and school levels, and techniques for overcoming barriers to the process. This part also emphasizes teamwork and shared effort among all professionals concerned about the educational success of all students.

CHAPTER 14

What Are the Major Strategies for Overcoming Barriers to Inclusion?

Implementing special education laws to serve students with disabilities has required schools to undergo rapid and complex change. Educators and policymakers agree that since the passage of P.L. 94-142 in 1975, great gains have been made for students with disabilities in enrollment in home schools and access to inclusive classrooms. Yet, there is more work to be done to improve the acceptance of students with disabilities in inclusive settings and to improve the overall quality of education provided.

BARRIERS TO INCLUSION. It is helpful to teachers who must manage inclusive classrooms to understand the breadth of organizational, knowledge, and attitudinal barriers that can affect the success of inclusion. This section presents some of the common problems and barriers to building inclusive education, as well as ways to overcome them. Barriers to implementing inclusion can be clustered into three categories: *organizational, attitudinal,* and *knowledge* (Kochhar & Erickson, 1993). The three kinds of barriers may be defined as follows:

- *Organizational barriers:* Barriers related to the differences in the way schools and classrooms are structured and managed, how they define their goals, and how they design instruction.
- *Attitudinal barriers:* Barriers related to the beliefs, motivations, and attitudes that different teachers have about educating children and youth, accommodating students with special needs in general education classrooms, communicating with parents, and the community participation of students.
- *Knowledge barriers:* Barriers related to the differences in the knowledge and skills of various teachers about instructing special needs students, providing support services, adapting curriculum and instruction, and structuring the classroom for optimal inclusion.

These barrier definitions are based on questions most often asked by teachers about including students in general education classrooms. There are a number of strategies, summarized in Tables 14-1, 14-2, and 14-3, which have been found effective in overcoming such barriers.

BUILDING ON CHILDREN'S STRENGTHS. Instead of concentrating on students' weaknesses, successful inclusion teachers identify the strengths that many students with disabilities possess and are using to compensate for their difficulties. Thus, instruction and curriculum modifications can be built around the existing strengths and special skills of these children. For example, many children may have well-developed kinesthetic abilities and may learn rapidly through more concrete learning experiences. Many may benefit from having information introduced through a variety of teaching media, including oral, visual, and tactile methods. For this reason, teachers and educational administrators need to be able to determine the strengths and weaknesses of the children and to devise appropriate instructional strategies and modifications. This assessment information can then be used to determine appropriate instructional levels and to modify instruction. With such small accommodations, children with special educational needs may lead fully normal lives and in some cases surpass their peers.

All students benefit when teachers work to improve the full participation of all children, enhancing their potential to succeed in the general education classroom. As individuals and as a nation, we can achieve equal opportunity in education and end discrimination in school programs and related activities. The barriers to inclusion discussed here can be overcome with commitment and careful planning. Case Example 14-1 provides a window into the struggles of one special education teacher to overcome the structural problems and multiple barriers to inclusion for his students.

TABLE 14-1. Organizational Barriers to Inclusion

Organizationl Barrier	Strategy to Overcome Barrier
Barrier 1: Lack of administrative commitment to implement inclusion: Many inclusion initiatives fail because there is a lack of strong commitment from administrators to provide teachers with the freedom and resources they need to revise their teaching strategies, modify curriculum and classroom organization, or form collaborative teams.	Educators need to add the goal of inclusion in the general school goals related to improving the teaching and learning environment for all students. Most important, the goals should include the outcomes expected from the teachers and students as a result of the inclusion effort. Teachers should examine other schools' or teachers' goals and policies on inclusion to learn what degree of freedom teachers have to implement inclusion, what resources are being provided, and what goals are being expressed.
Barrier 2: Tightening budgets threaten continuation of inclusion efforts: What help will the teacher get for including very diverse students? Where will the money for extra technology or teacher assistants come from? When education and social services budgets are tightening, the pressure can lead to disputes about the amount and kinds of resources that should be committed for inclusion purposes.	Efforts should be made to ensure that inclusion goals are built into the school's budget and improvement planning process. Educators must serve on committees for planning inclusion and for evaluating the success of inclusion. Records must be kept on the resources (time, staff, etc.) needed to serve students with disabilities in the classroom, so that additional costs can be anticipated and requested for future years. Teachers must share resources through teacher teams and interdisciplinary collaboration.
Barrier 3: Time and incentives for inclusion: Will teachers get extra pay for serving students with disabilities in general education classrooms, or fewer students? Many teachers claim they have no common planning time each day and often have to plan over lunch for the following day. The availability of classroom aides for teacher planning time is becoming more limited. Without a common planning time, teachers spend many hours outside of contract time planning for and reflecting on the progress of the children in their classroom.	Many schools are experimenting with ways of building in more planning time for collaborating teacher teams, particularly for general education teachers serving students with disabilities. Substitute teachers or student interns are being relied on to help provide such planning time. Other strategies for teacher planning include using a shortened school day one day a week, providing early morning sessions, or using teacher in-service days. Schools are also experimenting with ways to provide incentives for teachers serving students with disabilities, including smaller class sizes, targeted resources, support for team teaching, and extra planning time.
Barrier 4: Classroom management concerns: Increased class size and teacher workloads have been found to be major concerns of teachers who teach students with disabilities in regular classes (NEA, 1994). The common objections to inclusion are lack of teachers' time, impact on other students, diminishing resources, inadequate support for teachers and students, lack of teacher training, and mixed administrative support. Other concerns are related to how inclusion is affecting learning environments and which children are being moved from segregated schools and classrooms into more integrated settings.	Professionals should conduct a thorough assessment of a school's readiness to implement inclusion. Factors to be considered are interdisciplinary planning, physical environment, support services, educational accommodations, student assessment, administrative planning, commitment, teacher training, technical assistance, and parent involvement. In-service training in classroom management and use of resources, including generating new resources, is essential.
Barrier 5: Time-consuming requirements for developing the IEP, reporting, and data collection: There has been a long-standing concern of teachers, administrators, and the IEP team, that the instructional time of teachers and resources of the school are sacrificed in order to comply with heavy data collection and reporting requirements for students with disabilities.	Identify computer-based IEP software that enables teachers to easily and swiftly develop and store the academic components of the individualized instructional programs. Such software programs also make the review and revision process a lot easier. Team teaching involves at least two teachers in the process of creating the academic components of the IEPs, thus reducing the load for the individual teacher. This academic component, of course, is one element of the overall IEP developed by the full ITP team.
Barrier 6: Funding and resource barriers: In the past, special education funding formulas provided incentives for placing students into separate, more restrictive placements, and therefore rewarded segregated services. Use of funds to help students who are considered at risk of needing special education (prereferral interventions) has not been permitted. Thus teachers who have special education assistants or con-	Special education law allows the use of special education resources and equipment to benefit all students in a classroom, not just these with a disability. Revisions to the IDEA include giving more discretion on the part of schools and teachers to experiment with ways to improve the teaching and learning environments for individuals with disabilities in inclusive classrooms. Special education funds can be used to benefit

Organizational Barrier	Strategy to Overcome Barrier
sulting teachers in a class have been unable to use these additional resources to help other students in the class who could benefit from the knowledge and strategies of the consulting teacher.	students with disabilities through whole-school improvement efforts, which would include reducing barriers to inclusion and to team teacher coordination. Teacher teams must agree early in a semester on goals to work toward for the students with disabilities, and how resources will be shared. Regular meetings of teachers to discuss the coordination effort usually lead to continuous and constructive troubleshooting of most problems that arise.
Barrier 7: Legislative shifts complex regulations, and organization priorities: For years, many local school districts have had problems complying with complex special education requirements, particularly the requirements for due process, ensuring least restrictive environment, and developing students' IEPs. Now, school reform and improvement initiatives are changing the way teachers' and students' performance is measured and what is expected from them. Yet, in many of these initiatives, it remains unclear how students with disabilities are to be included.	Teachers must learn and help educate others about changes in special education and elementary and secondary education laws and what these changes means for teacher roles and expectations. They should ask the principal or coordinating teacher to gather resources about changes in laws and in state and local policies. Teachers can invite speakers in for in-service days to discuss these legislative mandates and what they mean for teachers' roles and responsibilities.
Barrier 8: Confusion about Section 504 and IDEA: The relationship between Section 504 of the Rehabilitation Act (now incorporated into the Workforce Development Act) and IDEA requirements remains confusing to most teachers and administrators. The Section 504 standard of "appropriate education" requires that schools meet the educational needs of students with disabilities *as adequately* as they meet the needs of nondisabled students (the comparability test), and that all procedural requirements be met. However, most educational agencies do not have a clear standard of what constitutes an "appropriate" education for students without disabilities.	The relationship between Section 504 and IDEA is linked to address two central issues related to disability and protection against discrimination. 1. There is a population of persons with disabilities who are not eligible for special education under IDEA but who still require protection against discrimination because of a disability defined under Section 504. 2. There is an obligation to provide services (special education, evaluation, regular education, and related services) regardless of eligibility for special education under IDEA.
Barrier 9: Problems with mediation and due process provisions in the IDEA: Until recently, there has been little attention paid to improving due process procedures for resolving disputes related to special education placement. The adversarial relationships between parents, teachers, and school officials are often made worse because there are few alternatives to due process proceedings. Educators are asking whether some form of mediation should be available to parents and teachers.	Amendments to IDEA (1997) now echo the Americans with Disabilities Act (ADA): "Where appropriate and to the extent authorized by law, the use of alternative means of dispute resolution, including settlement negotiations, conciliation, facilitation, mediation, fact-finding, minitrials, and arbitration, is encouraged to resolve disputes arising under this Act" (IDEA, 1997 Sect. 615; Senate Committee on Labor and Human Resources 1997). Schools are required to establish mediation options for students and parents to avoid the often lengthy, adversarial, and costly process of formal due process. These mediation options are also designed to facilitate swift and amicable resolutions early on.
Barrier 10: Need for school-linked community agencies to clarify the shared responsibility for inclusion: In many school districts, there are strong interagency agreements between schools and community agencies to share the responsibility and resources to support students with disabilities in inclusive schools. When interagency agreements are weak or nonexistent, the schools assume the primary responsibility for and cost of transition and related services.	Teachers should find out whether their school or district has formal interagency agreements with outside agencies to provide services such as rehabilitation, social services, mental health, juvenile services, family services, legal services, public health, employment, and speech and hearing services to students with disabilities and their families. In-service days are often used to bring local teachers together to meet with agency personnel, relate examples of interagency linkages and of successes in sharing resources.
Barrier 11: Barriers to participation in inclusive schools and classes (transportation, child care, service coordination): Often students who are placed into some schools or general education classrooms face many barriers particularly those students who have been in special schools or classes. These	Many schools are retrofitting school buses so that students with physical disabilities have better access. Schools are also adapting arrangements for before and after school care to include students with disabilities. Some schools are restructuring teacher roles so that each student with a disability is

TABLE 14-1. (*continued*)

Organizational Barrier	Strategy to Overcome Barrier
barriers can include lack of transportation, before and after school care, assistance with accessing counseling and support services, family linkages, and other support.	assigned a teacher advocate who is responsible for knowing the student and his or her needs and for determining additional service needs. Teacher-advocates often work closely with school social workers and psychologists to identify and link the student and family with needed services in the community.
Barrier 12: Problems linking assessments to educational services: There are concerns that special education law has resulted in (1) an emphasis on assessing students in order to label them with specific disabilities, (2) use of assessments that may not be reliable, or that may be culturally biased, and (3) assessment practices that fail to assist teachers in determining appropriate instruction and support services in the classroom. Labels only serve to stigmatize students. There is a need to strengthen the definitions and purposes, of assessment as well as the range of alternatives permitted in schools.	Schools that use assessment effectively use it not only to establish the existence of a disability or condition, but also to other useful and functional ends, such as (1) to understand the nature of the condition and how it impacts upon the individual's development and physical condition, (2) to understand how the disability affects the learning process and potential of the individual and, (3) to identify the specific educational or support services that are needed. Teacher labeling has been criticized as stigmatizing, but there are many ways that the use of labeling can be modified so that its benefits are preserved and its negative effects minimized.
Barrier 13: Dual system of general and special education: In the 1970s, the development of specialized educational services for children with disabilities resulted in the creation of two systems of education that until recently have been largely disconnected from each other. This dual system continues to create organizational problems in schools and provide barriers to the integration of special educational services within the general education framework. Special and general education have traditionally had different student target groups and different instructional purposes; this has made collaboration and shared goal setting for inclusion more difficult.	Educators must get involved in promoting additional training for all teachers, in blending special education services in general education classrooms, in developing team-teaching strategies, and in establishing teacher-advocate and peer-advocate arrangements to support students with disabilities. Teachers should be supported in learning all they can about instructional strategies such as student cooperative learning and team approaches.
Barrier 14: Personnel turnover and reorganization: One of the most severe barriers to inclusion is turnover among classroom teachers and aides and changes in school leadership. Inclusion efforts are most successful when there are school and community "champions" to lead the effort and promote collaboration and new ideas. For example, the loss of a respected principal who championed schoolwide inclusion and who fought to strengthen the effort in a time of economic constraint can cause a sudden halt to years of progress.	Administrators and teacher leaders must examine the staff recruitment, orientation, and training effort. Do they include team-building strategies, development of cooperative attitudes, and communication between teachers and administrators? Administrators should examine how new teachers and personnel are oriented to the school's inclusion model and expectations. They should look carefully at how well teachers document inclusion strategies and approaches that have been successful, so these can be passed on to assist incoming personnel. Incentives should be provided to keep teachers motivated; small expressions of support and appreciation make a significant difference.

TABLE 14-2. Attitudinal Barriers to Inclusion

Barrier 15: Attitudes and misconceptions about students with disabilities: Many teachers harbor attitudes about students with disabilities that prevent their commitment to inclusion. Examples of these attitudes or beliefs include the following: • Students with disabilities always become distracted in classes with other students. • When completing tests and assignments, these students always need additional time. • Such students have difficulty remembering to complete homework assignments. • Such students always need more help to take notes and maintain notebooks.	These stereotypes about students with disabilities may be partially true in some instances, but they are also partially true for many students in most general education class-rooms. Teachers who share their success stories about serving students with disabilities say that the strategies they implement with special education also benefit other students. For example, teachers help some students reduce distraction by changing physical location in the class. They offer more time to complete tests and assignments and provide extra structure and reminders to help students complete homework assignments. This extra structure is particularly helpful with longer term projects that have multiple components. They also provide extra help or team students to facilitate note taking and maintaining notebooks.
Barrier 16: Uncertainty about the effects of inclusion on students without disabilities: Many teachers are concerned about whether there will be negative effects of inclusion on	Research on inclusion has found that students who are appropriately placed into inclusive classrooms are more successful when their nondisabled peers are accepting and support-

Attitudinal Barrier	Strategy to Overcome Barrier
"regular" students. Teachers want to know how they can change the attitudes of nondisabled students and change their acceptance of their peers with disabilities. Some students have had bad experiences previously in other schools in which inclusion was poorly implemented.	ive. Many schools are establishing peer-mentor relationships to educate nondisabled peers and help build relationships for emotional and social support. The peer-mentor situation provides support and encouragement and "enables" the student with a disability to solve problems, make decisions, and adjust to the classroom and new expectations. Peer mentors also help students with disabilities to prepare for tests and project demonstrations, and in some schools they are provided special training to prepare them to understand the needs of students with disabilities.
Barrier 17: Political pressures from the community: As the economic pressures force schools to economize, inclusion efforts are vulnerable to political pressure inside and outside the school. Competing forces and pressures can cause school personnel and community leaders to change directions and reduce the commitment to inclusion. These forces can cause great conflicts among teachers, school officials, parents, and students.	Teachers must work with the PTA and school officials to demonstrate to the parents and to the wider community how inclusion is working and achieving results. Clear communication with the community about the school's goals for inclusion is helpful in battling detractors and naysayers.
Barrier 18: Territorialism: Teachers sometimes feel threatened that their "territory" is being encroached upon and that they will be asked to change the traditional ways of doing things in their class. Most teachers know that inclusion requires new teaching techniques, new teacher team relationships, and new attitudes.	Veteran teachers can informally help orient new teachers and aides about the school's commitment to inclusion. They can challenge new teachers and staff to accept changes in their roles, in traditional teaching practices, and in attitudes.

TABLE 14-3. Knowledge Barriers to Inclusion

Barrier 19: Lack of understanding between special education and general education teachers about their goals and missions: Inclusion is not likely to be successful when special education and general education teachers do not understand each other and the differences in their traditional missions. Nor will they be successful if they fail to recognize each others' complementary strengths.	As a first step toward collaboration, teachers who are forming teams should share their perceptions and understanding of each other's roles. Teacher-orientation and in-service sessions can also be devoted to promoting better understanding between general education professionals and special education and support service personnel.
Barrier 20: Lack of knowledge about whether and how inclusion programs work: Teachers often have little access to information about the benefits, successful strategies, and results of inclusion. They are often unclear about whether they will need to vary their expectations for students with disabilities or assess them differently.	Teacher in-service days can be used to share and learn new information about inclusive classrooms, strategies, and the lessons learned in other local areas and states. Local college and university personnel can help provide such information. Teacher seminars have been effective in many schools in bringing together teachers of inclusive classrooms within a school or from several schools to share, discuss, and demonstrate methods and techniques that are being used in their classrooms.
Barrier 21: Lack of knowledge about the continuum of placements: Teachers are often unclear about the reasons why certain students are placed into their classrooms. Often they are not told in advance, nor given much information about the students before they arrive. They are often unaware about special student requirements, such as medical needs, assistive devices, or behavioral problems. This lack of information and preparation by the teacher contributes to poor implementation of inclusion and to poor outcomes.	Teachers must be provided with appropriate training on the continuum of placements and the decision-making process for placing students into general education classes. They must also work to establish specific school policies that ensure that teachers receive adequate information about new students and the special educational accommodations they need. School policies should also include procedures for troubleshooting or constructively solving problems associated with student placements requiring additional support or intervention in the classroom. Teachers must remain alert to the kinds of placements that require special preparation or extra in-class supports, such as students with severe emotional or behavioral problems who are a danger to themselves or others, or those with complex medical needs who do not have adequate personal assistance or expert care. Teachers must communicate their concerns and advocate for the additional in-class supports.

TABLE 14-3. *(continued)*

Knowledge Barrier	Strategy to Overcome Barrier
Barrier 22: Lack of knowledge about teaching strategies for inclusive classrooms. Teachers often ask: How do I teach these students when my teacher education program did not prepare me to teac children with diverse abilities? Will I have to shortchange my other students? Are there reasonable adaptations I can make? Will I need more training?	General education teachers need to be provided with ongoing in-service training in new inclusion strategies for general education classes. To this end, teacher in-service days and teacher seminars are proving to be effective in many schools. They bring together inclusive teachers within or among schools to share and demonstrate innovative methods and techniques they use in their classrooms. Again, local college and university personnel can be useful in teaching, facilitating, and providing demonstrations of such strategies, in addition to sharing knowledge from other school districts outside the region or state.
Barrier 23: Lack of knowledge about individualized education programs: General education teachers often have not been provided training in individualized education programming. Hence, they may view it as too cumbersome and difficult, or they may not understand its essential purpose in the education and accommodation of students with disabilities.	General education teachers should be provided orientation and in-service training in developing and evaluating IEPs for students in inclusive classes. Teacher planning time is essential for developing IEPs that are understood by all teachers and related services personnel involved with the special student. For team teachers, it is very important that each agrees upon the educational goals and expectations for their students. Again, local college and university personnel can be useful in teaching and providing information about IEP planning and collaborative development.
Barrier 24: Parent orientation, participation, and support: Teachers are often concerned about whether parents will be involved with and supportive of their children's education and classroom placement. They are unclear about the rules regarding parental access to student records, confidentiality issues, and consent issues such as the use of tape recorders at the IEP meeting. There are additional concerns about the requirements for parent notification of meetings and of changes in the student's curriculum or IEP.	Parents and guardians play a crucial role in the success of inclusion. Each parent is responsible for the educational progress of his or her child and for protecting the rights to education and support services under the IDEA. By diminishing parental access to information, we diminish not only the power of parents to support their children's educational programs but also the goals of inclusion. Teachers in inclusive schools should communicate regularly with parents, not only about placement, but also about specific curriculum requirements and activities. In many schools, parents are invited to orientation sessions to introduce them to the inclusion goals and objectives of the school and to the inclusive classroom. Parents are invited to attend portfolio reviews and demonstration and exhibition sessions during the year to observe the skills gained by the students. Parents should be honored at these events for their participation and support both of their sons and daughters and of the school as a whole.

Note: Synthesized from materials from Kochhar & West, 1996; McCoy, 1995; National Center on Education Outcomes, 1993; National Council on Disability, 1994; NEA, 1994; Putnam, 1993; Searl, Ferguson & Biklen, 1985; Turnbull et al., 1995; U.S. Office of Special Education, 1997; U.S. General Accounting Office, 1994b.

CASE EXAMPLE 14-1. Lucas Thompson—A New Teacher Faces Multiple Barriers to Inclusion

"You have a job because of 11 eighth-grade students. Your job is to make them successful." These are the words I heard from the principal of Walker Middle School, where I had just been hired for my first teaching position. With heightened anticipation, I contemplated getting to know this group of students during their crucial year before entering high school. I was anxious to implement all that I had learned in my special education master's degree program.

Walker Middle School, which serves seventh- and eighth-grade students, had been engaged in inclusionary programming for 5 years. The administration had decided to make some scheduling changes so that the special education students placed in general education classes would be better dispersed throughout the school. The mainstreaming model had resulted in some unsatisfactory results. As the special education caseload rose, one special education teacher with his group of 15 to 25 students would be assigned to one general education teacher's subject area class each period. These classes were seen as special education classes of low-achieving students, which many of the general education teachers found undesirable. These classes, with their large numbers of students (averaging 30) and the concentration of students with identified learning needs, were difficult to manage, even with two teachers. In the new scheduling system, no more than five students with a need for special education services were assigned to a general education class. This improved integration approach proved to be a logistical nightmare for me.

I was one of three special education teachers in the school. My two colleagues, both in their second decade of teaching, were responsible for the seventh-grade students. I was responsible for all of the eighth-grade students. The 11 special education students in the seventh grade had two special education teachers working with them and their two general education teachers. The eighth-grade students had me. Thus, the seventh-grade students received twice the support as the eighth-grade students. My students were distributed across eight general education teachers, four of whom were first-year teachers like myself. The final part of the equation was that I averaged three special education students per general education class, while the seventh-grade special education teachers averaged five per class.

I was constantly faced with impossible scheduling decisions. While I was helping three students in English, the other eight were dispersed throughout various academic and elective subjects with no support available to them. I spent the first marking period in frantic activity, with the constant feeling that I was still trying to figure out how to do this increasingly impossible job. The end of the first marking period confirmed my doubts. Over half of my students were failing or close to failing one or more subjects. On reviewing their individual educational programs (IEPs), I determined that most of the students for whom I was responsible were receiving less than the level of services indicated on their IEPS. I went to my department chairperson with a list of questions.

1. Why am I the only special education teacher working with the eighth grade?
2. Why are there so few students with identified learning needs per class in eighth-grade compared with seventh-grade?
3. How can I offer students the level of services indicated on their IEPs when I barely see some students at all?

My questions and concerns were not welcomed. My department chairperson suggested that I schedule direct service "pull out" time with some students. After considering this option, I could not see how having them miss class time would help them or how I could manage coteaching with such a schedule.

I then addressed my concerns to my principal, who was displeased with my criticisms of the schedule. She had personally developed the eighth-grade schedule in consultation with the special education chairperson. Ultimately, we were able to make some schedule changes, but the result still left me with too many teachers to collaborate with and too little time to deliver the level of service indicated in some IEPS.

I spent much time and energy in developing study guides and practice tests for students and in keeping parents informed of upcoming tests and major assignments, to garner support at home. I put weekly monitoring sheets in coteachers' mailboxes in an effort to track student progress. Some teachers responded quickly; others did not.

I ended the school year exhausted and defeated. I was able to use very little of what I had learned during my teacher education program. I felt that I had rocked the boat at my school and was seen as a malcontent. I resigned my position. I know I want to teach, but not in a school or a school system that offers so little support. As I revisit the principal's first words to me, they sound like a tease: "You have a job because of 11 eighth-grade students. Your job is to make them successful."

Discussion Questions

1. Describe the implied philosophy in the new integration schedule.
2. What administrative supports would you suggest to make the program a success schoolwide and within the special education department?
3. What skills did Lucas Thompson need to be effective in his position? Is this a position appropriate for a first-year teacher?
4. If you were a parent of a student on Mr. Thompson's case load, what would you want to have happen?
5. What implications does the eighth-grade program have for students' success in high school?
6. On the basis of the issues presented in this case, develop five principles of effective inclusionary programs at the middle-school level.

Source: Adapted from Kinkaid, L. R. (1995). The trials and tribulations of a first-year team teacher (Weathering structural flaws: Experiences of a first-year multilevel teacher). In J.M. Tavmans (Ed.), *Cases in Urban Teaching,* (pp. 12–17). Washington, DC: George Washington University, Department of Teacher Preparation and Special Education.

CHAPTER 15

What Is the Continuum of Placement Options, and Why Is It Important?

CONTINUED PLACEMENT OF STUDENTS IN SEGREGATED SETTINGS. Several special education studies have revealed a great variation among states in the number of students with disabilities who are educated in separate classes or in separate facilities. For example, one state educates about 90 percent of its students with mental retardation in separate classes, while another state, only 27 percent. One state places over 49 percent of its students with mental retardation in separate public schools, while at least three states place no students with mental retardation into separate public schools (Fuchs & Fuchs, 1994; Hardman, Drew & Egan, 1999; Sawyer, McLaughlin & Winglee, 1992).

INCLUSION MEANS MUCH MORE THAN PHYSICAL PLACEMENT. Inclusion has come to be synonymous with physical placement of a student with a disability from one particular environment into another less restrictive one that allows closer integration with nondisabled peers. But the concept actually embraces an idea of much greater breadth than that of shifting physical environments. Inclusion is founded on two broad premises or beliefs:

1. All children have a right to basic physical access to community schools and public facilities.
2. For inclusion to succeed, society and the educational system must undergo comprehensive change.

The second belief expresses a vision of a world in which integration and acceptance of the student and his or her differences is broad and infused into all school programs and activities. The first goal, physical access, has been much more easily accomplished. *The second remains illusive.*

A SPECTRUM OF INCLUSION MODELS. Inclusion can take many forms and can be achieved in a variety of ways. Although there are several essential principles involved in implementing inclusion, there is no one specific way to achieve it. Inclusion is a way to encourage schools to build programs around individual student needs rather than try to force-fit students into existing programs (Dover, 1994). Dover described several models which represent a *continuum of placement options* available to schools.

- **Self-Contained Model:** The student stays in a special education classroom or resource room for 100 percent of the school day.
- **Mainstreaming Model:** The student takes part in activities in the regular class as long as he or she demonstrates an acceptable level of performance and behavior.
- **Nonacademic Model:** The student participates in regular class activities in elective subjects such as art, music, speech and drama, family life, and physical education.
- **Pull-Out (Resource) Model:** Special education staff provide instruction and support, as needed, to the student on a one-to-one basis outside the regular classroom.
- **Home Class Model:** The student participates in regular classroom opening and closing activities.
- **Social Mainstreaming Model:** The student is included during regular classroom instruction to provide him or her with appropriate exposure to nondisabled peers. The student is not required to complete instructional assignments.
- **Supported Instruction Model:** Special education staff provide support services within regular classroom instruction.
- **Collaborative Model:** Special education and general education staff work together and problem-solve to meet the student's needs.
- **Full Inclusion Model:** The student is placed in a regular

Inclusion is based on a vision of the world in which integration and acceptance of students' differences are broad and infused into all school programs and

This is a fourth-grade class taught by Cassandra Meisner and Jill Taylor at Mount Vernon Elementary School, Alexandria, Virginia. The class is composed of 12 students with learning disabilities and 10 regular education students. This is the first year that the inclusion class was implemented at Mount Vernon, and the two teachers elected to team teach. The improvement in reading levels and self-confidence level of the students with learning disabilities especially was greater than expected, and peer tutoring was routinely implemented. Reading levels at the beginning of the year ranged from reading readiness to six-grade level. One of the greatest increases in skills was a rise in reading level from a preprimer to a third-grade level. We are working with self-advocacy skills and pair students based on ability levels and personal skills that support learning in the classroom. Blending the class and eliminating pull-out resource services has minimized labeling and teasing and promoted success for all students in the class.

classroom 100 percent of the day. The special education staff provide consultative support to the teacher.

One Size Cannot Fit All: Keep the Focus on Individual Need. There are no uniform solutions to implementing inclusion. Most school districts use a variety of the models like the ones summarized by Dover, and several of these models are frequently implemented within a single school district. There is no one right model because each school has its own unique needs and student populations. There is, however, one common principle that inclusion implementors do need to share—the imperative *to keep the focus on the student's individual needs, not on the structure of the model. It is essential that inclusion decisions be made based on what is most appropriate for ensuring the educational success of the student.* This principle is based on the assumption that as appropriate

placement decisions are made, there must be choices and options, rather than uniform solutions for the students.

U.S. Department of Education Defines Inclusion. The U.S. Department of Education collects data from the states on the types of placements provided to students with disabilities in public and private schools. The Department *does not provide rules or prescriptions* on which placement options are appropriate for students with different disabilities. These decisions are left to the discretion of the state and local educational agencies. The U.S. Department of Education (1993a, 1997), therefore, has permitted wide experimentation and demonstration of different options in the field.

- **Regular class** includes students who receive the majority of their education program in the general education classroom and receive special education and related services outside the regular classroom for *less than* 21 percent of the school day. This option includes children placed in a regular class and receiving special education within the regular class, as well as children placed in a regular class and receiving special education outside the regular class (53.3 percent of all students with disabilities aged 6 to 11 are served in this type of class, 33.3 percent for students aged 12 to 17, and 26.6 percent for those 18 to 21).
- **Resource room** includes students who receive special education and related services *outside* the regular classroom for at least 21 percent, but not more that 60 percent of the school day. This placement option may include students placed into resource rooms but given part-time instruction in the regular class. According to the U.S. Department of Education, Office of Special Education (1997), of all students in the United States, 24.8 percent of those aged 6 to 11 are served in this placement option, 35.1 percent for students 12 to 17, and 28.1 percent for the aged 18 to 21 group.
- **Separate class** includes students who receive special education and related services outside the regular classroom for more than 60 percent of the school day. Students may be placed in self-contained special classrooms full time or given part-time instruction in regular classes. Of all students in the United States, 19.3 percent of those aged 6 to 11 are served in this placement option, 25.9 percent for ages 12 to 17, and 30.8 percent for those 18 to 21.
- **Separate school** includes students who receive special education and related services more that 50 percent of the school day in separate day schools for students with disabilities. Of all students in the United States, 1.9 percent of those aged 6 to 11 are served in this placement option, 3.7 percent for the 12 to 17 group, and 10.3 percent for students 18 to 21.
- **Residential facility** includes students who receive education in a public or private residential facility, at public expense, for more than 50 percent of the school day. Of all students in the United States, 0.3 percent of those aged 6 to 11 are served in this placement option; 1.1

percent for students 12 to 17; and 2.9 percent for those 18 to 21.

- **Homebound or hospital environment** includes students in and receiving special education in hospital or homebound programs. Of all students in the United States, 0.3 percent of those aged 6 to 11 are served in this placement option; 0.8 percent for students aged 12 to 17; and 1.3 percent for students 18 to 21. (Source: *Nineteenth Annual Report to Congress on the Implementation of the Individuals with Disabilities Education Act,* 1997, p. 70.)

The number of students with disabilities being placed into regular classrooms is increasing, according to U.S. Department of Education Data, particularly students with mild disabilities. The following facts summarize placement patterns across the United States.

FACTS ABOUT PLACEMENT IN THE U.S.

1. Younger elementary age students are more likely to be placed into inclusive settings because they are more easily accommodated. The elementary school curriculum may pose fewer significant challenges to the these children than does the junior high or high school curriculum.
2. Students with less severe disabilities, such as learning disabilities or speech and language impairments, are served in less restrictive settings (e.g., regular class or resource room).
3. Students with more severe disabilities, such as multiple disabilities, deafness and blindness, or severe mental retardation, are served in more restrictive settings.
4. Eighty-four percent of students with physical disabilities, orthopedic impairments and other health impairments receive their education in either a regular class or resource room; others receive services in separate classes or in homebound and hospital settings. (Source: *Nineteenth Annual Report to Congress on the Implementation of the Individuals with Disabilities Education Act,* 1997.)

Case Example 15-1 illustrates the challenges of seeking an appropriate placement option for an elementary student with significant learning disabilities.

CASE EXAMPLE 15-1. Maria—Searching for a Program

Maria is tall, slender, and full of energy. Adopted by a couple who had met her through the orphanage where she lived, she came to this country from Brazil when she was 5 years old. Maria adapted well to her new life in the suburbs of a large metropolitan area. She arrived in June and started kindergarten in September. She went to an ethnically diverse public school, which offered instruction in English as a second language (ESL) to about 20 percent of the school population, including Maria. Her school reports about her adjustment to her new country were very positive. Maria's joy in physical activity made her a good playmate at school. Her parents delighted in having a daughter and wondered what challenges first grade would hold for Maria. As new parents, they were anxious to learn how they could best support Maria's social and academic progress.

First grade offered a few challenges. The new ESL teacher felt that Maria was struggling to learn English and that with her Portuguese quickly leaving her, she was showing frustration with expressing herself. Maria's first-grade teacher was a veteran. She was firm yet gentle. She had definite rules but offered flexible assignments to meet the diverse learning levels in her class. Maria's report card was a mixture of Ses (satisfactory) and Ns (needs improvement); she needed improvement mostly in work habits such as paying attention and completing assignments. By the end of first grade, although Maria had shown much growth, she was identified as below grade level in reading and mathematics.

Maria's parents were concerned. They were trying to understand what part of Maria's uneven development was due to her acclimation to a new life and what part might be due to learning problems.

Second grade proved to be a challenge for Maria. Her attention in class was irregular at best. Friendships were quickly made and lost. Maria's second-grade teacher was more than firm. She had strict rules and procedures, a need for a quiet room, and homework that was at times difficult for parents to comprehend. Maria, on the other hand, never complained about school. Her teacher and parents tried a number of communication systems, none of which seemed to work for very long. Her mother was worried and frustrated. What problems were caused by the teacher, and what problems were caused by Maria's still uneven development? Maria's parents felt they did not have a good reference point for her school experiences. How typical or atypical was she as a student? It seemed that these questions were haunting her parents and that the responses given to them by Maria's teachers were difficult to interpret.

Third grade brought a more flexible teacher but a more rigid and rigorous curriculum. Maria was making slow progress in her academics. Socially, she had made a friend with whom she spent most of her time on the playground. Maria's parents again scheduled meetings with Maria's ESL and third-grade teachers. They wanted to try to help Maria more at home. They wanted guidance and insights into Maria. They left conferences appreciating the teachers' warmth toward Maria but still wondering what Maria needed to make better academic progress. They worried that Maria's teachers were developing low expectations for her and that they were seen as parents who needed to be handled carefully, rather than parents who were looking for answers as to how best to help Maria become successful in school.

Maria's parents, after much deliberation, employed the services of a private diagnostician to determine if Maria had learning disabilities. At this point, her parents did not trust the school enough to go through the regular school channels of requesting consideration for special education services. The possibility that Maria had significant learning disabilities had never been introduced to them by school personnel.

Maria's test results revealed significant learning disabilities. Her parents, in conjunction with the diagnostician, requested a meeting at school to determine Maria's eligibility for special education services. After four years of Maria being a student in the same school, working with the same ESL teacher, and the parents being active communicators with the school, it took the parents' initiative, with the support of the diagnostician, to initiate Maria's referral for special education services. At the eligibility meeting, there were no disputes. Yes, Maria certainly had significant learning disabilities. Yes, she would benefit from special education services. Yes, test results did indicate that she had made minimal progress in reading and mathematics during the first three grades. Maria's parents were astonished and chagrined at the readiness of the school personnel to agree with the test results. Why had no one at the school recommended that Maria be tested for learning problems?

The next struggle came with Maria's special education placement. The resource program at the school was taught by a strict and controlling teacher. On observing the class, Maria's parents found the instruction dry and unmotivating, with learning by rote. They could not see how the resource instruction would accelerate Maria's academic progress. Thus, Maria's parents fought for a more intensive special education program, one that would more likely offer Maria the environment she needed in order to achieve success. This program, which was offered within the same school system, was in a school 10 miles from Maria's house. It took a summer of meetings to obtain the placement, but by September of fourth grade, Maria was in a special education program.

The fourth grade was a whole new school experience for Maria. She was given work that was within her reach. Evening homework battles ceased. Spelling and mathematics papers came home with marks of 90 and 100 percent. Maria and her parents could see that she was learning, and the structure, level, and pace of the intensive special education placement met Maria's needs.

Maria's parents know that they and Maria have won something and lost something with this placement. They are not part of a neighborhood school. School communication is much more difficult, and this program is only minimally part of the school. School newsletters and Parent-Teacher Association meetings are not relevant to Maria's program. Maria misses her good friend from her neighborhood school, and as a fourth-grader in a new school, she has found that new friends have been slow in coming. Maria will return to the same program for fifth grade, but then elementary school ends; it will be time to determine her middle-school program. Maria's parents wonder what decisions await them and how satisfactory communications with school personnel will be. They know that they are known as vocal parents. Is that an advantage? How do they continue to obtain guidance on the mix of services that will best meet Maria's needs? What type of placement should they want for Maria?

Discussion Questions

1. Why do you think that school personnel did not refer Maria for consideration for special education?
2. What should be the major considerations given to Maria's middle-school placement?
3. What assistance do the parents need to best fulfill their role in Maria's placement decisions?
4. What inclusion principles and issues directly relate to this case?

CHAPTER 16

How Are Student Needs for Instruction and Support Evaluated, and How Is Their Progress Assessed?

EVALUATION IS REQUIRED UNDER IDEA. Evaluation procedures to determine whether a student is eligible for special education services are specified in special education law (IDEA, P.L. 105-17, 1997). However, the *legislation does not define a specific continuum of placements.* Instead, it provides the guiding principle of "least restrictive environment," and conveys a clear preference that *all* students should be included in general education classes and activities to the *maximum extent possible* while still obtaining an educational benefit for the student. It also requires that students receive regular reviews and evaluations of their educational and support service needs as the basis for developing individualized education programs. For the purposes of this chapter, the term *evaluation* refers to procedures used to determine (a) whether a student has a disability and (b) whether, as a result of that disability, the student needs special education and related services. *Assessment* refers to procedures for measuring a student's progress in the classroom and for accommodating students in districtwide and statewide academic performance assessments.

Student Evaluations and Needs Assessments Are Central to Placement Decisions. The individual needs of each student should take center stage in the decisions that surround the development of the IEP. There is no single and uniform test or procedure which can determine for all students the proper placement or individual constellation of services. Evaluation and placement decisions are made by a multidisciplinary team who examine the strengths and individual needs of each student. Determining the needs of the student should lead a multidisciplinary team to a placement decision that is strictly *student-centered*. Student-centered decisions are based on

1. Informal and formal evaluations both initial and ongoing reevaluations every 3 years.
2. Understanding of the student's disability in the educational environment.
3. Impact of the disability upon learning.
4. Curriculum and instructional modifications which will permit the student to benefit from the placement.

The placement of a child must be reviewed at least annually to determine if the placement has been successful and is meeting the needs of the student.

DEFINITION OF EVALUATION. Evaluation of a student's educational needs is an essential part of the special education process for students with disabilities. Students are evaluated initially to see whether or not they have a disability and whether, because of that disability, they need special education and related services designed to address their individual needs.

Individual evaluation is defined as the process of gathering and interpreting information about the education, health, or human service needs of individuals in the school and using this information to

1. Help determine the educational needs of the student.
2. Establish priorities for support services.
3. Determine the appropriate placement option.
4. Define individual goals and objectives.
5. Determine extent of participation in elective and extracurricular activities with nondisabled peers. (Kupper, National Information Center for Children and Youth with Disabilities, 1997)

The student's needs are documented in the individualized education program (IEP).

The *diagnosis* is a more specific term that refers to the process of identifying the presence of a disability by

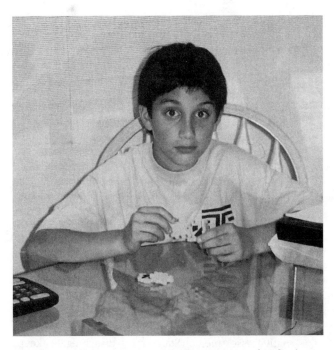

Diagnosis and assessment constitute a process of gathering and interpreting information about the student to help determine his or her educational needs.

using examinations, tests, and assessment instruments. One purpose of a diagnosis is to classify the condition, or place it into specific categories, such as learning disability, developmental disability, visual disability, cognitive disability, neurological disorder, hearing impairment, or traumatic brain injury. The diagnosis also serves the purpose of establishing eligibility for particular types of services, such as early intervention, speech and language services or mental health services.

Evaluation Requirements in IDEA. The Individuals with Disabilities Education Act is very specific about what is required in the process of conducting evaluations. The following points, summarized from IDEA, require that evaluations

1. Be conducted by a team of people which must include at least one teacher or specialist knowledgeable about the area of the child's disabilities.
2. Be individualized or centered on the single student, rather than on part of a group.
3. Be given in all areas of suspected disability to gather relevant functional, developmental, and instructional information.
4. Be conducted every three years to see if the student continues to have a disability and remains eligible for special education.
5. Be provided and administered in the student's native language or mode of communication, unless it is not feasible to do so.
6. Be conducted in a nondiscriminatory way, free of racial or cultural bias against the student.

7. Utilize only instruments and materials that are validated for the specific purpose for which they are being used.
8. Be selected and administered to ensure that if the child has impaired sensory, manual, or speaking skills, the test results accurately reflect his or her aptitude or achievement level being measured by the test.
9. Ensure that the tests, instruments, or materials used are administered by trained personnel and in conformance with instructions provided by producers of such tests. (IDEA, 1997 Amendments)

Once the evaluation is complete, the information is used to determine if the student has a disability and if he or she is eligible for special education and related services. This decision is made by a team of qualified personnel. If a student is found to be eligible for special education, then the information gathered through the evaluation process is used by the IEP team to discuss and determine the kinds of special education and related services the student needs. These decisions are then specified in writing by the IEP team leader.

If a student has a complete evaluation that was conducted 3 years ago, then the IEP team meets to review that data and determine if additional information is needed. Such information is needed to

1. Determine whether the student continues to be a child with a disability.
2. Determine present levels of performance and educational needs.
3. Determine whether the student continues to need special education and related services.
4. Determine whether any additions or modifications to the special education and related services are needed to enable the student to meet the annual goals set out in the IEP and to participate, as appropriate, in the general curriculum. (U.S. Office of Special Education, 1997)

Categories of Disabilities. The IDEA established specific categories of disabilities for eligibility for special education, and over the past few years, new ones have been added. The current categories in the statute include mental retardation; hearing impairments, including deafness; speech or language impairment; visual impairments, including blindness; emotional disturbance; orthopedic impairments; traumatic brain injury; other health impairments; developmental delay, or specific learning disabilities. The term *developmental delay* has been revised to now include students from ages 3 to 9 (formerly 3 to 5). This change was made because of the difficulty in determining the precise nature of a child's disability in the early years. The change also provides some flexibility to school personnel by allowing children with developmental delays to be eligible for special education and related services without being labeled with a specific disability. These labels have in the past been used to drive the student's IEP rather than the individual needs. Additionally, attention deficit disorder-hyperactivity disorder (ADHD) is referred to as a potential indicator of the need for further evaluation for special education and related services, but a diagnosis of ADHD alone does not automatically mean the student is eligible under IDEA.

Parents Must Be Notified. It is important to note that before a student can be evaluated for the first time, the Local Educational Agency must notify parents in writing. Parents must give their informed consent before their child may be evaluated. If the evaluation is not the first one, then the LEA must also notify parents if no further information is needed and the reasons for it. Furthermore, the LEA must also notify parents of their right to request additional assessment to determine whether a child continues to be a "child with a disability" as defined by IDEA, and the school must provide such assessments.

Inclusion of Students in State and Districtwide Assessments. Before the IDEA Amendments of 1997, the statute did not require that school districts and states include students with disabilities in their standardized achievement tests, no guidance was provided. According to the National Center on Educational Outcomes (NCEO, 1997), students with disabilities have been generally excluded from both state and national data-collection programs that measure academic achievement (Ysseldyke & Erickson, 1997). There are several reasons for this.

1. Concerns of teachers and administrators that these students' scores will depress the overall performance scores of the school or district.
2. Resistance of testing officials to adapt the test instruments or testing conditions because they are afraid that such changes may affect the validity of the results.
3. Lack of knowledge by testing officials about how to adapt test instruments and conditions without affecting the overall validity.

Under the 1997 Amendments to IDEA (effective June 4, 1997), students with disabilities are required to be included in and are encouraged to participate in statewide and districtwide academic performance assessments. Specifically, in regard to inclusion in such assessments, IDEA requires that

1. Individual modifications or adaptations must be made, as needed, in the manner in which the tests are administered. These adaptations may include modification in *timing* (e.g., extending time allotted for the test, altering time of day, using several sessions over the day or several days to complete the test); modifications in *setting* (e.g., small group administration, use of a study carrel, separate room administration, or homebound administration); modifications in *presentation* (e.g., use of audio cassette, reading aloud, large print, repeating directions, Braille versions, magnification devices); and

response (e.g., dictating the responses, sign language assistance, word processor, transfering answers from the booklet) (Erickson, 1997).
2. States must develop alternative assessments and, beginning no later than July 1, 2000, conduct these alternative assessments.
3. States must develop guidelines for the participation of students with disabilities in alternative assessments.
4. If an IEP team determines that the student cannot participate in a particular statewide or districtwide assessment of student achievement, even with modifications, then the team must include a statement in the IEP explaining why. They must also describe how the student will be assessed.
5. The states must make assessment information public in a similar manner for students both with and without disabilities (e.g., reporting as often and with the same amount of detail).
6. State assessment reports must include the number of children with disabilities participating in regular assessments, the number participating in alternative assessments, and their performance on regular and alternative assessments. States must disaggregate (keep separate) data on the performance of students with disabilities.
7. States must establish performance goals and indicators to judge students' progress toward these goals (U.S. Office of Special Education, 1997).

ADDITIONAL LAWS SUPPORTING EVALUATION AND ASSESSMENT OF STUDENTS WITH DISABILITIES. During 1993 and 1994 Congress enacted several additional laws that promoted educational restructuring and reform, encouraging states to establish world class standards that all the nation's students could meet, including those with disabilities. These laws include the Goals 2000: Educate America Act, Improving America's Schools Act, and School-to-Work Opportunities Act. If students with disabilities continue to be excluded from standardized academic performance assessments, then the states and the nation will never really know how we are doing in implementing IDEA or improving educational standards for all students. Furthermore, such exclusion prevents students from continuing on to postsecondary education (Senate Report on S.717).

School-to-Work Laws Require Student Assessments. The School-To-Work Opportunities Act (STWOA) defines student assessment for educational purposes. The STWOA defines assessment as ongoing consultation, interpretation, and problem-solving with students to identify academic strengths, weaknesses, and progress. It also requires assessment of work-place knowledge, as well as establishment of goals and needs for additional learning opportunities to master core academic and vocational skills. The Act requires each state and local school district to

1. Describe the performance standards that it intends to meet.

2. Describe how the state or local educational agency will include, in both academic achievement and vocational skills competencies, measures of learning and competency gains that are unbiased to special populations.
3. Describe how the state or local educational agency will assess the needs of students.
4. Develop an adequate plan to provide supplementary or support services to enable all students to participate in school-to-work transition programs.

Related Services That Support Evaluation and Performance Assessment. The IDEA defines related services that can be used to assist students with disabilities in benefiting from special education. These related services may also be used in the evaluation of a disability and may include medical and psychological services for diagnostic or evaluation purposes, including

- Medical services provided by a licensed physician to determine if a child's medical disability results in the need for special education and related services;
- Psychological services including psychological and educational testing;
- Other assessment procedures, including interpreting information about child behavior and conditions related to learning and classroom participation;
- Consultation with other staff members in planning school programs to meet the special needs of children as indicated by psychological tests, interviews and behavior evaluations;
- Planning and managing a program of psychological services including psychological counseling for children and parents;
- Diagnosing and appraising hearing loss and implications for learning;
- Diagnosing and appraising specific speech and language impairments and implications for learning;
- Evaluating vocational educational needs, employment preparation needs, and school-to-work transition needs;
- Evaluating the child's need for counseling, social work services, and school and community resources to enable the child to learn as effectively as possible in his or her educational program (Data Research Inc., 1997).

The IDEA regulations clearly state that the LEA may not use a *single procedure or test* as the sole criterion for determining an appropriate educational program for a student. Multiple measures must be used to determine the presence of a disability and the extent of its impact on learning. Furthermore, an important concern of the Congressional Committee on Labor and Human Resources (1997) during the reauthorization of IDEA was that determination of disability and eligibility for special education should not occur if the student has lacked instruction in reading or math or has limited English proficiency. The Committee stated that it "intends that professionals, who are involved in the evaluation of a child, give serious consideration at the conclusion of the eval-

uation process to *other factors that might be affecting a child's performance* (p. 19)."

Increasing the Inclusion of Students with Disabilities and Limited English Proficiency in the National Assessment of Educational Progress (NAEP). The U.S. Department of Education is developing strategies to increase the numbers of students with disabilities (SD) or limited-English-proficient (LEP) students who are included in the national assessment of educational progress. These strategies include changes to the inclusion criteria and the types of accommodations now being offered, development of new procedures for implementing national assessments, and ongoing research studies on inclusion issues. NAEP is in the process of examining and implementing new procedures to maximize the representativeness of students included in the assessment. The focus is on efforts to enhance overall participation by including more students with disabilities and LEP students.

NAEP's main purpose is to assess what the nation's students know and can do. This concept means that the NAEP results should represent *all students in the nation*. This is especially important because NAEP uses a sampling approach in which all students may be included, although, in actuality, some students with disabilities and limited English proficiency students do not participate in the assessment. Recent educational trends, reflected in the authorizations of Goals 2000: Educate America Act and Improving America's Schools Act (IASA), and the 1997 Amendments to the Individuals with Disabilities Education Act (IDEA), have called for assessments that are meaningful, challenging, and appropriate for *all* students.

NAEP's Approach Before 1995. In the past, students with disabilities and limited English proficiency were often excluded from NAEP for several reasons:

1. State and local policies had been designed to identify students with disabilities and LEP students and exclude them from testing based on certain criteria.
2. School staff may have believed these students were unable to participate meaningfully, or no test accommodations or adaptations were available that met the specific needs or requirements of the individualized education programs (IEPs) required by law for students with certain disabilities.
3. There has been a lack of available accommodations and adaptations (such as extended testing time or assessment instruments in other languages).

In order to standardize NAEP procedures, NAEP had previously developed policy guidelines for including students with disabilities or limited English proficiency, but some were excluded, particularly those with severe disabilities or students who would have required accommodations to the testing procedures. In previous years, about half or more of the students identified as having disabilities or LEP were excluded from the NAEP assessments. While the percentage of students excluded has remained relatively small in relation to the total population, these students make up a relatively large portion of the special education and LEP populations.

An evaluation of NAEP conducted by the National Academy of Education found that many of the students with disabilities and LEP students who had been excluded from the national assessment were, in fact, capable of participating (National Academy of Education, 1993). This was particularly true if certain types of adaptations and accommodations could be offered for the assessment. It also recommended that NAEP develop better criteria to promote inclusion, rather than exclusion, of students. During this same time period, various offices in the Education Department as well as other groups also were involved in examining the issues related to including more students in assessments. These groups provided additional valuable input to NAEP on ways to improve the inclusion and accommodations process (National Center on Educational Outcomes, 1994a; 1994b; 1996). In response to these concerns, NAEP explored ways to increase the inclusion rates even further. To meet these objectives, plans were made to try out new approaches toward inclusiveness in preparation for the 1996 assessment. Beginning with the 1995 NAEP field test, the criteria were revised to be more inclusionary. Other changes were made to make a better link between subject areas of instruction and the assessment and in response to concerns about the language used in the old criteria. The old and new criteria are presented in Table 16-1.

In all years, schools were instructed that students with disabilities and LEP students should be assessed if, in the judgment of school staff, they were capable of taking the assessment and that, in cases of doubt, the school should err on the side of inclusion.

In preparation for the 1996 assessment, NAEP field tested in 1995 the new inclusionary criteria for participation and the use of various accommodations and adaptations for the mathematics assessment. The field test also included science, but no accommodations or adaptations were tested for this subject. For mathematics, accommodations were made available for students with disabilities if they were part of the student's normal testing procedure, as specified in the student's IEP.

The accommodations for students with disabilities included

- Provision of large-print booklets and large-face calculators.
- Provision of Braille booklets and talking calculators.
- Accommodations in administration procedures, (e.g., unlimited testing time, individual or small-group administrations, allowing a facilitator to read directions, allowing students to give answers orally, allowing students to give answers using a special mechanical apparatus).

Accommodation and adaptation strategies for limited-English-proficient students (provided for mathematics only) included the availability of

- Spanish-English bilingual assessment booklets, with items in different languages presented on facing pages.
- Spanish-only assessment booklets.

In general, the 1995 field test results appear to be encouraging. Some students with disabilities and LEP students who would not have participated under previous assessment conditions were able to participate in the field test. The results of the field test showed that the new procedures could be implemented successfully in the 1996 national assessment.

Ongoing Research Studies on Inclusion Issues. Because this is a pioneering effort by NAEP, and the issue has many complexities, additional research is required. A

TABLE 16-1. Old and New Exclusion or Inclusion Rules for NAEP

	Old (1990–1994)	New (1995–1996)
Students with disabilities	*Exclude if:* Student is mainstreamed less than 50 percent of the time in academic subjects and is judged incapable of participating meaningfully in the assessment, *or* if the IEP team or equivalent group determine that the student is incapable of participating meaningfully in the assessment.	*Include if:* Student has an IEP, unless the IEP team or equivalent group determine that the student cannot participate, or if the student's cognitive functioning is so severely impaired that he or she cannot participate, even with accommodations.
Students with limited English proficiency	Student has a native language other than English *and* has been enrolled in an English-speaking school (not including bilingual education program) for less than two years, *and* has been judged to be incapable of taking part in the assessment.	Student has received academic instruction primarily in English for at least three years, *or* the student has received academic instruction in English for less than 3 years, if school staff determine that the student is capable of participating in the assessment in English, *or* the student, whose native language is Spanish, has received academic instruction in English for less than three years, if school staff determine that the student is capable of participating in the assessment in Spanish (if available).

number of studies are currently under way in NAEP to investigate further issues related to inclusion of students with disabilities or LEP in national assessments. This research includes studies of

- *Scaling issues*—an investigation to determine if there is a lack of fit between responses of students given under nonstandard assessment conditions with those given under standard conditions, and if so, what may account for it.
- *Reporting issues*—an examination of the implications of reporting NAEP results in alternate ways for students with disabilities and LEP students, when there is a lack of fit on the NAEP scale.
- *Appropriateness of the inclusion criteria for students with disabilities and LEP students*—for students with disabilities, a determination of the proper role of the IEP team; for LEP students, a closer look at whether the threshold for English-language study should be 2 or 3 years.
- *Construct validity of the assessment for students with disabilities and LEP students*—comparisons of the response patterns of students assessed under nonstandard conditions (e.g., with accommodations) with those of students assessed under standard conditions, and how they may differ; determination of whether NAEP is accurately measuring what accommodated students know and can do.
- *Language complexity issues*—an examination of whether native language proficiency of LEP students affects performance on NAEP and what language adaptations could be implemented into the assessment for these students; another study will examine whether training scorers to recognize typical syntax, spelling, and other errors made by LEP students can improve the scoring of their responses to extended constructed-response items.
- *Inclusion procedures*—an investigation and determination of whether there still are students being excluded who could be included in the assessment.

It is hoped that these studies will help NAEP make further progress toward the goal of full inclusion, while preserving the overall validity of the assessment. Research studies like these are essential in order to ensure that the reporting of what students know and can do, as well as gauging their academic progress over the years, is done in a reliable, valid, and meaningful way.

The maximum inclusion of students with disabilities or limited English proficiency is expected to result not only in an improved national assessment program but also in benefits to states, school districts, and other entities that conduct large-scale assessments. Many educators at these levels look to NAEP as a model for the best practice in assessment as NAEP proceeds in a thoughtful and thorough manner in its implementation of a more inclusive assessment.

EFFECTS OF THE STUDENT'S ENVIRONMENT ON INDIVIDUAL PERFORMANCE. It is important that teachers are aware of the range of factors in the student's environment, other than the disability, that can affect general performance or level of functioning. It is also important to understand how these factors interact in the student's environment and affect developmental or educational progress. For example, a student who needs academic tutoring but who is also troubled by a family divorce may not necessarily improve when given academic help. He or she may also need other support services such as counseling. Many other social, environmental, and developmental factors may impact academic needs and produce a child who is at risk for failing in the general educational environment.

The placement decision of the student is not simply a question of whether the student can keep up with a general academic program. Placement decisions should take into consideration the full range of functional areas in which the individual student may need help. These areas include all of the skill areas that students are expected to develop as they mature and move into adult roles:

- Physical development and health needs
- Independent functioning
- Social functioning
- Behavioral functioning
- Academic functioning
- Vocational development
- Employment skills
- Recreational and leisure needs
- Psychological functioning
- Family relationships

Inclusive placement may refer to integration with nondisabled peers in all activities except academic instruction, for academic and nonacademic activities, or, for recreational and leisure activities only. For example, the student with mild to moderate mental retardation may need an adapted curriculum in order to gain academic skills, but could benefit from inclusion into nonacademic activities for recreation and leisure- and social-skills development. Such a student could also benefit from additional functional skills training, as well as inclusion into general vocational classes and community-based work experiences that are available to all students. The student may also need additional assistance to help the family understand and reinforce learning in the home. Table 16-2 provides some examples of these needs of students that can impact learning and growth, together with examples of supports.

CHANGING NEEDS OF STUDENTS. Evaluations and assessments at any level should not be one-time events for students, but should be an ongoing process that extends throughout the students' tenure in school. Because the educational and support needs of students may change over time, IDEA requires reevaluation of the disability and eligibility for special education every 3 years. As

TABLE 16-2. Needs, Education, and Support in Inclusive Classrooms

Needs	Education and Support
Developmental and functional needs	Functional and independent living skills training, travel training, leisure education, sexuality and family life skills, survival skills, money management skills training, family relationships.
Physical, health, and nutritional needs	Medical services; drug treatments; physician's care; surgical procedures; hygiene training; nutrition; personal attendant services; assistive technology, medical devices and prosthetics; special diets; family nutritional education; neurological, medical, and health assessments.
Cognitive and wider educational needs	Special education; remedial education; assistive technology, speech and hearing; second language training; enrichment services; in-home teaching; educational consultation; guidance services; school-to-work transition support services; academic and vocational assessments.
Social, behaviorial psychological, and mental health needs	Mental health, psychological, and behavior management services; crisis management and support; psychological assessments; individual and family counseling.
Social service needs	Social services; juvenile and parole services; legal services; advocacy services; residential planning services, guardianship assistance, heath insurance assistance.

students' needs change so must the goals and priorities of the classroom support services and the goals in the IEP. Ongoing evaluations and in-class needs assessments can help teachers remain alert to the adjustments they need to make for the student.

TEAM ASSESSMENT OF INDIVIDUAL STUDENT PROGRESS. Each teacher who enters a collaborative relationship to educate students with disabilities in the general education classroom might define student educational priorities differently. So how do members of an interdisciplinary team of professionals reconcile their different viewpoints about goals for performance and achievement for the student and for the classroom environment into which that student is placed? What strategies are needed to form an effective working relationship that can assist the student in making genuine progress?

An interdisciplinary team is defined as a group of professionals, including a special education teacher, working in collaboration with general education teachers, counselors, and support services personnel, to design an IEP for a student with special needs. The interdisciplinary team would perform the following evaluation functions:

- Review school and medical records, vocational evaluation information, as well as social, behavioral, other information that would be pertinent to placement decisions.
- Make referrals for additional evaluations if needed.
- Consider the placement options within the schools and make appropriate recommendations for placement.

Negotiation is sometimes required between the professionals and parents in discussing the appropriate placement. In some instances a trial period in the classroom is needed to allow the interdisciplinary team to observe the student in the less restrictive setting. The duration of this trial period must be adequate (at least 1 month or more), to permit a full range of observations. During this critical period, the interdisciplinary team must be as supportive as possible to the student and the teacher or teacher team, in order to provide the student every opportunity to benefit from the inclusive classroom environment.

Technical assistance to the general education teacher or team may be required during this period. The interdisciplinary team should also focus on how it can better coordinate and link supportive services to the student in the classroom, for achievement of general education goals.

TRANSLATING STUDENT EVALUATION INFORMATION INTO INDIVIDUAL PERFORMANCE GOALS IN THE GENERAL EDUCATION CLASSROOM. One of the most significant changes in IDEA (1997) is that there is a new emphasis on including students with disabilities in the general education classroom and curriculum. The term *appropriate education* in the general education class means identifying appropriate goals and objectives for the student throughout the year, identifying what types of special education and related services are needed, and identifying the supplementary aids and services the student needs. This means that teachers must be able to translate student evaluation information into performance goals for students with disabilities that are consistent with the standards developed for other children in the school district and state.

A student evaluation should focus on *both the current level of skills or functioning and on the highest level of functioning before a more inclusive placement was sought*. Then, based on that evaluation appropriate placement, classroom accommodations, performance assessments, and support services can be established for the student. Evaluation activities for purposes of such placement and support decisions include the following:

- Conducting comprehensive evaluations of strengths and developmental needs of the student in a variety of functional domains (physical development and health status, independent functioning, social functioning, family relationships, behavioral functioning, emotional and psychological functioning, academic and vocational functioning, employment skills, and recreation-leisure functioning).
- Reviewing and renewing evaluations on a periodic basis.
- Communicating and interpreting evaluation information in terms of what the diagnostic information means to the teacher who will teach the student.
- Adapting evaluation and assessment tools for individuals with disabilities and eliminating cultural bias (IDEA, 1997).
- Documenting evaluation and diagnostic information in the individualized education program.
- Making specific recommendations for educational placement, additional evaluation and diagnostic needs, curriculum modifications, accommodations in performance assessments, classroom adaptations, social skills training, supportive services, or vocational-technical skills training, based on evaluation information in the relevant functional domains.

An important step for the interdisciplinary team is to utilize evaluation information to determine *the appropriate goals and expected levels of achievement (social and academic performance) for students placed into general education classrooms.* The present level of social, academic, and physical functioning provides the basis on which new target goals can be established. For example, Jeffry is a sixth grader with a learning disability who reads at a fifth-grade level but needs to achieve a seventh-grade reading level to enter the math-science program at the middle school. Once such a performance gap is determined, the interdisciplinary team can then decide what classroom accommodations and support services will be required to remedy it. As the IEP team translates evaluation information into IEP goals, the following questions are helpful:

1. What does the student evaluation tell the team about present levels of performance in the functional domains, such as academic, vocational, social, and physical?
2. What new goals will be set for students in relation to the functional domains?
3. What is the current level of performance for the student? What are the gaps between present functioning and targets goals for the year?
4. What does the student need to close the performance gap?
5. What are attitudes of the parents toward closing that performance gap?

6. How can the interdisciplinary team be supportive of the student and family and help to close these performance gaps?
7. How can the team explain to the student and parents what the assessment information means in terms of the student's learning needs?

The next step for teachers in inclusive classrooms is to determine *what the new goals or expectations will be for the student being transferred into the inclusive setting. What changes or outcomes can reasonably be expected within a year (or less) if the support services, curriculum adaptations, and physical accommodations are provided?*

Educational or social goals for students must be expressed in terms of specific outcomes for performance. Determining appropriate goals requires two additional pieces of information:

1. Reliable baseline information on students (status at the time of placement into the new classroom or school) against which to compare the current status.
2. Clearly defined goalposts for a future level of progress or achievement.

Goalposts mean the performance standards or target goals that are established by the IEP team for student progress or achievement within the quarter, or grading period, or year (Kochhar & Erickson, 1993). The elements of a comprehensive student assessment are described in Table 16-3.

EVALUATION AND ASSESSMENT TO PROMOTE SELF-DETERMINATION. In the responsive classroom and school, educators hold as a highest principle the belief in student options for the freedom to consider the life paths they will take. Students are encouraged to participate in the process of *self-determination,* a personal decision-making process that helps the student connect present educational experiences with future visions and goals. As part of the developmental process, these decisions must be *guided by accurate and comprehensive evaluation information upon which shared planning and decision making are based.* Such evaluation should encompass three domains: individual attributes, current and potential environments, and the comparability or interaction between the two (Leconte, 1994). Therefore, comprehensive evaluations of the educational needs of students being placed into general education classrooms must address the strengths and needs of the student, as well as the needs of the teacher and classroom environment, to provide appropriate education.

PRIORITIZING STUDENT NEEDS AT THE WHOLE-SCHOOL LEVEL. Schoolwide needs assessments can help identify many other environmental factors that place students at risk of failing in the regular educational environment. For example, competition for educational resources among several

TABLE 16-3. Elements of a Comprehensive Student Evaluation

Evaluation Component	Sources of Information for the Evaluation
Type of disability	• Evaluation and diagnosis of a specific disability for the purposes of (1) determining the student's needs for specialized educational and related services and (2) the student's ability to benefit from general educational programming, adapted educational programming, and supportive services.
Educational placement and academic skills	• Current school placement and grade level • Academic level and deficits • School attendance patterns and record • Extracurricular history, interests, and talents • School performance and grades • Certificates and awards received in the past
Ability to perform independent living activities	• Meal preparation • Self-help skills (dressing, bathing, cleaning, etc.) • Maintenance of home or personal space • Basic safety and self-protective skills (locking doors, turning off stove, knowledge of emergency numbers, etc.)
Management of personal health	• Personal hygiene, nutrition, and eating habits • Using medications appropriately • Routine health visits, vision, and dental care • Cooperation with ongoing medical treatment • Contacting physician in emergency
Social supports and social functioning	• Relationships with family, including siblings, and others • Parents or siblings with difficulties who are in need of services • Social skills and peer relationships • Sexual behavior and functioning • Record of antisocial activities or problems, criminal record • Leisure and recreational activities
Vocational and technical skills	• Employment history and patterns of performance • Formal vocational evaluation • Vocational education or job training program participation • Vocational and technical skills gained • Job skill certificates earned • Work behaviors and readiness
Previous services	• History of previous special education and related services • Experiences with previous services • Current services in use
Technology and adaptive equipment	• History of experience with classroom technology • History of technology accommodations provided • History of adaptive equipment used or requested • Current use of adaptive equipment or needs

groups of students with special needs requires school personnel to establish priorities for addressing these needs. Of course, the inclusion planning team must first consider the assessment and diagnostic information on each student to determine what specific educational strategies are needed in the general education classroom. The inclusion team can identify the largest at-risk group or groups in the school (e.g., students with limited English proficiency, emotional disorders, or learning disabilities), examine the educational and postschool outcomes for these groups, and then decide on and focus additional resources to improve these outcomes.

The Inclusion team can also consider the relative seriousness of the problems of different student groups or their impact on the total school environment. Some problems may be more serious than others or may represent threats to other children (violent behavior, substance abuse, conduct disorders). Finally, the inclusion team can focus special efforts on the special needs of students who have been excluded in the past from school classrooms and activities. For example, until recently students with disabilities were excluded from regular vocational and technical education classes and many sports because they were considered at risk of being hurt.

CASE EXAMPLE 16-1. A High School Tackles a Dropout Problem

Issue. The Meadowlark High School, in partnership with the High-Steaks Restaurant chain, wanted to design a program to address the problem of youth dropouts, particularly youth with special learning needs. The principal, teachers, and the owner of High-Steaks formed a team to discuss the problem and agreed that Meadowlark's top priority was to reduce the dropout problem among students with disabilities. The team had conducted a schoolwide needs assessment the year before, in which they polled only teachers about their impressions of the chief student problems in the school. Since students and parents were excluded from the survey, the root causes of dropout were still unclear and solutions to the problems remained a mystery.

This year, the partners decided they would set a goal to reduce to 15 percent the current dropout rate of 35 percent among high school students. They began by gathering information about how many students with disabilities actually drop out each year. Also, they asked questions not only of teachers, but of students who had dropped out, students identified as at risk of dropping out, and parents: What were the causes of the dropout problem, and what was needed? They also reviewed the assessment records of each student considered to have special learning needs and conducted additional assessments for students suspected of having learning disabilities.

After the second needs assessment, Meadowlark High School and High-Steaks realized that they had been working backwards. Students and dropouts said that what they needed was help in understanding their learning difficulties, setting short- and long-term goals for their own futures, and deciding where they were headed. The team learned that academic and vocational achievement goals could be defined only after this goal had been addressed. This revelation and understanding changed the focus of the services. The goal of the team was not to simply identify students at risk of dropping out, but rather to provide counseling and a combined academic and career development program to help students assess their career interests, make career decisions, and connect high school graduation with clear postsecondary goals. An additional goal of the team was to coordinate school and business resources to develop an inclusion coordination agreement and an annual action to help all students benefit from career opportunities.

The first assessment of needs conducted by Meadowlark and High-Steaks had been incomplete and one-dimensional (only teachers were surveyed). They realized that one of the primary problems of at-risk students was their inability to set goals for themselves and imagine a future (self-determination). The team had to first determine accurately the priority needs of the students before they could establish specific goals for the students.

Discussion Questions

1. What do you think the dropout problem has to do with inclusion?
2. What useful insight into the dropout problem did students and parents provide?
3. What does this example suggest about the relationship between present student academic achievement and future career planning?

Schoolwide needs assessments should be adapted to reflect variations and changing conditions among schools and communities. Case Example 16-1 is actually a composite of many examples of schoolwide needs assessments.

UNFORTUNATE REALITIES OF INCLUSION INITIATIVES. In reality, student placement decisions are often determined by many other factors, such as administrative convenience, availability of classroom space, teacher willingness and effort, fear of external legal pressures, and parent or political pressure. The failures of inclusion policies in many schools can often be attributed to pre- cipitous transitions to inclusive classrooms, failure to prepare administrators and teachers for the change, and lack of knowledge about effective inclusion strategies. When decisions *are not student-centered,* serious consequences often result for the student, teacher, peers, and for the classroom as a whole. While these decision factors can lead to unsuccessful inclusion practices, there are many instances in which students benefit from placement in the general education classroom, despite a poorly designed initiative. These successes in the context of poor inclusion policies are usually attributed to the commitment and creativity of individual classroom teachers.

CHAPTER 17

What Does Inclusion Mean for Teaching and Learning?

After a student is placed into the general education classroom, the teacher must make many decisions in preparation for accommodating the student.

ESTABLISHING CLEAR EXPECTATIONS. Clear expectations for the student's behavior, attendance, and achievement are essential to successful inclusion, so that

- The teachers involved understand their roles and responsibilities.
- The student understands what is expected and that a change is taking place in the classroom for his or her benefit.
- The student's peers understand the purposes of the changes in the classroom.
- The parents understand the modifications in the physical classroom, curriculum, or instruction for their child's learning.

RELATING CLASSROOM ACCOMMODATIONS TO FUNCTIONAL AREAS. The accommodations for the student must also take into account the many functional areas discussed in Chapter 16 (e.g., academic, social, behavioral, vocational, physical). The student, teacher, and parents must understand the functional areas in which the student is expected to be integrated with nondisabled peers. For example, it is important that the student and parents understand why an inclusion decision involves all school activities except academic activities—why the student will be receiving academic instruction in a resource classroom—or, in the case of a student with a physical disability, why he or she is being included with nondisabled peers in all school activities except for physical education.

TEACHER PLANNING TIME—AN ESSENTIAL ELEMENT. Teacher planning time is one of the most essential elements for implementing successful inclusion, especially when the student is new to the teacher and the classroom. Administrators must allow for such planning and facilitate the planning process. Teachers can also use a variety of supports for instructional planning, including enlisting parent volunteers, paraprofessionals or aides, or interns from local universities. Here are some examples of how planning time can be structured:

- Teachers hold a special meeting after the initial or annual IEP meeting to discuss new implications for curriculum or instruction in the general education classroom.
- Teachers have daily meeting times in the morning to plan instruction for the day.
- Teachers use part of their regular in-service days for semester planning or review of student progress.
- Teachers have an established afternoon or extended planning period to prepare for the following week; substitute teachers or parent volunteers are enlisted to cover for the period.
- Teachers use after-school time to prepare for the following day.

It is often a struggle to find adequate time for planning, but *regular meetings between general education, special education, and consulting teachers is an essential ingredient in the success of inclusion.* Many teachers cite the lack of planning time as the critical barrier to providing adequate supports to students with disabilities in the general education classroom.

SOCIAL RELATIONSHIPS AND INCLUSION: CREATING THE SENSE OF BELONGING. The success of inclusion is also determined by the degree to which the student with a disability feels a part of the general education classroom. The feeling of belonging positively affects the student's self-image and self-esteem, motivation to achieve, speed of adjustment to the larger classroom and new demands,

The feeling of belonging positively affects a student's self-image, self-esteem, motivation to achieve, and general adjustment to the general education classroom.

general behavior, and general level of achievement. The impact of the new student on the general classroom is a major consideration for inclusion planners. Fostering positive social relationships between students with disabilities and their peers requires the preparation of nondisabled peers in the classroom so that they understand the needs of their new classmates. A positive classroom environment can only enhance the mutual benefit an inclusive classroom can provide. Teachers use many strategies to help the student achieve a sense of belonging to the class and school. These strategies include the following:

- Discuss expectations with the student's peers and encourage interaction; the school counselor or psychologist can be helpful in preparing classes for a new student with a disability and in discussing the benefits of positive peer relationships.
- Use cooperative group learning, in which students are teamed for activities or projects and must cooperate, share ideas and materials, and share in the development of project products. Learning teams are also effective when students are required to prepare for classroom demonstrations and exhibitions.
- Assign peer advocates, a peer mentor, or a "buddy" who is responsible for interacting with and helping the student in classroom activities and social situations. The peer advocate provides support and encouragement and enables the student with a disability to solve problems with class activities and generally adjust to the new classroom environment.
- Assign a teacher advocate to the student, with whom the student can consult for guidance, general support, or crisis assistance.
- Include the new student in the daily roll call and in class pictures, and place the student's work on bulletin boards along with the work of his or her peers.

- Establish a lunch-buddy system (particularly helpful for younger students in the first weeks of class).

SOCIAL-COGNITIVE SKILL DEVELOPMENT. Social relationships are an important aspect of the learning process and the classroom environment. Research has demonstrated that a significant proportion of students who fail to adjust socially to the classroom environment lack effective social-problem-solving skills. Social problems include poor ability to be empathetic to others' perspectives, poor impulse control, and inability to generate multiple and effective solutions to problems faced in the classroom (McCoy, 1995; Parese, 1998). *Deficiencies in cognitive problem solving skills often lead to emotional and behavioral disorders requiring treatment.* The teacher in the inclusive classroom needs to address the social-behavioral domain as well as the academic domain. Research on teaching indicates giving training in social-cognitive skills to youth who are at risk of failure in general education classrooms can improve student's social effectiveness, achieving social goals, and reducing problem behaviors (Taymans, 1995, Schmidt & Harriman, 1998).

THE TEACHER'S POWER TO MODEL ACCEPTANCE. Research on inclusion has found that students who are appropriately placed into inclusive classrooms are more successful when their nondisabled peers are accepting and supportive. Many schools are establishing peer–mentor relationships to educate nondisabled peers and help build relationships for emotional and social support. However, probably the most important influence on positive classroom relationships and social attitudes is the attitude of the teacher and the degree to which the teacher models acceptance of students with special needs. Teachers must directly address the importance of mutual acceptance and support within the classroom, and they must reflect on their own attitudes and ability to demonstrate such acceptance.

Social relationships become an important aspect of the learning process and the classroom environment.

MODIFYING THE PHYSICAL CLASSROOM TO SUPPORT INCLUSION. The physical arrangement of the classroom is an important teacher consideration in preparing for a new student with a physical disability. For example, is there traditional individual seating, group table seating, or some other arrangement—and are changes desirable? Is the classroom crowded, or does it have adequate spacing for a wheelchair or a student with crutches? Can a student in a wheelchair maneuver adequately to get to the work stations or computer stations required by all students? Teachers use many strategies to make modifications in the physical environment, including the following:

- For students with cognitive or learning disabilities, assign buddies to assist students by reviewing assignments and organizing homework materials.
- For students with physical disabilities or limited muscular control in arms, secure papers to desk by using tape.
- For students with physical disabilities or who use a wheelchair, use nonskid devices, Velcro, and other common adaptations for carrying and securing materials.
- To expand learning environments, create opportunities outside the school for community-based instruction.
- Develop learning centers in the classroom for optimum use of classroom space; cluster tables and chairs into "centers" to open up spaces for movement.

ENRICHING CLASSROOM RESOURCES WITH COMMUNITY-BASED MATERIALS. Classroom resources may be required to assist the student who has a disability. Such resources include adaptations to computers and classrooms materials, and special instructional supplies. Businesses and other community organizations also offer a wide variety of useful instructional materials for the creative classroom teacher. These materials are excellent for promoting functional skill development and making curriculum more applicable to real life. For example, teachers have used actual banking materials to teach about personal finances and checking and savings accounts.

COOPERATIVE AND TEAM TEACHING FOR SUCCESSFUL INCLUSION

IDEA Requires That Teachers Be Prepared for Cooperative Teaching. As was mentioned previously, IDEA 1997 places a much greater emphasis on including students with disabilities in the general education classroom and curriculum. This means that as special and general education teachers and related services personnel consider the term *appropriate education* for students in general education, they must work closely together to (a) identify appropriate performance goals and objectives and (b) ensure that students receive the necessary special education, supplementary services, and related services. As schools focus on performance standards for students in the general education class, attention must necessarily turn to the qualifications and competence of teachers to provide services in the inclusive classroom. Currently most teachers agree they are "not prepared to deal with learners with disabilities and need a great deal of classroom support" (Waldron, 1996, p. 48). Those

who crafted the law realized that the effectiveness of inclusion depends upon the adequate preparation of those who will provide the services in the classroom. Toward this end, IDEA 1997 emphasizes the development of competent and well-trained professionals. Successful inclusion also depends upon the manner in which qualified special education and general education teachers and related services personnel can work together to support students in the general education classroom.

Cooperative and Team Teaching Arrangements. There are many teaching arrangements in which teachers share responsibility for assisting students to learn in the general education classroom. The broad term for such instructional shared responsibility in which teachers also share time and space is *cooperative teaching*. Under this broad practice, there are several types of shared arrangements:

1. *Collaborative consultation.* Collaborative consultation means joining general and special educators in inclusive classrooms to teach all students. This approach involves regular (daily, weekly, or biweekly) consultations in the general education classroom by a special education teacher or related services specialist. The consultant may help clarify student goals and objectives, help a teacher work on specific student problems or accommodations, or help evaluate a particular solution to a problem (Carkhuff, 1993; Friend & Cook, 1996; Smith, Polloway, Patton, & Dowdy, 1995; Walther-Thomas, Korinek, McLaughlin, & Williams, 2000).
2. *Team teaching.* Team teaching refers to the practice of "sharing the role of instructional leader through the stages of planning, delivering and evaluating instruction" (Friend & Bursuck, 1999; Schmidt & Harriman, 1998, p. 365). This means that teachers plan instruction together, evaluate student progress, communicate with parents, and generally work together with a group of students. When one general education and one special education teacher teach together in a single classroom, it is often referred to as coteaching. However when two or more teachers collaborate between classrooms and between subject areas, it is referred to as team teaching. Such teams can involve special education consulting teachers, coteachers, and general education teachers.

There are many kinds of teaching and consultation arrangements in which special and general education and related services professionals work together in teams to complement each other's expertise and support inclusion.

How Teachers Manage Their Time in the Teamed Classroom. Team teachers share their responsibilities in a variety of ways. They can divide subject matter instruction into content and process. For example, in the science class, one teacher delivers instruction on science content and the supporting teacher delivers instruction on the processes—such as assignments and activities—with special emphasis on ensuring that all students understand the instructions, and provides assistance to those who need extra help. Team teachers can divide students into teaching stations, or groups, that work on different goals and objectives, and the teachers divide their time among them. They can provide parallel teaching in which two teachers both teach the same content, but to two halves of the class. Or, one teacher can teach the class and the second teacher provide alternative teaching of the same content to a small group with adaptations to the instruction (Friend & Bursuck, 1999; McCoy, 1995). For example, a history teacher may provide instruction to the whole class on the Civil War, and then a small group of students grouped in one section of the class are given extra help to understand the historical sequence and interconnectedness of the events that were just taught. Another arrangement involves dividing students into collaborative learning teams in which students help each other on a study project. In some cases, three or four teachers may plan integrative instruction across four content areas, then rotate with their classes through the classrooms dedicated to instruction in each of those areas (Friend & Bursuck, 1999; Schmidt & Harriman, 1998).

Characteristics of an Effective Collaborative Team. According to special education experts, effective collaborative teams are characterized by members who have strong interpersonal skills and a positive attitude about the team concept, interest in gaining input from family members, ample classroom experience, knowledge of curriculum and materials, interest and ability in assessing learning and behavior problems and in individualizing instruction, interest in student goal setting and IEP implementation, and interest in gathering cultural information about students that may be useful in understanding the students' educational needs (Schmidt & Harriman, 1998; Waldron, 1996).

Case Example 17-1 illustrates the challenges and rewards of team teaching for an experienced special education teacher as her role changes in an inclusive school.

CASE EXAMPLE 17-1. Mattie Sullivan—An Experienced Teacher Finds the Secrets to Coteaching

I have been a special education teacher for 7 years in middle school. I began teaching in a seventh-grade self-contained program. I had 10 students with learning and emotional disabilities whom I taught all day. It was demanding and emotionally draining work, but I loved it. I enjoyed finding ways to motivate students to learn. I worked hard to forge relationships with their families, and at the end of each school year, I could see the progress the students had made in growing up. I was successful in integrating some of these students into general education classes, but for the most part, they worked with me for all their academic subjects. Most of these students were subsequently placed in the eighth-grade self-contained program. That program represented a step in maturity for them; rather than just having one teacher all day, they circulated among four special education teachers who were responsible for teaching different academic and functional curricula.

I am now a resource teacher; I coteach with four general education teachers and provide direct resource instruction to students for one or two periods a day. I am responsible for 20 students, 14 boys and 6 girls who range in academic achievement from second- to sixth-grade levels. I had a rough transition to coteaching, but I am now effective as a coteacher.

When the central school system administration decided that special education would take a more inclusionary approach, we were given little time to prepare for this new type of program. There was a 3-day summer workshop for all special education teachers who would be coteaching the next year. I left the workshop with good information and with the knowledge that the new school year would be dramatically different for me from previous years.

Three experienced teachers, none of whom I knew well, and one first-year teacher were to be my new partners. I tracked down these teachers and discussed the coteaching

with them. I made my first tactical error the first week of school. My coteachers and I decided that, during the first week, I would observe their teaching styles and classroom procedures. This approach would also allow me to observe the students with disabilities to determine their ability to handle basic classroom demands, such as listening, taking notes, getting along with classmates, and participating in discussions. I also devised some informal reading inventories that would help us to assess each student's ability to handle course reading demands.

I now realize my basic mistake: I never considered the coteachers' classrooms as also my own. Because I saw myself and my students as experimental visitors, I was not an equal instructor in the class. By starting out as an observer, I also confused the students. They didn't see me as a real teacher, but as an aide.

Another complication was that I never was able to establish a schedule of regular planning time with these coteachers. When we were able to plan, I was able to assume a viable teaching role in the classroom and to suggest useful modifications. When our planning meetings were disrupted, I was forced into the position of behavior management aide. Without advance planning I would enter the classroom with only a vague idea of the lesson content and no advance notice of the methods the teacher planned to use. On some days, class sessions did not go well because of student frustration, confusion, or lack of motivation. When students needed to be removed from class, I was always the person who left the class with the student. If student groups were off task in class, I took responsibility for getting them back on track. In the long run, this role did not help my relationship with the students, and it certainly threatened my sense of being a competent teacher.

I was successful in working with my coteachers in deter-

continues

CASE EXAMPLE 17-1. *(continued)*

mining grades and in structuring some assignments so that the students with disabilities had opportunities to express what they were learning in ways that would help them achieve passing grades. I also developed good communication with most of the families. As I ended the year and assessed the gains and losses in my new position, I felt that my sense of satisfaction and competence as a teacher had suffered most. Thus, with a year of experience under my belt, I made strategic changes in the way I began my second year of coteaching.

I met with the principal and the department chairperson to get approval and support for my plan for year two. Their understanding and support were crucial to the success of that year. With their help I made the following changes: I assisted in choosing a new group of coteachers so I could have a fresh start. The principal gave us planning time over the summer so that I could learn about their curricula and teaching methods prior to the opening of the school year. The summer work time also helped us do some long-term planning and to clearly identify an equal planning and teaching role for me. We also determined how we wanted to handle behavior management and again planned equal roles in how we would handle disruptive situations. By the beginning of the school year, I had developed a professional and cordial relationship with these teachers, and we all expected that I would function as a teaching professional in our team-taught classes. During the first week of school, I was an active presenter in all the classes, which made my role clear to all students. By the end of the first week, I was

learning directly about my coteachers' style, and they in turn were learning about mine. I also regularly informed the principal, my coteachers, department chairpersons, and my department chairperson of our scheduled planning times, with the expectation that these planning times would be honored and supported by the administration. My second year was a success.

Discussion Questions

1. Of the mistakes Mattie Sullivan made the first year, which ones do you think were the most costly to her effectiveness as a special education teacher?
2. What systemwide administration procedures would you recommend to make this inclusionary effort more effective for all teachers in Mattie Sullivan's position?
3. Mattie spends much more time describing her efforts at working with her coteachers than in describing efforts to meet her students' needs. Why? Does this concern you?
4. Develop a list of dos and don'ts based on this case. Who should take responsibility for each item (e.g., school principal, central administration, school staff, special education teacher, families, students, or those developing teacher education programs)?

Source: Adapted from Fried, M. (1995). A winding path to coteaching. In J. M. Taymans (Ed.). *Cases in urban teaching* Washington, DC: George-Washington University, Department of Teacher Preparation and Special Education.

Physical arrangement of the classroom is important when preparing for a new student with a physical disability. Is the classroom crowded, or is space available for optimum mobility?

CHAPTER 18

What Curriculum Modifications and Instructional Strategies Are Considered Best Practices for Inclusion Classrooms?

THE IMPACT OF NEW PERFORMANCE STANDARDS ON INCLUSION. The American educational system is undergoing reform in all aspects, especially in the area of curriculum standards aimed at helping all students achieve at higher levels. As states raise their expectations for students, they are selecting and mandating new methods of assessing student achievement. Standardized test scores represent society's demand for accountability, and school administrators and teachers are now being held accountable for students' learning. They are expected to show results. Consequently, teachers are struggling to decide how to implement curriculum to help them provide instruction to the standards selected by the state, to better prepare students to take the state assessments, and to prepare students for college and the workplace. To ensure that all students are learning, a variety of standards have been developed by various professional organizations, business and industry, and other educational associations. Standards-based curriculum is now a reality in schools and is drawing nationwide attention.

The trend toward standards-based curriculum presents a very real problem for special education teachers who must address individual needs of students; addressing the IEP goals and objectives are additional demands for them. Teachers are now also faced with the dilemma of what to teach to meet the IEP goals, as well as how to help all students prepare for state assessments. Students who do take the assessment specified by their state may require special accommodations in order to take the tests. Consequently, teachers are required to respond to all of these needs within the curriculum. This is a great challenge.

Curriculum modification is required by teachers to adjust the curriculum for the individual needs of students. Therefore, it is necessary that teachers have an in-depth understanding of the curriculum development process. Most teacher education programs at the undergraduate level do not adequately prepare teachers in the curriculum development process; rather, that is addressed in graduate programs. Professional development opportunities are essential to curriculum planning and development. However, it is difficult to integrate different components from various curricula without significant planning, development time, and opportunity for reflection.

There are three kinds of curriculum standards:

1. Content standards (a curriculum and instruction guide that determines what students are supposed to learn).
2. Performance standards (observable behaviors; what students need to be able to demonstrate proficiency).
3. Opportunity to learn standards (the guarantee that students have the opportunity to learn the standard before they are assessed on that standard).

State educational agencies have decided that in order to improve educational outcomes, more must be done to ensure that students are making progress through the curriculum. The choice of method for gathering this evidence is the standardized test. Students' scores on these tests determine their futures in school and beyond. Therefore, it is imperative that students with disabilities have the same opportunities other students have to learn the same content and to achieve the same standards, if they are to participate in standardized assessments. This requires a thorough understanding of the relationship between curriculum and outcomes and of ways to design and integrate curricula to meet the individual needs of all students.

Student Outcomes, Instruction, and Curriculum. Clearly defining outcomes for students with disabilities is a major element of the effective inclusive school. Since these student outcomes are the basis for providing educational and support services in the general education classroom, such outcomes must be clearly specified in terms of short- and long-term goals for each student. Without such clear specification, students cannot demonstrate that they have achieved a level of progress and achievement that qualifies them for graduation. Without that graduation record, students may be permanently locked out of postsecondary education, employment, or military service. According to the National Information Center for Children and Youth with Disabilities (1993), defining such specific outcomes for students with disabilities is a relatively new venture for special education (p. 3). New questions have emerged: What student performance outcomes should be defined? How should they be measured? How should they be used?

These questions and their answers have implications for the adaptation of curriculum and instruction, and for the degree to which students with disabilities will be included in standardized assessments in the general education class. For curriculum, teachers need to ask: In what way do I need to modify my curriculum sequence or pace of delivery to accommodate my students with disabilities, and how can I incorporate their IEP goals into the overall framework of my curriculum? For instruction, teachers need to ask: How can I modify the manner and the instructional setting in which I teach to help students learn and achieve their IEP goals? How can I accommodate their support service needs in the classroom? How can I enlist all the students in the classroom to help their peers with disabilities feel accepted and be successful? In terms of student assessment, teachers must ask: How can I develop alternatives to my standardized classroom assessments to measure the achievement and learning of my students with disabilities? Who is being successful in developing alternative approaches?

The general education teacher becomes central in the search for answers to these questions. The effectiveness of inclusion relies upon the manner in which the special education teachers, general education teachers, and support services personnel create clear connections between student IEPs, instruction, instructional settings, curriculum, student assessment, and student outcomes. All of these aspects of the teaching and learning process for students with disabilities must be connected in a coherent fashion and supported by all of the personnel involved.

Current technology must be integrated into the curriculum and all learners brought to proficiency in the use of computers for communication, computation, and research.

Inclusion and the Curriculum. Several curriculum modifications and instructional strategies are consistently found to be part of exemplary inclusion programs. Curriculum experts recommend that teachers consider the following 12 principles when they explore ways to modify curriculum to accommodate diverse learners (Hallahan & Kaufman, 1997; Marsh & Willis, 1999; Martin & Kohner, 1998; Schmidt & Harriman, 1998).

1. Expectations for schools must be raised by students, parents, teachers, educational administrators, and the community. Accomplishment and progress should be expected for all students—everybody counts.
2. Learners need a systematically integrated curriculum, not a fragmented one, with greater emphasis on coherence and more interrelationships and connections between subjects and disciplines.
3. Curriculum decisions should be focused not only on what to cover, but also on how the material fosters the ability of the learner to use and apply knowledge resourcefully.
4. Learning must be placed into real world contexts (contextualized) so the material makes sense in the world of the learner.
5. Though not all learners think alike, learn alike, or are alike all still need to be directed toward common general standards of achievement in using knowledge.
6. Evaluation of the learner should include nontraditional evaluations of performance, through strategies such as exhibitions, which call for the resourceful *application* of new knowledge more that just its display. The National Assessment of Educational Progress (U.S. Department of Education, Office of Educational Research and Improvement 1994) urges such engagement of the learner in concrete experiences.

7. Learners need the opportunity to be engaged in advanced academic work to prepare them for college placement.
8. Teachers need to become facilitators of learning, and learners need to become active doers and thinkers in the classroom, rather than passive recipients of information.
9. Each learner needs an advisor, advocate, or coordinator with whom the learner plans an academic program.
10. Current technology must be integrated into the curriculum and all learners brought to proficiency in the use of computers for communication, computation, and research.
11. Learners who elect to concentrate their studies in vocational education should have the opportunity to engage in advanced study through structured apprenticeships that are patterned after work-study arrangements in either traditional occupational fields or new ones. These advanced occupational opportunities serve as a bridge between secondary school and college or employment, and they provide for an organized transition into occupations.
12. The critical transition to college or work after graduation requires additional planning and supports for the learner.

Effecting these changes requires different responses on the part of the schools and community to support new initiatives. The existing familiar routines of schedules, courses, and teaching styles may not currently serve to reach these ends.

A NEW VIEW OF THE LEARNER. Inclusive models for educating all children require changes in the way learners are viewed and how the curriculum is structured. Inclusive education requires a reexamination and reformulation of (1) our view of who the learner is and (2) how curriculum, instruction, and learning environments must be restructured to accommodate this view. We are talking about preparing all members of the school system (e.g., teachers, students, parents, administrators, guidance counselors, and specialists) for a new kind of work that integrates our understanding about the learner and what we know about the promise of technology. As Jean Jacques Rousseau pointed out in 1911 (in *Emile*), education comes to us from many sources in nature, from each other, and from our experience and environment. Over the century, educational theorists have explored the concept of individual differences in the learner. Gardner (1983, 1992) and others have built upon the works of many theorists over the past century to develop new understanding about human intelligence and the various ways in which information is learned and understood.

NEW IDEAS ABOUT INTELLIGENCE ARE CENTRAL TO CURRICULUM MODIFICATION. Gardner (1983/1992) has questioned the assumption that intelligence is a single general capacity and that it can be measured by standardized verbal instruments commonly used today. He defines intelligence as the ability to solve problems or create products that are valued within one or more cultural settings. Human development is flexible and elastic. Intelligence involves a set of skills for problem solving and the potential for identifying new problems, thereby laying the groundwork for the acquisition of new knowledge. There is a broad range of human abilities which Gardner (1983/1992) has clustered into seven "intelligences," each of which is independent of the others and all of which are rooted in early sensory development.

1. Linguistic intelligence: rooted in the visual and auditory realms.
2. Musical intelligence: rooted in the auditory realm.
3. Logical-mathematic intelligence: rooted in the sensory-motor realm.
4. Spatial intelligence: not rooted in any particular modality.
5. Bodily-kinesthetic intelligence: rooted in the kinesthetic realm.
6. Intrapersonal intelligence: sense of self and access to one's own feelings, rooted in the combination of all senses.
7. Interpersonal intelligence or social intelligence: the ability to make distinctions among other individuals and personalities, rooted in the combination of all senses.

Inclusion efforts must be built upon understanding of different intellectual strengths and their variability within different environments.

RELATING NEW CONCEPTS OF INTELLIGENCE TO TEACHING AND CURRICULUM. Gardner's system for understanding the learner demands that we raise questions about different learning rates and styles and the interaction between the characteristics of the learner, the way we teach, and the characteristics of the learning environment. Examples of these areas of question include the following:

1. **Use of Symbols and Different Styles of Learning:** Since we rely on symbol systems to communicate meaning (e.g., number systems, musical notes, chords and symbols), a central question that arises from the recognition of multiple intelligences is whether information received in one medium is the "same" information as transmitted from another medium. We are challenged to explore different patterns and styles of learning and conveying information to different learners.
2. **The Cultural Context of Cognitive Accomplishments:** Cognitive accomplishments may occur in a range of domains. Some (logical-mathematical) are universal, and others are shaped and influenced by certain cultures. The question for teaching practice is this: To what extent should we consider the cultural context for learning in determining what should be learned and how it should be applied?
3. **The Context for Learning:** The understanding of the variety of cognitive abilities and patterns of learning re-

quires careful consideration of the classroom environments and methods that are most appropriate for delivering information to different learners. Teaching environments should combine concrete and abstract learning, using a variety of learning opportunities, such as the following:

- Direct, unmediated learning, or direct observation, in order to develop deeper knowledge through concrete experience.
- Active learning, including new technologies for learning.
- Imitation with observation—"know that" is joined with "know how."
- Real world settings.
- Novel or unique locations for learning.
- Transmittal of knowledge through the use of a variety of tools and techniques.

The assumptions we make about exceptional learners (and all learners) and the learning environment affect how we teach. Several assumptions that underlie the seven intelligences mentioned earlier are important for developing effective instruction for inclusive classrooms:

1. Within each domain of intelligence or capacity and the sphere of its application are a series of steps or stages ranging from the level of novice to expert or master.
2. Individuals differ in the speed with which they develop in these domains.
3. Success at negotiating one domain entails no necessary correlation with speed or success in others; they are independent.
4. Progress in one domain does not depend entirely on the solitary individual's actions within his world. But much of the information about the domain is better thought of as contained within the culture itself, because the culture defines the stages and fixes the limits of individual achievement.
5. The culture can mold or exploit capacities differently. The media through which the information in a domain is transmitted or communicated will affect the rate of progress, and this difference leads to different learning styles or responses to different media. (Gardner, 1983/1992)

MATH, SCIENCE, AND INCLUSION.   Greater emphasis is being placed on mathematics and science in general education today for all students. However, students with disabilities are often counseled out of math and science classes. This is unfortunate, since the instruction of abstract concepts in mathematics and science can easily be delivered using combined visual and concrete kinesthetic approaches in which students manipulate objects or data in real-world problem solving. Inclusion planning should emphasize the role of teachers and guidance counselors in explaining new approaches to teaching in the mathematics and science classes and in promoting access and participation. This should also include access to special enrichment opportunities offered by the schools such as "hands-on-science" and after-school classes. Teachers should also offer examples of mathematics and science

leaders who have disabilities; such role models can provide a sense of possibility for students with disabilities. Special resources are also needed to help teachers focus on curriculum modifications in mathematics and science to accommodate students with disabilities.

CURRICULUM DESIGN FOR INCLUSION.   The student with disabilities placed into the general education classroom should be expected to benefit and gain from the general education curriculum, with reasonable accommodations and adjustment in that curriculum. These reasonable adjustments are made to help a student with a disability catch up with peers or to modify the expectations for the student but permit the parallel work with peers. Such curriculum modifications can take many forms.

The Modular and Thematic Approaches to Instruction. The *modular* approach to instruction refers to small units of instruction that can be thematic, functional, or strictly academic. The *thematic* approach means use of integrated academic subjects. For example, three teachers may collaborate to combine lesson plans and develop common themes that connect math, social studies, and language arts, student activities and projects are then combined across the three subject areas so that they are linked. The project might involve "population" as the theme and students are assigned to write a paper on world population growth in the next decade, based on mathematical projections of population growth. The combined modular and thematic approach provides opportunities for success at many levels of academic or vocational skill training for every student, while allowing constant supervision and modification in the appropriate areas as needed. The advancement of integrated curriculum is also assisted by the very nature of the cross-curricular model. The thematic approach provides a means to constantly upgrade the curriculum, but it is the student who receives the greatest benefit. This approach gives each student a chance to achieve at an individual learning rate, providing immediate feedback on each activity. The thematic approach promotes a cooperative learning atmosphere, by teaming students and faculty members, giving the staff an opportunity to learn more about each student. It reflects a holistic view of the student as a learner, allowing more intensive individual or small-group learning lessons for remedial support.

The use of the modular approach to introduce information allows for a synthesis of the materials and methods that are most suitable for the instruction of students. Many students with special needs are hands-on learners who are trapped in a dominantly verbal environment. The incorporation of multimedia instruction using current technology provides students with a variety of methods with which to achieve success. Using interactive technology also gives students the hands-on experiences they need to be prepared for authentic work environments. The following are examples of curriculum modifications:

Multimedia instruction using current technology provides students with a variety of methods with which to achieve success.

- Including functional skills and applied academics in the curriculum.
- Building community service activities into the curriculum.
- Allowing flexible schedules for completion of assignments and for meeting annual curriculum objectives (include summer).
- Providing performance-based, authentic assessments for grading students.

- Allowing alternative certification of vocational skill proficiencies, including certification of levels of skill attainment.
- Integrating computer-based learning activities.
- Giving access to technology and technology labs for all students.
- Providing open enrollment for vocational programs and community-based programs.
- Using curriculum modules or units that permit flexible enrollment.
- Providing integrated academic and vocational instruction (academic instruction embedded within vocational-technical education and work-based programs).

Multilevel Instruction. In multilevel instruction, teachers use different instructional approaches within the same curriculum and adapt them to the individual needs and functional levels of the students. With this method the teacher must understand how the student's disability affects his or her ability to learn and cope socially in the classroom and must allow for a variety of student activities, assessment procedures, and student outcomes (Hardman, Drew, & Egan, 1999).

SOCIAL ASPECTS OF THE CURRICULUM. It is essential to provide the nondisabled students in the classroom with information and awareness about disabilities. Teachers can use numerous activities for explaining to nondisabled students the importance of integrating students with disabilities into the learning environment and why modifications in curriculum are needed. For example, teachers may show videos, have special education advocates or peer advocates talk with the class, discuss famous television and film personalities who have disabilities, assign readings about famous people with disabilities, or have students reflect on how their lives might change if they had a disability. Case Example 18-1 illustrates how students can become more sensitized to the needs and challenges that their peers with disabilities face each day.

CASE EXAMPLE 18-1. Sensitizing Students Toward Their Peers with Disabilities

Students at Jamestown Elementary School in Arlington, Virginia, were asked to do a few simple and familiar things, which they suddenly found hard to do—button a jacket, say their names, catch a ball. First the children had to wear socks on their hands, put marshmallows in their mouths, or not use any leg muscles. Now the tasks weren't so simple. The idea was to give students a better understanding of what their peers with disabilities may be challenged by throughout the day. Arlington and other school districts across the nation, challenged by IDEA, are moving steadily toward full integration of students with disabilities into regular classrooms. As they do, school and other professionals are working on ways to sensitize both students and teachers to the issues that arise when a child among them has trouble with hearing, or speaking, or general mobility.

"It makes me think they must have a hard time every day, waking up trying to put their clothes on," said one student, age 11, after struggling to button his jacket. Another kindergartner pulled herself across the floor on her stomach, using only her arms, and finally caught up with the beachball she was chasing. "It's really hard for people who can't use their leg muscles," she said thoughtfully, "and not fun."

All classes, from kindergarten through fifth grade took a half-hour turn in the gym, which was divided into four "sta-

continues

CASE EXAMPLE 18-1. *(continued)*

tions" designed to provide simulated experiences with four different types of disability:

1. *The fine motor station,* where students wore socks on their hands as they zippered coats and tried to piece together puzzles.
2. *The vision station,* where blindfolded students tried to catch a balloon with a bell inside.
3. *The language station,* where students tried to answer simple questions while their mouths were filled with marshmallows.
4. *The gross-motor station,* where students, without using their leg muscles, took turns on crutches and in wheelchairs and played volleyball sitting down.

Throughout the exercise, the teacher asked students how they felt when they could not complete a basic task and urged them to be patient with others in the class who

weren't as quick. She mentioned specific children with disabilities in the school who have these problems, and the students nodded in recognition. Several children said they would think more carefully about how they treat their fellow students with disabilities and would either help them more, refrain from teasing them, or just act naturally. "Treat them more like they are one of your friends, not like they are different," a student suggested.

Discussion Questions

1. What other strategies could the teacher use to encourage students to reflect on their attitudes and sensitivity toward their peers with disabilities?
2. Do you think the strategy described above is more effective than one involving lectures about characteristics of students with disabilities? Why?

(Source: *The Washington Post,* September 19, 1995).

CLASSROOM MODIFICATIONS. Many strategies are available for making reasonable accommodations in the classroom environment. They include the following:

- Creation of barrier-free settings for classroom access, including libraries, resource areas, and technology or learning labs.
- Modifications in physical groupings of desks.
- Modification in seating arrangements to permit improved access and viewing for those with physical and visual disabilities.

Modifications to seating and physical groupings are simple and reasonable accommodations enjoyed by most students in a classroom.

- Rearrangement or enlargement of visual tools or resources in room.
- Use of audiotape equipment or alternative communication devices for students with communication difficulties.
- Rearrangement of classes, with consideration given to their relationship to school building entrances and exits.

MODIFYING INSTRUCTION. The teacher can use many strategies for modifying teaching methods to maximize the adjustment and learning of the student with a disability, a student placed into the classroom with an expectation of reaching near grade level with peers by the close of the school year. The way the teacher delivers instruction in the classroom must be relevant to the student disabilities:

- *Task analysis to break down instructional objectives into smaller units.* Task analysis provides a way of dividing larger units of instruction or students' objectives into smaller, manageable activities and assignments. The teacher facilitates the step-by-step process. This is particularly effective for students who have short attention spans and who have trouble organizing and completing assignments. Task analysis provides more frequent opportunities for teacher feedback and for successful completion of assignments.
- *Strategic instruction.* Use of multiple instructional strategies aimed at matching the student's individual learning style to specific skill acquisition increases the opportunity for success.
- *Hands-on instruction.* Increasing students' opportunities to participate in active learning enhances the potential for success in the inclusive classroom. Active learning involves more hands-on instruction, which is particularly beneficial to students with disabilities be-

Student group projects help students learn cooperatively and share their talents and special abilities.

cause it combines the kinesthetic learning modality with the visual and auditory.

- *Collaborative team teaching.* The team teaching model offers an alternative instructional approach that is more effective and generally preferred over simply putting several students with disabilities, without support, into a traditional academic setting. Two or more teachers collaborate in the joint planning and the delivery of curriculum. Collaboration provides additional support for both the academic teacher and the special education teacher, as well as the students in the class.

Supplements to class instruction can be effective in enhancing learning abilities. These include the following:

- *Use of special materials or computers for one-on-one instruction and programmed instruction.* A vast array of commercially available instructional materials, as well as software, are available to supplement classroom instruction. This type of software is self-paced and allows students to feel a sense of control over their learning. Self-paced computer learning programs have helped many students with and without disabilities to achieve academic success. Students are often visually stimulated by computers and are motivated to achieve more in the classroom through computerized integrated learning systems and software for drill and practice, simulations, and electronic networks.
- *Use of peer learning teams in project activities.* Student group projects are becoming very popular in today's classrooms because such projects help students learn cooperatively as they share each other's talents and special abilities. Cooperative learning teams are examples of peer learning. For example, students are grouped into teams with a common assigned project to read chapters in the text and then to identify the basic concepts and paste them onto large newsprint or paper. The students then draw lines to show how these concepts connect to each other (webs). Each student is responsible for webbing notes on a particular section of the chapter, and all the notes are then brought together into the web. Students then assist and check each

other's notes to make sure they are complete. This activity combines the abilities of the stronger students with the students who are not academically as strong. Students are then given a group grade and an individual grade, based on their ability to answer questions related to information in their individual portion of the web.

- *Use of visual diagrams to reinforce classroom instruction.* Many students learn better through the visual modality. Therefore, teachers may use ready-made visual materials, as well as student-constructed visual materials, to supplement classroom instruction and readings. One of the best examples of using visual means to reinforce instruction is the use of visual images to teach fractions and mathematical concepts. Homework projects that emphasize construction of posters, collages, visual models, and diagrams are particularly effective for visual learners.
- *Writing to learn.* Teachers can help students with disabilities improve their writing skills and learn from their experiences by providing more opportunities to write about those learning experiences. The development of writing skills is closely associated with preparation of students for logical reasoning and critical thinking and how these can be applied in communicating about ideas. Students' capacity for critical thinking is greatly strengthened by their participation in writing, and such participation can influence the student's overall progress and quality of work in all subject areas. Writing assignments could include the following:
  - What students already know about a topic before a unit begins.
  - Experiences with activities they have completed in class.
  - Responses to field trip experiences.
  - Films seen in class.
  - The student's participation in learning teams or computer laboratory groups.
  - Students with whom they have completed an activity.
  - Homework experiences and how they learn best.
  - Unusual events that have happened in the classroom, school, or in their homes.
- *Practical writing for career development.* Finally, teachers should encourage students with disabilities to complete a job profile portfolio before completion of high school and to participate in interviews with prospective employers as part of their job search activities. A portfolio is a collection or compilation of a series of assignments or projects designed to integrate academic learning. Creation of the job profile portfolio involves a process that includes
  - Writing about a career interest or occupation
  - Participating in job search activities
  - Writing letters of interest
  - Obtaining letters of reference
  - Completing a job resume
  - Completing job applications
  - Participating in interviews
  - Writing the follow-up letter

PARTNERS FOR INSTRUCTIONAL MODIFICATION. Following are several ways in which personal relationships can provide additional support for students with disabilities in inclusive classrooms.

- **Peer mentoring to support students with special needs.** Each student is assigned to a peer-mentor team of two students. The participant's peer-mentors provide support and encouragement and enables the student with a disability to solve problems, make decisions, and adjust to the classroom and new expectations. Peer teams also help (enable) each other to prepare for performance demonstrations and exhibitions. Sometimes to help support peer-mentor teams or work through problems that arise, the psychologist, career counselor, or teacher advocates conduct group discussions.

- **Teacher–student mentor relationships.** Teacher-student mentor relationships provide additional support to students in inclusive classrooms. These relationships provide emotional and social support and help link the participant with needed support services. A student is assigned to a *teacher-advocate,* upon whom the student can depend for guidance, support, crisis assistance, and linkage with other professionals. The teacher-advocate is responsible for a group of students and meets with them on a regular basis.

- **Paraprofessionals and teacher aides.** Additional support within the classroom is always a benefit. Such support is particularly welcome and necessary to meet the demanding challenges of the inclusion classroom.

- **Volunteers: engaging the community.** Parents, the Parent-Teacher Association, and community representatives can volunteer to support instruction in the classroom. Typically, the volunteers assist by providing tutoring, preparing and organizing instructional materials, gathering resources, developing student materials, and performing many other services helpful to teachers in the classroom.

- **Peer tutoring.** Students in the class can also assist other students with the learning process. Students can also lead discussions or project teams. Peer tutoring, however, does not mean simply pairing students together. It means matching students who have common interests, discussing with the student tutor the purpose of the peer tutoring, and providing ongoing supervision of the peer-tutoring process. Peers can tutor individual students or groups.

- **Service coordination.** For assistance with coordinating a range of services to students with disabilities, some schools assign a teacher-advocate or case manager who is responsible for knowing the student, determining additional service needs, and making referrals for needed support services. Teacher-advocates work closely with the school social workers, psychologists, and others to identify and link the student and family with needed services in the school and community.

ASSESSING STUDENT ACHIEVEMENT IN EFFECTIVE INCLUSIVE SCHOOLS. There are several ways in which the assessment of student achievement in the classroom is being improved in many schools across the United States (Bernhardt & Higgen, 1992; Friend & Bursuck, 1999). However, these efforts to produce more positive outcomes for students have not always benefited students with disabilities in the inclusive classroom. In effective inclusive schools, for example, teachers are being educated to show how their instructional and student assessment strategies for students with disabilities relate directly to the expected outcomes for students and to the IEP objectives. They have begun to develop a logical progression of learning for these students. Effective instructional and assessment strategies for students with disabilities can be found across all grade levels, resulting in systematic, schoolwide improvement in student achievement as students with disabilities become part of the continuum of learning for all students. As a result, students with disabilities conduct self-assessments of performance in order to continuously improve, and these students show sustained improvements in achievement. Increased achievement for students with disabilities is evident across the school, and student morale, behavior, and attendance show significant improvement.

MODIFICATIONS IN STUDENT ASSESSMENT. Many teachers are experimenting with methods of assessing student learning that are different from the traditional standardized tests or paper-and-pencil tests. Methods such as student portfolios of completed work and exhibitions often provide more in-depth and richer information about what the student has learned about a subject and how the student learns. These methods of assessment are also often more interesting to students and help them integrate information about a subject by pulling together into a complete product all the bits of information they have learned. By increasing variety in student learning assessments, the teachers have a better opportunity to determine student progress on acquisition of specific skills. Authentic assessment, or assessment of students in performance-based activities, will enhance the inclusive classroom for all students. Examples of these approaches include the following activities.

Project portfolios and presentations. One method teachers have found to be particularly effective in the alternative assessment of learning is the completion of project portfolios and presentations of the portfolio before a panel of peers or parents in special demonstration sessions. Demonstrations require students to actively present their work and to discuss the process and products. Portfolio development can be directed by the teacher or the student and can involve teams of students using resources in the community. Portfolios can also be used at the end of the year as a framework for presenting student homework or long-range projects. Demonstrations and exhibitions can be used to evaluate individual and group learning and performance. Students can demonstrate proficiency in a variety of skills areas in either academic, vocational, or technology-related areas.

Participation in leadership activities. Leadership activities require students to cooperate in the planning and performance of a classroom demonstration or exhibition. Students may form teams to organize a science exhibit or a multicultural fair, produce a photographic exhibit, develop a videotape of an activity or process, prepare graduation materials for print, or to present to parents attending the exhibitions.

SUMMARY OF ADAPTATIONS AND ACCOMMODATION AT THE SECONDARY LEVEL

Curriculum Modifications

- Flexible or elastic completion times for assignments and for the annual curriculum objectives (to include summer completions).
- Open enrollment for vocational programs and community-based programs.
- Curriculum modules or units that permit flexible enrollment.
- Integrated academic and vocational instruction (academic instruction embedded within vocational-technical education programs).
- Alternative certification of vocational skill proficiencies, including certification of levels of skill attainment.
- Integration of computer-based learning activities.
- Access to technology and technology labs for all students.
- Inclusion of functional skill components in curriculum.
- Community service activities built into curriculum.

Classroom Modifications

- Barrier-free settings for classroom access, including libraries, resource areas, and technology or learning labs.
- Modified physical groupings of desks.
- Modification in seating to permit improved access for students who have physical disabilities and to permit best vantage for those with auditory or visual impairments.
- Rearrangement or enlargement of visual tools or resources in room.
- Use of audiotape equipment or alternative communication devices for students with communication difficulties.
- Rearrangement of classes, with consideration to their relationship to school building entrances and exits.

Equipment Modifications

- Access to technology labs and learning labs available to all students.
- Use of visual timers or alarms on equipment in vocational labs or centers.
- Peer teaming for use of equipment or projects requiring use of equipment.
- Simple modification of equipment.
- Relocation and reorganization of equipment in classroom or shop.

- Providing greater spacing between pieces of equipment.
- Providing visual and diagrammatic instructions for safety and use of equipment.
- Lowering and raising height of equipment or computers.

Instructional Modifications

- Use of computers for one-on-one instruction and programmed instruction.
- Use of peer teams in computer instructions.
- Using visual diagrams to reinforce classroom instructions.
- Testing adaptations and alternatives (portfolio assessments, demonstrations, and exhibitions of skills and proficiency).
- Structuring in teacher time for participation in IEPs and coordinated planning.
- Peer projects.
- Peer mentoring to support students with special needs.
- Teacher-mentor relationships.
- Task analysis to break down instructional objectives into smaller units.
- More frequent performance assessments.
- Strategic instruction aimed at matching the instructional method to the student's individual learning style or modality.
- Using multiple and varied instructional methods.
- Using concrete and contextualized instructional methods (hands-on).

Supplemental Personnel and Services

- Vocational assessment personnel, including community-based assessment of vocational and work performance in authentic settings.
- Classroom aides.
- Guidance counselor support.
- Service coordinators or case managers to link students to community services.
- Community-based (e.g., business personnel) mentors and guest instructors.
- Work adjustment personnel
- Community-based supervisors or job coaches.
- Training of work-based advocates.
- Post-secondary linkages and assistance with application to postsecondary programs.
- Linkages to adult services.
- Provision of information to students and families about postsecondary opportunities and transition supports.

CHAPTER 19

What Support Services Are Needed for Inclusive Classrooms?

SUPPORT SERVICES AND SPECIAL EDUCATION. Support services are special services that are provided to students with disabilities beyond their educational program. They include supplementary and related services.

What Are Supplementary and Support Services?
Supplementary and support services are provided to enable students with disabilities to succeed within the general education setting. This means aids, services, and other supports that are provided in regular education classes or other education-related settings to enable students to be educated with nondisabled children to the maximum extent appropriate. Supplementary services may include modifications to instruction, teaching preskills, modifying tests, modifying the physical class setting, use of alternative or supplementary materials and textbooks, use of technology, use of organizing strategies and study guides, adaptations to seat-work and homework assignments, alternative feedback strategies (Friend & Bursuck, 1999).

What Are Related Services? There are a number of related special education services that are essential to the provision of inclusive education. *Related services* means any of the following services that are needed in any setting to assist the student to benefit from instruction, particularly in relation to the general education curriculum:

1. transportation,
2. developmental, corrective and other supportive services,
3. speech-language pathology and audiology services,
4. psychological services,
5. physical and occupational therapy services,
6. recreation, including therapeutic recreation,
7. social work services,
8. counseling services, including rehabilitation counseling,
9. orientation and mobility services,
10. early identification and assessment of disabling conditions,
11. medical services for diagnostic and evaluation purposes.

Related services help a student to participate in and benefit from placement into an inclusive classroom and include early identification and assessment of disabling conditions, transportation, developmental and corrective services such as speech pathology and audiology, psychological services, social work services, physical and occupational therapy, recreation, and medical and counseling services. Such services may be required to assist a child with a disability in benefiting from education in the inclusive classroom.

Each related service by itself cannot guarantee success in the general education classroom, but if provided in addition to an adequate individualized education program, can contribute positively to the inclusion process. The following are examples of specific related and support services that should be available in the school and community:

- **Medical and health services.** Teachers can review existing medical and health reports for important information about the kinds of medical or health support services the student is receiving. Medical and health reports are important to the teacher for learning about potential medical alert procedures, changes in the schedule of in-school medications or procedures, or for determining any possible emergency arrangements or guidelines.

Supplementary services and supports in the classroom enable students to be educated with nondisabled peers to the maximum extent possible.

- **Social work and family support services.** These are the services of social workers or family service workers in the school or in the community. Such services are needed to intervene in family dispute situations, child neglect or abuse, truancy problems, or need for counseling for problems such as substance abuse or other self-destructive behaviors. Casework services include assistance in interpreting evaluation reports and making recommendations.

- **Rehabilitative services.** Rehabilitation workers help determine a youth's eligibility for vocational rehabilitation services as the student prepares for employment or postsecondary education. In effective inclusive schools, the rehabilitation counselor spends time on site identifying students (typically in grades nine and above) who will be eligible for vocational rehabilitation services and conducting the necessary assessments to determine eligibility. They also often provide counseling in work behavior and expectations, to prepare the student to use the vocational rehabilitation system as a transition support to employment or postsecondary education.

- **Personal counseling.** Personal counseling services for students and the family can assist in the inclusion process. The adjustment itself of moving into an inclusive classroom may create anxieties that could be alleviated through counseling. Often students are faced with family stresses such as the care of a sibling or ill health of a parent that may create barriers to learning. Individual or group counseling may help the student problem solve and provide guidance and emotional support during a difficult period.

- **Job coach and job placement services.** Providing vocational training requires the skills of a job coach who can provide one-on-one assistance during the occupational training. Job placement services are related to identifying potential job placement sites and requires a concentrated effort on the part of the counselor to know the community, the availability of job openings, the labor market needs at the local, state, and regional levels.

- **Occupational therapy.** The occupational therapist engages individuals or groups in activities designed to enhance their physical, social, psychological, and cognitive development in order to improve on-the-job performance in school and in work. Occupational therapists assess the combination of these capabilities and provide suggestions for accommodations (Meyer & Skrtic, 1995).

- **Reading specialist.** The reading specialist provides reading tutorial assistance designed to improve reading skills, comprehension, and academic performance.

- **Physical therapy.** The physical therapist manipulates, massages, and exercises body parts to assist the individual with motor control for optimal functioning; to prevent deterioration of physical abilities and to correct, relieve, or strengthen physical conditions.

- **Speech therapy.** The speech therapist provides services to remediate articulation problems, voice fluency disorders, and general language problems and fosters the communication skills of students within the classroom environment. Therapy services may be provided in individual sessions, group sessions or through consultation with the student's general education teacher.

- **Emergency management supports.** These supports include emergency response services for students who have medical conditions that may require emergency interventions (e.g., diabetes or seizures). Such supports may also be needed for students with emotional or behavioral disorders who might require the immediate intervention of a behavior management specialist, school psychologist, or the police.

Inclusive school teachers recognize that for students with disabilities who are transferred from segregated schools or classrooms, there are often many barriers to participation in the general education classroom. For many students, accommodations in the physical environment, instruction, or curriculum are not enough. These students may need additional support services provided by individuals outside the classroom or agencies outside the school. The purpose of these related and support services is to enable a student to participate in and benefit from placement in the inclusive classroom. A supportive environment is essential to the success of inclusive classrooms.

Case Example 19-1 describes the challenges of one family as they seek to have their son included in a school with limited related and support services.

CASE EXAMPLE 19-1. Chris—A Family's Quest for Neighborhood Schooling

Chris Della, 7 years old, is the youngest of three boys. He lives at home with me (his mother), his father, and his two brothers—Tom, who is 12, and Joe, who is 9. Chris has mental and physical challenges. His cerebral palsy requires the use of a wheelchair. His speech is limited and difficult to understand. Intellectually, he is more like a 4-year-old than a 7-year-old.

Chris has received special education services since infancy. We have continually worked with a group of professionals who have helped us set and meet goals for our special son's development. Chris is an integral part of our family. Like our other sons, he is comfortable in our community, attending church and local events and participating in recreation programs and scouting. Our goal for Chris is that he lead a happy and productive adult life, with as little assistance from others as possible. We know that at age 7 it is impossible to project the possible and it is desirable to shoot for the stars.

Fortunately, we have formed strong bonds with other parents who have children with multiple challenges. Through a parent-support group we belong to we have developed our vision of the school program we want for Chris. We want Chris included in our neighborhood school, which will help him to remain part of our community. Our focus on inclusion has put us at odds with many of the professionals who are part of our lives. This desire for inclusion and the resulting conflict with professionals is a common bond within our parent support group.

The school system wants Chris in "special programs," which are either wholly or partially separated from mainstream education. As we look back, we think we made a mistake by placing Chris in a therapeutic preschool program. The teachers and staff were wonderful, but once we had placed him in a restrictive program, we found that it was impossible to remove him from it. This was an unexpected disappointment. We did not like being in conflict with professionals who truly cared about Chris.

Professionals who work with students who have disabilities seem to be an overworked group of individuals. Formally scheduled meetings with parents have a tight time frame. Many meetings are structured so that parent questions come at the end of a presentation of what the professional team has already planned. We know that we are seen as troublemakers, as parents who are in denial of our son's problems. This label does not help us, Chris, or the professionals who work with him. We expect that Chris will develop slowly, but we also know that spending the school day in a separate school with other students with limited mobility and language will only slow his development and marginalize Chris in our community. We have been able to integrate Chris into community activities. Why can't he be a part of our neighborhood school? We are involved in due process hearings to obtain a determination on our request that Chris be released from the special center and be placed with an aide in our neighborhood school. Yes, this may mean complications for the school's transportation systems, and it may require the school to hire a paraprofessional who can be supervised by a professional special educator to meet Chris' wide-ranging needs during the day.

We want to give it a try for a year and see if Chris' development is slowed or harmed in any way. Our best guess is that it will not slow his development. Other parents' experiences tell us that he will be more motivated and stimulated in his neighborhood school and thus make greater progress. Isn't this what federal legislation guarantees—that all students be allowed the most appropriate placement to meet their long-term needs? We know Chris will receive less intensive special education and related services, that it will be an adjustment for all individuals involved with Chris' inclusion into his neighborhood school, and that it will take valuable professional time to make this all work. But we also know that inclusion is the intent of federal legislation—to meet individual needs, not to impose a service delivery template based on disability categories. Our best guess is that Chris and his classmates will make the adjustment most easily and that the professionals will have the greatest adjustment because they are stymied by their professional ideas of what makes sense to them.

Chris is successful and appreciated at home and within the community. Why does the school system have to be different? What do all those degrees and salaries mean in relation to what is best for my son? We are at a stage in our relationship with the school system where it is us versus them; yet I sincerely believe that we all want what is best for Chris. Our problem is in what the school system will allow themselves to consider as possible for Chris. My only choice is to remain steadfast in my role as Chris's mother to be his advocate. Unfortunately, the school system sees its only role as cost containment and defense of convenient service delivery structures. I wonder after all these years what federal legislation has accomplished.

Discussion Questions

1. How would you describe this parent's definition of inclusion?
2. What are her reasons for wanting her son included in his neighborhood school? Is she being reasonable?
3. What barriers is she facing?
4. What legislation supports including Chris in his neighborhood school?
5. What steps could the school system have taken to prevent an adversarial relationship from developing?
6. What advice would you give the parents as they continue to advocate for full inclusion?

CHAPTER 20

What Is the Role of the Interdisciplinary Team and the Student in the IEP and Inclusive Placement?

Students with disabilities have many unique needs and often require the services of a variety of professionals in order to succeed in the general classroom. These professionals are responsible for developing, reviewing, and revising the individualized education program (IEP), or central planning document. They are also responsible for ensuring that the student is involved in the process of individualized planning and is making adequate progress in relation to the IEP goals and objectives. The IEP team has a dual role in both the creation of the planning document, as well as the coordination of services written into the student's IEP. This second function of coordination is not adequately carried out in schools in which there is not clear assignment of responsibility for monitoring the student's progress on the IEP. Furthermore, in many schools, the role of the student in the IEP process remains unclear to many personnel, and as a result the student is personally left out of the process of setting goals and planning for the future.

NEW IEP REQUIREMENTS UNDER IDEA SUPPORT STUDENT INVOLVEMENT IN THE GENERAL EDUCATION CURRICULUM. The Senate report on the reauthorization of IDEA states that the

> majority of children identified as eligible for special education and related services are capable of participating in the general education curriculum to varying degrees with some adaptations and modifications. This provision is intended to ensure that children's special education and related services are in addition to and are affected by the general education curriculum, not separate from it . . . The law and this bill contain a presumption that children with disabilities are to be educated in regular classes and that every decision made for a child with a disability must be made on the basis

of what that individual child needs. (Committee on Labor and Human Resources, 1997, pp. 20–21)

Although much of the IEP and many of the placement processes, such as the type of information that must be contained, IEP team membership, how the document should be developed, reviewed, and revised, remain much the same, the 1997 Amendments to IDEA made several changes in the IEP and the placement processes, effective July 1, 1998 (U.S. Office of Special Education, 1997). One of the primary new emphases or areas of modification is on the student's involvement in the general curriculum. There are several issues that must be addressed for students with IEPs in the general education classroom (see Figure 20-1).

A Statement of Commitment: General Purpose of the IEP for Students in Public and Private Educational Settings and for Students Who Move Between LEAs. The IDEA requires that an individual education program (IEP) be developed for each student with a disability who is receiving special education and related services. The state educational agency must ensure that every child with a disability in the state has a free, appropriate public education, regardless of which agency is responsible for the child. Therefore, IEPs are also required for students with disabilities who are (1) placed in or referred to a private school or facility by a public agency, or (2) enrolled in a parochial school or other private school and receive special education and related services from a public agency. Furthermore, if a student is receiving educational services under contract to or through interagency agreement with a state agency such as a mental health, welfare, or state correctional facility, then that agency is responsible for ensuring that an IEP is developed and implemented for the child. For example, IEPs

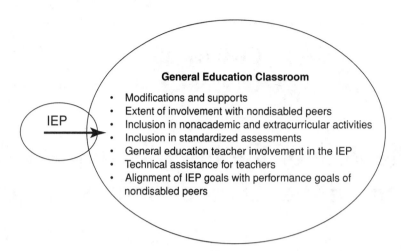

FIGURE 20-1. Issues for Students with IEPs in the General Education Classroom

must be developed and implemented for students in any of the following situations:

- A local educational agency (the school district or basic administrative unit that operates the schools within a relatively small geographic area) (LEA) places the student into a school or program operated by another state agency.
- A state or local agency other than the SEA or LEA places a child in a residential facility or other program.
- A parent initiates a placement from a private to public institution.
- The court system makes a placement of an adolescent into a juvenile correctional facility.

If the LEA initiates a placement into a state-operated facility, then the LEA has responsibility for the development of the child's IEP, and that IEP must be developed before the child is placed (U.S. Office of Special Education, 1997). If the student is placed out of state, then the placing state (rather than the receiving state) is responsible for developing the IEP and ensuring its implementation. If a student who has been receiving special education services moves from one LEA to another, then a new IEP meeting is not needed if

1. A copy of the student's current IEP is available.
2. The parents are satisfied with the current IEP.
3. The receiving LEA determines that the current IEP is appropriate and can be implemented as written.

If the IEP from the sending LEA is not available, or the parents believe it inappropriate, then an IEP meeting is needed and should occur within a short time after the student enrolls with the new LEA (within one week).

The IEP is a written record of the decisions that are reached at the meeting of the interdisciplinary team. There are several purposes and functions of the IEP, which include the following:

1. Puts into writing a commitment of resources necessary to enable a student with a disability to receive needed special education and related services.

2. Serves as a management tool used to ensure that each child with a disability is provided appropriate special education and related services.
3. Serves as a compliance and monitoring document and a source of data for governmental agencies at all levels (e.g., the school, district, state, or U.S. Department of Education) that are monitoring the degree to which students with disabilities are actually receiving a free, appropriate public education.
4. Serves as an evaluation tool for individuals, schools, and other agencies to determine students' progress toward individualized goals.

The IEP must be in effect at the beginning of each school year and before the special education and related services are provided to the students. It must be implemented as soon as possible following the IEP meeting, allowing no delay between the time an IEP is finalized and the beginning of the services. In order to avoid extended delays in services, the IEP meeting must be held within 30 calendar days after the student is found to need special education and related services. If the identified student is being placed into the school or classroom for the first time and has not previously had an IEP, then the IEP must be developed before the placement decision is made. The student may be placed in a temporary "evaluation" placement until a final decision is made about placement for the year. For example, if a group of rising eighth-grade middle-school students with disabilities are being identified for placement into general education classrooms in the ninth grade, then their IEPs must be developed in advance of their actual transition to the school. This placement may represent a trial period to carefully evaluate the student in the general education classroom. The IEP, however, must be prepared in advance of the transition and must set out the specific conditions and time lines for the trial placement. A time line for completing the evaluation and setting the IEP team meeting to make final placement decisions for the student must also be established before the placement. The parents must agree to the trial placement before it is carried out and must be involved throughout the process of developing, reviewing, and revising the IEP.

The IEP team meets at least once a year to review and revise the IEP. There is no prescribed length of the IEP meeting; initial placement meetings may be longer than continuing placement meetings. The meeting should allow sufficient time to ensure meaningful participation by the parent and the student.

Who Participates in the IEP and What Is the Parents' Role? The IEP meeting serves as a communication vehicle between parents and school personnel and it enables parents, as equal participants, to jointly determine the student's needs, the services that will be provided to meet those needs, and the anticipated outcomes (U.S. Office of Special Education, 1997). Figure 20-2 describes personnel who are typically involved in an IEP meeting. The general education teacher is now expected to participate in IEP meetings for students with disabilities in the general education class. Parent participation is key to the success of both the IEP process and the student's inclusion. The parents are expected to be equal participants along with the other IEP team members and to take an active role in discussions about their child's needs for special education and related services and in the decisions about placement and services. The IEP process allows the team to resolve any differences between the parents and the school concerning special education needs of the student, first through the IEP meeting, and if needed, through due process procedures available to the parents. This second protection refers to the required mediation options that schools must now provide parents and students for resolving differences in a constructive and nonadversarial manner.

The LEA is required to ensure that one or both parents of a student are present at each IEP meeting, that they are notified of the meeting early enough and at a mutually agreed upon time, and that the purpose of the meeting is explained. If a meeting must be conducted without a parent's attendance, then the school personnel must have a record of its attempts to encourage and invite the parents to the meeting. The parents should also be informed that they may bring to the meeting other people who may be helpful in the development or review of the IEP. These may include friends, neighbors, or specialists.

Parents' signatures on the IEP are not required by law, but the practice is used widely in states, because the signatures document who attended the meeting, are useful for monitoring and compliance, and indicate that the parent has approved of the student's program and placement (U.S. Office of Special Education, 1997). Parents do have a right to a copy of their child's IEP. They also have the right to be informed that they can appeal the team's decisions about the student, if they disagree, and can request a hearing to resolve the differences. Parents also can expect the school to provide for regular reporting on the progress of their child through the general reporting procedures in place for all children (e.g., parent-teacher conferences, report cards, parent letters, and notes).

Functions of the IEP. The individualized education program, a written statement for each child with a disability, does the following:

1. Identifies present levels of performance in academic, social, vocational and other areas, beginning with how the student is currently doing in school.
2. Identifies strengths and needs of the student, or areas of skills to be addressed. This information is drawn from recent evaluations, observations, and input from parents and school personnel.
3. States how the student's disability affects his or her *involvement and progress in the general curriculum.*
4. Defines annual goals and benchmarks, or short-term objectives. The goals must be annual and measurable (i.e., what can the student reasonably achieve in a year?), and they must be related to helping the student be involved in and progress in the general education curriculum.
5. Describes the special education and related services that the student needs in order to achieve the annual and short-term goals. The IEP must specify the supplementary aids and supports needed to enable the student to be involved in the general education curriculum, to participate in extracurricular activities, and to be educated and participate with other children with and without disabilities.
6. Specifies any program modifications or support from school personnel that will be provided for the student.
7. Specifies the individual modifications, or adaptations made to district or state assessments of achievement, how the tests are administered, and the specific modifications that will be made to enable students to participate in these assessments.

☞ Student
☞ Parent
☞ General education teacher
☞ Special education teachers
☞ Related services professionals
☞ Nonschool-agency representatives
☞ Other relevant professionals

FIGURE 20-2. Members of the Interdisciplinary Team

8. Clearly and specifically states when the student's special education and related services (including modifications) will begin, their duration, and the location in which the student will receive the services.

9. For students age 14, and every year thereafter, includes a statement of transition service needs in their courses of study. The purpose of this requirement is to focus attention on how the student's educational program can be planned to help the child make a successful transition to postsecondary placement.

10. For students one year before reaching the age of majority (as defined by the State), includes a statement that the student has been informed of the rights, if any, that transfer to him or her upon reaching the age of majority.

11. Includes a statement of how the student's progress toward the annual goals and objectives will be measured. This is to include how the parents of the student will be kept regularly informed about their child's progress toward the annual goals in the IEP and the extent to which that progress is sufficient to enable the student to achieve the goals by the end of the year. They must be informed at least as often as the parents of nondisabled students (for example, through the use of IEP report cards that are issued at the same time as the general school report cards).

12. Explains the extent, if any, to which the student will *not* be participating with nondisabled children in the general education classroom, in the general curriculum, and in extracurricular and non-academic activities. The new requirement reaffirms IDEA's preference for educating students with disabilities with their nondisabled peers to the maximum extent possible and in the most appropriate (least restrictive) educational setting. Furthermore, the U.S. Department of Education has recently defined criteria for "Great IDEA schools" which includes the following: Students with IEPs are included in all aspects of the school—extracurricular and other non-academic activities. (Final IDEA Regulations, 1999)

The box "Elements of an Individualized Education Program" describes the typical elements of an IEP.

What Is the Difference Between the IEP and a Section 504 Plan? Section 504 of the Rehabilitation Act of 1973 is closely related to IDEA and shares the goal of ensuring the inclusion of students with disabilities in educational programs and services. Section 504 is a nondiscrimination clause in the Rehabilitation Act that states

> No otherwise qualified individual with disabilities . . . shall solely by reasons of his disability, be excluded from the participation in, be denied the benefits of, or be subjected to discrimination under any program or activity receiving Federal financial assistance.

Elements of an Individualized Education Program

1. Date of entry into the inclusive setting, date of IEP meetings, placement information.
2. Identifying information (name, date of birth, address, sex, grade level, etc.).
3. Assistance needed to establish appropriateness for placement and eligibility for special educational services or to make application to other needed services.
4. Names of service coordinator or program advocate and parents or guardians.
5. Names of individuals and agencies represented in the development or review of the plan.
6. Summary of assessments and observations of the individual that indicate student strengths and needs and needed services.
7. Types of services the individual and family are receiving.
8. Persons providing services.
9. Short- and long-range measurable objectives for the services, as well as priorities in all relevant functional areas.
10. Vocational-technical training and employment assistance objectives.
11. Methods or strategies of service delivery, including responsible persons and agencies to which the individual may be referred.
12. Service coordination supports needed and methods of monitoring the receipt of such services.
13. Special supports needed by the student to participate in the service (e.g., transportation or assistive devices).
14. Criteria for evaluation of services, with explicitly stated and measurable outcomes.
15. Expected and realistic dates of completion for each service to be delivered.
16. Potential barriers to accessing or using services recommended in the IEP (e.g., placement criteria, enrollment procedures, unavailability of services, attitudes of the individual, lack of family agreement or support, etc.).
17. Service or supports needed to exit from the placement and transition to an alternative placement or program (if appropriate).
18. Extent to which the student will be integrated into the general education curriculum, nonacademic activities, and other school activities with his or her nondisabled peers.
19. Signatures of student, parents, and professionals participating in the planning meeting.

Note. Synthesized from a review of many individual service plans and individual education plans from several states and localities.

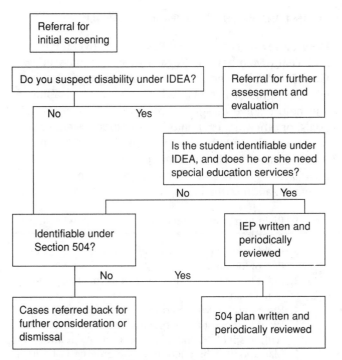

FIGURE 20-3. Considerations for Disability (IDEA and Section 504)

While the Rehabilitation Act did not provide funds to the states to provide education for students with disabilities, the law made it illegal for any program receiving federal funding to discriminate against any student on the basis of disability. Section 504 refers to nondiscrimination and does not include the resources and supports that are guaranteed under IDEA (Rothstein, 1995). It does, however, indicate that some reasonable accommodations must be provided to meet the nondiscrimination standard.

Section 504 applies to students of all ages who have, or have a record of having, physical or mental impairments which substantially limit one or more major life activities. Major life activities include caring for oneself, performing manual tasks, walking, seeing, hearing, speaking, breathing, learning, and working. Section 504 is frequently invoked to protect children who are not eligible for or identified under IDEA. Some schools have 504 Coordinators to assist students who are not eligible under IDEA but who may need special accommodations to participate in general education or educational activities. If the student qualifies under 504 but not under IDEA, then a 504 plan is developed instead of an IEP (See Figure 20-3). For example, a student with a physical disability may not need or be eligible for special education services because she is performing well in the general education class and requires no supplemental services. However, to participate with peers in the activities in a new technology lab, the student may need some minor accommodations. Section 504, and not IDEA, would be invoked in this case, and the student would have a 504 plan.

Deciding a Student's LRE. In 1994, the U.S. Department of Education offered a memorandum to clarify for the states the LRE provisions (Heuman & Hehir, 1994). This memo explained that the student's placement in the general education classroom is the *first* option the IEP team must consider. The 1997 Amendments to IDEA continued this presumption that children with disabilities are most appropriately educated with their nondisabled peers. The most important question for the IEP team in determining whether or not a student will be educated in the general education classroom is, What is the possible range of supplementary aids and services needed to ensure that the student can be adequately educated in that setting? If the IEP team decides that the student cannot be educated in the general education setting, even with the supplementary aids and services, then an alternative placement must be considered. Schools are required to

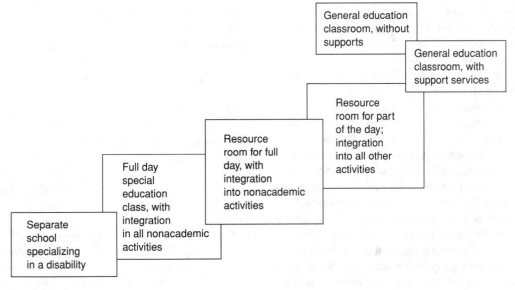

FIGURE 20-4. LRE Placement Options

make available a continuum of alternative placements to meet the needs for special education and related services of students with disabilities. This required continuum reinforces the importance of the individualized determination of the least restrictive environment, and not a one size fits all approach (Heumann, 1994).

THE STUDENT AND THE IEP: BUILDING SELF-DETERMINATION OF THE STUDENT. The terms self-advocacy and self-determination are becoming widely used, especially as they relate to students with disabilities. *Self-determination* refers to the act of making independent choices about personal goals and directions, based on accurate information about one's own strengths and needs and the available placement, service, or program options. Self-determination is most effective and rewarding within an environment that promotes and facilitates independent decision making (Racino, 1992; Field & Hoffman, 1998). It does not mean going it alone or relying only upon oneself. Rather, the idea should be placed within the context of shared decision making, interdependence, and mutual support (Racino, 1992). Many children and youths with disabilities have difficulty assuming control of their lives and participating in the IEP goal setting and educational decisions that are made each year about their futures, and, thus, self-determination is an important issue.

The term *self-advocacy* has been defined as a social and political movement started by and for people with disabilities to speak for themselves on important issues, such as housing, employment, legal rights, and personal relationships (Smith & Lukasson, 1992). The term is related to self-determination in that the student with a disability is directly and actively involved in the decisions that are being made about his or her education and future. In 1974, a consumer-directed movement, called Self-Advocacy, was established in Oregon by a group of individuals with disabilities. Now, most states have self-advocacy groups and organizations, such as those associated with the Association for Retarded Citizens or the Disability Coalition, which are active in starting peer-support and self-advocacy groups.

The process of building self-determination depends on greater shared decision making among the student, the family, and professionals in decisions that affect the future of the individual being served. Along with building individual capacity to make informed choices and decisions comes a greater responsibility and accountability for the outcomes of those decisions. Students with disabilities and their parents, therefore, become equal partners and share the responsibility for developing IEPs and for the results of those plans. It is logical and necessary that students be actively engaged in the process, as the IEP is the central planning document for the student, family, teachers, and support services personnel who will be involved with the student's educational development.

STUDENT AND PARENT PARTICIPATION IN THE IEP

How Can Disagreements Be Resolved Between Parents and Team Members in Regard to Placements or IEP Goals? IDEA has certain procedural safeguards that protect the rights of parents and students with disabilities and help resolve disagreements about placements, IEP goals, or other matters related to the student's education or participation in school activities. IDEA 1997 has modified some of the requirements for procedural safeguards. Safeguards that remain in place from the 1990 reauthorization of the law include the following:

1. Right to a copy of the child's IEP and all educational records.
2. Right to obtain an independent educational evaluation of the child.
3. Right to content of the child's placement and educational plan.
4. Right to prior written notice about safeguards.
5. Right to request a due process hearing on any matter with respect to the identification, evaluation, or placement of the child, or to the provision of a free, appropriate public education.
6. Right to a due process hearing conducted by an impartial hearing office.
7. Right to a child's placement while a due process hearing is pending.
8. Procedures for students who are placed into interim alternative educational settings.
9. Right of parents for unilateral placement of children into private schools at public expense.
10. Mediation.
11. Right to appeal the initial hearing decision to the State Education Agency if the SEA did not conduct the hearing.
12. Right to bring civil action in an appropriate state or federal court to appeal a final hearing decision.
13. Attorney's fees.

Parents must be provided information about these procedural safeguards and how they can seek assistance in understanding them. Parents must be sent a copy of a detailed description of the safeguards whenever any of the following events occurs: (1) initial referral for evaluation for special education services, (2) parental notification of an IEP meeting, (3) reevaluation of a child, (4) refusal to evaluate, (5) change in identification of disability, (6) initial placement or change in educational placement, and (7) filing of a due process complaint. This notice must be in the native language of the parents (if feasible to do so). IDEA 1997 added several new requirements for both the parents and the schools.

1. Parents must notify the school when they plan to remove their child from the public school and place him or her into a private school at public expense.
2. Parents must notify the SEA or the LEA when they intend to file a request for a due process hearing.

3. States must establish a voluntary mediation process as a way of helping parents resolve disagreements with LEAs
4. Mediation procedures must be in place (OSEP, 1997).

While the 1990 IDEA permitted mediation, the 1997 amendments require states to create mediation processes in which parents and the LEAs can *voluntarily* participate. The mediation process must:

1. Be voluntary on the part of the parties involved, and not be used to deny or delay a parent's right to a formal due process hearing.
2. Be conducted by a qualified and impartial mediator.
3. Be publicly paid for.

The purpose of the mediation procedures are to encourage, whenever possible, the early constructive, and amicable resolution of disagreements and to reduce costly litigation (Senate Committee on Labor and Human Resource, 1997).

How Involved Should Students Be in Their IEP Meetings?
The participants in the IEP meeting include the student's teachers, transition services participants (if the purpose of the meeting is to consider transition services), other individuals who are knowledgeable about the student and his or her needs and qualified in the area of the student's disability, and one or both of the student's parents. The student is required to attend the IEP meeting unless the parents believe that attendance would not be beneficial to the student. Older students in middle and secondary school should be encouraged to participate in their IEP meetings. This is particularly important for students who are developing transition services plans (see Chapter 23 on transition). The IDEA states that if the purpose of the IEP meeting is to consider transition services for a student, the public agency must invite the student and a representative of any other agency that is likely to be responsible for providing or paying for transition services. If the student does not attend, the public agency shall take other steps to ensure that the student's preferences and interests are considered. If the agency invited to send a representative to a meeting does not do so, the public agency shall take other steps to obtain the participation of the other agency in the planning of any transition services.

Toward Self-Determination: Student-Led IEP Meetings.
Traditionally, the IEP process has been controlled by professionals within the school system. However, the 1997 Amendments to IDEA strengthen the role of the student in transition planning (self-determination). The assumption upon which these requirements are based is that students who are engaged in planning for their own futures will become empowered in the process. This means that students will show improved self-reliance, self-esteem, and self-knowledge about their own career interests and strengths, motivation, and knowledge

about postsecondary opportunities. Furthermore, they will feel less passive, more confident in their choices of future goals, and will experience a greater sense of control over their own destination. These feelings of control and confidence lead students to a heightened motivation and excitement about future directions.

There are several key elements to defining student-centered planning. These elements include a combination of (1) an organized and monitored planning process, (2) problem-solving strategies, (3) natural supports, and (4) high quality transition services that are based on the needs and preferences of the student. Student-centered planning requires the following elements:

1. *Group support:* circle of friends, action planning team, personal network.
2. *Unique descriptions:* Who is the individual? What are his or her gifts, talents, strengths, interests, and contributions to family and friends?
3. *Vision:* "great expectations"; visioning questions: what if or why not?
4. *Action:* steps to make vision a reality (connections, risks, surmounting barriers, solving problems, promises by others).
5. *Empowerment:* through the process of supported self-determination.
6. *Transition:* IEP and ITP development, encompassing all of the above (Field & Hoffman, 1998; Forest & Lusthaus, 1990; Mount & Zwernik, 1988; Turnbull & Turnbull, 1992).

There are several strategies for student-centered planning used in schools today. These include the McGill Action Planning System (MAPS), which is designed for students included in the general education classroom. The McGill system bases individual future plans on a student's personal history, dreams, nightmares, and strengths (i.e., gifts, abilities, needs, ideal day, what can be done?). The Gray Action Planning (GAP) constructs student plans through a method that includes the following steps:

- Inviting support
- Creating connections
- Developing a vision for future
- Solving problems
- Celebrating success

Student-centered planning is not currently required under IDEA, but the law does require that students be invited to their IEP and transition planning meetings and be assisted to participate in their own future planning to the extent possible. Parents should be integrally involved in transition planning, along with their children, and learn to support them as they learn to shape their own directions. Such support by parents and other professionals should only be as much as is needed to help the student participate to the extent possible. Teachers and related services personnel all need to be involved in supporting the student in his or her own future planning. Some students, of course, have limitations in this process, but the emphasis on individual transition planning should be on enhancing the capabilities of the students and their contributions to the planning process.

CIRCLE OF COMMITMENT: THE INTERDISCIPLINARY TEAM PLANNING AND COORDINATION FOR INCLUSION. Students with disabilities typically require a variety of related and support services to successfully participate in an inclusive classroom or other least restrictive setting. These services are best coordinated by a single responsible individual who serves as a point of contact for the student, parents, and professionals associated with the student's IEP. While the IDEA 1997 does not require LEAs to use case management procedures in the development of students' IEPs, many local educational agencies have found systematic coordination particularly effective in supporting the inclusion of students. The traditional principles of service coordination found in other settings, such as health care, rehabilitation, and adult mental health and mental retardation services, are now being applied in the delivery of special education services (Friend & Bursuch, 1999; Kochhar & West, 1995; Kochhar, 1987).

Service Coordination and the Student's IEP. While the IEP team is responsible for the planning and monitoring of the IEP, for continuity, some schools have assigned the responsibility for IEP coordination to one single individual in the school. This individual, who might be a social worker, counselor, special educator, or psychologist, serves as the case manager of the IEP process and has primary responsibility for (1) monitoring the student's progress in attaining IEP goals, and (2) ensuring that the student receives the related and supplementary services written into his or her IEP. The service coordinator is attentive to the needs of students with a range of needs in the variety of functional domains (e.g., physical development and health, social functioning, academic progress, behavioral functioning, and vocational functioning). The coordinator works to link educational and related goals and objectives in the IEP, related and support services, school extracurricular experiences, and community-based opportunities for the student. The service coordinator with special education expertise can help the general education classroom teacher to connect instructional and curriculum modifications with IEP goals.

The Basic Functions of Inclusion Coordination. The procedures that many schools have created to coordinate the services required by the IEP and to ensure the implementation of the IEP can be referred to as "inclusion coordination functions" (Kochhar & West, 1995). This section defines the essential elements or functions of inclusion coordination, which are adaptations of traditional service coordination models in human service agencies. Though many researchers have identified different elements of coordination, a synthesis of the litera-

ture reveals agreement on eight basic functions or clusters of activities. These eight functions represent the procedures and activities that schools create to coordinate the needs of students in inclusive environments.

1. Information and referral for classroom placement
2. Review and initial assessment of student needs
3. Assessment and diagnosis of disability and educational needs
4. Planning and development of the individualized education program
5. Coordination and linking of related and support services
6. Monitoring of the individual education program plan and follow-along
7. Inclusion of advocacy and support
8. Evaluation of the inclusion program and follow-up of the student (Kochhar, 1987, 1995).

Studies of service coordination show great variety in the types of activities that are included in each of the eight functions. The following definitions have been synthesized from the experiences of many coordination programs in operation in human services today (Kochhar, 1987, 1995). These functions are being transferred for use in schools for purposes of coordinating support services to students who need special supports to succeed in the home school.

FUNCTION 1: Information and Referral for Classroom Placement. Procedures for providing information and placement referrals vary widely among schools. The information-and-referral function is defined in two ways:

- Narrowly, as the giving of information to teachers receiving students into inclusive classrooms,
- Broadly, to include activities by inclusion planning teams or principals gathering information about general changes in placement policies, extensive outreach activities, parent orientation, and information to identify groups of students who might be appropriate for placement into inclusive classrooms or placement from segregated schools to home schools.

When students with severe disabilities and complex needs are considered for placement into inclusive settings, assertive and creative attempts at outreach to families are necessary. Individual information and referral includes activities such as

- Identifying and conducting outreach to students' families.
- Providing advance information to teachers about students who may be identified as ready to transition into their classrooms.
- Disseminating information to the community about inclusion goals, philosophies, and benefits.
- Developing a single contact person for teachers and families to discuss and problem-solve issues for students being transferred into inclusive settings or attempting to adjust.
- Managing classroom placement referrals and follow-ups.

- Decreasing the amount of time between the family's initial contact for information or assistance and the coordinator or teacher's response.
- Providing information to teachers about strategies and methods of accommodating students with disabilities.

Many schools are working toward improved identification and referral procedures for students who are not currently placed into more inclusive settings but should be. When families learn about inclusion efforts and goals through an organized and coordinated information and referral strategy, they are more likely to perceive the school as accessible, responsive, and supportive.

FUNCTION 2: Review and Initial Assessment of Student Needs. Initial review and assessment, at the *individual student level,* involve review procedures for determining individual appropriateness for placement into inclusive classrooms, as well as anticipating student needs for related and supportive services long before the students are placed into the classroom. Review and initial assessment activities may include

- Maintaining reliable data on the progress of students in inclusive classrooms.
- Developing appropriateness criteria for placement into inclusive settings.
- Ensuring that support services are accessible to students in classroom, library, laboratory, and other settings before placing students into the school or classroom.
- Facilitating interim placements for students transitioning in from other schools or agencies.
- Obtaining and documenting the consent of the student and family for a change in educational placement.
- Developing and maintaining student records.
- Understanding the needs of families and communicating with them about initial eligibility evaluation and the transition into the general education classroom.

At the *administrative level,* initial review and assessment means developing schoolwide data collection and placement determination processes. Through data collection, schools can compare information about groups of children and youth served in different inclusion options and can help each other anticipate classroom needs. Schools can share enrollment and placement information to help match individuals with classroom environments, services, personnel, and to project future service and budget needs. Finally, they can create quality criteria for inclusive classrooms.

FUNCTION 3: Diagnosis and Evaluation of Disability and Educational Needs. Evaluation is a process by which information is collected and analyzed in a systematic, student-centered, and collaborative way among educational personnel, support service personnel, parents, and students in order to answer the following key questions:

- What is the current functioning of the student in the range of functional domains (e.g., social, intellectual,

physical, vocational, behavioral), and what are the student's strengths and needs?
- What features of the student's environment or classroom milieu support or inhibit improved functioning?
- Based on evaluation data on the student's disabilities, what goals and objectives for improved functioning in the range of domains should be identified and included in the IEP, and what are the priorities?
- What resources and support services are necessary to accomplish these goals and objectives in the classroom and in nonacademic activities outside the classroom?
- What procedures and schedule will be utilized for monitoring progress toward these goals and objectives both in and outside the classroom?
- What outcome criteria will be used to evaluate results of the inclusive placement? (Adapted from Hare & Clark, 1991)

The inclusion coordinator facilitates and supports the process of eligibility determination and evaluation of educational needs.

FUNCTION 4: Planning and Development of the IEP. Facilitating the development of the IEP is an essential function of the inclusion coordinator. Written plans are essential for students and families in inclusive classrooms because they represent the service "agreement," or contract between the student and the instructional and related service personnel. The IEP documents the planned activities and responsibilities of the student, the teachers, related and support service personnel, family members and others concerned with the student's development. It also indicates the criteria by which all parties will determine if the student's educational and related goals have been achieved and if the required support services have been provided. The IEP team is made up of a variety of professionals who are responsible for providing the specialized educational services and support services the student may need. The IEP team also includes the student and his or her family. The IEP team initially identifies students, on a case by case basis who are ready for appropriate placement into an inclusive setting. However, in districts where inclusion is supported and encouraged, it is easier for an IEP team to make a recommendation for placement into a general education classroom. The IEP coordinator can facilitate the acquisition of services the student may need from outside agencies and provide coordination of such services. Facilitation of the IEP by the inclusion coordinator includes activities such as the following:

- Scheduling and leading the interdisciplinary team in educational planning.
- Identifying agencies and individuals who can provide support services.
- Including in the IEP the necessary linking or transition services as the individual moves from one school or setting to another, or from one level to another (e.g., middle school to high school).

- Providing information to students and families about the IEP process and their roles and responsibilities;
- Ensuring active student and family participation and decision making in the IEP planning and review.
- Facilitating the transfers of IEPs to other LEAs, state agencies, or private institutions when students are placed outside the school.

Inclusion coordination at the *student level* results in effective implementation of the IEP process. Inclusion coordination at the *team or school level* results in the development of an *inclusion coordination agreement, or interagency agreement,* that links the school with agencies that can provide related services for students.

FUNCTION 5: Coordination and Linking of Support Services.

Service linking means identifying appropriate related and support service providers who can provide the services required by the IEP. For example, for families of students with emotional disabilities, it may mean providing a central contact person in the school to help the family locate needed community services (e.g., health services, mental health services, counseling, assistive devices, or evaluation and diagnostic services). For students with speech and hearing problems, it may mean providing information and linking the family with speech and hearing evaluation services, clinics, and specialists. For secondary youth preparing for postsecondary placement, it may mean providing additional linking services to vocational technical schools and community colleges. Such linking activities at the *individual student level* may include

- Establishing a school coordinator or contact for each individual or family.
- Identifying and contacting needed services within the school district or outside, if appropriate.
- Arranging school contacts or visits for the student and family.
- Arranging special support services for students who are transferring from more restrictive settings to inclusive settings, or from segregated to inclusive schools. This many mean arranging visits to the school and classroom before the transfer occurs, providing extra counseling or guidance during the transfer or transition, providing information about the new environment and expectations, and arranging meetings with new teachers.
- Tracking and documenting changes in student placements or in movement between schools or classrooms.
- Documenting support services used by students and families.
- Documenting referrals to other related agencies for assessments or additional services.

Inclusion Coordination at the Administrative Level. At the *administrative level,* linking activities include coordination among schools and community agencies for sharing resources for the provision of related and supplementary services. Shared resources include financial, personnel, and material resources that belong to the schools and cooperating agencies, but that could be dedicated to inclusion activities defined by an agreement between the school and the agency. Interagency linking activities can help prevent the duplication of services between schools and community agencies, thus resulting in cost savings and system efficiency. Linking functions also join professionals from different fields and disciplines to share in common problem solving, which can expand capacity to provide needed services and improve their quality. Inclusion coordination activities should be included in a school's School Improvement Plan.

The Interagency Agreement Formalizes the Linking Function. The interagency agreement is a written collaboration with an agency that provides related services to students with disabilities in the school. Such agencies may include vocational rehabilitation services, mental health or developmental disability services, social services, juvenile services, public health services, and employment services. The purpose of these agreements is to establish joint responsibility for providing necessary support services to students with disabilities, to secure commitments for services, and to establish ongoing collaboration and communication about present and future needs for services.

Interagency agreements generally include a mission statement, coordination goals and objectives, and a timetable for activities. The mission statement describes the *broad purpose* of the agreement and the broad areas of joint responsibility of professionals who will be involved. It is a statement of what the agencies and school units will and will not provide. An inclusion mission statement may include one or more of the following parts:

1. *A statement of the context or history of the agreement,* or a brief introductory paragraph that defines how the cooperative arrangement was established or how it expands what has been in place before.
2. *The authority for the cooperative relationships,* which describes the legal or policy basis for the agreement and typically lists the local, state, and federal laws, statutes, or regulations that may give authority to or mandate this inclusion initiative and agreement.
3. *A general statement of purpose of the agreement and expected outcomes* offers a rationale for entering into the inclusion coordination agreement and broadly defines the benefits and outcomes that the inclusion team hopes to achieve.
4. *The broad goal or outline* of what the agreement provides lists the agreement's specific goals and objectives.

The interagency service coordination agreement defines the scope of activities, responsibilities and contributions of each team member or agency, and the expected outcomes for each participating partner. Interagency agreements should address four essential features related to the linking and coordination of school-linked services for students with disabilities:

1. Identify resources available to support the inclusion initiative and expand related service availability to students.
2. Identify activities of the interagency coordination team to be accomplished within a year.
3. Identify expected results of the interagency agreement, in terms of its impacts and benefits for students.
4. Establish timetables for the interagency initiative.

The statement of goals and shared activities of first-time interagency agreements provide only a blueprint for defining new relationships and procedures. Like the student's IEP, these agreements for the school as a whole must be reviewed and modified annually or periodically. The inclusion coordinator can greatly facilitate the development and implementation of interagency agreements.

FUNCTION 6: IEP Monitoring and Follow-Along. IEP monitoring and follow-along are essential functions of inclusion coordination. The purpose of IEP monitoring at the *student level* is (1) to evaluate the student's progress in achieving the goals and objectives included in the IEP and (2) to assure that the student is receiving services and accommodations required by the plan and which are appropriate to enabling the student to benefit from the educational program in the general classroom. This is usually the role of the teacher or teacher team.

Monitoring requires that the teachers maintain ongoing contact with the students in the inclusive classroom and with the professionals providing related services (Friend & Bursuch, 1999; McCoy, 1995; Levine & Fleming, 1986). Monitoring of the IEP also enables the teacher to observe and gain direct knowledge of the types and quality of the support services received by the student. Another important aspect of monitoring is that it allows the student to evaluate the services he or she is receiving and allows the teacher to understand those services from the student's perspective. *Monitoring* activities may include:

- Documenting and maintaining a chronological record of support services received by each student.
- Documenting student progress in academic achievement, vocational skills development, social and family relationships, or independent living skills.
- Documenting student achievement of educational goals included in the IEP and modifications of the plan.
- Documenting services actually received, those not received, and reasons why services were not received.
- Documenting and communicating gaps in services for the student and efforts to locate services outside the school.
- Documenting barriers to services for the student.
- Maintaining continuity in communication among service providers and the coordination of support services throughout the year.
- Facilitating the reporting of progress to parents through the general progress-reporting procedures of the school, such as report cards and letters.

Monitoring at the Administrative Level. Service monitoring at the *administrative level* means observing the educational progress of students and monitoring the delivery of support services for inclusive classrooms as a whole. It is usually the role of the school's inclusion coordinator or principal. It means ensuring that such services are

1. Being provided according to the intended schedules.
2. Reaching the students they were intended to reach.
3. Being provided in a manner that complies with established local, state, and national laws, regulations, guidelines, standards, and ethics.
4. Being provided with an acceptable level of quality.

Examples of monitoring activities at the *administrative level* include

- Documenting progress and performance of collaborating personnel and school units, as well as the achievement of goals, objectives, and timetables of the inclusion team.
- Collecting information from students and parents about how they perceive the quality, appropriateness, and accessibility of educational and support services in their new classrooms.
- Examining and improving inclusive policies related to placement criteria, assessment procedures, discipline procedures, and policies governing related services for benefiting and participating in inclusive classrooms and nonclassroom activities.
- Conducting projections of needs for related services, needs for personnel, and additional spaces in inclusive classrooms.

The monitoring function can offer valuable information about the quality and effectiveness of inclusion practices in a school.

Follow-along. Follow-along activities are an important part of the monitoring function. In some schools where case loads of students with disabilities are high, the monitoring function is often a paper tracking activity. In other schools, monitoring includes ongoing and close contacts with the student and family to provide direct interpersonal support throughout the year. The follow-along function includes those activities by the teacher or coordinator to provide encouragement, to foster relationships of trust with the student, to maintain close contact and communication with the family, and to help troubleshoot problems before they become major concerns. Examples of follow-along activities include

- Home visits to families with students with special needs.
- Visits to youth in their school or work-based programs.
- Visits with students in their classrooms or in nonclassroom-based activities.
- Informal counseling with students or families.
- Supportive counseling with families and siblings.
- Providing for regular face-to-face contact with a school counselor or coordinator.
- Addressing family involvement and communication needs.
- Providing behavioral (or other) crisis intervention.

The follow-along function represents the personal support component of inclusion coordination and is very important for increasing the retention of students placed into inclusive classrooms (i.e., preventing dropout).

FUNCTION 7: Advocacy for Inclusion. Definitions of student advocacy are not always clear and are often circular (e.g., "advocacy is any attempt to advocate for services"). Advocacy is a very broad term that has evolved over the past few decades to mean different things to professionals in different fields, but it is a particularly important function of inclusion coordination. This discussion of advocacy can be divided into two components: *(1) advocacy for the individual student* and *(2) advocacy for a schoolwide inclusion initiative.*

Advocacy at the Student Level. Advocacy for an individual student can mean promoting the placement of that student into a more inclusive setting, (acting on the student's behalf) or it can mean assisting the student to *advocate on his or her own behalf* (self-advocacy) for an inclusive placement or for needed supportive services. Student advocacy promotes informed decision making by both students and their families.

These advocacy activities, rather than being two separate types of activities, should actually be viewed as two aspects of a *continuum* (see Table 20-1). Inclusive teachers continually strive to maximize the extent to which students and families are empowered and en-

abled to make decisions for management of their educational experiences and personal affairs in as independent and self-sufficient a manner as possible.

Advocacy at the School Level. School-level advocacy means advocating on behalf of whole groups of students. Examples of school-level advocacy activities include

- Developing a schoolwide understanding of the needs of groups of students with special needs.
- Addressing multicultural and multilingual issues with teachers and related service personnel to negotiate the development of special supports or accommodations.
- Identifying and targeting students with the greatest need for inclusive programs and support services.
- Communicating service barriers and service gaps to principals and other decision makers.
- Communicating and protecting human rights and due process procedures for groups of students.
- Promoting an emphasis on self-determination and informed decision making for students and their families.
- Linking students with advocacy organizations and working with local agencies to help them meet new inclusion goals and requirements.
- Providing attitudinal leadership to improve school and community attitudes that are supportive of inclusive classrooms.
- Working to increase supports during transitions between schools, programs, or classrooms.
- Reinforcing the family and informal support network.

TABLE 20-1. Student Advocacy Activities: A Continuum

Advocacy on Behalf of a Student	Assisting in Student Self-Advocacy
• Assisting the individual in receiving all the benefits to which he or she is entitled.	• Assisting the individual in requesting information about the variety of benefits to which he or she is entitled, and in making decisions about which to apply for.
• Intervening to ensure that individual human rights and due process procedures are protected.	• Providing information about human rights and due process procedures to both the individual and family, for their own self-advocacy.
• Helping the individual gain access to a service from which he or she has traditionally been excluded.	• Offering strategies to help the individual independently gain access to a service from which he or she has been excluded.
• Directly intervening on behalf of the individual to negotiate admission to a program.	• Offering strategies, information, or coaching that will help the individual negotiate admission to a program.
• Negotiating with a service agency to provide supports services or accommodations that will enable an individual to participate in a service.	• Offering strategies, information, or coaching to enable the individual to negotiate with a service agency for special supports services or accommodations that will make it possible to participate in a service.
• Educating the family, to allay fears and encourage cooperation and participation.	• Offering strategies, information, or coaching to help the individual negotiate with the family to support participation in a service or program, or to agree to enroll as a family in a needed service.
• Helping an agency understand the special language or cultural conditions and barriers that prevent an individual's enrollment and participation in a service and negotiating special supports for such an individual.	• Offering strategies, information, or coaching to help the individual explain the special language or cultural conditions or barriers that prevent enrollment or make it difficult to participate in a service or program.
• Intervening with a potential employer to provide information about an individual and explaining his or her skill, training, and supervision needs.	• Providing coaching to help the potential employee describe his or her own strengths and weaknesses, relevant job skills, and training needs.

Reducing Conflicts of Interest. As schools respond to new requirements for inclusion, advocacy can help build a shared capacity to meet the multiple needs of students and their families. Advocacy activities can help stimulate creative approaches to reducing resistance and barriers to inclusion and collaboration. In addition, *advocacy can lead to reduced conflicts of interest for the teacher, an issue raised by many teachers in inclusive classrooms.* For example, teachers employed by large school systems which contract for related support services are often caught between the student and the administration which controls funding to all parts of the system. The independence and authority of the teachers to truly advocate on behalf of the students can sometimes be compromised by forces within the school. If this occurs, advocacy becomes an ideal that is written into every mission statement, but is seldom actually realized. *When teachers and related service personnel set goals for the advocacy function, their emphasis on the benefits and outcomes for the student can help empower them and thereby focus the advocacy effort, bringing it closer to students and their individual needs.*

FUNCTION 8: Evaluation of Inclusion and Student Follow-Up. Service evaluation and follow-up are essential to effective inclusion coordination. Although evaluation may be a *final step* in assessing the value and quality of inclusive services to students, it is the *first step* in their improvement. It may be helpful to view the evaluation process as a continuous spiral that gradually lifts the inclusion initiative continuously upward toward greater improvements.

WHY IS INCLUSION COORDINATION IMPORTANT? Resources to plan, develop, implement, evaluate, and sustain inclusion practices are usually difficult to obtain. *When educational and human services budgets are being reduced, coordination activities become carefully scrutinized and may be the first activities to be eliminated.* In many states and localities today, resources for related services, service coordination activities, and state and local interagency cooperative team activities are falling under the budget scythe. Sound and comprehensive evaluation and needs assessments can prevent this from happening. Decision makers will ask for sound rationale for inclusion coordination activities and inclusion coordinator roles, especially to justify additional personnel positions. The inclusion planner needs to be able to *show a clear relationship between the role of the inclusion coordinator and the requirements of the school to ensure IEP implementation and sound inclusion practices that are consistent with IDEA.* Inclusion coordinators must help administrators understand how the service-coordination functions directly address the needs of students and their families and help facilitate efficient and effective use of resources.

CHAPTER 21

What Is an Appropriate Class Size for Inclusion and Classroom Management?

CLASS SIZE BECOMES A FOCUS FOR THE NATION. Class size issues are important for all classrooms in all school districts, yet in the past they were rarely discussed because of their implications for educational funding in schools. More recently, because of the national emphasis on improving education for all students, classroom size has become a central focus in school districts around the nation (Hardman, Drew & Egan, 1999; Turnbull, Turnbull, Shank & Leal, 1995). For inclusive classrooms it is particularly important as teachers are called on to attend to the needs of a very diverse group of students with a range of challenges. The teacher is expected and required to make accommodations and produce reasonable outcomes in the classroom, while often facing substance abuse, aggressive and violent behavior, disrespect for property, school code violations, and nutrition and health problems among students. The teacher is also expected not only to design curriculum and utilize technology in the classroom, but also form cooperative learning groups, and provide alternative assessments and interdisciplinary instruction.

CLASS SIZE AND SUCCESSFUL INCLUSION. Few resources on inclusion address specific issues of class size. When Sailor (1991) outlined six components for inclusion, he suggested that schools work to achieve a "natural proportion" of students with disabilities in schools and classrooms. In other words, according to Sailor, one of the characteristics of an effective inclusive school is that the population of students with and without disabilities reflects the population of the community as a whole. He also applied this natural proportion to classroom placements. Therefore, if 10 percent of the total population of students in a community have disabilities, then the percentage of students with disabilities among the popula-

tion of students in each inclusive classroom within the community schools should be no more that 10 percent (or 2 to 3 in a classroom of 25 to 30). Also, rather than their being concentrated in a few selected classrooms, students with disabilities should be distributed as equitably as possible among all educators. This equalizes the responsibility within the school and allows greater opportunities for social interaction between students with and without disabilities (Turnbull, 1995).

National Education Association Recommendations. In 1994, the National Education Association (NEA) recommended a much higher placement proportion than Sailor suggested. NEA reported recommendations from teachers who conducted research on the inclusion of students with disabilities (Dalheim, 1994). In general these teachers recommended that class size should not exceed 28 students, the number of boys and girls being roughly equal. In addition, these teachers recommended that for students with learning disabilities, the "proportion of students with disabilities should not exceed one quarter, or 25 percent, of the class. The remaining three quarters should be a heterogeneous group of both talented and general education students" (NEA, 1994, p. 21). They also recommended that a balance between boys and girls improves the experience for all students.

Considerations in Determining Ratio of Students with Disabilities to Nondisabled Students. To determine acceptable classroom ratios of students with disabilities to nondisabled students, school administrators should consider several factors related to students and classroom environments:

- Severity of the disabilities of all students identified for placement in a specific classroom.

- Funds available for classroom restructuring and curriculum and instructional adaptation.
- Resources and support services available to the classroom.
- Teacher access to support services in the school and community.

Severity of Disability. School administrators must be realistic about learning environments for all students, including those with disabilities. The severity of the disability must be considered in determining the ratio of students with disabilities to nondisabled in a classroom. Students with more severe disabilities will require additional supports, planning time, intervention, and physical accommodations.

Funds and Resources Available for the Classroom Restructuring. Special education funds are structured to follow the student into the classroom. This means that the special education dollars provided to the state and local educational agency are used to supplement the per-pupil amount spent in the district. By law, funds must be made available to schools and teachers to supplement the per-pupil expenditures, including these for students in the general education setting. These funds are to be used and should be accessible to provide additional resources in the classroom as needed. In some cases, additional funds may be needed for specific equipment, resources, or instructional supports. Ongoing communication between the IEP team, classroom teachers, and administrators about resources needed in the classroom is essential for successful inclusion.

Resources and Support Services. The availability of supplementary related services, equipment, and technology is an important consideration in determining appropriate placement of students with disabilities in general education classrooms. The teacher has a right to be informed in advance about the placement of a student with a disability into the general education classroom. Adequate advanced notice enables teachers to plan for physical, curriculum, and instructional modifications. Teachers also have a right to know the nature of the new student's disability and if the student has a physical, medical, emotional or behavioral problem that might result in the need to make special accommodations or may require emergency response. The IDEA law promotes, within reasonable limits, the inclusion into the regular classroom of children with chronic health impairments and those dependent on medical technology. An unreasonable situation is one in which no classroom aide is available and the teacher is required to perform physical assistance activities for students with disabilities, at the expense of classroom instruction and management for all students. Teachers should have in writing for the classroom (and written into the IEP) specific expectations for physical assistance, assistance of an aide, or special procedures that may be required in the classroom.

Teacher Access to Support Services. Teachers expect technical assistance and support services in order to accommodate students with disabilities. *The teacher team has the right to expect that information about the student will be available and that they will be able to access the range of needed student support services in general education classrooms, particularly those that are written into the student's IEP.* These services should include the following:

- Guidance and counseling.
- Consultation with the school psychologist or social worker.
- Collaboration and support from teachers who coordinate peer-mediation and conflict-resolution services (these teachers often have special knowledge and background and could get involved in helping promote positive peer relationships).
- Health services or consultation with the school nurse.
- Consultation with special education teachers and specialists for better understanding of the implications of the disability for both student learning and for teaching modifications.
- Consultation with vocational teachers and career counselors to learn about how to make the academic curriculum relevant for student career interests and preferences.
- Access to transition services and community-based job training and placement opportunities for youth.
- Assistance in promoting the student's participation in nonacademic and extracurricular opportunities and activities involving technology.
- Assistance and consultation for making accommodations in such extracurricular activities.
- Adaptations to equipment that may be necessary for use of the technology and for participation in student group activities which rely upon the use of computers or other technology.

CLASS SIZE, CLASSROOM MANAGEMENT, AND DISCIPLINE. A reasonable ratio of students with disabilities to nondisabled students is important to ensure that all students receive the time and attention they need in the classroom, although such ratios should not be rigidly adhered to without some room for flexibility. Appropriate class size is also important to ensure adequate classroom control, so that students who are at risk for behavioral incidents (with or without disabilities) can be given the appropriate attention and support. Students with disabilities who are new to the general education classroom often need additional supports and the understanding of their teachers and peers to help them adjust to new demands and expectations. Often for these students, the general education classroom is larger, more stimulating, and more challenging than their previous smaller special education classrooms. Time and patience in allowing students to adjust are a major requirement for teachers in inclusive classrooms and for students' parents.

The goal of teachers and parents is to prevent formal disciplinary actions by identifying potential signs of adjustment problems and providing appropriate and timely interventions. Some students may have difficulty adjusting academically or socially and may require an adjustment in the kinds of in-class accommodations or supports they are receiving. Or they may need counseling or a behavioral intervention plan as part of their IEP. An intervention plan is essential for students who show signs of adjustment problems that could potentially lead to actual violations of class or school rules and codes of conduct and trigger a disciplinary action. Such signs include repeated failure to turn in homework; disruptive behavior such as agitation and inability to remain in one's seat; physical or verbal aggressiveness with peers during group learning activities; use of abusive language; defiance or refusal to respond to teacher instructions or requests; wandering the halls during class periods; and breaking classroom equipment or defacing materials or books. These behaviors cannot be ignored.

Teachers should request consultation from special educators to learn how to recognize the signs of adjustment problems and implement behavior management techniques in the classroom. Teachers also need to know about the changes in discipline requirements for students with disabilities under IDEA 1997. The manner in which school personnel respond when there are clear signs of student adjustment problems is very important information in a formal hearing to determine disciplinary action or expulsion. A pattern of failure to respond to students' adjustment problems in the general education classroom has been viewed as neglect in previous court cases involving discipline of students with disabilities

(*Stuart v. Nappi,* 1978; OSEP, 1997). The following section describes these changes in discipline provisions.

NEW DISCIPLINE REQUIREMENTS UNDER IDEA 1997. New discipline requirements and guidance have been added to the 1997 IDEA. These are very complicated requirements that have evolved over the past decades in response to litigation in the courts, from U.S. Office of Special Education Memoranda, and the U.S. Office of Civil Rights (OSEP, 1997). The U.S. Department of Education has received numerous requests for guidance concerning the discipline provisions of IDEA 1997. The IDEA statute contains four basic themes on discipline:

1. All students, including those with disabilities, deserve safe, well-disciplined schools and orderly learning environments.
2. Teachers and school administrators should have the tools they need to assist them in preventing misconduct and discipline problems and to address these problems, if they arise.
3. There must be a balanced approach to disciplining children with disabilities that reflects the need for orderly and safe schools and the need to protect the rights of children with disabilities to a free appropriate public education.
4. Appropriately developed IEPs with well developed behavioral intervention strategies decrease school discipline problems. (OSEP Memorandum, September, 7, 1997)

IDEA 1997 incorporates several precedents set in the courts regarding discipline and students with disabilities. It brings together for the first time the rules that ap-

Effective inclusive classes are characterized by the shared responsibility between the general education and special education teacher-consultant team.

ply to students with disabilities, clarifies the roles and obligations to provide free, appropriate public education for students who are under disciplinary action, and clarifies procedures that involve the relationship between the student's misconduct and the disability. The law includes the regular education teachers in the child's IEP meeting and gives the teacher an opportunity to better understand that student's needs, thus decreasing the likelihood of disciplinary problems. It allows school personnel to move a student with a disability to an interim alternative educational setting for up to 45 days if that student violates certain school policies related to weapons and illegal substances.

The Stay-Put Requirement. One of the central provisions in the special education law is known as the *stay-put provision*. This provision was established in 1975 within P.L. 94-142, to protect students from being removed from their current placements to interim placements when a due process hearing or complaint process was pending. The stay-put provision required that the student remain in the current placement until the hearing was completed. The 1997 IDEA continued this provision, with some exceptions. One of the most complex issues debated in Congress during the reauthorization of IDEA was the stay-put provision and the discipline of students with disabilities. How could the rights and procedural safeguards available to students with disabilities be balanced with the needs of school systems to maintain safe environments for all students? Discussions related to the stay-put provision included the following:

1. What if maintaining a student in a placement during a hearing may result in self-injury or injury to other students?
2. How should behavior problems be addressed?
3. Since suspension or expulsion is essentially a "change in placement," can a student be subject to this if the stay-put provision is in effect (OSEP, 1997)?
4. How many times can a student be suspended or expelled before it is considered a change in placement?

The boundaries of the stay-put provision have been discussed, debated, and challenged through the courts by students, parents, and LEAs. Several key court cases over the past two decades represent instances in which behavior issues and disciplinary procedures have met head on with the provisions of P.L. 94-142. These have resulted in a few important findings and precedents set by various courts, including the Supreme Court:

1. If the school fails to provide a student with appropriate educational services, then it is inappropriate for the school to resort to the use of disciplinary measures with the student (*Stuart v. Nappi,* 1978).
2. Expulsion of 10 days or more is considered a "change in placement" which triggers the procedural safeguards of the act (*Stuart v. Nappi,* 1978).

3. The interdisciplinary team would be convened to consider alternative placement and the student's individual needs.
4. A student's misconduct needs to be examined for its potential relationship to the disability, and such a connection must be determined by a trained and knowledgeable group of people (*S-1 v. Turlington,* 1981).
5. Expulsion is a proper disciplinary tool under IDEA and Section 504, but a complete discontinuation of educational services is not.
6. While a student's placement may not be changed during a complaint proceeding, the school can still use normal procedures for dealing with students who are endangering themselves or others (e.g., time-outs, detention, or restrictions of privileges) (*Honig v. Doe,* 1988). If a student poses an immediate threat to the safety of others, school officials may temporarily suspend the student for up to 10 school days.
7. Changes in a student's placement cannot be made without the consent of the parents. The stay-put provision, sustained by the courts in the cases referred to above, sought to prevent schools from permanently excluding students with disabilities through use of suspensions and expulsions.

Further Requirements. The 1997 IDEA adds other new requirements that further guide the discipline of students who (1) violate school rules or codes of conduct; (2) carry weapons to school; (3) possess, use, or sell illegal drugs while at school; or who (4) are likely to injure themselves or others if left in their current educational placement. A weapon is defined as a "device, instrument, or substance that is used for, or can cause death or serious bodily injury" (Committee on Labor and Human Resources, 1997). Excluded from this definition are pocket knives with a blade of less than 2-1/2 inches in length. Following are nine sections that describe these new discipline provisions.

1. Authority of School Personnel. School personnel may apply the same discipline procedures to students with disabilities as to others who commit very serious offenses. School personnel may order either a change in a student's placement to an appropriate interim alternative educational setting or a suspension, for no more than 10 days (i.e., to the same extent such alternatives would be applied to children without disabilities). If the violation of school policy or the behavior is extremely serious (e.g., the student carries a weapon to school, possesses or uses illegal drugs at school), then the student's placement may be changed to an appropriate interim alternative educational setting for the same amount of time that a child without a disability would be disciplined, but for no more than 45 days. Either before, or no later than 10 days after taking a disciplinary action, the school must convene an IEP meeting to develop an assessment plan to address the behavior. If it has not already done so before the suspension, then the IEP team must conduct a functional behavioral assessment and put a behavioral intervention plan in place. If the student already has a behavioral intervention plan, then the IEP team must review that plan and make modifications to it as necessary to address the behavior (IDEA, 1997).

2. The Hearing Officer's Role and Authority. A due process hearing must be conducted by an impartial hearing officer who is not employed by the public agency (Underwood & Mead, 1995). Hearing officers may be attorneys, certified special education teachers, or others who have completed state training. The hearing officer hears the case, considers the evidence, reaches a decision and puts that decision in writing within 45 days of the request for the hearing. IDEA 1997 expands the authority of hearing officers to place students into appropriate interim alternative educational settings in some circumstances. A hearing officer may order a change in the placement of a student for no more than 45 days if the officer

a. Determines that the school or LEA can show by "substantial evidence" (or, beyond a preponderance of evidence) that maintaining the student in his or her current placement is likely to result in injury to the student or to others.
b. Considers the appropriateness of the student's current placement.
c. Determines whether the school or LEA have made reasonable efforts to minimize the risk of harm in the student's current placement (including the use of supplementary aids and services).
d. Determines that the interim alternative educational setting meets the requirements of providing "appropriate educational services" to the student.

Determining the "Appropriate Interim Alternative Educational Setting." The alternative setting must be determined by the IEP team and must be a setting that enables the student to (a) continue to participate in the general curriculum; (b) continue to receive those services and modifications (including those described in the current IEP) that will enable him or her to meet the goals set out in that IEP; and (c) include services and modifications designed to address the behavior that resulted in change of placement.

3. Manifest Determination Review. The IEP team is required to review the connection between the student's disability and the misconduct that resulted in suspension or change of placement. A *manifest determination review* is conducted to find out to what extent the behavior is a manifestation of the disability. If a disciplinary action is decided on which would involve a change in placement of a student for more than 10 days, then the parents must be notified on the same day that decision is made and provided information about procedural safeguards that apply. Then immediately, if possible, but no later that within 10 school days, a manifest determination review must be conducted to examine the relationship between the student's disability and the behavior or

actions subject to disciplinary action. The IEP team may find that the behavior of the student was not a manifestation of the disability only if the team

a. First considers all relevant information that could be pertinent to their review, including evaluation and diagnostic results, information supplied by parents, observations of the student and study of the student's IEP and placement.
b. Determines that the student's IEP, placement, special education and supplementary services were all appropriate and consistent with the IEP and placement.
c. Determines that the disability did not impair the student's ability to understand the impact and consequences of the behavior subject to disciplinary action.
d. Determines that the disability did not impair the student's ability to control the behavior subject to disciplinary action.

4. IEP Team Determination That the Behavior Was Not a Manifestation of Disability. If the IEP team finds that the misconduct was not a manifestation of the student's disability, then the relevant disciplinary procedures and consequences that apply to all students will also apply to the student with a disability. The exception to this is that for a student with a disability, schools are required to continue to provide a free, appropriate public education to students who have been suspended or expelled from school.

5. Parent Appeal. If an IEP team determines that a student's behavior is not a manifestation of his or her disability, then the parents have a right to disagree and to request a hearing on the matter. The state or local educational agency shall arrange for an expedited hearing, and the hearing officer must determine whether the school or LEA has demonstrated that the student's behavior was not a manifestation of the disability.

6. Placement During Appeals for Disciplinary Action. This part of the law provides *an exception to the stay put provision of IDEA 1990,* and it is one of the most complicated to understand. When there is an appeal of an IEP team's decision regarding disciplinary action, change in placement, or manifest determination, two conditions apply.

a. The student must remain in the interim alternative educational setting pending the decision of the hearing officer or until the 45 days expire (45 days refers to the maximum amount of time that a child without a disability would be subject to disciplinary removal).
b. If the 45 days expires and the due process hearing is still pending, then the student must return to the general education classroom (or current placement before removal to the interim placement) even if school personnel were proposing to change the student's placement at the end of the 45 days.

An exception to item b. may apply if school personnel maintain that it is dangerous for the student to be in the general education classroom (or original placement) while the hearing is pending. School personnel may then request an expedited hearing.

7. *Protection for Students Not Yet Eligible for Special Education and Related Services.* In many cases students who have violated school rules or codes of conduct may not yet have been found eligible for special education. In such cases, the student could be protected under IDEA 1997 if the school or local educational agency had knowledge prior to the behavior violation that the student was a child with a disability. Whether the LEA had knowledge of the disability before the violation is based on any of the following conditions:

a. A parent has expressed concern in writing to school personnel that the child is in need of special education and related services.
b. The behavior or performance of the student demonstrates the need for such services.
c. The parent has requested an evaluation of the student.
d. The teachers of the students (or other personnel of the LEA) have expressed to the director of special education concern about the behavior or performance of the student.

An expedited evaluation may be made during the time period in which the student is subject to disciplinary action, and if a student is found to have a disability, then the LEA must provide special education and related services.

8. *Referral to and Action by Law Enforcement and Judicial Authorities.* According to IDEA 1997, LEAs are not prohibited from reporting a crime committed by a student with a disability, nor are law enforcement authorities prohibited from exercising their responsibilities. The agency reporting a crime, however, must ensure that copies of the special education and disciplinary records are provided to the appropriate authorities for their consideration.

9. *Attorneys' Fees.* Attorneys' fees are appropriate during a formal due process hearing; however, the IDEA 1997 prohibits attorneys' fees and related costs for *certain services,* such as

a. An IEP meeting, except if it is ordered by an administrative proceeding or judicial action.
b. At the discretion of the state, for a mediation that is conducted before a formal complaint is filed.

The Senate Committee on Labor and Human Resources (1997) commented in its report to Congress that the IEP process should be devoted to determining the needs of a student and planning for the student's education with parents and school personnel. Attorneys' fees can be reduced in cases in which the court finds any of the following: (1) the parent causes unreasonable delays in the final resolution of the due process proceedings; (2) the attorneys' fees exceed the prevailing hourly rates for similar services; (3) the time and legal services were exces-

sive; and (4) the attorney representing the parent did not provide the school district the appropriate information in the due process complaint (OSEP, 1997).

STRATEGIES FOR MANAGING LARGE INCLUSIVE CLASSROOMS. Most students with disabilities being placed into general education classes are coming from smaller special education classrooms. The experience of the large, general education classroom is often a major adjustment for these students. It is also an adjustment for the teacher, who now has an additional challenge in time and classroom management, to ensure that the students with special needs receive the time and attention they need. The classroom environment is characterized by multiple events occurring at the same time, rapid pace of activities, and unpredictability (Waldron, 1996). The specific ratio of students with disabilities to nondisabled students, however, is an equally important factor in the classroom environment as are teacher and peer acceptance, administrative support, support services, instructional aids, and planning time.

Teachers have found several strategies to be successful in managing large classrooms that include students with disabilities (NEA, 1994; Putnam, 1993; Waldron, 1996). These strategies include the following:

1. Team teaching in which teachers share their ideas, knowledge and techniques.
2. Grouping students into "learning teams" including students with disabilities (team sizes are determined by the nature of the activity, with teams of two, three, or four the most commonly used).
3. Using alternative assessment tools to evaluate the achievement of the students in the groups (project evaluations, student exhibitions, performance demonstrations, science fairs, and other performance-based assessments).
4. Providing special reminders to students or calling them at home to remind them to complete their homework.
5. Checking notebooks regularly to make sure students with disabilities are able to maintain them in an organized fashion.
6. Using and checking assignment schedule books which students write in every day.

These strategies are generally beneficial for nondisabled students as well.

Team Teaching: Sharing the Responsibility. Effective inclusive classrooms that create positive and productive experiences for students with disabilities are characterized by the shared responsibility between the general education and special education teacher-consultant. Team teaching, however requires a relationship of trust between the teachers. Teachers must have previously agreed upon goals for their students and common planning time each day.

Managing the Paperwork: Strategies for Teachers. A frequent complaint of teachers is the paperwork associated both with documenting IEPs and with the referral process for determining if a student is eligible for special education services. Once the eligibility has been determined and the student is moved into special education, the IEP process is also at times viewed as time-consuming. Consequently, teachers are always searching for strategies to help reduce paperwork. The most common strategies include use of the following:

1. **Instructional aides.** Assistants help complete or prepare sections of the IEPs in advance of the IEP meetings, or make copies of updated IEPs for the teachers.
2. **Easy-to-use forms and checklists.** Many schools have revised their IEP forms and other documentation forms to make them easy to complete. Utilizing forms and checklists are efficient ways of communicating or of documenting important information for a student's file.
3. **Computers.** Some schools are using computers to develop and adjust individualized education programs. Identifying goals and objectives from a database saves time, but there is one caution: student goals and objectives, and instructional strategies selected from a database must be carefully matched to the individual student's needs.
4. **Case meetings.** Holding regular strategy meetings on a quarterly basis, for example, to monitor a student's progress and share information, can reduce the amount of paperwork and can engage the assistance of the inclusion coordinator. The designation of an inclusion coordinator can also be helpful for assisting teachers in their responsibilities for reviewing the student's IEPs and ensuring a match between student needs and classroom activities. Inclusion coordinators can help teachers by
   - Providing information about available supplementary and related services.
   - Linking students and families with related services.
   - Helping teachers interpret student evaluation information in terms of its implications for student learning and classroom accomodations.
   - Acting as a liaison with administrators to communicate teachers' needs for classroom resources, materials, or consultation.
   - Linking teachers with specialists for classroom consultation.
   - Assisting with the development of in-class behavioral interventions for students.

CHAPTER 22

What Are Important Considerations Related to the Use of Technology?

In schools, there is an increasing gap between the technological "haves" and "have nots." Students with disabilities have a right to access the full range of technology that is available in the classroom for instruction, including access to computers, libraries, information centers and technology laboratories, school-based weather stations, and other centers. Whether or not a school is rich in technological resources, access to technology is generally more limited for students with disabilities than for their nondisabled peers. The same holds true for students' access to computers in the home. The questions of access and equity are unavoidable when we consider the high cost of computer equipment adaptations for students with disabilities and of assistive technology, much of which has to be customized to the needs of individuals. Access to these devices and financial support for purchasing them are lacking for many individuals with disabilities. For these students, it is essential that school administrators give special attention to computer station adaptations and instruction early in the student's school career. This form of early intervention for technology access promotes independence long before the individual begins the process of transition to the technology-centered world of secondary and postsecondary education and work.

TECHNOLOGY INTEGRATION: IS IT HAPPENING FOR STUDENTS WITH DISABILITIES? Billions of dollars are spent each year on educational technology that lies unused in our schools, while research demonstrates exciting links among technology, literacy, achievements by students with disabilities, and improved student motivation and performance. Over the past decade, school improvement efforts have focused on using technology in the classroom. However, its effective use remains an elusive goal for most teachers as well as for most students with

disabilities. Reasons for this include the following:

- Inadequate staff training for effective integration of technology into instruction.
- Lack of support services.
- Lack of incentives for schools to accommodate technology.
- Lack of understanding of how to use technology to accommodate diverse students in regular classrooms.

The Technology Assistance Act of 1998. Access to assistive technology for a student with a disability can mean independence, the ability to attend school and participate in the range of educational activities, and the opportunity to participate in community life. Conversely, the lack of access can mean dependence and isolation. The Technology Assistance Act of 1998 (ATA), signed into law by President Clinton in November 1998, is designed to support states in sustaining and strengthening their capacity to address the assistive technology needs of individuals with disabilities. The ATA builds on the success of the earlier Technology-Related Assistance for Individuals with Disabilities Act of 1988 (referred to as the "Tech Act"). State assistive technology programs have increased community awareness of the value of assistive technology; educated individuals with disabilities about how to select and purchase appropriate assistive technology; expanded the knowledge of school personnel about assistive technology; and expanded the number of individuals with disabilities in inclusive school, workplace, and other community settings.

Technology and Goals 2000. Technology can increase the likelihood that students with disabilities will also achieve the outcomes related to the National Education Goals, namely, that all students will participate in educa-

The use of technology reinforces learning and promotes independence and motivation.

tional programs designed to meet their present and future needs within a global community (National Council on Disability, 1993; 1997, National Education Goals Panel, 1994). Educators need to advance their understanding of the benefits of technology for students with disabilities who are mainstreamed into regular classrooms.

NATIONAL INITIATIVES SUPPORT TECHNOLOGY IN THE CLASSROOM. Several national education and training initiatives under the Clinton administration have placed instructional technology at the center of education and employment training policies. One of these—the Goals 2000 initiative—establishes broad national education goals and challenges each state to achieve them by the year 2000 (National Education Goals Panel, 1994). Goals 2000 requires that all students be prepared for work and be technologically literate. Goal 5, Adult Literacy and Lifelong Learning, specifically highlights technology in education, stating that by the year 2000, every adult American will be literate and will possess the knowledge and skills necessary to compete in a global economy and exercise the rights and responsibilities of citizenship (National Education Goals Panel, 1994). These national educational goals and objectives require that children become technologically literate as early as possible in their educational programs.

USES OF TECHNOLOGY FOR INCLUSION. There are many uses of technology that can support the successful inclusion of students in the classroom. Adaptive technologies and equipment enable students with disabilities to access technology for assessment purposes, for IEP decision making, and in instruction. Students can incorpo-

rate technology in developing their vocational-technical skills for future employment and independent living. For example, for a student with a severe disability, a multidisciplinary team might involve a general education teacher, a special education teacher, an assessment specialist, and an augmentative communication specialist to determine individual needs and technology access. Students can utilize keyboarding, word processing, database tools, and graphic tools in addition to classroom-related software to reinforce learning. Again, for students with disabilities, it is essential to provide such adaptations, instruction, and training to promote independence while the learner is still in school.

Students with more severe disabilities would be unable to compete in society without access to technology for basic communication and productivity. For example, students with cerebral palsy, brain injuries, vision impairments, epilepsy, and degenerative muscular disorders must be provided with early training and preparation for technology access. Each student's unique cognitive, motoric, and sensory needs present challenges in the classroom because learning stations need to be customized to match the experience, capabilities, and career interests of the student.

USES OF TECHNOLOGY IN INSTRUCTION. Computers can also provide a means of helping students with disabilities remain in the general education classroom (Behrmann, 1984; King, 1999). Behrmann (1984) outlined six reasons why computers are a valuable instructional medium for teachers.

Six Reasons Why Computers Are Valuable in Instruction

1. *They can be used in individual or group instruction.* Computers can assist teachers with many of the tasks designed to provide individualized and small-group in-

Teachers combine the use of computers with small groups or teams.

struction and to free the teacher to work on children's needs (e.g., as indicated by social interaction or withdrawal). The computer can present information to groups or individuals. Some activities combine use of the computer with experiential activities in small groups or teams.

2. *They can provide immediate feedback and reinforcement to students.* Computers are intrinsically motivating because they provide immediate feedback, allow the student to work at his or her own pace, and can present information in a game format. Computers can also be programmed to provide the student with personalized reinforcement and to call the teacher's attention to good work.

3. *They can collect and analyze student performance data.* The IEP requires a plan for evaluating student progress toward short-term and long-term goals. Computers can be helpful in evaluating student performance data on such things as rate, accuracy, duration, and frequency of responses. They can also be used to store data collected by the teacher about other student behaviors such as seat behavior, social behavior, and tardiness.

4. *They are flexible in terms of level of instruction and type of child–computer interaction.* Computer programming can be varied to customize the way information is put into the computer by the learner (input) and the way it is taken out by the learner (output). For example, students put information into the computer by keyboard. For students with severe physical disabilities, who may have no cognitive disabilities, the keyboard can be adapted so that only one key is used for input. Information can also be entered in a computer by electronic pads or communication boards or adapted switches or sensors that detect touch, movement, light, sound, or temperature. For example, sensors are being used to control wheelchairs by head movements, and computers can be activated by voice commands. Information provided to the student by the computer can be in the form of graphics, text, or voice. In this way, the computer varies the output or may combine the output (text and voice). The computer also varies the mode of presenting information so that it can be adapted to different learning styles. For improved visual learning, computers can also be connected to peripheral devices such as video discs, videotapes, and filmstrips. For improved auditory learning, computers can use voice synthesis to control tape recorders, record players, and other devices.

5. *They allow self-paced instruction.* Computers allow students to work at their own pace, to slow down the learning or to speed it up. Computers are infinitely patient and allow students as much time as they need to respond to questions without pressure or anxiety.

6. *They allow errorless practice.* Computers allow students time for as much practice as they need to master a skill or understand a concept. The teacher can determine the mastery level needed by a student, and the computer can then use that information to decide whether to move to the next level of instruction, provide more time to practice a skill, move to a remedial

With more technology use in the educational and work environment, all students need to learn how to access and be comfortable at the computer.

level, or alert the teacher that the student is having difficulty. (*Source:* information synthesized from Behrmann, M. (1984). *Handbook for microcomputers in special education.* San Diego, CA: College-Hill Press, pp. 30–39).

INCLUDING CHILDREN WITH SEVERE AND MEDICALLY RELATED IMPAIRMENTS. The 1997 Amendments to IDEA (P.L. 105-17) promote the inclusion of children with chronic health impairments and those dependent on medical technology in the regular classroom. Schools are required to include children who are in transition from medical care to special education, including those with traumatic brain injuries, those with chronic health impairments, and those who are dependent on medical technology, who may require individualized health-related services to enable them to participate in or benefit from education. Such individualized health-related services include services that could be provided by school nursing personnel or others with appropriate training, rather than by a physician. Examples of these services include suctioning, tracheotomy care, administration of oxygen or intravenous medication, intermittent catheterization, and gastrostomy or nasogastric tube feedings. Students with severe disabilities may also require technological devices that assist them to participate in the classroom. Such devices are termed *assistive technology.*

Assistive Technology to Support Inclusion. The term *assistive technology device* means any item, piece of equipment, or product—whether acquired commercially or purchased off the shelf and modified, or customized—that is used to increase, maintain, or improve the functional capabilities of individuals with disabilities. *Assistive technology service* means any service that directly assists an individual with a disability in the selection, acquisition, or use of an assistive technology device, including

a. an evaluation of the needs of a student with a disabilities, including a functional evaluation of the students in his or her customary environment;

b. purchasing, leasing, or otherwise providing for the acquisition of assistive technology devices by individuals with disabilities;

c. selecting, designing, fitting, customizing, adapting, applying, maintaining, repairing or replacing assistive technology devices;

d. coordinating and using other therapies, interventions, or services with assistive devices, such as those associated with existing education and rehabilitation plans and programs;

e. training or technical assistance for a student with a disability, or where appropriate, the student's family;

f. training or technical assistance for professionals, employers, or other individuals who provide services to, employ, or otherwise are substantially involved in the major life functions of individuals with disabilities. (The Assistive Technology Act of 1998)

Inclusion plans that include technology integration should respond to the Technology Assistance Act of 1998 and the 1997 Amendments to IDEA. These laws address the need for access of students with disabilities to the range of technology and media supports available within schools.

MAXIMIZING STUDENTS' PERFORMANCE USING TECHNOLOGY.
With more technology use in the educational and work environment, individuals are spending much more time at the computer. Ensuring proper access and comfort at the computer is important for maximizing performance and enhancing productivity. For persons with disabili-

ties, issues of access and comfort often make the difference between success and failure in the use of technology. The use of assistive technologies for persons with disabilities can also help to eliminate barriers that previously prevented access and success in school and at work. For example, adapting the computer through a DOS extension software program can open doors for a one-handed typist or a mouthstick user. Similarly, using a wrist rest can help an individual with muscular dystrophy or rheumatoid arthritis access the keyboard and increase his or her work productivity.

TYPES OF EQUIPMENT MODIFICATIONS FOR TECHNOLOGY IN THE CLASSROOM. Special education means adapting curriculum and instructional methods to enable the student to learn. Educators have realized for some time that computers are able to incorporate many of the best practices in instructional methods in special education. The following are examples of using technology to accommodate students with disabilities in the classroom:

- Providing access to technology labs and learning labs for all students.
- Use of visual timers or alarms on equipment in vocational labs or centers.
- Peer teaming for use of equipment or projects requiring use of equipment.
- Simple modification of equipment.
- Relocation and reorganization of equipment in the classroom or shop.
- Providing larger spaces between pieces of equipment.
- Providing visual and diagrammatic instructions for safety and use of equipment.
- Lowering and raising the height of computers or other equipment.
- Using auditory and visual alarms or timers.

CHAPTER 23

How Do School-to-Career Transition Services Support the Inclusion of Students in the Community After High School?

INTEREST IN TRANSITION ON THE RISE. Interest in career development and transition is greater than it has ever been before, both in the United States and in other nations. Successful transition of the young adult from school to employment and adult living is becoming recognized as a chief indicator of the effectiveness of our national investment in education, youth development, and employment preparation. Transition from school to adult life involves changes in the self-concept, motivation, and development of the individual, and is a fragile passage for the adolescent seeking to make difficult life choices (Michaels, 1994). This passage is even more delicate for youth with disabilities who need additional support and preparation to make the journey. For professionals seeking to help the student in such a journey, the process involves forming linkages among education and other human service agencies, including employment and training, adult services, and rehabilitation. As we face the next millennium, it is important to recognize that this is an era of great experimentation in education and employment preparation that will have profound effects on the lives of youth with disabilities throughout the next century.

HOW IS TRANSITION DEFINED? Transition, which generally means a continuing process of movement toward independent adulthood (Schill, 1988), appears in the literature well before the 1960s. The following provides a summary of some of the definitions of transition that have shaped the field and of the legislation that now requires states to provide transition services to all youth with disabilities.

1. **1976: Scharff and Hill** described the transition process as a critical stage in life in which an individual "brings together his internal resource and those gained from adults at school and home to make the first major independent choice which has lasting implications for the future. Young people were required to cope with 'the personal turbulence inseparable from adolescence, while at the same time experiencing an abrupt change in their institutional environment' " (p. 68).

2. **1977: The U.S. Department of Health, Education and Welfare** studied barriers in the transition to employment and postsecondary education and determined that the schools should be responsible for the following activities:
   - Providing students with information about the nature and requirements of different occupations, employment prospects, and educational and experience requirements for career entry and progression.
   - Providing students with information about their own abilities and aptitudes which would be useful in selecting an appropriate career or considering further educational experiences.
   - Providing early socialization of young people into occupational roles.
   - Ensuring that occupational competencies learned in school are certified as useful to students' continued education or to entry and progression into various occupations.
   - Providing job seeking skills and assistance in finding work.
   - Strengthening students' work habits and basic skills required for entry level employment and preparation for advancement in careers. (HEW, 1977, p.xvii)

3. **1983: An Amendment to the Education for All Handicapped Children Act** (P.L. 98-199) was passed, which defined "transition services" and authorized a voluntary and discretionary program, encouraging states to implement it. This definition has been modified and greatly expanded since 1983, adding new services and expected outcomes for youth.

4. **1984: Madeleine Will,** then director of the Office of Special Education and Rehabilitative Services (of the U.S. Department of Education), defined transition as an outcome-oriented process encompassing a broad array of services and experiences that lead to employment and were to be a "bridge" from secondary school to employment. Services to assist youth in successful transition into employment were divided into three categories: no special services, time-limited services, and ongoing services.

5. **1985: Halpern** expanded upon Will's definition and added outcomes other than employment, such as community living and social and interpersonal networks (Halpern, 1985).

6. **1986: Wehman, Kregel, Barcus, and Schalock** (1986) expanded and redefined transition as an "extended process of planning for the adult life of persons with disabilities" and included the domains of employment, independent living, and recreation. They viewed transition as beginning in the early secondary school years and involving students, families, school-linked agencies, employers, and other organizations, and they recognized the importance of student's informal networks and home environment upon the success of transition services.

7. **1986: Bates, Suter, and Poelvoorde** (1986) also defined transition as a "dynamic process" involving a partnership of consumers and local communities providing school-age and postschool services, resulting in maximum levels of employment, independent living, integration, and community participation.

8. **1987: Halpern** defined four "pillars" for secondary education and transition curriculum: academic skills, vocational skills, social skills, and independent living skills (Halpern, 1987).

9. **1994: The Council for Exceptional Children, Division on Career Development and Transition (DCDT)** developed a new definition of transition that combined the concepts of continuous career development from early schooling through high school, recognized the multiple domains that are encompassed by the term, and emphasized the central role of the individual in the planning process. The DCDT definition is as follows:

Transition refers to a change in status from behaving primarily as a student to assuming emergent adult roles in the community. These roles include employment, participating in post-secondary education, maintaining a home, becoming appropriately involved in the community and experiencing satisfactory personal and social relationships. The process of enhancing transition involves the participation and coordination of school programs, adult agency services, and natural supports within the community. The foundations for transition should be laid during the elementary and middle school years, guided by the broad concept of career development. Transition planning should begin not later than age 14, and students should be encouraged to the full extent of their capabilities, to assume a minimum amount of responsibility for such planning. (Halpern, 1994, p. 117)

10. **1996: Patton and Blalock** also agreed that transition involves many domains that are interrelated, including the following:
    - Advocacy and legal
    - Communication
    - Community participation
    - Daily living
    - Employment
    - Financial/income/money management
    - Health
    - Self-determination/self-advocacy
    - Transportation/mobility
    - Independent living
    - Leisure/recreation
    - Lifelong learning
    - Personal management
    - Postsecondary education
    - Relationships/social skills
    - Vocational evaluation
    - Vocational training

These evolving definitions reflect a continuing dialogue about what transition means and who should provide it for students with disabilities in secondary schools. Several elements of these definitions are reflected in the amendments to IDEA.

SUCCESSFUL TRANSITION DIFFICULT FOR HIGH SCHOOL STUDENTS WITH DISABILITIES

Poor Outcomes for Youth Underscore the Need for Transition Support. There is ample evidence that the past 20 years of mandatory free and appropriate public education for youth with disabilities have not adequately prepared these youth for employment, and the outcomes for youth in transition from high school remain alarming (Benz & Halpern, 1993; GAO, 1996; Halloran & Simon, 1995; Hoyt, 1990; Kochhar & West, 1996; Sitlington, 1992; Wagner, 1995; Wehmeyer & Ward, 1995). However, the number of students exiting the schools *has* increased over the past 10 years because there have been many improvements in the education of special learners in secondary education. As has been discussed in previous sections, schools have improved the identification of students who need specialized services, expanded accommodations and improved teaching strategies in general education classrooms, increased access to technology in the classroom, and initiated system change within the overall transition service system. Yet the capacity to provide transition supports, employment assistance, and postsecondary services has not kept pace with the need (Eighteenth Annual Report to Congress on IDEA, 1996; Wehman, 1992).

Federal and State Commitment to Transition Services for Youth: There Is a Lot of Work to Be Done. Since the 1960s and 1970s, the federal and state governments and many other institutions have focused considerable attention on ensuring that assistance is provided to all youth with disabilities for making a successful transition from school to employment and postsecondary settings. Over 19 years ago, the National Commission on Employment Policy (1981) stated,

> The school-to-work transition process is complicated by the extended education required in our society, by the separation of classrooms and work places, by the focus of pedagogy on continued schooling rather than preparation for employment, by the failure to provide basic skills to many graduates and dropouts. . . . A variety of interventions have been implemented to ease the transition process. They seek to improve the labor market awareness and occupational choices of students, to develop the basic employability skills demanded in the labor market, to remediate where severe educational and behavioral problems act as barriers to employment, to provide help in securing and successfully navigating labor market entry, and . . . to offer first work experiences . . . as stepping stones. (1981, p. 24)

From the mid 60s to the late 80s, many transition-related policies were crafted to ease transition for all youth, including those with disabilities (e.g., Manpower Development and Training Act in the 1960s, 1973 Comprehensive Employment and Training Act (CETA), the 1977 Youth Employment Demonstration Act, and the 1983 Transition Amendment to the Education of the Handicapped Act (P.L. 98-99). More recently congressional leaders have called for studies of outcomes of educational and career preparation programs, including special education, vocational education, job training and rehabilitation. The results of these studies have highlighted a lack of coordination among education and training agencies in addressing the complexities of youth unemployment (U.S. General Accounting Office, 1989, 1992, 1993, 1994c, 1996). Experts conclude that a more aggressive and comprehensive effort must be made to address the continued poor outcomes of America's youth with disabilities.

Youth with Disabilities Are at High Risk for School Dropout. By some estimates, over 55,000 special education students between the ages of 16 and 21 drop out of school each year, an average of over 300 students each school day (West, 1991; U.S. Department of Education, 1994b). The national dropout rate for youth who have exited special education is currently about 25 percent, with many state and local agencies reporting higher rates (e.g., between 31 and 35 percent) (Blackorby & Kortering, 1991; Eighteenth Annual Report to Congress on the Implementation of the Individuals with Disabilities Education Act, 1996). High school dropout rates remain high, and approximately 90 percent of dropouts are between 16 and 17 years of age (Kortering & Braziel, 1998; OJJDP, 1995).

According to Wagner (1995), there is a 38 percent dropout rate across all disabilities, compared to approximately 20 percent in the general population. Categorically, 47 percent of these students are labeled as having learning disabilities, 23 percent as having mental retardation, and 21 percent as having emotional disabilities (U.S. Department of Education, 1991). The Eighteenth Annual Report to Congress (1996) indicates school dropout rates for students with disabilities at about 27 percent (compared with 16 percent for the general population) and over 50 percent for students aged 15 and 16. Furthermore, students with disabilities are even less likely to be served in community colleges, 4-year colleges, or vocational-technical centers, despite evidence that with small program modifications and supportive counseling, many can benefit from such opportunities (Council of Chief State School Officers, 1998; Halpern, 1991). The following information summarizes why transition services are essential for youth with disabilities.

Why Transition Services for Youth with Disabilities?

- Although the Individuals with Disabilities Education Act (IDEA) requires each school to provide transition services for all students with disabilities and the School-to-Work Opportunities Act requires the same; most students with disabilities are still not being provided with a systematic transition from school to work.
- Approximately 50 to 75 percent of all adults with disabilities are unemployed.
- Many students with disabilities and other special needs can and should benefit from appropriate vocational education programs, but their enrollment in vocational education remains very low—now close to *4 percent nationally.*
- There is a high rate of underemployment for these youth who must work in jobs that do not use their skills.
- Studies show that students with disabilities and other special needs drop out more frequently than their nondisabled peers.
- A Washington state study followed 1,292 leavers of special education and found only 58 percent employed. Only 18 percent were making more than $135 per week (Benz & Lindstrom, 1997).
- The dropout rate for students in urban areas was 36.6 percent, for suburban, 24.6 percent, and for rural, 31.4 percent (Eighteenth Annual Report to Congress on the Implementation of the Individuals with Disabilities Education Act, 1996).
- Dropout rates for students with different disabilities (as compared with 19 percent for individuals who are nondisabled) are as follows:

With learning disabilities: 37 percent
With emotional disabilities: 42 percent
With hearing impairments: 28 percent
With speech impairments: 24 percent

- Students are more vulnerable at different ages. Dropout rates are highest at ages 16 and 17 (55 and 34 percent respectively) (Eighteenth Annual Report to Congress on the Implementation of the Individuals with Disabilities Education Act, 1996)

The Educational Environment Contributes to School Dropout. Dropout prevention experts believe that there is a strong link between the problem of school dropout and the educational environment of the school (Fennimore & Tinzman, 1990; Sitlington & Frank, 1993; West, 1991). This is particularly true for students with disabilities. In addition, a large proportion of in-school and out-of-school youth with disabilities who are at risk of delinquency or already involved with the juvenile justice system need specialized educational services to succeed in their community schools (Leone, Rutherford & Nelson, 1991b). The chances of having delinquent behavior and being adjudicated were 220 percent greater for youths with learning disabilities and emotional and behavior disorders than for adolescents with no disabilities (Dunivant, 1986; McDaniel, 1992; Zionts, 1997). Even as schools experiment with innovative alternatives to traditional educational approaches, students with disabilities are often denied access. What Kvaraceus (1963) stated over 30 years ago is still true: the imbalance in the curriculum in the public schools today "favors the academically talented middle-class child and is highly prejudicial to both the non-academic and lower-class youngster" (p. 204). Many schools are seeking answers both to why students are dropping out and how to develop new responses to the situation.

Several reasons for high dropout rates are offered by the research and practitioner community:

1. There is a rising number of at-risk youth who are not succeeding in the regular classroom nor receiving the additional attention they need. This leads to alienation from peers and teachers.
2. There is inadequate development of skills (academic, vocational, and personal) that are essential for entry into employment, postsecondary training, and responsible citizenship, particularly for youth with disabilities.
3. There is a lack of systematic career planning incorporating vocational assessment and counseling, work readiness, career and transition planning, and exposure to the work world for students with disabilities.
4. Junior and senior high school programs do not integrate academic and career vocational skills, particularly for students who are applied learners.
5. Youth with disabilities do not have access to the range of vocational-technical and community-based training options available to nondisabled youth.
6. Secondary programs often fail to consider the context for learning—the variety of cognitive abilities and patterns of learning that require educators to carefully consider the sites, contexts, and methods for delivering information to different learners (Bussey & Bandura, 1992; Clark & Kolstoe, 1995; Gordon, 1973; Kiernan & Schalock, 1989).

The inflexibility of secondary school curricula is also blamed for the increasing dropout rates. Improving out-comes for school dropouts requires committed responses on the part of teachers, schools, and communities to support new transition services.

REFORMS ARE RECOMMENDED IN SECONDARY EDUCATION AND TRANSITION. Policymakers and other leaders in education and job training are demanding a systematic redesign of transition service delivery for all youth, particularly those with disabilities. Some educational researchers observe that it is often the inflexible structure of the school itself that contributes to the conditions that breed academic failure. According to experts, change in the school system is paramount. Experts have concluded that schools must do the following to improve employment outcomes for youth and reduce school dropout:

1. Develop innovative secondary programs to integrate academic, vocational and employment skills.
2. Provide access for out-of-school youth, both high school completers and noncompleters, to the range of vocational-technical and community-based employment training options.
3. Assess cognitive abilities and learning styles and, as teachers, carefully consider the learning environments and methods for developing academic and vocational skills in special learners.
4. Raise expectations for students with disabilities.
5. Provide each learner with an advisor, advocate, or coordinator with whom the learner plans the transition to employment programs.
6. Develop alternatives to traditional assessment of the learner's progress in school-based employment settings.
7. Restructure the high schools and offer non-college-bound students a 13th year of technical training.
8. Provide remedial education and on-the-job training for poor youths.
9. Create apprenticeship programs and increase high schools' ability to prepare students for the work place.
10. Teach all students basic math and English skills by 10th grade.
11. Emphasize critical thinking, problem solving, independent learning and communication skills for all students in the 11th- and 12th-grade curricula.
12. Encourage students not planning to attend college to couple their academic courses with a work internship.
13. Allow high school students to pursue a 13th year of professional or technical learning in the field of their choice.
14. Allow students completing their technical training to take a voluntary national competency test in their chosen area and receive a certificate of competency recognized by employers in the field (Edgar, 1991; National Longitudinal Transition Study, 1992; O'Brien, 1992; Reich, 1993; West, 1991).

According to U.S. Secretary of Education Richard Riley, "We're the only industrial nation that has no formal strategy for helping students make the transition to work." (*Education USA*, Vol. 35, No. 13 (March 1, 1993), pp. 1,2).

Reformers are promoting comprehensive and flexible youth development approaches that can embrace academic development, social-psychological development, career development, and preparation for work and broader life roles. Box 23-1 presents common concerns about the readiness of young people for work.

Box 23-1. Common Concerns About Youth Readiness for Work

The Commission on the Skills of the American Workplace report, *America's Choice: High Skills or Low Wages* (1990), summarized the concerns of a variety of federal government, and academic, and community organizations and outlined six broad problems associated with poor worker performance and youth preparation for employment:

1. Lack of clear standards of achievement and motivation to work hard in school.
2. The high percentage of dropouts.
3. A very small segment of non-college-bound students prepared for work.
4. The lack of employer investment in high-performance work organizations.
5. A passive public policy on high school preparation and worker training.
6. An inefficient job training system.

These concerns underscore the need for secondary education reform and new strategies that link academic and career-vocational-technical components to education, blending both school-based and community-based approaches.

Broad National Goals Support Transition and Inclusion in Career Development. Major national reform initiatives by the federal government reflect society's recognition that all youth need assistance at the stage of exit from secondary school. These reforms stress high academic and occupational standards and improved teaching, and have called for broad-based partnerships for designing comprehensive statewide school-to-work systems. With the passage of the Goals 2000: Educate America Act of 1993 (P.L. 103-227), the nation wrote into law eight challenging educational goals which state and local educational agencies are expected to attempt to achieve over the balance of this decade. These goals were designed to raise standards and the performance of schools in preparing children and youth to enter formal schooling and exit prepared for employment, advanced education, and adult responsibilities. Table 23-1 summarizes these goals and corresponding adjustment of these goals for students with disabilities.

These goals have affected the inclusion movement by raising expectations for all students in general educa-

TABLE 23-1. GOALS 2000: Provisions for Students with Disabilities

Goal for All Students by the Year 2000	For Students with Disabilities
1. All children will start school ready to learn.	1. Students will have access to preschool programs.
2. High school graduation rate will increase to 90%.	2. Students will have specialized supports and transition services to assist them.
3. Students will leave grades 4, 8, & 12 with demonstrated competency in English, math, science, history, geography; each school will ensure that all students learn to use their minds well and be prepared for responsible citizenship, further learning and productive employment.	3. Students will have classroom supports and accommodations needed to access and achieve more challenging subjects; programs of applied academics will be available for non-traditional learners.
4. Students will be first in the world in science and math achievement.	4. Will have supports and accommodations needed to access and achieve in math and science.
5. Adults will be literate and exercise the rights and responsibilities of citizenship.	5. Will be held to similar standards but provided with counseling and supports aimed at preventing discipline problems.
6. Every school will be free of drugs and violence and will offer a disciplined learning environment.	6. Parents will be informed about educational programming, accommodations, and student performance.
7. Parents will be involved in their children's education.	7. Educators will be prepared to work with students with disabilities.
8. Professionals will be well trained. (National Council on Disability, 1995)	

tion classes, including students with disabilities. They also address school-to-work transition services for all secondary youth preparing for employment or postsecondary training. Goals 2, 5, and 7 are particularly relevant for the expansion of school-to-work transition services for students with disabilities. Goal 2 requires innovative dropout prevention strategies, as well as outreach to students who have dropped out of school. It also encourages transition support strategies to ensure that all students get the support they need to make a smooth transition to postsecondary education, employment, and adult life. Goal 5 specifically addresses strengthening the connection between education and work. Goal 7 challenges schools to increase parental involvement in the education of their children and to respond to actively engage parents and families in shared educational decision making. In order to increase the likelihood that all youths will prepare for participation in their communities, educators and policymakers have concluded that schools must assist young people in making a successful transition from school to adult life and constructive citizenship.

The Aim of Inclusion Also Includes Career and Work Skills.
A U.S. Office of Vocational and Adult Education study (1991) examined the role of vocational-technical education in the redesign of high school curricula and in the transition from school to careers. The traditional approaches, including apprenticeship, cooperative education, and school-based student enterprise, make deliberate use of work as part of the learning experience. The latest innovations, including vocational academies and tech-prep programs, are reconstructing the high school curriculum to unite vocational with academic disciplines. The report emphasized the important role employers play through business-school partnerships. Studies of innovative programs for youth have found that the best vocational education programs feature educators who view vocational education as an integrated "learning system" and make use of techniques on the cutting edge of school reform: team teaching, cooperative learning, alternative assessments, applied learning, and experimental learning (Clark & Kolstoe, 1995; William T. Grant Foundation, (1988). Educators of youth with disabilities recognize the strong link between school dropout, differences in students' learning readiness and styles, and the educational environment's capacity to respond to learner differences.

SUMMARY OF ASSISTANCE YOUTH CAN EXPECT TO RECEIVE UNDER CURRENT LAWS, TO SUPPORT THEIR PARTICIPATION IN SCHOOL-TO-CAREER TRANSITION.
The Individuals with Disabilities Education Act (P.L. 105-17) was reauthorized in 1997, and several amendments strengthened (1) transition services requirements, (2) the role of parents and guardians in the educational programming for students, (3) the role of the student in his or her own educational planning, and (4) the role of community agencies in sharing the responsibility for providing such services. The following information expands upon areas touched on in previous sections of this handbook.

New IEP Requirements Under IDEA Shift Emphasis to Inclusion in the General Education Curriculum.
The 1997 Amendments to IDEA made several changes in the IEP and placement processes, emphasizing students' participation in the general curriculum with some adaptations and modifications. The goal of this provision is to make sure that special education and related services are provided "*in addition to the general education curriculum,* not separate from it. . . . The law presumes that children with disabilities are to be educated in general education classes (both academic and vocational) and that every decision made for a child with a disability must be made on the basis of what that individual child needs" (Senate Committee on Labor and Human Resources, 1997, pp. 20–21).

WHAT CAN STUDENTS EXPECT AT AGE 14?

IDEA Emphasizes Transition Planning. The IDEA 1997 requires that at *age 14 and every year thereafter,* the IEP must include a statement of the student's transition service needs in his or her courses of study. The purpose of the requirement is to focus attention on how the student's educational program can be planned for successful transition to the student's life goals after secondary school.

At Age 14 and Above, How Involved Should Students Be in Their IEP and Transition Planning Meetings? Traditionally, the IEP process has been controlled by professionals within the school system. However, the 1997 Amendments to IDEA strengthen the role of the student in the transition planning, through self-advocacy and self-determination. *Self-determination* refers to the act of making independent choices about personal goals and directions, based on accurate information about one's own strengths and needs and the available placement, service, or program options. Self-determination is most effective and rewarding within an environment that promotes and facilitates independent decision making (Field & Hoffman, 1998; Leconte, 1997; Racino, 1992; Wehmeyer & Ward, 1997). Self-determination does not mean "going it alone" or relying only upon oneself. Rather, the idea should be placed within the context of shared decision making, interdependence, and mutual support (Racino, 1992). Many youths with disabilities have difficulty assuming control of their lives and participating in the IEP goal setting and educational decisions that are made each year about their futures.

The term *self-advocacy* has been defined as a social and political movement started by and for people with disabilities to speak for themselves on important issues such as housing, employment, legal rights, and personal relationships (Smith, 1998). The term is related to self-determination in which the student with a disability is directly and actively involved in the decisions that are being made about his or her education and future.

The assumption upon which these requirements are based are that students who are engaged in planning for their own futures will become empowered in the process. This means that the students will show improved self-reliance, self-esteem, self-knowledge about their own career interests and strengths, motivation, and knowledge about postsecondary opportunities. Furthermore, they will feel less passive, more confident in their choices of future goals, and will experience a greater sense of control over their own destination. These feelings of control and confidence lead to a heightened motivation and excitement about the future directions that the student chooses to take.

The Student Is in Charge of His or Her Future: Participating in the IEP/ITP Meeting. The 1997 Amendments of

IDEA strengthened the student's role in transition planning, through self-determination, which means making independent choices about one's personal goals and directions, based on accurate information about one's strengths and needs and the available programs and services in the community. Self-determination is most effective and rewarding within an environment that promotes and facilitates independent decision making (Field & Hoffman, 1998; Leconte, 1997; Racino, 1992; Wehmeyer & Ward, 1997). The idea of self-determination is based on the belief that when students plan for their own future, they become empowered in the process, increasing their self-reliance, self-esteem, and self-knowledge about their career interests and strengths, motivation, and knowledge about postsecondary opportunities. Furthermore, they feel less passive and more confident in their choices of future goals, experience a greater sense of control over their own destination, and feel more excited about the future directions they choose. Self-determination does not mean "going it alone" or relying only on oneself; instead, it means sharing decision making and learning from each other (Racino, 1992).

The student can take control of his or her future by actively participating in the IEP goal setting and educational decisions that are made each year. To take the lead role, students should be encouraged to

1. Learn as much as they can about the transition process and how to take a lead role.
2. Learn to cooperate with all who are there to support them (i.e., parents, teachers, others).
3. Understand their strengths and needs, the importance of support services, and how they must develop their own unique abilities in order to advocate for themselves and their goals.
4. Think carefully about their long-range plans for postsecondary education and how their decisions about their educational program today will affect their ability to achieve their goals.

Parents, teachers, and other service representatives from the school and community must also attend IEP meetings to assist students in transition planning. The goal of the transition planning process is to *enhance the student's ability to contribute to the planning process, in consultation with the student's parents and teachers.*

Can Vocational Education Be Included in the IEP Before Age 16? The definition of special education, as redefined in the 1997 Amendments to IDEA, strengthened the expectation that all students would have a right to career education and transition services appropriate to their needs. In some cases the student's participation in vocational education must be included in the IEP at age 14. The term *special education* was clarified to include:

- Vocational education if it consists of specially designed instruction, at no cost to the parents, and meets the individual needs of the student.

- Vocational courses as an organized educational program offering a sequence of courses which directly prepare students for paid or unpaid employment.
- Preparation for employment in current or emerging occupations requiring other than a baccalaureate or advanced degree.
- Competency-based learning in which specific learning objectives and outcomes are specified.
- Applied learning strategies in which instruction is delivered in real-world settings or applied to real-world problems.
- Competency-based and applied learning strategies that contribute to a student's development of academic knowledge, higher order reasoning, and problem-solving skills, as well as the development of work attitudes, general employability skills, and the occupation-specific skills necessary for economic independence as a productive and contributing member of society.
- Applied technology education.

Furthermore, it is important that students, at age 14, begin the process of career counseling and vocational assessment in order to provide additional evaluation information to support transition decisions. If a student is determined to be able to participate in the regular vocational education program without any modifications, it would not be necessary to include vocational education in the student's IEP. However, if modifications to the regular vocational education program are needed in order for a student to participate in that program, then those modifications must be included in the IEP. Additionally, if the student needs a specially designed vocational education program, then vocational education must be described in all applicable areas of the student's IEP (e.g., students present levels of educational performance, goals and objectives, and specific services to be provided) (Horne, 1996, U.S. Office of Special Education, 1997). It is important that the vocational educator attend the IEP meeting if the student is participating in vocational education and has written goals and objectives in the IEP.

What If the Student Does Not Need Transition Services? According to IDEA 1997, if the interdisciplinary team decides that the student does not need transition services, then the IEP must include a statement to that effect and the reason for making that determination. However, it was the *intent of Congress to ensure that all students do receive some kind of transition support or services to begin to prepare them for graduation.* It is widely recognized that these services can have a significantly positive effect on the employment and independent living outcomes for many of these students in the future, especially for students who are likely to drop out before age 16. These provisions in IDEA ensure that each student who needs special educational services is given assistance early to develop a transition plan and goals for career preparation and postsecondary planning.

WHAT CAN STUDENTS EXPECT AT AGE 16 AND ABOVE?

How IDEA Can Help Students Get Ready for Postsecondary Education and Employment. High school students with disabilities can benefit from careful planning for the post-high-school years. IDEA requires that the student have an individualized transition plan (ITP) in place as part of his or her IEP at *age 14 and every year thereafter.* At age 16, the ITP must include a plan of specific transition services to assist the student to achieve transition goals and to adjust to life after secondary school. Transition services are defined as a coordinated set of activities aimed at achieving a specific outcome for the student. Transition activities promote movement from school to postschool activities such as 2- or 4-year college enrollment, vocational or technical school training, continuing and adult education, full-time or part-time employment, supported employment, independent living, participation in community activities, and citizenship responsibilities. These coordinated activities should be based on the individual needs of the student and take into account the student's career preferences and interests. They should include needed activities in the areas of instruction, community experiences, the development of employment and other postschool adult living objectives, and, if appropriate, daily living skills and functional vocational evaluation.

The IEP and the Services of Noneducational Agencies. The IDEA requires that when the student reaches age 16, the IEP should describe the specific transition services that are to be provided to the student. These transition services may include instruction, community experiences, the development of employment and other postschool objectives, as well as independent living skills and functional vocational evaluation (Senate Committee on Labor and Human Resources, 1997). In planning what types of transition services a student needs in order to prepare for adulthood, the IEP team considers preparation for transition goals such as postsecondary education, vocational training, adult service agencies and community agencies, employment, independent living, and community participation.

The 1997 Amendments to IDEA also address the role of other noneducational agencies in supporting transition of youth from school to employment and postsecondary education. The IDEA requires that the IEP include a statement of interagency responsibilities or any needed linkages. When an IEP meeting is convened to consider transition services for a student, the IEP coordinator must invite a representative of any other agency that is likely to be responsible for providing or paying for transition services. If the agency representative does not attend the meeting, then the IEP coordinator must take other steps to obtain the participation of the other agency in the planning of transition services. There are several implications of these changes in IEP requirements for interagency collaboration and shared responsibility for transition services. These include the following:

- Rehabilitation agencies, postsecondary institutions, community-based service agencies, adult services, and business must form interagency partnerships.
- Schools and community agencies must share resources.
- LEAs must develop a seamless system of supports to assist youths in making a successful transition to postsecondary life.
- Students and families must be engaged in transition planning well before graduation.
- Interagency coordination for transition must be strengthened.
- The financial responsibility of each agency must be addressed in formal interagency agreements.

In order to ensure availability of services from noneducational agencies in the student's IEP, the new law clarifies that the state educational agency's supervision *does not limit or lessen the obligation of other than educational agencies to provide or pay* for some or all of the costs of a free and appropriate public education (including transition services), and it describes ways to do this. Each state must have a state interagency agreement. The governor or designee is required to ensure that an interagency agreement is in effect between the SEA and public agencies assigned responsibility to pay for needed services. The agreement must include services considered special education or related, including assistive technology, supplementary aids and services, and transition services. The current IDEA (1997) regulations state that

> If a participating agency fails to provide agreed-upon transition services contained in the IEP of a student with a disability, the public agency responsible for the student's education shall, as soon as possible, initiate a meeting for the purpose of identifying the alternative strategies to meet the transition objectives and, if necessary, revising the student's IEP. Nothing in this part relieves any participating agency, including a State vocational rehabilitation agency, of the responsibility to provide or pay for any transition service that the agency would otherwise provide to students with disabilities who meet the eligibility criteria of that agency.

What Kinds of Services Can Be Sought from Noneducational Agencies? School-linked agencies are required to share the responsibility for transition support services. LEAs and SEAs are actually required to provide the services that are written in IEPs, but funding may come from other sources by formal agreement:

- If medically necessary, then services can be sought and provided from Medicaid; private insurance; early periodic screening, diagnosis, and treatment programs; or intermediate care facilities for persons with mental retardation.
- If transition-related, then services may be sought and provided from vocational rehabilitation agencies, employment services, Job Training Reform Act programs,

School-to-Work Opportunities Act programs, Workforce Investment Act programs, supported employment projects, Projects with Industry, Projects for Achieving Self-Sufficiency, or disability-related work expenses.

- If independence oriented, services may be sought and provided by independent living centers, under the Rehabilitation Act;
- If related to specific disability categories, services may be sought and provided by the Division of Services to the Deaf, Division of Services to the Blind, State Technology Act programs, or others.
- If related to the need for specific purchases, services may be sought and provided by organizations such as Elks, Lions, Easter Seals, and United Cerebral Palsy.

Congress believes that teachers, administrators, and schools have a responsibility to ensure that the transition process is a *shared responsibility that does not end until an initial postsecondary placement goal has been achieved.*

What Can Students Expect in Their Last Year of High School?

Reaching the Age of Majority. The student needs to make sure that several things occur before graduation. First, the student should learn about the provision in IDEA that is called the *age of majority* requirement. This refers to the age at which the student is considered to be an adult rather than a minor (typically age 18). IDEA 1997 has outlined a procedure for the transfer of parental rights to the student when he or she reaches that age. Schools must now notify the student and both parents about the student's rights when he or she reaches the age of majority. Under this provision, 1 year before the student reaches the age of majority under state law, the IEP must include a statement that the student has been informed of the rights that transfer to the student when he or she reaches the age of majority. This transfer of rights is an enormous step toward independence and the student's participation in decision making for his or her education and future planning (Kupper, 1997). Educators will provide additional training and opportunities for the student to understand the impact of this responsibility (OSEP, 1997).

Students should be provided with career counseling to understand their vocational interests, strengths, and needs based on assessments conducted over the previous few years. They should also obtain assistance to identify 2- or 4-year colleges that (a) they can qualify for, (b) have programs that match the student's interests and abilities, (c) have available student support services, and (d) have a strong record of supporting students with learning disabilities. Students should ask for help from their teachers and career counselors. If a student is planning to enroll in 2- or 4- college or technical school, he or she should ask for assistance with the selection of colleges, applying and negotiating for support services, information about how to access campus resources, guidance in interview techniques, guidance in discussing self-advocacy and how to promote his or her strengths, and advantages and disadvantages of self-disclosure of his or her disability. If the student is planning to enter employment directly after high school, he or she should ask for help in job search strategies, developing a résumé, and working with business personnel in simulated job interviews before actual interviews to gain experience and receive real-world feedback from employers. It is important that students obtain assistance in matching their career interests and abilities to available employment opportunities in their community. It is also important that they find out which employers provide supports to students with disabilities.

What Kinds of Career Vocational-Technical Education and Work-Based Services Can Be Expected? IDEA redefined special education to include career-vocational education and transition services. *Congress was responding to the fact that the highest rates for dropout for youth occur between ages 15 and 17 and that 35 percent of students with learning disabilities do not finish high school. The majority of students with learning disabilities (62%) were not fully employed 1 year after graduating from high school* (Wagner, 1992). For many students with disabilities, career-vocational and transition activities must begin earlier than 11th grade in order to provide adequate developmental time to prepare for postsecondary education or employment. Career vocational services can include (a) vocational education, if it consists of specially designed instruction, at no cost to the student's parents, and meets the student's individual needs; (b) vocational courses as an organized educational program offering a sequence of courses that directly prepares the student for paid or unpaid employment; (c) a program that offers preparation for employment in current or emerging occupations requiring other than a baccalaureate or advanced degree; and (d) applied technology education. The IDEA and the Carl D. Perkins Vocational and Technical Education Act, 1990 and 1998 Amendments, contain language promoting the inclusion of students with disabilities into general vocational education classes. The term inclusion is not actually used, but instead the term *full participation* is defined. The Act requires each recipient to use Perkins funds to improve vocational education programs with "full participation of individuals who are members of special populations." The U.S. Department of Education interprets full participation to mean that programs must provide "the supplementary and other services necessary for them to succeed in vocational education." States receiving federal funds under the Act must provide assurances that

- Members of special populations will be provided equal access to recruitment, enrollment, and placement activities and to the full range of vocational education programs.

- Individuals with disabilities will be provided services in the least restrictive environment and will be afforded certain rights and protection.
- Vocational education planning for individuals with disabilities will be coordinated with special education and rehabilitation agencies.
- The provisions of vocational education will be monitored to determine if that education is consistent with the IEP for each student and ensure that disadvantaged students and students with limited English proficiency have access in the most integrated setting possible.

The Act also requires each organization or agency receiving funds to provide assurances that it will

- Assist students who are members of special populations in entering vocational education programs, and with respect to students with disabilities, assist in providing certain transitional services.
- Assess the special needs of students participating in programs using Perkins funds, with respect to their successful completion of vocational education programs in the most integrated setting possible.
- Provide certain supplementary services to students who are special populations members, including individuals with disabilities.
- Provide guidance, counseling, and career development activities.
- Provide counseling and instructional services designed to facilitate the transition from school to postschool employment and career opportunities. (Sections 118 & 235)

This definition helps protect and promote the inclusion of students with disabilities into regular vocational-technical education opportunities, as well as activities in which students work in their communities. Career vocational education programs are required under the Carl D. Perkins Vocational and Technical Education Act of 1998 to provide the following assurances of full participation of all youth, particularly members of special populations:

1. Equal access to recruitment, assessment, enrollment, and placement activities related to career vocational-technical education and school-to-work programs.
2. Equal access to the full range of career vocational-technical education and school-to-work programs, including job readiness and work preparation, social skills training, vocational assessment matching students strengths and interests to work requirements, and on-site job supportive supervision and training.
3. Coordination of career vocational-technical education and school-to-work programs and programs with existing related career and transition programs for special populations.
4. Provision of information about available career vocational-technical education and transition to students, parents and guardians 1 year prior to the age that such programs are generally available to students in the state.
5. Provisions for vocational-technical education teachers to be involved in IEP development and review.

6. Provision of supplementary services and accommodations in the general vocational-technical education class, including adjustments to the vocational and technical education curriculum, adapted instructional materials, physical accommodations in the class and work sites, follow-up support and monitoring, case management and coordination of students' community-based programs, and supportive guidance and counseling.
7. Provision of supplementary services and accommodations in work-based learning activities in the school, such as paid and unpaid work experience, instruction in general work-place competencies and work behaviors, work adjustment activities, instruction in and orientation to reasonable work accommodations and job restructuring, job shadowing, job exploration activities, work-based vocational skills assessments, school-sponsored enterprises, or on-the-job training for academic credit.
8. Provision of career exploration and counseling, beginning prior to the 11th grade year of the students, or as early as 9th grade if necessary for students who need additional time for preemployment training, or who are experiencing particular difficulties in the learning environment. These services are helpful for students who may need extra preparatory time or who are interested in identifying, selecting, or reconsidering their interests, goals, and career majors.
9. Provision of regularly scheduled assessments and evaluations involving ongoing consultation, interpretation, and problem solving with students to identify academic strengths, weaknesses, academic progress, work-place knowledge, goals, and the need for additional learning opportunities to master core academic and vocational skills.

If the student's IEP/ITP includes career-vocational education and community-based experiences, and the school provides such services under the Perkins Act, then the school must ensure equal access to recruitment, enrollment, and placement activities and to the full range of vocational education programs. Schools must provide supplementary services and accommodations in the general vocational-technical education class, including adjustments to the curriculum, adapted instructional materials, physical accommodations in the class and community sites, follow-up support and monitoring, supportive guidance and counseling, accommodations in work-based learning activities (e.g., paid and nonpaid work experience, job exploration activities, work-based vocational skills assessments, school-sponsored enterprises, on-the-job training for academic credit).

Vocational education planning must be coordinated with special education and rehabilitation agencies and must be consistent with the student's IEP. Career vocational teachers should be involved in the IEP development and review. Beginning prior to the 11th grade, or as early as 9th grade if necessary, career exploration and counseling should be provided for students who need additional time for pre-employment training, or who are experiencing particular difficulties in the learning environment. These services are helpful for students with disabilities who may need extra preparatory time or are interested in identifying, selecting, or reconsidering their interests, goals, and career majors. It is important that at age 14 students begin the process of career counseling and vocational assessment in order to provide additional evaluation information to support transition decisions. Students' needs for career-vocational education services—with or without modifications—should be included in the IEP/ITP (Horne, 1996, U.S. Office of Special Education, 1997).

Can Students with Disabilities Participate in Programs Under the School-to-Work Opportunities Act (STWOA)?

IDEA requires schools to coordinate with other system change and reform initiatives such as programs under the School-to-Work Opportunities Act (P.L. 103-239, 1994). The definition of transition services under IDEA is closely aligned with the definition of school-to-work activities under this Act. STWOA services can include activities related to developing and providing leadership, supervision, and resources for comprehensive career guidance, vocational counseling, and placement programs. The STWOA was designed to provide transition services for all students with all kinds of learning needs, including students with disabilities. The chief purposes are to (1) offer opportunities for all students to participate in a performance-based education and training program; (2) encourage all youths, including youths with disabilities, to stay in or return to school and strive to succeed; (3) promote the formation of local partnerships that are dedicated to linking worlds of school and work, parents, community-based organizations, and human service agencies; and (4) create a universal, high-quality, school-to-work transition system that enables youths to identify and navigate paths to productive and progressively more rewarding roles in the work place.

School-to work (STW) programs provide opportunities in school and work arenas. The *school-based learning component* promotes awareness of the variety of careers that exist, assistance in career selection, support for developing a study program consistent with career goals and interests, integration of academic and vocational learning, regular evaluations of student performance and assistance with entry into postsecondary education. The *work-based learning component* involves work experience that is relevant to the student's career, choice workplace mentoring, and academic instruction in the work setting. Finally, *connecting activities* designed to match students with work experiences and employers also provide a means for linking the school and employer, collecting data on program outcomes for students, and providing outreach to employers to engage them directly in program development.

Placement and Transition Support. There are several supports available to aid students in job placement or in

their application for postsecondary training. These include career counseling and information about employment and postsecondary training opportunities. Students who desire to enter a 2 or 4-year college or technical school can request assistance with the following:

- Selection of colleges.
- Applying and negotiating for needed support services.
- Learning about how to access campus resources.
- Arranging for sessions with the career counselor to discuss job search strategies.
- Discussing interviewing techniques.
- Discussing self-advocacy and how to promote one's strengths.
- Discussing the advantages and disadvantages of self-disclosure of the disability and how to negotiate for needed job accommodations.
- Working with business leaders in simulated job interviews before actual interviews to gain experience and receive "real-world" feedback from employers.

WHAT CAN STUDENTS EXPECT AFTER HIGH SCHOOL?

What Does the Age of Majority Provision Mean for Students *After* High School? Once the student has graduated from high school, there are several things to consider that are important. As mentioned earlier, 1 year before the student reaches the age of majority under state law, the student must be informed of the rights, if any, that transfer to him or her upon reaching the age of majority, and the IEP must include a statement of such notification. This transfer of rights is an enormous step toward empowering students as adults and encouraging them to become much more involved in their education and future planning (Kupper, 1997). The following considerations are important for the student and family upon graduation:

1. The postsecondary, adult service and rehabilitation systems deal directly with individuals, not their parents. Those involved in the rehabilitation system are very alert and cautious when someone else wants to intervene in the decision of the individual.
2. Students no longer have IEPs or 504 plans but may be connected with student support services in the postsecondary institution.
3. A student receiving services from the rehabilitation system will have an Individual Written Rehabilitation Plan (IWRP) and can then receive services such as employment assistance, postsecondary education, counseling, and vocational evaluation and assessment.
4. If the student is determined incompetent under state law, then the rights remain with the parents. Some students may not have the ability to provide informed consent for their IEP but have not been determined to be incompetent by the state. To protect these children, IDEA requires each state to establish procedures for appointing the parents (or other appropriate person) to represent the student's educational interests).

Students need training to prepare for and understand the implications of this transfer of rights.

What Can Students Expect in 2- and 4-Year Postsecondary Institutions? While there are no student IEPs, 504 plans, or IEP team meetings in postsecondary institutions, these are requirements under the Americans with Disabilities Act and the Higher Education Act that these institutions provide reasonable accommodations for students with disabilities. Colleges have much more latitude in complying with ADA requirements than schools have in complying with IDEA. However, students can expect in most colleges and universities to apply for and receive services from the offices of support services. For example, in the case of one recent college graduate (a student of the author) who was a traumatic brain injury survivor,

> My supervisor at the university and my support services counselor bent over backwards to either "give me a kick" or provide additional motivation to keep me from getting discouraged. A friend or colleague would edit or constructively critique papers before I handed them in to the professors. Professors have allowed me extensions of time when taking tests and have allowed me to tape record lectures to compensate for missed information. Professors and students have withheld their pre-judgements and given me the same opportunities as all student have to participate, speak in front of the class, and complete all graduate assignments.

Often students have support service plans that are similar to 504 plans, since they specify the kinds of accommodations the student is to receive in the classrooms and in other nonacademic activities. Accommodations that can be requested in postsecondary education include testing and physical accommodations, adaptations of technology, special software for large print, note-takers, extensions of time for papers and homework, tutors, and group support sessions.

What Can Students Expect from Rehabilitation Services After High School?

Summary and Intent of the Law. Section 504 of the Rehabilitation Act of 1973 (new part of the Workforce Investment Act) is closely related to IDEA and shares the goal of assisting students to make a successful transition from high school. Section 504 is a nondiscrimination clause in the Rehabilitation Act that states: "No otherwise qualified individual with disabilities . . . shall solely by reasons of his disability, be excluded from the participation in, be denied the benefits of, or be subjected to discrimination under any program or activity receiving Federal financial assistance" (Rehabilitation Act of 1973, Section 504). While the Rehabilitation Act did not provide funds to the states to provide education for students with disabilities (as IDEA does), the law made it illegal for any program receiving federal funding to discriminate against any student on the basis of disability. Section 504, however, does indicate that some reasonable accommodations must be provided to meet the nondiscrimination standard.

Who Is Eligible? Section 504 applies to students of all ages who have, or have a record of having, physical or mental impairments that substantially limit one or more of the major life activities. The major life activities include caring for oneself, performing manual tasks, walking, seeing, hearing, speaking, breathing, learning, and working. Since learning is a major life activity, students with learning disabilities and attention deficit disorder (ADD) are covered under the Act.

What Are 504 Plans and How Do They Differ from IEPs? Section 504 is frequently invoked to protect students who are not eligible for services or identified under IDEA. Some schools have so-called 504 coordinators to assist students who are not eligible under IDEA but who may need special accommodations to participate in general education or education-related activities. If the student qualifies under 504 but not under IDEA, then he or she can have a 504 plan developed instead of an IEP. For example, a student with attention deficit disorder (ADD) may not need to be assessed and identified for special education services and may be able to perform acceptably within the general education class with some minor instructional accommodations. Often 504 plans include fairly minor accommodations for students with ADD or learning disabilities.

What Transition Services Can Students Expect? The 1997 Rehabilitation Amendments (P.L. 102-569) strengthened the role of rehabilitation agencies in providing transition to employment services. Vocational rehabilitation service agencies must now coordinate with educational agencies responsible for transition of students from school to employment or postsecondary settings. Students with disabilities are entitled to accommodations to help them succeed in the postsecondary program, but the individual is responsible for making his or her disability known and for asking for the accommodations needed. The state rehabilitation unit must create and annually update a plan that transfers responsibility for transitioning students from the state education agency to the state unit providing vocational rehabilitation services. This provision *links the IEP and the individual written rehabilitation plan (IWRP) in accomplishing rehabilitation goals prior to high school graduation.* Vocational rehabilitation will provide funds for eligible students with disabilities to attend postsecondary education or technical education programs. Colleges, universities, and other educational institutions that receive government funding must comply with the law under the ADA and Section 504 of the Rehabilitation Act.

The 1997 Amendments to the Rehabilitation Act also help students make informed choices about services and providers by requiring that in the final 2 years of high school they receive information about available services and providers. Rehabilitation services such as early assessment for eligibility for services, vocational assessments, and counseling in work behaviors are now available to students in their final years of high school and after graduation. If a student has not been referred to vocational rehabilitation before graduation, then he or she may be referred upon graduation for assessment for eligibility and assistance with employment or postsecondary placement.

How Does the Americans with Disabilities Act Protect and Support Students After High School?

Purpose of the Act. The Americans with Disabilities Act (ADA, P.L. 101-336) prohibits discrimination against people with disabilities, including individuals with learning disabilities and ADD. ADA requires that public and private institutions make accommodations for persons with disabilities in the areas of employment, transportation, public accommodations, state and local governments, and telecommunications. The ADA promotes accommodations in both public and private organizations, including public and private schools, colleges and universities; postsecondary vocational-technical schools, employer-based training programs, and other private training programs. While private schools do not have to provide special education programs, they cannot deny reasonable accommodations to students who have disabilities.

How Can the ADA Support Students in a Postsecondary Institution? ADA prohibits discrimination against individuals with disabilities in postsecondary applications, postsecondary education, job training, job application procedures, hiring, advancement, and employee compensation. Under ADA, transition activities can include preparation for college interviews, preparing for job interviews, learning about reasonable accommodations, comprehending essential job functions, and gaining assistance with applications and supporting documentation. Additionally, the ADA promotes participation in higher education through its antidiscrimination provisions. In other words, colleges, universities, and postsecondary institutions are required to fairly consider applicants with disabilities in their recruitment of teachers, professors, and support personnel. In postsecondary institutions, "reasonable accommodations" include modifications to a postsecondary education admission procedure to enable students to be considered for admission, as well as modifications in classrooms, test administration, and instructional methods that would help the student participate and learn in the college setting. If students will be using telecommunications equipment as part of their educational program or on the job, then accommodations for sensory deficits must be made.

While students may not have IEPs or 504 plans in college, postsecondary institutions are required under ADA and the Higher Education Act to provide reasonable accommodations. Colleges have much more latitude in complying with ADA requirements than schools have in complying with IDEA. In most colleges and universities, students can apply for and receive services from a department or office with a title such as "student support services." For example, a college student with severe learning disabilities reflected on accommodations that helped him complete his program: "Professors have provided me with extra feedback on my writing, have allowed me extensions of time when taking tests and have allowed me to tape record lectures to compensate for missed information. Professors and students have withheld their pre-judgments about my abilities and given me the same opportunities as my peers have to participate, speak in front of the class, and complete all graduate assignments" (Personal communication, May 1998).

Often students have support service plans that are similar to 504 plans since they specify the kinds of accommodations that the student is to receive in the classrooms and in other nonacademic activities. Accommodations that can be requested in postsecondary education include testing accommodations, physical accommodations, adaptations of technology, special software for large print, notetakers, extensions of time for papers and homework, tutors, and groups support sessions.

How Does the ADA Help in Employment? The ADA prohibits discrimination by employers against "qualified individuals with disabilities," or individuals who possess the skills, experience, education and other job-related requirements of a position and who, with or without reasonable accommodations, can perform the essential functions of the job. This antidiscrimination provision covers all aspects of employment, including application, testing, medical examinations, promotion, hiring, layoffs, assignments, termination, evaluation, compensation, disciplinary actions, leave, training, and benefits. Examples of reasonable accommodations include job restructuring; modified work schedules; reassignments of position; modifications to equipment; modifications of examinations, training materials, or policies; and provision of readers or interpreters. Employers are not required to lower their standards to make such accommodations, nor are they required to provide accommodations if they impose undue hardships on the business through actions that are very costly or disruptive of the work environment.

What Additional Services and Opportunities Are Available to Graduates Under the Workforce Investment Act of 1998?

The Workforce Investment Act (P.L. 105-220) establishes a state workforce investment board responsible for developing the state's 5-year strategic plan for providing job training services in the state. The law requires that a one-stop delivery system be established in each local area, which may include postsecondary educational institutions and various agencies including employment services, private, nonprofit, or governmental. The one-stop delivery system is to provide core services such as outreach and intake, initial assessment of skill levels, job-search and placement assistance, career counseling, assessment of job-skills, case management, short-term prevocational services, and training-service information. The law also authorizes Individual Training Accounts (vouchers) through which participants choose training from among providers. This law encourages coordination among multiple service sectors. States may submit "unified plans" to ensure the coordination of (and avoid duplication of) services such as workforce development activities for adults and youth, adult education, secondary and postsecondary vocational education, vocational rehabilitation, and others.

What Supports Can Employed Graduates Expect Under the Fair Labor Standards Act (FLSA)? The key provision of the FLS Act of 1938 and its Amendments is the "right to fair wages" and provision of overtime compensation to workers for more than 40 hours work. The Act, administered by the U.S. Department of Labor, covers private and state or local public employees and also addresses special categories of workers, such as youths and young adults with disabilities. For youth and adults with disabilities, the severe restrictions on earnings have been removed and special alternative wage structures have been established to allow for work internships or employment training programs. The FLSA also addresses work-related issues such as

- Minimum wage (established in 1981).
- Labor standards protection for prison inmates.
- Strengthening of child labor law.
- Status of model garment seamstresses and industrial home workers.
- Labor standards for blind and disabled workers.
- Overtime pay revisions to allow for more flexibility.
- Allowing employers the benefit of volunteer services for 6-months.

The FLSA has many provisions that allow for training and work internships at modified wage structures. Many youths with disabilities participate in work-based training using special wage arrangements with businesses.

What Services and Supports Can Graduates Expect Under the Job Training Reform Act (JTRA) of 1993 (P.L. 102-367)? The JTRA (formerly the Job Training Partnership Act, JTPA) has been a federal program for over 30 years that provides job training to economically disadvantaged youth and adults, including persons with disabilities. It has encouraged the involvement of private business and industry in partnerships with the public sector to provide programs and services to assist young people to prepare for and enter employment. The earlier JTPA also established Job Corps centers for disadvantaged youths in need of additional education, vocational and job skills training, and other support services in order to make a successful transition into employment.

What Can Postsecondary Students Expect from the Higher Education Act (HEA)? Several Sections (Titles) of the Higher Education Act can directly assist students with disabilities. Title I of the HEA (P.L. 89-329) encourages partnerships between institutions of higher education and secondary schools serving low-income and disadvantaged students, including students with disabilities. Such partnerships may include collaboration among businesses and labor, community-based, and other public or private organizations. Title IV is aimed at increasing college retention and graduation rates for low-income students and first-generation students with disabilities. Here a high priority is placed on serving students with disabilities who are also low income. This priority challenges colleges and universities to collaborate with schools and other community agencies for outreach and support of students.

Chapter 4 of Title IV allows for grants for experimentation and development of model programs that provide counseling for students about college opportunities, financial aid, and student support services. It also encourages creative collaborations among colleges, universities, financial aid institutions, and support service agencies. Title V is intended to provide assistance to the teaching force to improve professional skills, address the nation's teacher shortage, and support recruitment of underrepresented populations into the teaching force. This includes special instruction for college and university teachers to introduce them to the needs of students with disabilities.

Title XI provides incentives to vocational-technical schools, colleges, and universities to encourage them to work with private and civic organizations to (1) address problems of accessibility of students with disabilities to institutions of higher education and (2) reduce attitudinal barriers that prevent full inclusion of individuals with disabilities within their academic communities, including the social and cultural community of the campus. Activities to achieve this can include student visits to postsecondary settings, provision of information about student support services on campus, special seminars for college teachers and administrators about student accommodation needs, and accommodations in the classrooms and on campus.

INCLUSION STRATEGIES FOR TRANSITION. The following inclusion strategies can be used successfully to assist teachers in the transition planning for students with special needs:

1. Students are viewed as unique learners who learn differently and at different rates, and therefore transition services are initiated at different points in time for different students (e.g., in middle school for some and high school for others).
2. Individuals have significantly different interests and varying degrees of ability but all students can gain work skills; career learning experiences are presented in a variety of ways to appeal to the different learning styles of students.

3. The educational program for each student in the transition phase is based on the student's Individual Transition Plan to ensure that each student achieves the required standards established for the common core of learning in the occupational area, and to motivate youth to achieve their maximum potential.

4. A transition curriculum combines academic, vocational-technical, and work-skills development and also emphasizes

   • *Social responsibility:* The student learns positive attitudes towards peers and learns the importance of the adult roles of career and work.

   • *Technology:* The curriculum makes effective use of technology, developing in students both the competence and the confidence they will need in technologically enriched work environments. The curriculum, to the extent possible, exposes students to the types of technology they will face in actual work settings.

• *Problem solving, critical thinking, analysis and synthesis, creativity, and application of knowledge:* Students learn how to use academic knowledge to solve real world problems.

• *Integration and interrelatedness of knowledge:* The student learns that subject matter is not separated but is closely linked in the real world. For example, knowledge and skills in mathematics and English are linked together when the student has to measure the dimensions of piping and write up a report on the specifications needed for replacement of such piping.

• *Multiple learning styles:* Students learn subject matter through a variety of teaching techniques such as project work, constructing objects, developing portfolios, using technology, exhibits, and demonstrations of work.

• *Developmental appropriateness:* This factor addresses the developmental level of the student for

---

Craddock Boat Building School, Alexandria Seaport Foundation, Alexandria, VA

Established in 1992, in part through the generosity of the Craddock family, our boat building school hearkens back to Alexandria's glory days as a major ship-building and outfitting center. Through an assortment of vocational and scientific programs, the not for profit foundation works to bring young people from all walks of life in contact with the Potomac River and America's maritime heritage. One of the programs offered is the Apprentice Program for middle and high school age students and is taught by Joe Youcha. Mr. Youcha provides the support and direction for students and volunteers working closely together in a program focused on

boat design and construction for young people who come to the program often uninspired and considered at-risk for dropping out. This program accepts students with a variety of learning abilities and disabilities many of whom realize, for the first time, that when working in the shop they can succeed. They also see the practical application of learning a skill and receive guidance and exposure to the work habits required to hold a job in today's workplace. Working with the local schools and employment officials, job placement assistance is provided to ease the transition from street life back to school and to work.

A transition curriculum combines academic, vocational-technical, and work skills to help students apply knowledge to real-world problems and challenges.

Students learn that subject matter is not separated from the real world and is directly relevant for business and industry skill standards.

which the curriculum is designed. Students are introduced to subject matter that is appropriate for their age and experiences.

- *Curriculum relevance:* This factor addresses the relevance of the curriculum to the community and to business and industry skill standards. Students learn about available job opportunities in their community and how the subject matter they learn in school is relevant for the real world of work.
- *Flexibility and collaboration:* This factor addresses the ease with which the curriculum can be modified for a variety of learning environments and student learning styles (as in the multiple learning styles item in this list), and can be adapted to promote collaboration among teachers and students.

These strategies are now common in most school districts, but the extent to which students with special needs are included in these activities is sometimes limited, for a variety of reasons.

Why Are Transition Services Not Yet Fully Implemented? Since transition services were only mandated (i.e., included in the definition of 'special education') in 1990, school-to-work transition services are in a relatively early stage of design and implementation in the states. Furthermore, the extent to which such services have been developed in states and localities has been uneven. For example, career education and transition services vary widely among states and communities in the following ways:

- They may be limited to a few hours each week during the school year.
- They may or may not be summer services.
- They may or may not be offered in integrated settings.
- They may be initiated only after the student completes Carnegie units and leaves school.
- They may not be available at all to students who have completed graduation requirements.
- They may be comprehensive and include vocational training in early grades.
- They may or may not include vocational assessment.
- They may be integrated as part of an alternative education curriculum.
- They may be "added on" to the high school curriculum.
- They may involve integrated academic and vocational education.
- They may be limited to work skills only and not include social or functional skills training.
- They may or may not be delivered within the framework of an interagency cooperative agreement.
- They may or may not offer alternative credit to youths.
- They may or may not involve cooperative planning with business and industry.
- They may or may not aggressively seek the involvement of the family.
- They may or may not comply with current labor laws and guidelines (Clark & Kolstoe, 1995; Ianacone & Kochhar, 1996, 1999; Leconte, 1995).

There are several reasons for difficulty in implementing transition services. First, transition is a very complex set of services to provide. (Johnson & Guy, 1997). Second, linkages among disciplines (e.g., general education, special education, and vocational education) must be improved, and linkages between schools and a variety of community agencies (e.g., Higher Education, Vocational Rehabilitation, Education, businesses, Developmental Disabilities, and Social Services) are needed to ensure successful transition to employment and postsecondary settings. Third, secondary schools must be organized to provide the instructional, educational, and support services appropriate to students' needs. Fourth, the skills of personnel responsible for providing transition services must be adequate for implementing a transition system. Fifth, policies at the state and local levels must be realigned with current IDEA mandates and provide structure for new levels of transition services and interagency linkages. Sixth, administrative structures at the state and local levels vary, resulting in variations in leadership for system change efforts. Seventh, resource variations lead to variations in priorities for educational services at the local level and uneven development of transition services. Eighth, variations exist when states view system change as a long-term rather than short-term initiative. When states view the system change as long term, then efforts to institutionalize (make permanent) the changes occur earlier and resources are marshaled from multiple sources to continue the achievements of the first few years. Johnson & Guy (1997) also cited regional perspectives, geography, and economic stability as additional factors that affect approaches to system change by local communities within a state.

Several other problems have been identified in the literature that have led to weak implementation of transition services:

- Problems with integrating the ITP into the IEP process.
- Challenges in developing effective transition evaluation instruments and follow-up measures.
- Difficulties in increasing postsecondary options and securing funds for services.
- Problems in informing parents and securing their involvement in transition planning.
- Conflicting administrative and regulatory mandates that create barriers to collaboration among service agencies.
- Lack of financial responsibility of each agency addressed in formal interagency agreements.
- Challenges to developing ways to promote meaningful involvement of students with disabilities in transition planning.
- Inadequate funding to support transition services and a pattern of transition "haves" and "have nots" among LEAs within states.
- Problems of developing career and transition programs that are relevant for local community employment.

- Lack of procedures for reviewing the transition plan if the services could not be provided as planned.
- Inadequate transition training for personnel, parents, and students (transition training is the strongest predictor of IDEA transition policy implementation).
- Lack of availability of community-based experiences, paid work experiences, and social skills training.
- Weak guidelines governing interagency linkages, particularly in rural communities; linkages tend to be loosely managed with a great deal of local flexibility and discretion over the types of relationships among service agencies.
- Lack of co-location of service agencies or poor access to agencies needed to provide related and support services.
- Lack of procedures for sharing of interagency resources. (*Note.* Some material synthesized from Baer, Simmons & Flexer (1997); Cobb & Johnson, 1997; Johnson & Guy, 1997; Johnson & Halloran, 1997; Kohler, 1994; West, Taymans, Corbey, & Dodge, 1995.)

To improve students' access to and the availability of transition services, professionals must look within the IDEA and related laws, at their own state transition requirements, and at their local implementation guidelines. They must work together to develop a comprehensive, seamless system of supports to assist youths to make a successful transition to postsecondary life.

THE TRANSITION COORDINATOR ROLE. Many secondary schools are focusing attention on helping students think about and plan their lives beyond high school and on preparing them for the transition to postsecondary education or work. During the transition phase for special learners, there is a need for transition coordinators (who are often teachers) who can link the student with other people and agencies that can help with transition. These may include postsecondary schools, employers, community service and rehabilitation agencies, and others. The teacher or the transition coordinator, therefore, becomes an important link between the student and the post-high-school world.

Schools are experimenting with many new ways to build transition support services into instructional or related service roles in the schools. Here are some strategies used in schools today:

1. Additional transition-related responsibilities are added to the teacher's role; in many schools, the transition coordination responsibilities are attached to existing roles such as the special education teacher, the related services specialist, the vocational education specialist, or the guidance counselor (West, Taymans, Corby & Dodge, 1994).
2. Transition responsibilities are assigned to teams of teachers (subject matter teachers and consulting special education teachers).
3. Transition coordinator roles are established that focus entirely upon transition supports for students.

The roles these individuals may play in linking the student and the community may vary greatly, although the functions usually have common elements. Transition coordinator roles may vary in

- The types of transition coordination and support functions that are performed.
- The kinds and amounts of direct contact with a student and family.
- The relationship of the coordinator with the student and the family.
- The primary goals of the transition coordination activities.
- The size of the transition caseload (group of students who need transition services).
- The scope of school and interagency responsibility and of authority in the coordinator role.
- The degree to which the transition coordination functions are attached to a primary role such as teacher, counselor, administrator, or specialist.
- The way that the role is evaluated.

There is also considerable variation in how teacher-coordinators view the scope of their roles. There is no "right way" to craft the role of the transition coordinator. *What is important is that the coordination functions are appropriate for and responsive to the needs of students preparing for graduation and transition from school.*

What It Takes to Be a Transition Coordinator: Essential Skills. There are several competencies (necessary knowledge, skills, and attitudes to do the job) needed by transition coordinators. Some of the many "hats" that transition coordinators wear include

- Assessment specialist.
- Counselor who responds to the needs of individual students.
- Problem solver who resolves conflicts.
- Human resource developer who trains others and understands collaborating agencies.
- Manager who keeps records and arranges the schedules of others.
- Evaluator who assesses the progress of students and helps evaluate the effectiveness of transition coordination services to students.
- Diplomat who negotiates with sensitivity within political environments.
- Coordinator who links students with community service agencies and other community sectors.
- Public relations agent who comes into contact with citizens and community agencies.

Greatest Challenges Facing State Transition Coordinators. In a national study (West, Taymans, Corbey & Dodge, 1995), transition coordinators were asked to indicate the greatest challenges they face in their role as state transition coordinator. The following areas were most often identified:

- Working through barriers to interagency collaboration such as conflicting administrative and regulatory mandates.

- Developing ways to promote meaningful involvement of students with disabilities in transition planning.
- Working with inadequate funding to support transition services.
- Receiving consistent information from multiple local-level agencies.

COMPLIANCE WITH IDEA REQUIREMENTS IS ASTONISHINGLY LOW. Baer, Simmons, and Flexer (1997) set out to define the status of transition practice in local educational agencies in the state of Ohio and to identify factors related to compliance with transition mandates and implementation of best practices. IDEA outlines five essential components of transition that can be summarized as (1) planning based on student needs, taking into account interests and preferences; (2) outcome-oriented planning; (3) a coordinated set of activities that offer instruction, community experiences, and development of employment and postschool adult living objectives; and (4) activities that promote movement from school to postschool settings; and (5) linkages with adult services (p. 62). According to Baer, Simmons, and Flexer, research on factors influencing transition policy have been less well researched. These researchers found that in the state of Ohio that *there was less than 50 percent overall compliance with IDEA transition mandates in the LEAs and a serious lack of transition opportunities at many schools.* The specific findings are as follows:

- Ninety percent of LEAs reported that transition plans existed for transition-age students.
- Less than 50 percent reported transition services were made available as required.
- Less than 25 percent reported any system for calling together the transition team if services in the transition plan could not be provided as planned.
- There appeared to be little coordination of services among transition providers, and the IEP/transition plan was not driving the provision of transition services.
- The uneven implementation of transition mandates revealed a pattern of transition "haves" and "have nots" among LEAs.
- More than 30 percent of respondents reported less than 2 hours of transition training.
- Transition training was the strongest predictor of IDEA transition policy implementation, and there is an uneven pattern of training and advocacy to support transition implementation in the LEAs.
- A higher percentage of minority students negatively correlated with transition policy implementation, suggesting that there are unique minority issues related to transition program development. (p. 69)

These findings support earlier findings about the weak implementation of the IDEA transition mandate. For example, Kohler (1994) found only four "best practices" that were well supported by empirical research: parent and employer involvement, vocational training, paid work, and social skills training.

PROLIFERATION OF STATE INTERAGENCY POLICIES AND PLANNING MODELS FOR TRANSITION. Since 1990, states have responded to the transition initiative in many different ways. A majority of states have developed some transition policies and initiated interagency activities in their efforts to develop transition services delivery systems (Bates, Bronkema, Ames & Hess, 1992). For example, Virginia has established a state-level interagency coordinating council and transition coordinating teams for LEA throughout the state (Virginia State Improvement Plan, 1998). Many states have developed interagency agreements and committees to guide the policy process. Table 23-2 provides a summary of several states' initiatives for transition development. Some researchers have observed that many transition models were developed for students with more severe disabilities and who have more limited postsecondary options (Patton & Blalock, 1996). Often students with milder disabilities require no special services to make a successful transition. Rojewski (1992) recommended that transition services be viewed in terms of the *processes,* or *pathways,* required to make a successful transition to postschool settings. Rojewski's model embraces four main paths to employment and adult life that incorporate the variety of possible postsecondary options appropriate for students with mild disabilities:

Four Pathways to Transition

1. Direct path from high school to employment. This path would involve assistance with direct placement into employment.
2. Path from high school to postsecondary education or training. This would involve formal transfer of responsibility to adult service providers for assistance in enrolling in postsecondary programs.
3. Path from high school to postsecondary education and training and then to employment. Support begins in high school, continues through postsecondary training, and ends with employment.
4. Path from postsecondary education and training to employment. Services are initiated once the student enters postsecondary employment and continue through to placement into employment. (pp. 21–22)

The kinds of services provided to the students are determined by the processes required to help individuals reach their long-term goals.

FINDINGS FROM STUDIES OF STATE IMPLEMENTATION OF TRANSITION SERVICES: REPORT FROM THE 5-YEAR SYSTEMS CHANGE GRANTS. Since 1990, The U.S. Department of Education has funded transition system change grants to stimulate the development of systems of service delivery to students preparing to transition from secondary education. To study just how transition has been implemented in the states as defined by IDEA, and to identify best practices, the U.S. Department of Education funded

Table 23-2. Summary from States: Key Role of Supplemental and Support Services in Including Youth with Disabilities in Career-Vocational Education Services

States and Localities Reporting Improved Access and Clear Benefit from Vocational Education Cite with the Following Services as Essential	Outcomes That Correlate with Participation in Vocattional Education with Special Supports
• Job-readiness and work preparation. • Vocational staff involved in IEP development and coordination. • Social skills training. • Vocational assessment to match students' strengths and interests to work requirements. • On-site job supportive supervision and training. • In-class supports and assistance. • Adjustments to the vocational and technical education curriculum. • Adapted instructional materials. • Physical accommodations in the class and work sites. • Follow-up support and monitoring. • Case management and coordination of students' community-based programs. • Supportive guidance and counseling.	**In-School Outcomes and Indicators** • Reduced dropout rates. • Increased attendance rates. • Reduced rate of conduct or behavioral incidents. • Reduced suspension and expulsion rates. • Improved academic achievement and grades. • Greater number of Carnegie units gained. • Greater likelihood of graduation with diploma. • Greater likelihood of obtaining job skill certification before graduation. • Increased participation in community-based work experiences and paid work experiences. • Increased access to summer work experiences. **Postschool Outcomes** • Greater likelihood of obtaining competitive employment after high school. • Greater likelihood of continuing technical training or community college after school. • Greater likelihood of obtaining full-time rather than part-time employment. • Higher wages in initial employment. • Improved job retention. • More likely to live independently rather than with parents and to support own living expenses. • Greater participation in community activities and citizenship responsibilities (voting, etc.). • Reduced dependency on federal assistance programs.

Source: Synthesized from Bonz & Lindstrom, 1997, Guy & Shriner, 1997; Halpern, 1992; Micheals, 1994; NCRVE, 1994; RVSCH, DeStefano, Chadsey-Rush, Phelps, & Szymanski, 1992

a large evaluation of transition implementation. The practices that were examined included: (1) planning based on student needs, taking into account interests and preferences; (2) outcome-oriented planning; (3) a coordinated set of activities that offers instruction, community experiences, and development of employment and postschool adult living objectives; and (4) activities that promote movement from school to postschool settings; and (5) linkages with adult services.

Results of an evaluation of the system change grants funded by the U.S. Office of Special Education have shown that while transition service delivery has advanced since 1990, the changes have been very uneven within and across the states. Guy and Schriner (1997) reported that "strategies that were most likely to be effective in producing this change included (a) the use of interagency teams and cross-agency training; (b) sustained commitment of highly skilled individuals; (c) strategic integration of transition activities and resources of other system change initiatives; (d) knowledge and understanding of stakeholder systems, and (e) ongoing evaluation" (p. 2). The findings resulted in recommendations

for a coordinated system of appropriate educational and transition services and supports that would be characterized by the following:

1. *A long-range, coordinated, interagency plan for a system of education and support services* for students in integrated settings, from early intervention through to postsecondary transition, and special supports for the critical "passages," or transitions between educational settings.

2. *A statewide system of personnel development* dedicated to the long-range coordinated interagency plan for the system of services, which includes preservice and in-service personnel preparation and the training of parents.

3. *Innovative cooperative partnerships* among public schools, area colleges and universities, private providers, related services agencies, parents, and the private sector to achieve common goals for the inclusion of students with disabilities into the mainstream of education and in all aspects of educational reform (Benz & Kochhar, 1996; Clark & Kolstoe, 1991; Cobb & Johnson, 1997; Eighteenth Annual Report to Congress on IDEA, 1996; Epstein,

TABLE 23-3. How Business Can Support the Goals of Transition and Inclusion

Goal of Restructuring	Examples of Employer Partnership Activities*
1. Ensure that all students learn well.	Serve as tutors, mentors, career advisors; offer summer jobs, special courses, and after-school activities; develop entrepreneurial clubs, sponsor activities in subject areas such as science fairs; organize academic competitions; provide funds to experiment with flexible staffing; help teachers and students link with community and social service agencies.
2. Extend the capacity of teachers.	Help teachers develop new instructional strategies; provide opportunities for teachers to learn more about a subject; bring in academic consultants to work with teachers; extend teacher internships at companies; sponsor workshops; develop training programs; train volunteer teams.
3. Create school systems that encourage innovation.	Work with educators to assess school system needs; help set goals; help the district hire qualified individuals to oversee the restructuring process; bring in outside experts or advisors to help teachers and school leaders develop new strategies; provide training sites and programs; help schools appeal for community support.
4. Develop effective assessment tools.	Help schools generate, manage, and use assessment information; identify and develop measurable goals; create performance-based assessment strategies; institute an interactive evaluation process.

* *Source:* Kochhar & Erickson (1994). Business-Education Partnerships for the 21st Century, with permission of the Council for Aid to Education, © 1991.

1995; Janney & Meyer, 1990; Johnson & Guy, 1997; Johnson & Halloran, 1997; Kochhar, 1995; Lueking, Fabian & Tilson, 1995; Meers, 1991; Meyer & Skrtic, 1995; Neubert, 1996; Rifle, 1990; Schattman & Benay, 1992; Skrtic, 1990; West, Taymans, Corbey & Dodge, 1995).

4. *Ongoing evaluation* of systematic service delivery efforts and transition outcomes (Guy & Schriner, 1997; Johnson & Guy, 1997; Johnson & Halloran, 1997).

Service coordination and multiagency collaboration continue to be primary factors in the transition success or failure for individuals with disabilities and their families; gains made by students can be lost in the critical stage of transition to employment and independent living. One of the purposes of the system approach fostered by these grants was to facilitate interagency linkages and to improve the ability of systems to respond to changing population needs, as well as to reduce fragmentation of local services. Continued national commitment is required to strengthen the nation's capacity to provide and improve the preparation of professionals to strengthen collaboration across agency lines (Guy & Schriner, 1997; Johnson & Guy, 1997; Johnson & Halloran, 1997).

HOW CAN THE BUSINESS COMMUNITY SUPPORT INCLUSION INTO OCCUPATIONAL PREPARATION PROGRAMS?

Assessing Skill Achievement in the Inclusive Vocational-Technical Program. Students who are in inclusive career-vocational and technical education need to have their skill achievements assessed to determine how ready they are to actually perform tasks in a given occupational area. Many occupations have published skill criteria that are being used in vocational-technical education classrooms to develop curricula and design assessments of

student achievement. These skill assessments are based upon classroom and work-based skill performance attainment, completion of the national standards certifications for specific vocational areas, and course completion requirements. For example, in the graphics arts industry, students would be required to complete certification in at least one of the eight certification areas before placement into employment in the field. These certifications would be provided by the Printing Industry of America. Similarly, auto mechanics trainees would be expected to complete certification in one of the major certification areas through an area community college certification program. Students in child care and medical assistant vocational areas would be expected to meet state standards and guidelines for child care workers and national standards for medical assistants.

Use of authentic training environments and training outcomes in the community have been found to be particularly effective for adolescent special learners, allowing them to integrate academic and vocational skills development in real-world work-environment applications.

The business community is equally concerned with academic programs and the transition of youth to contemporary work environments. Table 23-3 summarizes transition and inclusion strategies to support business involvement with the schools.

EFFECTIVE STRATEGIES AND APPROPRIATE PATHS TO THE WORKFORCE. The school-to-work transition process is a shared responsibility between schools and community agencies, one that does not end until an initial postsecondary placement goal has been achieved. It is widely recognized that the provision of school-to-work transition services can have a significantly positive effect on the employment and adult independent living outcomes for all students in the future, especially for students who are likely to drop out before age 15. For students with disabilities for whom employment after graduation is an appropriate goal, career and vocational education opportunities have reduced dropout rates and grade retention (holding the student back one or more years) for youth. School inclusion plans should offer opportunities for all students to participate in a performance-based education and training program that will

1. Enable the students to earn portable work credentials (verification to employers of occupational skills students have achieved).
2. Prepare the students for skilled jobs in careers that have relevance in the community.
3. Teach students general skills that are transferable between occupations and that provide the foundation for productive and progressively more rewarding roles in the work place.
4. Increase their opportunities for further education, including advanced technical or on-the-job training, or education in a 4-year college or university.
5. Be consistent with effective transition practices in the field.

Assurances of Full Participation in Paths of Opportunity into the Workforce. Career-vocational education programs should provide the following assurances of full participation of all youth, particularly members of special populations. These programs should include

1. Equal access to recruitment, assessment, enrollment, and placement activities related to school-to-work program.
2. Equal access to the full range of school-to-work transition programs.
3. Coordination of school-to-work transition programs with existing related career and transition programs for special populations.
4. Provision of information about available school-to-work programs to students and parents or guardians 1 year prior to the age (age of majority) that such programs are generally available to students in the state.

Work-Based Learning. The work-based learning component of a vocational-technical program or School-to-Work Opportunities program should also include

1. Paid work experience, and, as appropriate for career exploration and preemployment work preparation activities, unpaid experience.
2. Instruction in general work-place competencies, including instruction and activities on developing positive work attitudes and work behaviors, work adjustment activities, and employability and participative skills.
3. Instruction in and orientation to reasonable work accommodations and job restructuring, if needed.

4. Activities such as job shadowing, job exploration, work-based vocational skills assessments, school-sponsored enterprises, or on-the-job training for academic credit.
5. Career exploration and counseling, beginning prior to the students' 11th grade year or as early as ninth grade, if necessary, for students who need additional preemployment training time or who are experiencing particular difficulties in the learning environment. This counseling is to help students who may need extra preparatory time or who may be interested identifying, selecting or reconsidering their interests, goals, and career majors.
6. Regularly scheduled assessments and evaluations involving ongoing consultation, interpretation, and problem solving with students to identify academic strengths, weaknesses, academic progress, work-place knowledge, goals, and the need for additional learning opportunities to master core academic and vocational skills.
7. Input and outcome focus for youth transition: An outcome focus is vital to facilitating inclusion since positive outcomes for youth offer evidence that the programs are working (Wagner, 1993). Outcomes for youth placed into inclusive vocational education classrooms will improve if the resources, supports, and specialized services (inputs and processes) are available to address their individual needs. Outcomes need to be realistic and consistent with the students' IEP goals, and should correlate with supported participation in vocational-technical education.

Emphasis on outcomes alone, however, will not guarantee positive outcomes unless schools ensure the appropriate resource inputs into the overall improvement of career and vocational and transition services.

Skill Certificates. The term *skill certificate* means a portable, industry-recognized credential issued by a School-to-Work Opportunities program under an approved plan. It certifies that a student has mastered skills at levels that, to the extent feasible, are at least as challenging as skill standards endorsed by the National Skill Standards Board established under the National Skill Standards Act of 1993. Until uniform skills standards are developed, the term *skill certificate* means a credential issued under a process described in an approved plan of a state. The opportunity to receive a high school diploma, skill certificates, or other diplomas upon completion of high school should be available to all students, including those with disabilities. It is also important to recognize that there is a rapidly growing number of youth who are failing in the general education setting, are at risk of dropping out of school, and who need alternative paths to the diploma, such as occupational certification.

SUMMARY OF BEST PRACTICES FOR TRANSITION. The following provides examples of practices states have found most effective for student inclusion in school-to-work transition.

Transition Services for All Students

- Establish a student-centered approach.
- Establish transition or careers academies which will offer technical and preapprenticeship training in four high-demand occupational areas.
- Develop a regional consortium of LEAs and community agencies to strengthen regional transition planning to improve the quality and quantity of career-vocational and transitional services, improve at-risk students' inclusion in occupational training with nondisabled peers, and improve the preparation of teachers, counselors, and community support personnel to serve students with disabilities.
- Develop unique strategies to identify, recruit, train, and place youth with disabilities who are at risk of dropping out of school or who have already done so.
- Develop interagency partnerships for long-range planning to assist youth with selection of, application to, enrollment in, and adjustment to postsecondary institutions.
- Develop an LEA systemwide change plan for transition support for all youth with disabilities who have dropped out of school or who are at risk for dropping out.
- Utilize a unique partnership among school and community organizations for the outreach, recruitment, assessment, and planning for students who have dropped out of school.
- Incorporate planning for dropout prevention and outreach to dropouts into the school's strategic planning and systemwide change initiative to expand services for students with disabilities.
- Provide intensive support to students who return to school to complete their education, including transportation, peer mentoring teams, teacher-advocates, and monetary incentives for time spent in the program.
- Incorporate recent achievement research and outcomes in vocational-technical areas into alternative performance assessments (exhibitions and demonstrations).
- Provide an innovative linkage with the local Private Industry Council Regional Consortium to provide transition and follow-up support for program completers.
- Promote self-determination and self-advocacy for youth with disabilities through peer teams and incentives.
- Provide preapprenticeship training and opportunity for skills certification; allow out-of-school students to also work toward completion of the GED.
- Provide employer assessment, references, and certification of skills.
- Promote access and inclusion in work-based training opportunities.
- Develop and implement procedures for a regional dropout study to analyze factors that influence students' decision to drop out, profile significant characteristics and risk factors for youth currently enrolled in school, and modify school barriers to the participation of youth who have left school.

- Provide parents with a broader support network through the local Parent Resource Center and include parents in school exhibitions and demonstrations of student performance to make training concrete and product(outcome)-focused.
- Include parents in the transition planning process.
- Develop integrated academic-vocational-technical education which meets industry-based performance standards.
- Develop business-education partnerships.
- Provide orientation and training to teachers, which includes the context of broad school reform and restructuring activities.
- Build on youths' natural attraction to applied work experiences and use of innovative technology.
- Promote students' goal setting and cooperative learning and encourage students to engage in self-evaluation of their own performance and progress.
- Stimulate sharing of resources among schools, employment and training agencies, and businesses.
- Enable school-based staff to have a major role in making instructional decisions.
- Place a major emphasis on professional development.
- Ensure that health and other social services are sufficient to reduce significant barriers to participation and learning.
- Expose students to technology and current real-world work environments.

Placement and Transition Support. There are several strategies available to the transition teacher to directly place students into jobs or assist them in applying and enrolling in postsecondary training. These include providing career counseling and information about employment and postsecondary training opportunities. For students who desire to enter a 2- or 4-year college or technical school, the teacher can

- Assist the student in selecting colleges.
- Assist the student in applying and negotiating for support services.
- Assist the students in learning about how to access campus resources.
- Arrange for student sessions with the career counselor for discussion of job search strategies.
- Discuss interviewing techniques.
- Discuss self-advocacy and how to promote one's strengths.
- Discuss the advantages and disadvantages of self-disclosure of the disability and how to negotiate for needed job accommodations.
- Have cooperating business leaders host near graduates in simulated job interviews before their actual interviews, to gain experience and receive real-world feedback from employers.

These practices usually require long-term change strategies to address the needs of youth with disabilities, most of whom are at risk of dropping out of school and of long-term dependence. Youth learning environments, as early as possible, must relate what is taught in school with what is required in the world of work or postsecondary educational settings. Learning to know must not be separated from learning to do.

Case Example 23-1 provides a sample local school guideline for supported inclusion in vocational-technical education.

CASE EXAMPLE 23-1. Prince William County (PWC) Public Schools Guidelines for Supported Inclusion in Vocational-Technical Education

Prince William County Public Schools has as its goal to integrate as many students with disabilities into the regular classroom and to provide access to technology enriched vocational-technical education and work-experience opportunities in integrated settings. To that end, the following objectives are in place:

1. Students with disabilities must be educated with students without disabilities.
2. Special classes, separate schooling, or other removal of children with disabilities from the regular educational environment should occur only when the nature or severity of the disability is such that education in the regular classes cannot be achieved satisfactorily with the use of supplementary aids, services, and support (PL. 94-142, Section 300.50).
3. An effective delivery system of specialized services at the local level *will be established to reduce the need to remove the student from his/her neighborhood school to obtain special education and related services* [emphasis added].

Similarly, PWC's objectives for mainstreaming include the following:

1. To educate all children with disabilities in regular school settings regardless of the degree or severity of

their disability unless the severity of the disability is such that education in regular classes with supplementary aids and services cannot be achieved satisfactorily.
2. To allow special education students to participate in regular education classes with support provided as needed by the special education staff, related services staff, support personnel, and other local school personnel.

Although PWC seeks to develop a continuum of support services, the existing continuum poses many barriers to fulfilling a commitment to mainstreaming or supported inclusion. These barriers include (1) determining educational, vocational, and transition service needs through comprehensive assessment, (2) providing services in integrated education settings, (3) preparing personnel for integrated instructional and community-based programs, (4) restructuring classrooms and related services to accommodate students with severe disabilities, (5) accommodating students with disabilities with technology instruction, and (6) integrating services across agencies.

Source: Prince William County Public Schools, Manassas, VA.

WHO SHOULD I TALK TO FOR INFORMATION?

- Student's special education teacher
- County or district transition coordinators
- School's vocational education teachers
- County or district community services agency managers or directors (e.g., developmental disabilities personnel)
- State or local Department of Rehabilitative Services supervisor
- Department of Rehabilitative Services school unit
- School or county job placement coordinators
- District or county offices of Adult and Community Education (they typically offer apprenticeship and external diploma programs)
- County or district office of Business/Industry Relations
- County or district office of Vocational Education
- County or district office of Special Education Programs
- County or district Community Services Act coordinator
- County or district school-to-work coordinator
- County or district Parent Resource Center
- County or district Human Services Administration
- County or district Commission for Disabled Persons or human rights organization
- State Department of Motor Vehicles (for special permits for students with disabilities)
- State or local Employment Commission or Department of Manpower Services
- Local job training offices
- Local or state Department of Social Services

For schools seeking linkages with business, the Angelito Unified School District Partnership Program Data

Information Form provides an example of a structured record of information on a school–business partnership.

CHECKLIST FOR PARENTS, TEACHERS, SERVICE COORDINATORS, AND ADVOCATES

PREVOCATIONAL

___ What vocational preparation opportunities are available before ninth grade?

___ What vocational preassessment services (preferences, aptitudes) are available?

___ Know your rights: Get familiar with vocational education, special education, Americans with Disabilities Act, and school-to-work legislation.

CAREER AND VOCATIONAL PREPARATION

___ Is there a vocational component in the IEP (goals and plans for the student with disabilities? *Be involved*)

___ Is there a team approach to planning (special education, vocational education, rehabilitation, regular educators, etc.)?

___ Is there a central listing of the vocational programs that are available to choose from?

___ What vocational assessment services are there?

___ What support services are available?

___ Can students explore different vocations?

___ Can students get actual real-world work experiences (community-based training)?

___ What school-based employment opportunities are there?

___ Are there semicompetitive employment options if the student is not ready for competitive employment, and what are the rules?

___ What decisions does the student have to make and when? (What grade; what career or occupational area; what program; what long-range goals for employment and independent living?)

___ What help is available for making career choices?

___ Are there physical or job accommodations that should be made?

___ Do regular education, special education, and vocational education teachers work together?

___ Are there summer programs for students, and how do they get in?

___ Is there a central contact person (service coordinator or advocate) who has continued contact with the student?

___ What transportation is available for different vocational programs?

___ Know your rights: vocational education, special education, rehabilitation, Americans with disabilities Act, and school-to-work legislation.

TRANSITION FROM SCHOOL TO WORK

___ Are there transition goals and plans in the IEP?

___ Is there a team approach to transition planning (special education, vocational education, rehabilitation, and regular educators, as well as community-based personnel and employers)?

___ Is there a policy that tells what happens if an agency identified on the IEP does not fulfill its responsibility for a transition objective?

___ Is there a central listing of the transition services and support services that are available to students with disabilities?

___ What placement assessment and counseling services are there?

___ Are students prepared for job interviews and placement?

___ Are there on-the-job supports available once the student is placed into employment?

___ Are there job coaches for community-based work? Is there supported employment?

___ What decisions does the student have to make about postschool placement and when?

___ Are there physical job accommodations that should be made?

___ Do regular education, special education, and vocational education teachers work together for transition?

___ Are there summer programs for students and how do they get in?

___ Is there a central transition contact person (transition coordinator or advocate) who has continued contact with the student? Who is that person?

___ Is there an emphasis on self-advocacy?

___ Know your rights: special education, rehabilitation, community services, Americans with Disabilities Act, and school-to-work legislation.

POSTSECONDARY TRAINING

___ What area postschool programs are available to my son or daughter?

___ Are there any area programs under the School-to-Work program and Job Training Partnership Act (JTPA)?

___ Who and where are the counselors who can help make postschool enrollment decisions?

___ Should my child think about community college?

___ If community college is a possibility, what colleges have special support services and counselors to help the students?

___ Is my son or daughter prepared for self-advocacy? Can he or she tell the employer about preparations to overcome barriers, without waiting to be asked?

___ Know your rights: rehabilitation, school-to-work, Americans with Disabilities Act, and higher education legislation.

EMPLOYMENT

___ What area job opportunities are best for youth with disabilities?

___ Which businesses have special programs to hire youth with disabilities?

___ What is the general outlook for employment in the region? (Service industry: computer-related fields and data entry, clerical, health, child care, and preschool occupations; horticulture; home-improvement industry; personal services; and telecommunications).

___ What job descriptions are there for entry level jobs? (ADA now requires specific descriptions for any jobs advertised).

___ Is my son/daughter prepared for self-advocacy? Can he/she tell the employer how he/she is prepared to overcome the barriers and not wait to be asked?

___ Know your rights: Americans with Disabilities Act, rehabilitation and fair labor standards legislation.

INDEPENDENT LIVING AND LIFE ENRICHMENT

Is my son or daughter preparing or prepared for

___ Independent living in the near future? What are the short- and long-range goals?

___ Social participation in postschool activities?

___ Involvement in community activities?

___ Involvement in avocations and hobbies?

___ Serious relationships and marriage?

THE ANGELITO UNIFIED SCHOOL DISTRICT
PARTNERSHIP PROGRAM DATA INFORMATION FORM

SCHOOL/OFFICE: _____ DATE: _____ LOCATION CODE: _____

FILL OUT A SEPARATE FORM FOR EACH PARTNERSHIP PROGRAM

SURVEY DIRECTIONS: *Using a #2 pencil*, fill in *all* the appropriate bubbles () and provide additional information as requested.

A. PARTNERSHIP NAME

() Adopt-A-School
() Applied Economics
() Business Issues in the Classroom
() Focus on Youth
() Invent America
() Law Day
() Los Angeles Beautiful

() Math, Engineering, Science Achievement (MESA)
() Project Business
() Regional Occupational Program (ROP)
() Small Grants for Teachers
() Young Astronauts
() Youth Motivation Task Force (YMTF)
() Others (list): _____

B. DATE PROGRAM BEGAN

Month_____ Year 19___

C. PROGRAM STATUS

() Planning Stage   () Operational
() To Be Expanded   () To Be Discontinued

D. PARTNER INFORMATION

(NOTE: If this Partnership has more than one partner, attach additional partner information to this form.)

COMPANY/ORGANIZATION NAME: _____

ADDRESS: _____
              (Street)   (City)   (State)   (Zip)

CEO/SENIOR EXECUTIVE: _____ TITLE:_____

CONTACT PERSON: _____ TITLE: _____ PHONE: () _____

SIZE OF COMPANY/ORGANIZATION:
() Large (more than 500 employees)   () Medium (50 to 500 employees)   () Small (less than 50 employees)

E. KIND OF COMPANY/ORGANIZATION

() Advertizing/Marketing
() Agri-Business
() Armed Services
() Association/Foundation
() College/University
() Community Agency
() Construction

() Entertainment
() Financial/Banking
() Fine Arts/Humanities
() Government
() Health Care
() Hospitality/Recreation
() Insurance

() Manufacturing
() Media/Publishing
() Professional (Dr., Lawyer, etc.)
() Public Relations
() Restaurant/Food Service
() Sales
() Science/Technology

() Service
() Sports/Fitness
() Transportation
() Utilities
() Other: _____

F. PROGRAM TARGET GROUPS

1. STUDENTS

() PreKdg   () Grade 3   () Grade 7   () Grade 11
() Kdg   () Grade 4   () Grade 8   () Grade 12
() Grade 1   () Grade 5   () Grade 9   () Special Ed.
() Grade 2   () Grade 6   () Grade 10   () Adult Ed.

2. ADULTS

() Teachers   () Parents
() Administrators
() Others (list): _____

G. SUBJECT AREA FOCUS

() Bilingual/ESL
() Career Awareness
() Computer Tech.
() Fine Arts (music, art, drama, dance)
() Health
() Language Arts

() Mathematics
() Parenting
() Physical Education
() Reading
() Safety
() Science
() Social Studies

() Substance Abuse prevention
() Vocational Education (write in subject
   areas): _____
   _____
   _____
() Other: _____

H. PROGRAM OBJECTIVES AND ACTIVITIES

() ENHANCE INSTRUCTION
    () Guest Speaker/Lecturers/Demonstrator
    () Reading Incentive Programs
    () Specialized Contests
    () Tutoring in Subject Areas
    () Educational Tours and Field Trips
    () Other: _____

() IMPROVE CAREER EDUCATION AND
PREPARATION FOR WORLD OF WORK
    () Career Day Programs and Fairs
    () Classroom Presentation/Demonstration
    () Business and Industry Visitations
    () Career Shadowing
    () Employment (jobs/skills development for students)
    () Other: _____

() IMPLEMENT SHARED DECISION
MAKING
    () Management Training
    () Staff Development
    () Curriculum Design/Redesign
    () Teacher Internships
    () Resource Centers
    () Other: _____

() PROVIDE IN-KIND ASSISTANCE, MATERIAL
AND FINANCIAL RESOURCES
    () Awards and Incentives
    () Equipment Donation
    () Material Donations (meetings, newsletters,
       events, video, etc.)
    () Scholarships
    () Other: _____

() REDUCE DROPOUT RATE
    () Attendance Incentive Program
    () Self-Esteem Programs
    () Tutoring
    () Citizenship Program
    () Mentoring
    () Other: _____

() IMPROVE SCHOOL CLIMATE/LEARNING
ENVIRONMENT
    () School Beautification Programs
    () School Pride Program
    () Student, School and Community Service Programs
    () Anti-Vandalism Programs
    () Extracurricular Programs
    () Other: _____

() EXPAND PROFESSIONAL DEVELOPMENT AND
STAFF RECOGNITION
    () Staff Recognition
    () Teacher Internships
    () Staff Grants
    () Staff Development (teachers, parents, volunteers)
    () Team Teaching (business and education)
    () Other: _____

() IMPROVE COMMUNICATION WITH LEGISLATORS,
BUSINESS, COMMUNITY AND PARENTS
    () Attend PTA/School Site Council Meeting
    () Development of Communication Tools
    () Partner/Volunteer Recognition
    () Grants (staff development, curriculum, etc.)
    () Promote Advocacy
    () Parent Programs (cultural, health, parenting, etc.)

I. PROGRAM DATA AVAILABLE THROUGH: (FILL IN AS APPLICABLE)

() Records (Example: attendance)   () Surveys   () Tests
() Teacher Judgement   () Observations   () Interviews
() Other (list): _____

J. SPECIAL SCHOOL NEEDS
(Choose *two* school needs and, on the lines provided, list activities to meet the needs):

() Enhance Instruction _____
() Reduce Dropout Rate _____
() Improve Career Education and Preparation for World of Work _____
() Improve School Climate/Learning Environment _____
() Implement Shared Decision Making _____
() Expand Professional Development and Staff Recognition _____
() Provide In-Kind Assistance, Materials and Financial Resources _____
() Improve Communication with Legislators, Business, Community and Parents _____
() Other _____

PRINCIPAL SIGNATURE _____

CHAPTER **24**

How Can a School's Readiness for Inclusion Be Assessed?

As a school prepares for inclusion, or prepares to expand the inclusive practices it has already begun, it is useful for administrators to assess the readiness of the school and its personnel for the changes ahead. Because of the emotionally charged issues surrounding the inclusion process, it is important to determine if, in fact, the school environment is ready for and conducive to expanding inclusion initiative. Frequently, schools move to adopt inclusive practices with little understanding of their demands and impacts on the whole school. In other words, they fail to engage in *strategic planning for inclusion*. The following assessment tool has been used in classrooms and by inclusion planning teams to determine if the current school organization and personnel and general resources are adequate for, or in alignment with, their inclusion initiative. It has also been used by schools who have been implementing inclusion for a year or more to determine if the school's inclusion practices (personnel, curriculum and instruction, and school "culture," or attitudes) are consistent with best practices for inclusion. Inclusive classrooms and schools provide opportunities for access and full participation of all students, to the extent possible, in the full range of academic and nonacademic activities.

Are You Ready? Assessing Readiness to Implement Inclusion in the Classroom and School

INCLUSION RATING KEY

5 = Consistently achieved with high quality (high performing)

4 = Progressing well, but could improve in some areas

3 = Progressing, but still have many problems to solve

2 = Initiated, but showing very limited progress

1 = Not initiated, or experiencing many barriers (low performing)

Note: These assessment items reflect research-based best practices in inclusion, as well as the 1997 Amendments to the Individuals with Disabilities Education Act

READINESS FOR STUDENT EVALUATION AND ASSESSMENT	5	4	3	2	1
Students with disabilities are diagnosed and their educational needs assessed in advance of the decision for inclusive placement.					
Student evaluation and assessment is comprehensive and addresses the range of functional domains that may impact upon the student's ability to benefit from the inclusive classroom.					
Initial vision, speech and language, and hearing screenings are available for students who need them.					
Students are provided accommodations to participate in district and statewide performance assessments					
Diagnostic test information is interpreted for teachers so that the teacher understands the implications of the disability on learning and on the teaching environment.					
Diagnostic test information is interpreted for the parents, in understandable terms, so that they understand the implications of the disability on learning and on the teaching environment.					
For students with disabilities, evaluations are current within 3 years.					
Procedures have been developed for obtaining record information about the previous placement, particularly for students being transferred in from other school districts or from private or other public agencies.					
Medical evaluations and medication needs are communicated to teachers and related personnel who will be working with the student; this is done before the student placement into the classroom (if these are conditions that may require intervention in the classroom or may impact the learning).					
Initial and annual assessments of functional skills are available for students who need them.					
Vocational evaluation and assessment is available to students who are developing transition components in their IEPs.					
Vocational evaluation information is interpreted for teachers and parents in terms of its implications in the identification of transition service needs, courses of study, and career goals.					
Administrators know the percentage of students with disabilities in the vocational-technical education classes.					
Administrators seek to identify students with disabilities who might benefit from vocational-technical education.					
Administrators know the percentage of students with disabilities participating in work-based and transition services and activities and seek to identify those students with disabilities who could benefit from such experiences.					

continues

READINESS FOR STUDENT ASSESSMENT *(continued)*	5	4	3	2	1
Administrators know the numbers of students with disabilities who are participating in nonacademic and extracurricular school activities with their nondisabled peers; they and seek to identify students with disabilities who could participate.					

READINESS OF THE EDUCATIONAL ENVIRONMENT					
Information is recorded and shared among personnel about the number of students enrolled in their home schools who have transferred from more restrictive settings, such as hospitals, rehabilitation agencies, institutions, correctional facilities, or residential programs.					
Individualized education programs (IEPs) are developed before placement and continued for each student after placement into an inclusive classroom.					
If an interim placement is identified for a student transferring between schools or from one grade level to another, an interim IEP is developed in advance of the placement; parental consent is obtained.					
IEP reviews are held annually, with representation from an interdisciplinary team, including the student, parents, teacher, consultant, and pertinent support-service personnel.					
Functional and social-skill training goals are addressed in the IEP as needed.					
For students enrolled in vocational education who need modifications or support services in order to participate, vocational education and the support services and accommodations are written into the IEP, along with specific goals and objectives.					
Students' IEPs include short- and long-range goals and identify specific personnel who will be primary points of contact for the student's IEP and progress.					
IEPs include a statement of how the child's progress toward achieving annual goals will be measured, how the parents will be regularly informed (e.g., periodic report cards) at least as often as parents of nondisabled students, and the extent to which that progress is adequate to enable the student to achieve the goals by the end of the year.					
The IEP identifies service barriers or services needed by the student but not available in the school or community.					
The IEP specifies expected dates for achievement of goals and provision of needed services.					
Needed related and support services are documented in the IEP with specific dates of provision, amounts of services, and person identified as responsible for providing them.					
Students with disabilities are provided opportunities to participate in school-to-work and transition activities that directly address the needs of the students.					
At age 14 (or earlier, if appropriate), the student's IEP includes a statement of needed transition services that focus on the student's course of study (such as participation in vocational education, community-based experiences, or advanced placement classes, for example).					
At age 16 (or earlier, if appropriate), the student's IEP includes a statement of needed transition services, including a statement of the interagency responsibilities or any needed linkages.					
At least 1-year before a student reaches the age of majority under state law, the IEP contains a statement that the student has been informed of the rights that will transfer to the student on reaching the age of majority.					

READINESS OF THE EDUCATIONAL ENVIRONMENT (continued)	5	4	3	2	1
Teachers and related service personnel make necessary accommodations for students with disabilities to participate, to the extent reasonable, in nonacademic and extracurricular opportunities generally available to all students, including student clubs, sports (as appropriate), drama and theatrical productions, chorus, debate teams, trade-related clubs, student governance organizations, booster clubs, student fund-raising activities, science fairs, and other extracurricular opportunities.					
Students with disabilities are offered guidance counseling in their high school years and assisted in gaining access to the guidance counselor.					
Administrators know the numbers of students with disabilities who are participating in guidance counseling and seek to identify students who could benefit.					
When appropriate, students with disabilities are included in college preparation seminars or career counseling sessions available to nondisabled students.					
Students with disabilities who are placed into general education classes are included in instructional activities in which technology is used.					
Teachers and related personnel provide necessary accommodations for students with disabilities to participate in technology-related activities generally available to all students, including libraries, computers for on-line activities, information centers, technology laboratories, school-based weather station (with accommodations in the physical layout of these centers and adaptations to equipment as necessary).					
To the extent reasonable, students with disabilities are included with all students in the same state or school district in standardized testing and evaluation experiences required of all students (e.g., national or state competency tests, achievement tests, and others).					
Teachers are provided with adequate technical assistance and support services needed to help the student benefit from the inclusive placement, and to help other students accept the student and create a positive environment.					
In advance of a student's placement into the general education classroom, teachers receive the administrative and IEP team's rationale for a decision to place a student into the classroom.					
When a student is placed into the general education classroom, teachers receive a statement of the expectations of the IEP team for the benefits of the placement and for the progress of the child in the classroom within the year.					
Teachers are knowledgeable about the range of inclusive options within the school.					
Teachers are provided with technical assistance, as needed, to help students with disabilities be accommodated in the full range of nonacademic, extracurricular, and technology-related opportunities generally available to all students.					
Teachers are provided technical assistance, as needed, to help students with disabilities be accommodated in the full range of career-vocational and school-to-career programs and services available to all students, including vocational education, career planning activities, job training and placement opportunities, transition services, school-to-careers programs, community-based experiences, and assistance in planning and making applications to colleges and other postschool programs.					
Teachers are provided with constructive problem-solving strategies and a fair and accessible process in which the teacher may raise issues or concerns at any time about a placement of a student, the student's progress, or the student's behavior, and the teacher may request a consultation or assistance in problem solving or seeking additional support.					

continues

READINESS OF THE EDUCATIONAL ENVIRONMENT *(continued)*	5	4	3	2	1
Teachers who work in teams and need to modify the curriculum and instruction for students with disabilities in the general education classroom are provided with opportunities for common planning time each week to develop plans that meet students' IEP goals.					
Teachers have examined the system of classroom performance assessment they will use and have considered accommodations and nontraditional assessments for students with disabilities, or they have considered using the assessments for an interim period in order to measure learning and competency gains in academic, social, and behavioral achievement.					
READINESS OF THE PHYSICAL AND SUPPORT SERVICES ENVIRONMENT					
When students with disabilities are placed into the general education classroom, they have access to a range of support services that they may need to benefit from the educational program (including speech and hearing, assistive technology, vocational assessment, special education consultation, health supports, guidance, and counseling).					
There is adequate time provided in advance to students, parents, and teachers about a classroom placement for all to determine (1) appropriate accommodations and support services that the student will need, (2) time for orientation of the student to the new classroom, and (3) need for advanced orientation and preparation of teachers in the use of new materials or adaptive equipment.					
Students are informed about potential emergency situations that may arise out of the disability and that may require them to receive emergency treatment or procedures in the classroom or school; they are provided with advanced training in actions or responses they must take, if any.					
Receiving teachers or the teaching team are informed about the student's disability and whether the student has a physical, medical, emotional or behavioral problem that might result in the need to take an emergency action in the classroom.					
Students and parents are informed about the emergency management policies and procedures of the school, which are clearly defined to guide actions of teachers and other personnel in the event of a behavioral, medical, or natural emergency.					
Teachers, related service personnel, and administrators are trained and knowledgeable of the emergency procedures or actions that may be needed with a student with a disability, including medical, behavioral or other emergency.					
To the extent possible, in advance of their placement, students are provided with information about the needed supplemental materials, equipment, or personnel deemed necessary by the IDT to enable the student to benefit from the educational social program in the classroom, including, but not limited to, physical assistive devices or equipment, technology adaptations (computer adaptations), physical adaptations to the classroom, personal or classroom aides, instructional materials, interpreters, recording devices, or other equipment.					
Teachers are provided with the supplemental materials, equipment, or personnel deemed necessary by the interdisciplinary team for the student to benefit from the educational and social program in the classroom, including, but not limited to, physical assistive devices or equipment, technology adaptations (computer adaptations), physical adaptations to the classroom, personal or classroom aides, instructional materials, interpreters, recording devices, or other equipment.					
Teachers are informed in advance of placement about classroom accommodations and are trained in the use of such equipment and materials in advance of or, minimally, at the time of the student's placement into the classroom.					

READINESS OF THE PHYSICAL AND SUPPORT SERVICES ENVIRONMENT *(continued)*	5	4	3	2	1
A support service directory, with contacts of key professionals and representatives of service agencies, is available, is updated, and is used by teachers and inclusion implementors.					
Each student included in the regular classroom is assigned to a teacher mentor, advocate, or coordinator (a *single point of contact*) who can assist and support the student is his or her effort to succeed in the new classroom.					
READINESS OF THE ATTITUDINAL CULTURE AND ENVIRONMENT					
Teachers, administrators, and related service personnel believe that, to the maximum extent possible, students with disabilities belong in classrooms and other school and community settings with students who are not disabled, and that special classes, separate schooling, or other removal of children with disabilities from the regular educational environment should occur only when the nature or severity of the disabilities is such that education in regular classes cannot be achieved satisfactorily with the use of supplementary aids and services.					
Teachers, administrators, and related service personnel believe that social inclusion is an essential element of successful full inclusion and that students must feel that they belong.					
Teachers, administrators, and related service personnel believe that students with disabilities placed into general education classrooms should be as equally involved in cooperative learning and peer instruction as are all students.					
Teachers, administrators, and related service personnel are committed to the development of a caring school community which fosters mutual respect and support among personnel, parents, and students.					
Teachers, administrators, and related service personnel are committed to the belief that students without disabilities can benefit from friendships with students with disabilities.					
Teachers, administrators, and related service personnel *actively intervene* in student behaviors which violate the belief that all students must demonstrate respect for each other and that all students belong (e.g., taunting, teasing, or isolating a student with a disability in the classroom or other school setting).					
The administration creates a school environment and culture of support and commitment to inclusion and the development of inclusive practices.					
Inclusive principles are modeled to the community: Communication and information to the community about students with disabilities are integrated into general school reports or newsletters, rather than prepared as separate documents.					
Teachers and administrators celebrate the successes of inclusion by rewarding excellence in teaching of diverse classrooms, team teaching, special education consultation, and creative accommodations (e.g., through awards, commendations, posters, announcements at staff meetings and school assemblies, and highlights in newsletters).					
Teachers and administrators celebrate the successes of inclusion by rewarding excellence in the achievement of students with disabilities in inclusive classrooms, in classroom climates of acceptance, in peer mentoring and support, in student participation in nonacademic and extracurricular activities, and in general school participation.					
Teachers and administrators celebrate the parental role in inclusion by rewarding excellence in parent involvement, parent-to-parent mentoring, and parent volunteering in the school.					

continues

READINESS FOR WHOLE SCHOOL PLANNING AND COMMITMENT	5	4	3	2	1
The inclusion plan states that students with disabilities are expected to be educated with students without disabilities; this plan is linked to the General School Improvement Plan.					
The school inclusion plan includes assurances that the school will promote the inclusion and full participation of all students, including students with disabilities, in the full range of nonacademic and extracurricular programs and activities, including outreach, recruitment, assessment (or tryouts), and enrollment in those activities.					
The school inclusion plan includes assurances that the school will promote the inclusion and full participation of all students, including students with disabilities, in the full range of school-to-work transition programs, including outreach, recruitment, assessment, enrollment, and placement activities.					
The school inclusion plan states that special classes, separate schooling, or other removal of children with disabilities from the regular educational environment should occur only when the nature or severity of the disability is such that education in the regular classes cannot be achieved satisfactorily with the use of supplementary aids, services, and support.					
The school inclusion plan requires that an effective delivery system of support services and instructional supports in the school and in each inclusive classroom be established to minimize the need to remove the student from his or her classroom or home school to obtain special education and related services (i.e., the school seeks creative methods to integrate the needed supportive services into the regular class).					
The school inclusion plan addresses the needs of all students to participate in classroom activities and to access materials and technology.					
The school inclusion plan addresses coordination of inclusion efforts with other school-linked agencies, such as vocational-rehabilitation service agencies, social and human service agencies, health service agencies, and other agencies responsible for coordinating services to children and youth.					
The school inclusion plan describes how the services in the students' IEPs will be coordinated through a single point of contact for students, parents, and teachers.					
The school inclusion plan describes the manner in which the school will provide vocational-technical, transitional, and school-to-work activities to youth with disabilities, and will provide the necessary support services to enable them to participate.					
The school inclusion plan describes the manner in which IEP implementors will ensure that needed transition services are available to the students, that needed external agency services are coordinated, and that there is a procedure for monitoring delivery of these services to students.					
The school inclusion plan clearly states that teachers will be supported and provided assistance in adapting curriculum, classroom setting, materials, assessments, and teaching strategies in order to accommodate students in the classroom and enable them to benefit from the educational program.					
The school inclusion plan describes how the school will provide leadership, supervision, and resources to establish, advance, and improve inclusive practices throughout the school.					
The school inclusion plan relates its initiative to the laws that promote and strengthen effective inclusion practices, including the Individuals with Disabilities Education Act, the Americans with Disabilities Act, Rehabilitation Act (Section 504), the Carl D. Perkins Vocational and Technical Education Act, the School-to-Work Opportunity Act, the Community Services Act, and the Improving America's Schools Act. These statutes contain several provisions in their statutes designed to ensure full participation of youth with disabilities in the range of educational opportunities.					

READINESS FOR PLANNING AND COMMITMENT *(continued)*	5	4	3	2	1
The school inclusion plan describes its relationship to the school's activities and programs under the School-to-Work Opportunities Act.					
The inclusion plan addresses the inclusion of students in state or national testing or assessments of academic achievement, performing arts performances, or other competency testing.					
The school inclusion plan describes its outreach policies for students with disabilities who have dropped out of school, and addresses services and supports to reintegrate them into the school programs.					
The school inclusion plan addresses how administrators will intervene to fill absolute gaps in services, as in cases in which needed support services in students' IEPs cannot be provided because they are not currently available in the school.					
The school inclusion plan ensures that waivers of statutory and regulatory requirements do not undermine the efforts to promote inclusion and full participation.					
READINESS FOR SCHOOL AND COMMUNITY INVOLVEMENT					
The school has a plan to inform parents, students, and consumer organizations, such as the PTA, parent advocacy groups, and student organizations, about the plans for inclusion.					
The school informs teachers and key support-service personnel who will have primary responsibility for any new programs or initiatives that will affect instruction or student services.					
The school has a plan to inform school-linked agencies and support-service agencies about the inclusion initiative and has established formal interagency agreements for needed services.					
The school provides for information seminars for parents and other community members about the inclusion initiative and respective roles and responsibilities.					
The school has informational brochures and materials that explain the missions and benefits of inclusion initiatives.					
The school informs collaborating business partners about the inclusion initiatives and makes modifications to partnership agreements, as appropriate.					
School personnel reach out to the local colleges and universities to obtain both technical assistance with inclusion and professional development opportunities.					
READINESS FOR INDIVIDUALIZED PLANNING, STUDENT AND PARENTAL INVOLVEMENT					
Teachers, administrators, and related personnel have knowledge of support and related services and community resource agencies.					
Teachers make contact with the families regularly and have methods of making themselves more accessible to families (telephone, regular reporting journals, e-mail, teacher call-in lines, appointment hours).					
Teachers make special efforts to involve parents of students with disabilities in class events, field trips, student demonstrations or exhibits, and other activities.					
Each student with a disability is assigned a teacher or a service coordinator who is identified to the family as a single point of contact.					
Teachers are oriented as to how to identify and refer students to needed support services both inside and outside the school.					
Students with disabilities who are placed into general education classrooms are informed about their disabilities and the special accommodations to be implemented for their entry into the classroom.					

continues

READINESS FOR INDIVIDUALIZED PLANNING, STUDENT AND PARENTAL INVOLVEMENT *(continued)*	5	4	3	2	1
Parents are informed of the reasons for their child's placement into the general education classroom, and they receive information in advance about the administrative and IEP team's rationale for such a decision. They are provided with an explanation of the expectations of the IDT for the benefits of the placement and of the child's expected progress in the classroom within a year.					
Parents and students with disabilities are informed in advance about a change in placement.					
The student with a disability is notified of the IEP meetings in advance and invited to such meetings.					
The student participates, to the extent possible, in the development of the IEP and its goals and objectives—academic and nonacademic—as established for the school year, is assisted in such participation, and is encouraged to take an increasingly more active role.					
Students are generally present at the IEP meetings; if they are not being generally included, then the school has a procedure to determine why students are not present.					
Students actively participate in their own transition planning and in determining the course of study and needed transition services for the school year; they are assisted in their participation and are encouraged to take an increasingly more active role.					
Students and parents are provided access to the student's IEP/ITP at any time after the student has been placed into the classroom.					
Teachers, as appropriate, are provided adequate time to participate in their students' IEP meetings and in the development of students' IEP, and to be present and participate in the IEP placement meeting prior to placement in order to discuss and learn about student needs and anticipate accommodations.					
Parents are informed about the variety of activities—academic and nonacademic—in which their children are involved.					
Parents are informed about the accommodations that are needed to enable the student to be included in the general education classroom; if these accommodations are modified or added to, the teacher communicates with the parents about these changes through regular weekly reporting methods.					
Parents are contacted to establish IEP meetings at mutually agreeable times, and they are invited to attend each IEP meeting.					
Parents are informed of their right and expectation to participate in the development of the student's IEP and the right to be present and participate in the IEP placement meeting prior to placement in order to discuss and learn about needs and available accommodations.					
Parents are informed when their child has been determined to have a physical, medical, emotional, or behavioral condition that might result in the need for teachers or other school personnel to take an emergency action.					
As needed, the student's IEP includes goals in the range of domains, including physical status, vision, hearing, speech, mobility, functional skills and adaptive behavior, academic, vocational, and transitional.					
Teachers, administrators, and related personnel are informed about parents' due process rights and of the procedures available to parents for requesting a due process hearing.					
The school has established a mediation process as a voluntary and informal method of dispute resolution, and teachers, administrators, and related personnel are informed about school mediation procedures for assisting parents in resolving disagreements with the IEP team.					

READINESS FOR INDIVIDUALIZED PLANNING, STUDENT AND PARENTAL INVOLVEMENT *(continued)*	5	4	3	2	1
The school informs parents of the established voluntary mediation process to assist them in resolving disagreements with the IEP team, of the relationship of that process to formal due process hearings, of their legal right to a formal due process hearing, and how to request such a hearing.					
To prevent the mediation step, parents are provided with and informed about procedures for a fair and accessible process in which to raise issues or concerns at any time about their children's placement and progress, requests for consultation or assistance in problem solving or seeking additional support, or suggestions on how the home environment may support the problem-solving process.					
Teachers convey information and communicate in the family's native language, or use appropriate accommodations (e.g., sign language); supports for language assistance are provided as needed.					
READINESS FOR PROFESSIONAL DEVELOPMENT AND TEACHER IN-SERVICE TRAINING					
The school recruits qualified special educators who can provide consultation or team teaching, who understand the needs of students with disabilities and methods and materials needed to provide specialized educational services, and who are available within the school to work with general education teachers.					
The school administrators provide resources for ongoing in-service training of teachers and related personnel to prepare them for team teaching, special education consultation in the classroom, and general accommodation of students with disabilities in their classrooms.					
The school administrators provide resources for technical assistance to teachers and related service personnel to support and guide their inclusion efforts.					
The school or district has trained personnel in career-vocational-technical education, and there is an adequate number for preparation of direct support service and instructional staff to ensure access to the range of educational, career-vocational, technical and technology-related, and transition services.					
The school actively recruits individuals with disabilities into the roles of administrator, teacher, noninstructional support personnel, consultants, volunteers, and guest speakers.					
The school's in-service training for inclusion includes school-linked agency personnel (who are essential to the success of inclusion) for joint training (including regular educators, special educators, career-vocational educators, as well as rehabilitation, school-to-work, and related services personnel).					
LEADERSHIP AND RESOURCES					
The school has a plan for providing clear leadership, supervision, and adequate resources to support inclusive practices throughout the school.					
The school budget reflects a commitment to providing adequate resources to address the goals in the inclusion plan and to develop activities which promote the full participation of all students, including students with disabilities, in the full range of school programs and activities.					
The school budget reflects a commitment to providing adequate resources to develop supplementary and support services that promote the full participation of all students in school activities.					
The school ensures that the career-vocational and transition programs are preparing students for occupations in which job openings are projected or are available within the community, based on a labor market analysis.					

continues

DATA COLLECTION, EVALUATION, AND CONTINUOUS IMPROVEMENT OF INCLUSION PRACTICES	5	4	3	2	1
Decision making about students' placements is systematically documented and communicated with teachers.					
There is documented information on both the numbers of students with disabilities placed into inclusive settings and on the changes in the number of students transferred to more inclusive settings.					
Information is collected on referrals to external agencies for related services.					
There is recorded data on the number of students who participate in district and statewide performance assessments.					
Follow-up information is collected on students who graduate from high school.					
Information is recorded on the time delay between referral and entry into the inclusive classroom or program after the student and parents have been notified and have consented.					
There is documentation of reasons for rejection of placements into the general education classroom.					
Enrollment in advanced training or into postsecondary education is documented as part of a follow-up system.					
Job placement and retention data are gathered as part of a follow-up system.					
The ratio of students with disabilities to students without disabilities in general education classrooms is tracked and documented.					
Teachers and administrators conduct student and parent satisfaction questionnaires related to placement and supports.					
The school conducts questionnaires related to teacher and related personnel satisfaction with inclusive practices, resources, and supports.					
Students and families are involved in evaluating inclusion practices.					
Teachers and administrators review parent problem-solving and mediation strategies to determine if changes are needed.					
There are annual evaluation reviews by the inclusion planning team regarding the effectiveness of planning, in-service training, and resource development.					
Teachers document student crisis incidents that disrupt class, disciplinary actions, suspensions, and expulsions.					
Teachers document parent visits and teacher consultations.					
Teachers provide input into evaluation of parental involvement in student's overall programming and of changes in such involvement.					
Teachers and administrators "reinvest" the evaluation results, or utilize them for improvement of inclusive practices (e.g, share the evaluation reports with the inclusion planning team and other personnel and use results for further dialogue about improvement and future needs).					

CHAPTER 25

What Factors Should Be Considered When Planning for Inclusion?

Once a school or classroom personnel have assessed their readiness to initiate inclusive practices or to strengthen those now in place, they should consider a number of crucial elements in the planning process. These include administrative sensitivity and support, collaboration and support, planning time, teacher incentives, personnel development, support services, technical assistance, teacher team relationships, and common fears about inclusion. Successful inclusion is the result of deliberate, focused planning efforts that can guide inclusion implementors in setting priorities, making resource and budget decisions, and achieving the results they have envisioned.

ADMINISTRATOR SENSITIVITY AND SUPPORT Administrators provide instructional leadership, and they set the climate for acceptance and a positive approach to including students with disabilities in general education (Dalheim, 1994; Friend & Bursuch, 1999). Among the most important factors in the success of inclusion are interpersonal relationships and support. Administrators and teachers who are regarded as supportive demonstrate qualities of interpersonal communication that include good rapport with others, enthusiasm, positive attitude, flexibility, and a low-key and nonthreatening manner. *Teachers need to know that the administrative staff notices and appreciates their efforts and considers the time and energy spent in advancing inclusion as necessary and meaningful to the educational process.*

PLANNING TIME Inclusion requires additional planning time to develop appropriate curriculum, modify instruction, consult with parents, meet with school personnel, plan community-based instruction, and train peer tutors to work with the students with disabilities. Teachers

need to work as a team and take the problem-solving approach. They need to implement collaborative student-centered planning teams and develop good communication between general and regular education teachers. Administrators must help teachers carve out time from their school schedules to accomplish the additional tasks required when serving students with disabilities in the general education classroom.

TEACHER TEAM RELATIONSHIPS *The personal relationships of the individuals involved in inclusion are the cornerstone of a successful inclusive classroom.* The most powerful of these relationships occurs among those closest to the students (teachers, instructional support staff, and volunteers). Often both the successes and difficulties with the inclusion process can be traced to problems in individual relationships. Collaboration for inclusion is much more effective if teachers are familiar with and alert to these barriers to cooperation. Box 25-1 presents some of the fears and perceptions that can arise among school personnel as they work to develop or strengthen inclusive education.

COLLABORATION AND SUPPORT General and special education teachers need to find ways to become informed about their students' abilities, needs, and goals. They first do this by participating in the student's IEP. Second, they can communicate frequently with the student about his or her disability and strengths and needs. Rarely are students asked to discuss their own thoughts and feelings about their disability and what they need in the classroom. Such communication should not be reserved only for the IEP team meeting but should be an ongoing conversation between the student and teacher. Teachers should not be afraid to discuss in a constructive and sup-

BOX 25-1. Common Fears Related to Collaboration for Inclusion

Fears Related to the Environment for Inclusion

1. There won't be any funds available for collaborative initiatives.
2. We won't have the needed administrative support for this initiative.
3. We won't have the technical assistance that we'll need.
4. There will be tension based on personality conflicts, turf wars, organizational boundary conflicts, prejudices, and broken trust.
5. There will be competition for students and scarce resources.

Fearful Attitudes About the Impacts of the Initiative

1. We will become influenced or controlled by the professionals in external agencies, or by other school units.
2. Our failures or inadequacies will be discovered and exposed to the school community.
3. Funding sources will not approve new collaborative arrangements, and they will end support.
4. Exchanging resources will mean losing them or receiving less than you give.
5. Innovation or change will mean more work or may threaten our jobs.
6. Students will not receive adequate services if they are served in less restrictive settings.

7. Students will not receive the necessary information from other partner agencies.
8. The quality of education and the teaching environment might be compromised.
9. Students might be labeled or categorized negatively by a partner organization.
10. Our energy will be drained from being forced to deal with the whole, complex bureaucracy.

Lack of Knowledge and Skills to Implement Inclusion

1. We don't have the knowledge and skills to implement inclusion in our classes; we don't know enough about strategies or methods for adapting our curriculum or teaching.
2. We don't know how to conduct "team teaching" between special and general educators, and we don't know how to negotiate the roles.
3. We aren't aware enough about external agencies, and lack understanding of other organizations, their functions, and resources.
4. Our colleagues may not be able to "stand outside" their disciplines and see new approaches to collaboration and creative ways of finding resources.
5. We won't be involved in the planning for this initiative, even though our positions, roles, and responsibilities will be greatly affected. (Hiltenbrand, Brown & Jones, 1992)

Ability to collaborate and personal relationships of the individuals involved in inclusion are the cornerstone of a successful inclusive classroom.

George Washington Middle School
Alexandria City Public Schools Alexandria, VA

Ms. Laura Russell and Mrs. Felicia Baskin are two seventh-grade inclusion team teachers at George Washington Middle School. Their class subject focus is U.S. history designed for a group of 16 students, 5 of whom receive special education services. The teachers work well together and have developed a real sense of closeness as professional peers. The class lessons are organized into activities such as group worksheets, role playing, research papers with presentations, and frequently varied hands-on activities. Within any given activity, students are paired with peer coaches/tutors. Students are not treated differently, regardless of their status as students receiving special education services. This commitment has helped to foster an atmosphere where all students fit well into the classroom and are an integrated part of the class group. The results this year have demonstrated that students can and have shown marked improvement in participation, public speaking, writing, and composition skills.

portive manner the student's disability and its implications for learning and accommodations.

Mutual planning and cooperation among general and special education teachers are essential. Input should be obtained from general education teachers about where and how to integrate the student's abilities and needs, when assistance is required, and when consultations would be most useful to the teacher in the classroom. These decisions have to be negotiated between teachers. It is also important that there not be too much intervention by the special education teacher or consultant unless needed by the student. The sharing of observations of the students by both the general and special education teachers can help prevent "errors of commission," or the situation of "oversupport." Conversely, such observations can also help prevent "errors of omission," or the situation of "undersupport."

TEACHER INCENTIVES While increased pay for inclusion activities might be most ideal for teachers, it is not likely to be the primary method of providing incentives to teachers for their effort. Many administrators are searching for answers to the question: What incentives are necessary and most appropriate? Teacher incentives are a way to acknowledge that inclusion is important, valued, and understood. Examples of teacher incentives include granting of the following:

- Professional leave to visit other inclusion classrooms.
- Assistance of substitute teachers to release general education teachers to meet with other professionals involved in planning, or for in-service training.
- Support of an aide in the classroom to assist with additional activities.
- Summer stipends to attend graduate training courses.
- Classroom assistants.

PROFESSIONAL DEVELOPMENT AND TECHNICAL ASSISTANCE Technical assistance and training and preparation of administrators, teachers, parents, and related agency personnel are crucial to the effectiveness of inclusion. Professional development is important to help general education teachers to understand the needs of students with disabilities, how to adapt curriculum and instruction, and how to collaborate with special education teachers to support students in the classroom. Chapter 27 in this book takes a more detailed look at professional development for inclusion teachers.

Technical Assistance. School districts involved in inclusion efforts frequently call on outside consultants and specialists to assist them in planning, organizing and conducting professional development needed for successful inclusion. Outside consultants or technical assistants can

serve a variety of valuable functions that can support the inclusion initiative. These include the following:

1. Provide assistance with the development of the school's inclusion plan and the setting of goals and objectives that are consistent with IDEA 1997.
2. Provide assistance with the evaluation plan for the inclusion initiative and help the school establish or modify its data collection procedures to aid in evaluation. Consultants may also be involved in designing surveys, analyzing data, and writing evaluation reports.
3. Provide assessments of the inclusion practices within the school, such as teacher teaming, classroom accommodations, parent communication, student involvement in nonacademic and extracurricular activities, and make recommendations to assist the school in reaching inclusion goals.
4. Provide assistance in the establishment of informal, voluntary mediation procedures used as a method of resolving parent-IEP team disagreements in a constructive manner and preventing formal, and often costly, due process hearings.
5. Provide assistance in the development of interagency agreements with school-linked agencies for the reliable and ongoing provision of related and support services.
6. Provide technical assistance in the development, evaluation, or improvement of transition services or transition follow-up activities in the school or district.
7. Making available specialists, such as mediation specialists, and professionals-in-training, such as graduate students, to help with projects in the school.
8. Provide multiagency training for school personnel and parents in collaboration with other partner agencies such as rehabilitation, social services, adult services, postsecondary, or juvenile services.
9. Be available to administrators and teachers to help troubleshoot problems with the implementation of inclusion and to answer technical questions they might have.

SUPPORT SERVICES There are a number of district support services available which can contribute to inclusion efforts. Inclusion is not the sole responsibility of one school, but rather a collective responsibility of the district. This means that if the supportive services required by students to participate in their least restrictive environment are not available, then it is the school district's responsibility to ensure that these services are obtained. If the service is one that is required in the student's IEP, and is generally available in school districts in the state, then under IDEA, the school or district cannot say: "We simply can't provide it!" Examples of support services include health, counseling, physical therapy, speech therapy, rehabilitation, vocational evaluation, case management or service coordination, interpréter services, and adaptive technology assistance.

CHAPTER 26

Ten Steps in Developing and Implementing Inclusive Practices

The 10 steps discussed in this section are designed to provide a "path" and map of activities and strategies for those who are either (1) beginning the process of developing inclusive practices or (2) embarking on a self-assessment or a renewal of their inclusive practices in the school. These steps can serve as goals and help inclusion planning teams develop relationships and processes that are uniquely suited to the local school, service system, or community. These steps are not meant to be prescriptions; rather, they are offered as guideposts for developing school-based and classroom-based inclusion action plans, and they are based on the experiences of inclusion implementors and inclusive schools around the nation. As such, they offer a *menu of options for inclusion planning,* rather than presenting a fixed model. The process must remain flexible!

- Can be initiated either by *a single teacher* or, jointly, by *several teachers* who are interested in implementing or strengthening their inclusion practices in the classroom.
- Are relevant for schools that have *not yet initiated* inclusive practices and which may also *desire to strengthen* their collaborative practices or relationships.
- Are relevant for schools that have already begun to implement inclusive practices and have developed *more advanced collaborative relationships.*
- Can guide the *design of evaluation* of inclusion initiatives, relationships, and outcomes.

It is helpful to view the planning and evaluation or self-assessment process as a circular process, rather than a linear one, as shown in Figure 26-1. In the field of strategic planning, the process of planning and development for any group or organizational initiative eventually leads the team back to evaluation and the reexamination and renewal of the processes once again.

STEP 1: CONDUCT A NEEDS ASSESSMENT AND SCAN THE ENVIRONMENT. Performance of a needs assessment is an essential first step for schools that are reorganizing for inclusion. Such an assessment involves collecting the important information necessary to planning inclusion activities, for example,

- Data on the size of the population of students with disabilities.
- Information from parents, teachers, and support personnel, to identify strengths and weaknesses of the present level of services available for students with disabilities.
- Self-assessment by school personnel about the readiness for inclusion and adequacy of available resources.
- Analysis of current resources by an independent, objective professional conducting a needs assessment for the school.

Preplanning assessment involves (1) defining the local "picture" or landscape of the school organization and existing services for students with disabilities in order to identify a foundation for an inclusion initiative or for improvement of inclusive practices and (2) determining the level of "readiness" of personnel and related services professionals to collaborate (Kochhar & Erickson, 1993; Kochhar & West, 1996). It is important to understand that there are many kinds of collaboration required of teachers and related service personnel in schools and community agencies serving the educational needs of children and youths with disabilities.

How Ready Is the Inclusion Team for Collaboration? Inclusion planners should know what each team member brings to the relationship in terms of resources, knowledge, and philosophy about inclusion. Those just beginning the process of implementing inclusion may

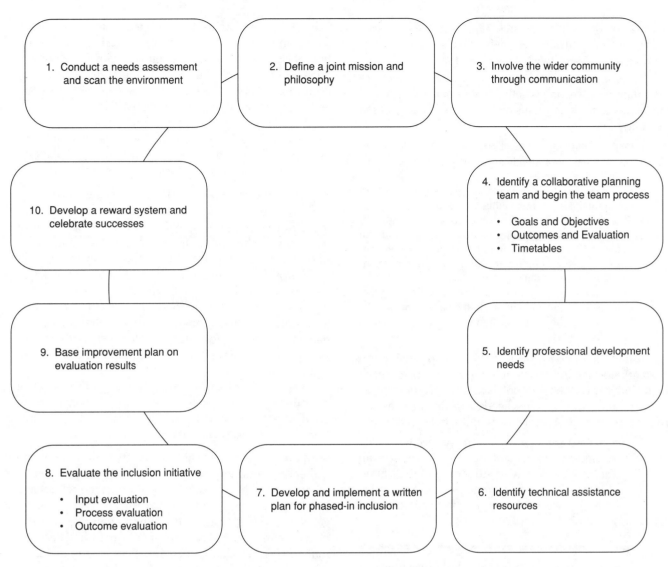

FIGURE 26-1. Ten Steps in Developing and Implementing Inclusion

find it useful to consider some basic questions:

1. What *community agencies* are most appropriate for collaboration?
2. What are the *attitudes* of the inclusion team members toward inclusion and toward the population of students to be served?
3. What is the *knowledge* level of each team member about the population of students to be served, the collaborative team process, and the principles and strategies of inclusion?

Strategies for Assessing Readiness for Inclusion. The following sections offer strategies, methods, and resources for assessing the readiness of potential inclusion team members. These strategies can be used by inclusion planners or by individual teachers in self-assessments for their classrooms.

Are Personnel Ready for Team Collaboration and Coordination? In an inclusion initiative, it is important

to first assess the needs of professionals who will form the inclusion implementation team.

> **Assessment of inclusion team needs:** *is the process of gathering and interpreting information about (1) the educational and support service needs of students, (2) the "goalposts," or progress measures, toward which the collaborating teachers and support personnel are working, and (3) the operational needs of the inclusion team members as they invest in real change in the teaching and learning environments.* (Kochhar & West, 1995)

Need for Periodic Assessment of the Inclusion Team's Needs. Like students, the needs of school personnel change over time and, therefore, needs assessments must be done with some regularity so that as needs shift, so can the inclusion goals and procedures. The first set of goals and activities defined among collaborating team members will provide only a blueprint or map for defining educational needs. Just as student IEPs are revisited and modified, so must the goals and procedures of inclusion teams. Ongoing needs assessments for the inclusion team helps teachers and administrators remain sensitive to any changes.

Assessing Inclusion Readiness. Several activities are important for assessing whether a school is ready to begin implementing an inclusion initiative. These include the following:

- Defining the range of local services available in the existing system, thus identifying an existing foundation for an inclusion initiative.
- Identifying service gaps and any service needs that are currently not being met within the system.
- Determining the level of readiness of teachers, support personnel, and cooperating agency personnel to form a collaboration for meaningful change in the service environment (e.g., change in education, employment, health services, social services).
- Determining the expertise and resources that each discipline or organization brings to the partnership.
- Determining the needs of the cooperating community agencies.

A thorough needs assessment can help provide important information for determining how prepared each inclusion team member or unit is to develop effective inclusion practices. Ongoing needs assessment is as important at the school level as it is at the individual level.

Levels of Assessment in Inclusion. Assessment of the school's readiness to implement inclusion has to do with knowing the needs not only of students and their families, but also the cooperating agencies. It is also an essential step in the process of defining the goalposts that the school will work toward.

1. **Needs assessment at the individual or consumer level** is the process of gathering and interpreting information about the educational and support service needs of students in the school. Needs assessment at the individual level means identifying the range of developmental, health, academic, vocational, transitional, social, and support needs of individuals and families. Teachers and support personnel can establish, through an assessment of individual needs, appropriate goals and priorities for services.
2. **Needs assessment at the school level** involves determination of:
   - The readiness of personnel to take on the initiative.
   - The resources needed to help prepare them.
3. **Needs assessment at interagency level** involves determination of:
   - The level of readiness of cooperating agencies to form a partnership that creates real change in the service environment.
   - The relative strengths and weaknesses of each agency in the partnership.

School Factors Facilitate or Impede Inclusion. Many factors in the school structure, organization, or distribution of resources can serve to either facilitate or impede inclusion (see Table 26-1). Planning teams will find it useful to consider and discuss these factors as they examine their school and anticipate barriers.

Understanding the environment and existing resources in the school—financial, human, material, and service—is an essential first step in building a platform from which to launch a school inclusion plan.

A "Circle of Commitment": The Resource Environment. The concept of a Circle of Commitment, applied to inclusion implementors, helps to define the range of resources in the environment, both human and material, that must be invested in an inclusion effort, both to improve supportive services and outcomes for students with disabilities, and to improve the overall learning environment. Members of the school community (key stakeholders), along with other material and financial resources, form the six elements of the inclusion planning team's Circle of Commitment, shown in Figure 26-2.

The Circle of Commitment includes the range of tools that *inclusion pioneers* need to make changes in the educational and human service system to better serve students with disabilities and their families.

Scan the School and Local Community Environment and Collect Information for Planning. For inclusion implementation to obtain a scan or a picture of the school and local community environment, collect information regarding the preparation of teachers, parents, and students for inclusion. Teachers should read and learn as much as possible about best practices for the inclusion process, especially in regard to the following questions:

- How should teachers and support personnel be prepared for inclusion?
- How should the physical environment be modified for inclusion?
- What modifications in curriculum and instruction are needed?
- How should the IEP and interdisciplinary team process be modified or strengthened?
- What additional classroom supports are needed?
- How can students access available and new technologies?
- How can students be helped to access and participate in vocational, occupational, technical education, and transition services?
- How can students be helped to participate in nonacademic and extracurricular school activities?
- How can students be helped to participate in community-based and community-service experiences?

STEP 2: DEFINE A JOINT MISSION AND PHILOSOPHY. Defining a joint mission and philosophy involves meeting with key inclusion planners, discussing a joint vision of inclusion implementation, and hammering out broad goals and strategies for achieving that shared vision. This step

TABLE 26-1. Addressing School Factors That Facilitate or Impede Inclusion

Action	Explanation
1. Understand the diversity of the individuals and groups with whom you will need to collaborate.	Inclusion involves groups of professionals who cross disciplinary lines, agency lines, and school-community boundaries makes collaboration for inclusion a challenge. Each team member has his or her own philosophy, educational approaches, knowledge and skills in the classroom, understanding of curriculum and subject matter areas, classroom procedures and regulations, standards, professional roles, and responsibilities. This diversity and culture of the school enriches the process of setting shared goals and is important in the implementation and evaluation of the inclusion effort.
2. Determine what written collaborative agreements and planning processes are already in place.	Many inclusion planning initiatives lack formalized agreements and documents to guide their activities. These agreements or operating procedures are crucial to the development of the inclusion initiative because they define the common goals and objectives and the authority for teacher action.
3. Find out the policies and funding restrictions of the school-related service agencies involved in the inclusion partnership.	Often different school programs and cooperating school-linked agencies have evolved from separate funding streams, local policies, state laws, federal laws, or historical initiatives. They, therefore, have different eligibility requirements and target different student groups. It is important to examine and understand these differences when developing agreements and cooperative activities and in defining inclusion outcomes. Also, recent changes in special, general, vocational-technical education and related disability laws will affect school priorities and the way programs can operate together.
4. Assess the existing data collection and reporting capability of team members.	Teachers and related service professionals both define and report differently their activities and performance goals and outcomes. Inclusion team members must understand these differences and seek to integrate their performance goals and outcomes. For example, a consulting resource teacher and a general education teacher teamed to teach science must both agree upon student achievement measures for all students, including those with disabilities. They must also agree on how they will collect assessment information for all students and how they will report progress on students with disabilities in academic, social, functional, and other domains.
5. Consider the economic health of the school and its impact on the ability of key professionals to collaborate	When funds for schools are eroding, the demand for educational accountability tends to increase. These forces can serve either to erode confidence of school personnel in their goals or to strengthen the collaboration and sharing of resources within and among schools and community agencies. Collaboration and shared resources make education for all students more efficient.
6. Assess the Level of parental involvement and family supports needed.	Parental involvement is considered one of the most important factors in the success of students' readiness for inclusion and their successful transition to inclusive classrooms. Therefore, a school's capacity to enlist parents in the process must be assessed. Inclusion efforts will remain weak if parents are not viewed as, and given the resources to be, essential players in the assessment of needs and in the development of the inclusive initiative. Capacity for direct involvement of parents, by means of training and information dissemination, must be assessed.

Assessing Team Member Attitudes

Action	Explanation
7. Be sensitive to political pressures and pressure groups.	As local economic pressures force schools to economize, inclusion planners must be prepared to show how school inclusion activities and community linkages can contribute to cost-effective programs.
8. Be sensitive to territorial attitudes.	Encroachments of professionals and school units into each others' "territory" can sometimes threaten people's comfort with traditional ways of operating and making decisions. Collaborative initiatives like inclusion changes the way everyone in a school conducts business, and this should be made clear to all professionals from the beginning of the inclusion initiative.
9. Consider issues of morale and carefully select team leaders who can provide long-term attitudinal leadership.	Many inclusion failures can be traced to high turnover rates among key personnel in the schools. Established relationships, and the emergence of "champions" (energetic and enthusiastic attitudinal leaders), contribute to confidence and trust among inclusion planners, and can accelerate collaborative efforts.
10. Work to build early understanding among inclusion team planners and implementors of their respective goals and missions.	General and special education teachers and related service personnel must understand each other's common goals, missions, and complementary strengths. This is essential to early crystallization of team collaboration. Early inclusion readiness seminars are worth every hour of time, and continued training can keep the momentum high.

continues

TABLE 26-1. *(continued)*

Assessing Team Member Attitudes	
Action	**Explanation**
11. *Explore and share* existing models for inclusion and team collaboration.	Model practices are necessary for the development of inclusion and team collaboration. Explore a variety of existing models and development practices, and discuss these ideas with inclusion team planners and school leaders.
12. *Explore relationships* with local universities for assistance in the inclusion development process.	Many colleges and universities have entered relationships with schools, local and state education agencies, and community service organizations to provide resources and technical assistance for new initiatives. Universities can provide the time and expertise of graduate students for in-service training, as well as the expertise of faculty to design instructional materials, provide technical assistance, and develop grant proposals for additional resources. Universities can also help champion local initiatives in communities in which there are political or resource barriers. Frequently the availability of grant funding for an inclusion initiative has provided the very stimulus needed for action in the event of "foot-dragging" from school administrators.

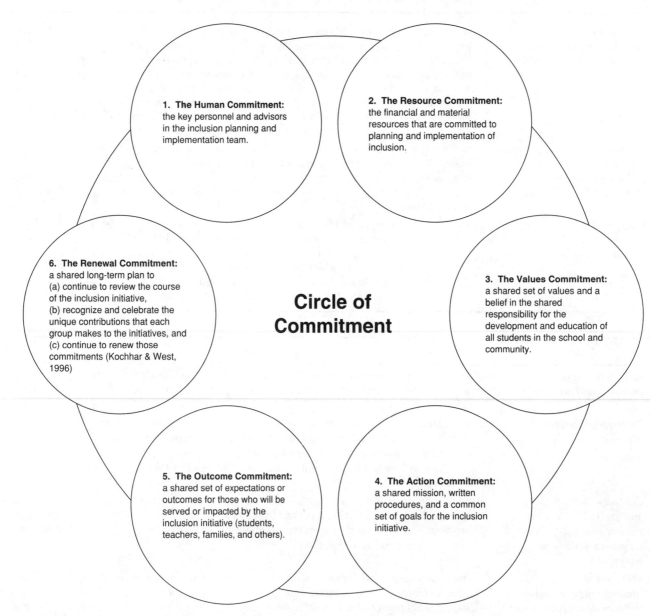

FIGURE 26-2. Circle of Commitment

will help in designing a written *mission statement* for the inclusion initiative, as well as in developing formal agreements with collaborating non-school-agency partners. The inclusion team may think about its initiative in terms of two kinds of strategies:

1. **A classroom-level strategy** or intervention designed to (a) improve the availability of and access to supportive services in the classroom and (b) help solve specific problems and overcome the barriers to inclusion identified by teachers in the individual classroom.
2. **A schoolwide strategy** designed to assist all school personnel, both instructional and noninstructional, in understanding the inclusion goals and strategies and in being a part of changing the school's culture to support the participation of all students.

Develop the Mission Statement for Inclusion. Each school will define its inclusion mission differently, so no two mission statements will look the same. However, a few fundamental rules should be followed in developing mission statements. A mission statement should describe the *broad purpose* of the initiative, its collaborating people and units, and the specific areas of joint responsibility. Effective mission statements generally include one or all of the following four parts:

1. **Statement of context.** This is usually a brief introductory paragraph that broadly describes the initiative, how it was started, and how it addresses current educational needs of students, or, if the school is revising a previous mission statement, how it differs, expands or improves upon what is currently in place to support inclusion. This section helps school personnel, as well as parents and community members, understand the broader context for the initiative.
2. **Statement of the authority for the initiative.** This is an introductory section in the mission statement that refers to the legal basis for the initiative (e.g., IDEA, Section 504 of the Rehabilitation Act, and the Americans with Disabilities Act) and lists the local, state or federal laws, statutes, regulations, or policies that give authority to this agreement. This section helps school personnel, parents, and members of the community understand the importance and necessity of the inclusion initiative.
3. **General statement of philosophy, purpose of the initiative or agreement, and expected benefits and outcomes.** This includes a broad statement of what the initiative does, what the inclusion planning team expects to accomplish, and the anticipated results for students. This section helps school personnel, parents, and members of the community understand the principles and values that underpin inclusion, as well as how the initiative is to benefit students and the school.
4. **Broad goals, roles, and responsibilities.** This part defines the goals of the initiative and the roles of key planners and implementors and cooperating agencies or community agency personnel. This section helps school personnel, parents, and members of the community to understand the specific activities and key persons and agencies involved in the initiative.

Case Example 26-1 provides a sample mission statement.

CASE EXAMPLE 26-1. When All Children Belong—Flora County Public Schools Inclusion Initiative

Context/History. Flora County Public Schools and the community it serves have recognized the need to expand upon and improve the education and preparation for transition of its children and youth. As a result of a 2 year evaluation of the current status of providing special education and related services to students in the range of placement options, and based on the recommendations of both state special education monitors and federal Office of Special Education monitors, the school has determined that it needs to improve the overall services and supports. Therefore, in 1998, Flora County Public Schools establishes this inclusion initiative, in cooperation with the State Educational Agency, the Division of Vocational Rehabilitation, the Department of Public Health, the Department of Mental Health and Developmental Disabilities, the Department of Social Services, the Department of Juvenile Services, and the Chamber of Commerce.

Purpose. The purpose of the initiative is to

1. Increase the number of students who have been determined by their IEP teams to be appropriate for placement into general education classrooms, but until now have not been placed, or have been maintained in general education due to inadequate resources.
2. Improve the overall Interdisciplinary Team process and involvement of students and partners in the process.
3. Improve the overall student eligibility evaluation process and the availability and quality of related support services to students.
4. Improve the overall availability and quality of technical assistance and support services to the teachers in the general education classrooms.
5. Establish formal interagency agreements to provide related support services to students and families.
6. Increase the participation of students with disabilities in nonacademic and extracurricular activities.
7. Increase both the availability of career-vocational-technical education and services to students and their participation in the transition services.
8. Improve parent participation in their children's educational programming and school activities.

continues

CASE EXAMPLE 26-1. *(continued)*

Authority. This agreement is in accordance with the Flora County School Board's mandate to expand, improve, and increase access for all youth to appropriate educational and related services and general school activities. The agreement is consistent with state regulations regarding special education and related services for students and with federal law and regulations under IDEA 1997.

Roles and Responsibilities. Flora County Public Schools es-

tablishes this inclusion initiative, in cooperation with the State Educational Agency, the Division of Vocational Rehabilitation, the Department of Public Health, the Department of Mental Health and Developmental Disabilities, the Department of Social Services, the Department of Juvenile Services, and the Chamber of Commerce. Each of these agencies will provide related and support services in accordance with cooperative agreements with the Flora County Public Schools system.

Case Example 26-2 provides a sample general guideline for inclusion.

CASE EXAMPLE 26-2. Prince Albert County General Guidelines for Inclusion

Prince Albert County Public Schools has as its goal to integrate as many students with disabilities as necessary into the regular classroom and, in integrated settings, to provide access to technology-enriched academic and vocational-technical education and to work-experience opportunities.

1. Students with disabilities must be educated with students without disabilities;
2. Special classes, separate schooling, or other removal of children with disabilities from the regular education environment should occur only when the nature or severity of the disability is such that education in the regular classes cannot be achieved satisfactorily with the use of supplementary aids, services, and support.

3. An effective delivery system of specialized services at the local level is to *be established to reduce the need to remove the student from his or her neighborhood school in order to obtain special education and related services.*

Objectives for inclusion:

- To educate all children with disabilities to the maximum extent appropriate in regular school settings regardless of the degree or severity of their disability.
- To allow special education students to participate in regular education classes, with support provided as needed by the special education staff, related services staff, support personnel, and other local school personnel.

Mission statements are usually followed by supporting statements of well-defined goals and objectives that are written in measurable terms so the inclusion planning team can determine whether the goals written into the mission statement have been accomplished.

STEP 3. INVOLVE THE WIDER COMMUNITY THROUGH COMMUNICATION. Involving the community is an important step in implementing a collaborative planning process to develop or strengthen inclusive practices. The success of any inclusion initiative depends upon the ability of the planning team to create a supportive environment for the development of professional collaboration. This process of collaboration begins by *informing key populations within the school and wider community—particularly parents—about intentions to develop, expand, or improve inclusive practices.*

Informing and Involving the School Community. In an environment that supports inclusion, key stakeholders (persons who care about and are invested in seeing inclusion successfully implemented) become knowledgeable and informed about the need for improved collab-

oration and the benefits of inclusion for the student, school, and community.

Under current laws, state and local educational agencies are required to increase opportunities for inclusion into general education classes and general school activities and to improve working relationships with students, families, teachers, and related services personnel concerned with the development of students.

Strategies for Involving the School Community in Plans for the Inclusion Initiative. Table 26-2 presents 15 strategies for involving the school, communities, agency personnel, parents, students, and community leaders in inclusion initiatives.

By involving the school community, inclusion planners can begin identifying future participants in the planning process. Often community leaders must be sought out and invited into the process. Different schools will require different strategies for involving their community.

STEP 4: IDENTIFY A COLLABORATIVE PLANNING TEAM AND BEGIN THE TEAM PROCESS. The concept of *collaborative planning* is helpful when inclusion planners try to deter-

TABLE 26-2. Fifteen Strategies for Involving the School Community in an Inclusion Initiative

Strategy	Objective
1. Inform parent, student, and consumer organizations.	Inform parent, student, and consumer organizations, such as the PTA, parent advocacy groups, and student organizations, about the plans for inclusion. Distribute information and solicit input on the plans and roles of these groups in the development of the initiative.
2. Inform educational leaders and school principals.	Inform educational leaders and school principals who have primary responsibility for any new programs or initiatives that will affect instruction or student services. Most school districts and schools establish well in advance their educational priorities (e.g., expansion of special education programs or new agency agreements). *Principals should be* among the earliest to be informed of the effort (if they are not the prime initiators) and should be helped to see how the initiative will aid them in achieving their educational goals and objectives for all students.
3. Inform staff and directors of community and adult services agencies.	Inform staff and directors of community and adult services agencies because their support is vital to interagency agreements and service coordination initiatives (new or renewed). Each cooperating (or potential) partner needs to know about an intent to collaborate and the process for forming the collaborative arrangement.
4. Develop concept papers and rationale statements.	Develop concept papers and rationale statements to help the potential cooperating agencies understand the relationship between the collaborative endeavor and their own individual agency's mission, goals, and objectives. Agencies must understand how the new collaboration will help them to achieve their individual agency goals, improve services and resources, or evaluate agency efforts. The mutual benefits to all cooperating agencies must be defined and stressed early on.
5. Inform relevant teacher unions and educational associations.	Inform relevant teacher unions and educational associations about new initiatives that involve teaching personnel to help them understand the potential benefits of the collaboration for the students and professionals. It might also be helpful to have the county or district educational associations go on record as supporting the initiative.
6. Conduct local educational reform seminars.	Include in local educational reform seminars information about the inclusion initiative and new interagency partnerships.
7. Conduct special seminars.	Conduct special seminars on inclusion and interagency service coordination and provide cotraining with members of a variety of agencies and organizations.
8. Plan coffees for teachers, principals, and parents.	Plan coffees for teachers, principals, and parents to discuss the initiative.
9. Conduct brainstorming meetings.	Conduct brainstorming meetings with school personnel and heads of community agency personnel to discuss inclusion and interagency service coordination.
10. Develop informational brochures and materials.	Develop informational brochures and materials that explain the mission and benefits of the inclusion initiatives. These include information packets in the local budget documents that are distributed to educational and community agency planning boards. Develop interagency logos and brochures to inform the community of the key partners in the initiative and to promote the initiative as a distinct entity.
11. Conduct business-education seminars.	Include in local business-education seminars information about the inclusion initiative, or in Chamber of Commerce meetings, or Private Industry Council meetings (Job Training Partnership Act).
12. Utilize local newsletters and newspapers.	Use local newsletters and newspapers for editorial and feature article coverage about the inclusion initiative, and its goals and benefits for all students.
13. Conduct meetings with community leaders.	Conduct meetings with community leaders who can help champion the inclusion initiative.
14. Develop links with local colleges or universities.	Develop links with local colleges or universities to facilitate meetings or seminars related to the new initiative, or to engage them in the development of grant proposals.
15. Utilize annual reports of cooperating agencies.	Include in the annual reports of cooperating agencies descriptions of the inclusion initiative and the agency's partnership with the school.

mine which key individuals are most appropriate and needed in the short- and long-term planning processes.

The Collaborative Planning Process. With many educational innovations or restructurings, inclusion planning and development have been primarily viewed as the responsibilities of administrators. However, the inclusion planning process must be viewed as much more than an extension of administrative activities. The basis for *inclusion planning activities should be student-centered (or consumer-centered) and teacher-centered, rather than procedural.* In other words, rather than benefiting (or being convenient for) administrative functions, the inclusion processes and procedures established should primarily benefit students and teachers. They should benefit the teaching and learning environment as a whole. As the planning team works to develop new processes and procedures, they should adopt the habit of asking each other regularly: How will this new procedure benefit our students?

Outcomes View: Inclusion Is an Intervention. To be successful and beneficial for teaching and learning, inclusion planning must be viewed as an *intervention—a planned effort designed to produce intended changes, or outcomes, in the target population*. This "outcomes view" requires a change in the methods used to define and measure the effectiveness of inclusion planning. The intended changes in the target population (students with disabilities) must be clearly specified and school and community resources focused to pursue those outcomes. An outcome orientation, with its vigorous focus on measuring both benefits to students and teachers and impacts on the total learning environment, becomes central to evaluating inclusive classrooms and schools. *In a student-centered service system, student benefits and impacts drive the development of inclusion planning and implementation, from initial definition of the mission and goals to annual evaluation.*

Planned Change as a Management Practice. Many forces at work in the school systems affect the work of inclusion planning teams and the "durability" of the change process. Change and innovation can decay in a short time if school environment factors that support the change process are not identified and "engraved" into the inclusion planning process. *Planned change is now coming to be viewed as essential* to the planning and implementation of inclusion initiatives. *Collaborative planning* strategies can help teachers and school leaders develop planning teams to manage a continuum of inclusive placements.

Defining Planning Terms for Inclusion. Two terms important to an understanding of the development of inclusive practices are *collaborative planning* and *planned change*. Collaborative planning refers to how teachers and administrators make decisions and develop actions in cooperation with one another. The term *planned change* refers to the implementation and management of the relationships needed for an initiative such as inclusion, or the carrying out of the actions agreed upon through strategic planning (Goodstein, Nolan & Pfeiffer, 1993). Both processes are essential to the change process to implement inclusive classrooms (Walther-Thomas, Korinek, McLaughlin, & Williams, 2000).

Another related term, *strategic planning*, was defined by Bryson (1988) as a "disciplined effort to produce fundamental decisions and actions that shape and guide what a school or organization is, what it does, and why it does it" (p. 5). Collaborative planning is a form of strategic planning because it is conducted by a team of teachers, administrators, and others to identify and understand how to implement an initiative within the given school environment. Strategic planning also helps inclusion planners to understand and identify ways that different parts of the school environment can be integrated to improve access to general education classrooms and general school activities. The school environment includes the political, economic, professional, and social influences that characterize and influence the school.

Planned Change and Flexibility. *Planned change* focuses on the implementation and management of the change process for inclusion, and helps teachers to use and modify these forces to achieve a *shared mission*. The inclusion planning process must be viewed as a dynamic process that may be imperfect and sometimes not particularly orderly. The essential guiding principles and goals are of primary importance. *The planning process must support flexibility in the placement process so that schools can respond to changing needs of students and learning environments*. The concept of strategic planning provides a foundation for understanding, creating, and implementing inclusive practices that are responsive to the needs of students and their families (Kochhar, 1995b).

The planning team members. The inclusion planning team should include individuals who will have primary responsibility for the implementation of the plan. The most effective team should include:

- The principal
- General education teacher leaders
- Special education teacher leaders
- A transition coordinator
- A representative from vocational-technical education
- A representative from related services
- Representatives from key external agencies (rehabilitation, social services, mental health, and others)
- A parent representative
- A university or an in-service training-unit representative
- A business or industry representative
- Key community leaders to help solicit community support

These team members should be selected on the basis of (1) their commitment to inclusion principles and the inclusion initiative, (2) their availability to attend ongoing meetings throughout the year, and (3) their leadership and interpersonal skills in teams. After establishing a regular schedule of meetings throughout the year, the team should begin the series by having team members share information about their roles and responsibilities in the inclusion initiative.

STEP 5: IDENTIFY PROFESSIONAL DEVELOPMENT NEEDS. Inclusion requires increased awareness, thoughtful consideration, and meaningful dialogue. Teachers and parents need the opportunity to discuss the complexity and importance of inclusion and to air their concerns. Well-planned training and professional development programs can help the teacher learn how to implement inclusion effectively. However, change can create resistance among the very people who are needed to implement the inclusion initiative. When teachers sense that the traditional ways of doing things are being abandoned, some may resist or become negative about the future. The inclusion pioneer needs special know-how to help champion change and transfer the spirit of opportunity to others who will be involved in the inclusion process.

1. To prepare general education teachers to understand the nature and needs of students with disabilities, as well as the strategies and methods of curriculum and instructional adaptations for students with disabilities, and methods of collaborating with special education teachers to share the effort.
2. To prepare special educators for team teaching and support in the general education classroom.
3. To prepare all teachers, administrators, and related service personnel to understand their relative roles and responsibilities in the inclusion effort.
4. To prepare all teachers, administrators, and related service personnel to work with school-linked agencies to acquire needed support services for students.
5. To prepare all teachers, administrators, and related service personnel to work with the families of students with disabilities.
6. To prepare all teachers, administrators, and related service personnel to implement the individualized education program planning process in accordance with the requirements of IDEA.
7. To prepare all relevant personnel to be engaged in the process of developing the school's inclusion plan and determining realistic goals for the initiative.
8. To prepare all relevant personnel to be engaged in the process of evaluating the school's inclusion effort.

Staff development can be conducted through workshops, use of teacher in-service days, consultant seminars, graduate training courses or in-service sessions, federal or state grant projects, and mentoring by master teachers. The inclusion planning team must try to assess the knowledge base of the key personnel who will be affected by the inclusion initiative—teachers, related services personnel, administrators, and others. This can be accomplished through surveys, interviews, and meetings to brainstorm priority training needs. Chapter 27 in this book takes a more detailed look at professional development for inclusion teachers.

Forging an "Adoption Plan" for Inclusion Through Training. How can inclusion implementors foster a sense of investment or ownership in the initiative? How should teachers be oriented to the changes that the new collaboration may bring? What kinds of training are needed? How can the teachers share and celebrate their successes and honor those who have made important contributions? Change requires teachers to adopt new teaching methods, relationships, procedures, norms, values, and attitudes. An inclusion initiative will *not* be

successfully adopted or fully implemented by teachers and related service personnel unless they are *adequately trained in their field, understand the purposes of the collaboration initiative, and are prepared for change*. New training and development activities are needed to help key personnel *adopt new practices*. Two important concepts relate to preparing teachers for change:

1. The *adoption plan* is a strategy for fostering the constructive involvement of teachers and related personnel in the development and support of the inclusion initiative. It involves preparing teachers for new practices related to inclusion, enlisting the help of volunteers, and securing the support of students and families.
2. The *knowledge sharing plan* defines the specific areas of new knowledge that teachers and related personnel need to have to successfully implement inclusion.

The knowledge sharing plan includes a series of professional development, training, and organizational development activities aimed at ensuring that the inclusion initiative is adopted, or fully accepted, by all who will be involved. The term *knowledge sharing* is used because some school personnel may have much more knowledge and experience than others and can be enlisted in the training of their peers.

Six Components of the Adoption Plan. There are six important components of an effective adoption plan. These activities are important for establishing a plan that can reach many school professionals efficiently and therefore increase the likelihood that the plan will endure over time.

1. Establish links with professional development and training programs of local and state educational agencies: Most local educational agencies organize in-service training days for teachers, administrators, and support personnel. Inclusion planners should use these existing training activities as a vehicle for providing an introduction and orientation to the new inclusion initiative and to changes in teacher roles.

2. Ensure participation of all cooperating agencies: The adoption plan must include all cooperating community agencies in the training, because the inclusion relies upon interagency partnerships. This does not mean that all training sessions must include personnel from each of these agencies, but planners should include some regular training meetings that include staff from cooperating agencies. This increases the likelihood that over time inclusion planning team members will come to share a common understanding and vision of the direction of the initiative. Representatives of cooperating school-linked agencies could be invited onto a panel with education personnel to share and discuss the mission and goals of the initiative. Families, students, and community leaders could be invited to attend and join the discussion. These are good opportunities for sharing information, presenting inclusion concepts and philosophies in a community context, and discussing the benefits of inclusion for all students. The mission statement and inclusion plan should include the schedule for training and staff development.

3. *Develop inclusion planning materials for training and distribution:* Materials must be developed for use in in-service training for teachers and collaborating personnel. These materials should include specific information about the inclusion mission; philosophy; associated laws, goals, strategies, teacher and student information, key roles, and contact persons; and the mission and goals as they relate to inclusion and new support services that will be offered through the initiative.

4. *Adopt new educational and human service practices:* Inclusion planners must help key teaching personnel reassess their teaching practices and adopt new ones. Once inclusion practices have been in place for 1 or 2 years, teaching personnel will need advanced training. For advanced training, the results of the past year's inclusion implementation efforts can provide valuable information to the team to renew and strengthen the initiative, identify barriers and weaknesses, and further define and improve its outcomes.

5. *Evaluate the adoption plan:* Evaluation of the adoption plan is extremely important to an inclusion initiative. Inclusion planners must ask if the training is having the desired effect on teachers and the classrooms. Is the training reaching all the key school personnel that need it? Is cross-agency training occurring? Are the teachers involved in evaluating the adoption plan and the training effort? Are teachers satisfied with the training, and what are their recommendations for improvement? Such ongoing evaluation should be included in the inclusion mission statement.

6. *Provide technical assistance:* Inclusion planners should also make sure that they are linked with experts who can provide assistance during the development, implementation, and evaluation phases. Expert consultants, such as university personnel, private evaluation firms, independent consultants, education association personnel, and others, can be very helpful on a short-term basis to

- Problem solve during inclusion implementation
- Develop assessment and monitoring tools
- Design training materials
- Provide orientation to planners and related personnel
- Conduct advanced or refresher training for staff
- Assist the teachers and administrators in using evaluation information

Inclusion experts can also provide information about other programs and their successes and help link new local inclusion teams with more experienced teams. (Chapter 27 addresses professional development and training in greater detail.)

In summary, the partnership adoption and knowledge sharing process includes the broad range of activities aimed at recruiting, orienting, educating, preparing, and renewing personnel who will be key players in inclusion planning and improvement. An irony in this process is that those who resist change in the beginning of a new initiative are often the most likely to call themselves pioneers as the initiative moves forward successfully!

STEP 6. IDENTIFY TECHNICAL ASSISTANCE RESOURCES. Many resources are available to school districts to support inclusion. The more a local educational agency seeks and uses information from other schools, districts, and states, the better informed it will be to develop its own initiative. School districts involved in inclusion efforts frequently call on outside consultants and specialists to assist them in planning, organizing, and conducting professional development. These professionals provide a variety of valuable services that support the inclusion initiative. These include the following:

1. Provide assistance with the development of the school's inclusion plan and the setting of goals and objectives.
2. Provide assistance with the evaluation plan for the inclusion initiative and help the school establish or modify its data collection procedures to aid evaluation. Consultants may also be involved in designing surveys, analyzing data, and writing evaluation reports.
3. Provide assessments of the inclusion practices within the school, such as teacher teaming, classroom accommodations, parent communication, and student involvement in nonacademic and extracurricular activities, and make recommendations to assist the school in reaching inclusion goals.
4. Provide technical assistance with the evaluation of the LEA improvement initiatives, report on LEA activities, and collect information on achievements and best practices that could be shared statewide.
5. Provide assistance in the establishment of informal, voluntary mediation procedures used as a method of resolving parent-IEP team disagreements in a constructive manner of and preventing formal, and often costly, due process hearings.
6. Provide assistance in the development of interagency agreements with school-linked agencies for the reliable and ongoing provision of related and support services.
7. Provide technical assistance in the development, evaluation, or improvement of transition services or transition follow-up activities in the school or district.
8. Making available specialists, such as mediation specialists, and professionals-in-training, such as graduate students, to help with projects in the school.
9. Provide multiagency training for school personnel and parents, in collaboration with other partner agencies, such as rehabilitation, social services, adult services, postsecondary agencies, or juvenile services.
10. Be available to administrators and teachers to help troubleshoot problems with the implementation of inclusion and to answer technical questions they might have.

Specific University Resources. Local colleges and universities can provide many resources to assist schools and administrative agencies at the local and state levels in planning for inclusion. Universities with special education, transition, vocational education, social work, or rehabilitation counseling departments can be of special assistance. Some universities have interdisciplinary programs that can offer expertise in collaborative planning. Explore university programs such as the following for the kind of expertise needed to support a comprehensive inclusion initiative:

- Special education training programs
- Vocational-technical education and evaluation programs
- Early intervention specialist training programs
- Alternative education for at-risk students
- Rehabilitation counseling programs
- Social work services
- Nursing and health services administration
- Learning disabilities training programs

College and university programs may participate in contracts for services or provide technical assistance on a subcontract basis with individual faculty. Many schools are developing close working relationships with college and university faculty and including them in advisory and planning meetings. They are often knowledgeable about or can help the planning team locate resources related to inclusion models and practices in other localities and states.

STEP 7: DEVELOP AND IMPLEMENT A WRITTEN PLAN FOR PHASED-IN INCLUSION

Documenting System Change. Written plans are essential to ensure the continuity and sustainability of the inclusion initiative and the process of system change with the school. These plans do not have to be extensive, but they do help teams keep focused by providing documentation and setting goals for achievement. The written plan should have a well-defined set of activities, with accompanying timelines and assigned responsibilities. The following recommendations are offered to new teams for their initial planning sessions:

1. Determine what each team member's role will be for the year.
2. Determine what each team member will contribute to the team's work over the year (in terms of specific goals, objectives, and outcomes).
3. Determine how the team member's goals will be reviewed periodically through the year (quarterly is optimal) and at the end of the year.
4. Determine how the overall team goals, objectives, and outcomes will be reviewed at the end of the year.
5. Determine how the individual team members will evaluate the team planning process at the end of the first year.
6. Determine a process by which team members can make suggestions and recommendations—or raise concerns—about the process during the course of the year.
7. Decide how minutes of meetings and team decisions will be recorded.
8. Set forth in writing all of the above commitments.

While these steps may sound bureaucratic to some, they represent sound management practice. These procedures outlined above also greatly aid evaluation at the end of the year, generate a document history of the work of the team, provide essential information about the team should there be changes in team membership, serve as a reference if team members need clarification about earlier decisions made, and serve as the basis for developing the plan for the second year of work. *They are essential to the continuity and sustainability of the change process.*

Case Example 26-3 provides a sober glimpse at the challenges and barriers to implementing a high school inclusion program.

CASE EXAMPLE 26-3. Crosswinds High School—A High School Begins an Inclusion Program

Five years ago, Crosswinds High School was in a severe decline. Lax discipline, continuous teacher turnover, low academic standards, and directionless school policies offered an unproductive school program to the growing multicultural school population. Today Crosswinds is an up-and-coming school. A strong administrative team has engaged the faculty in school restructuring efforts. Discipline is tight. The labyrinth of halls at Crosswinds is quiet and quite empty while classes are in session. Between classes, bustling groups of students walk quickly to their next classes. Students know they cannot enter class late without a pass and that three occasions of tardiness result in suspension. The rules are clear and consistently enforced.

Teachers now like working at Crosswinds, and teamwork is a consistent part of their operation. Departments meet regularly to address curricular needs, and ample time is given in the summer for curriculum development. Teachers also work in interdepartmental teams to integrate the curriculum across academic disciplines. The instructional staff, led by the principal, takes the school system's standardized testing program very seriously. Student grades and standardized test scores are a clear and closely scrutinized accountability measure for each teacher and department and for the school as a whole. The school's slowly rising standardized test scores are being used by the school system to gauge whether the reforms at Crosswinds are working.

continues

CASE EXAMPLE 26-3. *(continued)*

The largest department in this 2,000-student school is the special education department. The department offers comprehensive special education services from special education classes for the full school day to full inclusion of students with disabilities, with monitoring. This year the department actively participated in restructuring the ninth-grade program. Each ninth grader was assigned to one of five teams of teachers. Each teacher team served 130 students, and teams comprised teachers of English, social studies, mathematics, science, technology, special education, and English as a second language. The teams had two goals for the first year: to begin to integrate their curriculum across academic areas and to infuse technology into all academic areas.

In order to integrate into the teams all students receiving special education services, the special education staffing was modified so that only two levels of special education services were available to ninth-grade students—inclusion in the ninth-grade team or self-contained special education. The option to take one or two academic subjects within special education was no longer available for freshman students with disabilities.

It was a challenging year for the veteran special education teachers who chose to work on the ninth-grade teams. They were responsible for team planning and team teaching with the academic teachers. Each teacher also offered a one-period class in study skills each day for all the students on the team who had been identified as needing special education services. As in any school year, there were the fluctuations of frustrations and successes. The integration into a regular classroom was a difficult adjustment for many of the students with learning and emotional disabilities. The special education teachers struggled to determine the most productive way to use the time in the study-skills class, and student behavior in that class was also an issue. Students seemed to resent the one period of being in special education, and behavior management was a challenge in these classes all year.

The match between the academic curricular expectations and student skills and comprehension levels was tenuous for about 25 percent of the identified special education students. The first half of the year was stressful for both teachers and students, as the teams struggled to integrate the academic material they were teaching. Grades for the first and second marking periods were generally low for identified students with disabilities. By midyear, 11 students had been moved to one of the two self-contained programs, 7 had left the school for various reasons, and 40 remained in the program, with grades averaging from D− to B+. The teams also identified about 15 percent of the general ninth-grade student population who were in danger of failing ninth grade at midyear.

The school administration, concerned about grades as well as the overall progress of the program, sent a strong message to the teams that grades for all students were a measure of program success. The message was also sent that, for ninth-grade students, grades on standardized tests given in the third marking period were of the utmost importance. Each team experienced various crisis points as the pressure to increase student performance grew. The special education teachers, accustomed to celebrating small student victories and measuring growth in terms of individual performance, at times felt overwhelmed and defeated by this new system. They could see progress and growth as their students struggled to adjust to this demanding ninth-grade curriculum, but grade point averages and standardized test scores were inadequate measures of *some* students' growth.

By the end of the year, exhausted ninth-grade team members took time to reflect. The special education teachers agreed that the weekly meetings of the ninth-grade special education teachers with the special education department chairperson had been a crucial support mechanism. There they could share strategies, express concern for specific students, and share their small victories. By working as a special education team, as well as by teaming with their academic counterparts, they had been able to support the success of students with disabilities in their ninth-grade year. All students with disabilities passed ninth grade, although some did so with solid grade-point averages, some by the skin of their teeth, and some by moving to a more restrictive special education placement.

At the end of the first year of the ninth-grade team approach, the following events occurred:

- Because of cuts in the school budget and redistricting, the school lost 20 teaching positions. The number of ninth-grade teams was reduced from five to three, with each team serving 150 rather than 130 students. Students identified as needing special education services would be distributed across two teams.
- Thirty percent of the team teachers (in all disciplines) decided not to continue in the ninth-grade program.
- Of the five special education teachers who had worked with the ninth-grade teams, one left teaching, one was transferred to another school because of decreased school staffing, two chose to continue with the program, and one took a position with the self-contained program.
- Ninth-grade test scores and grades did not show significant improvement from the previous year. The school principal met with all ninth-grade team members at the end of the school year and informed them that the program would be in jeopardy if important indicators did not improve the next year.

Discussion Questions

1. What factors were present in the first year to help make the ninth-grade inclusion program a success?

CASE EXAMPLE 26-3. *(continued)*

2. What factors are now working against the program?
3. What are your major concerns for the program as it enters its second year?
4. What additional evaluation indicators should be used to determine if the program is a success?

5. If you were a parent of a student with a reading disability in the program, what questions would you have for the team of teachers working with your child?
6. Based of the information presented, would you consider this program a success?

STEP 8: EVALUATE THE INCLUSION INITIATIVE

Measuring the Effectiveness of Inclusion. This section provides an introduction to the concept of evaluation for improving inclusion practices and to the basic evaluation principles. It also focuses on practical uses of evaluation for measuring inclusion outcomes and provides an overview of how to design evaluation for inclusion and use evaluation results for decision making and planning. Although evaluation is the *final step* in the process of developing inclusion initiatives and teams, it is the *first step* in their ongoing improvement. It may be helpful to view the evaluation process as a continuous spiral that gradually lifts the students, teachers, and related personnel ever upward toward greater improvements in teaching and learning for all students.

Evaluating Inclusion Means More that Just Placement of Students. Inclusion has come to be synonymous with physical placement of a student with a disability from one particular environment into another which is less restrictive or more closely integrated with nondisabled peers. The success of inclusion, therefore, is often measured quantitatively by numbers of students with disabilities moving from special education classes into regular classes or by the number of actual class periods these students spend in a regular classroom. Measures of quality and outcomes often are ignored, as are numerous factors in the environment of a classroom and school which may impinge upon the quality of the regular classroom accommodation and the adaptation of the student with the disabilities and his or her peers.

Teachers in Inclusive Classrooms Affect Inclusion Outcomes and Quality. Teachers in inclusive classrooms provide a powerful *intervention* that affects student achievement and many other outcomes. The following summary provides a few examples of how the inclusion teacher can enhance or protect access to and quality of educational services for children and youth.

How Inclusion Teachers Improve the Quality of Education for All Students

1. *Increase access to education and school activities:* Teachers help improve access for students who would not be able to participate in education or school activities without additional supports. They match student and family needs with available services and supports

and conduct interdisciplinary team planning for the student to ensure that needed services are provided.
2. *Affect distribution of inclusive services and placement decisions:* Teachers provide information about the degree to which they can accommodate students with disabilities and their willingness to make such accommodations.
3. *Identify service gaps:* Teachers identify barriers to inclusion and service gaps for students and bring them to the attention of inclusion team planners and administrators. They act as the eyes and ears of the inclusive system in communicating student needs to administrative personnel.
4. *Enhance communication across disciplines and school units:* Teachers help develop a common language across disciplines, assess student needs, and conduct individual service planning. They assist with communication among all people involved in the successful placement of the student.
5. *Provide quality assurance and monitoring:* These teachers are aware of and help other teachers and personnel to understand local, state, and federal regulations and quality standards. They adhere to local guidelines for inclusion and can help monitor the provision of interdisciplinary educational services for the student.
6. *Solve inclusion problems:* Teachers facilitate solutions to disagreements about student placements, they seek alternative services as needed, intervene in students' rights issues, and troubleshoot conflicts and barriers.

Inclusion planners and implementers must be viewed as key players in inclusion practices that lead to positive outcomes for students and for the general teaching and learning environment. The following scenario provides a context in which to place the evaluation concepts that will be discussed. The scenario is based on the experience of one of the authors, along with additional elements drawn from a composite of many inclusion initiatives.

An Evaluation Scenario. Educators and community services leaders in Hillbrook Valley wanted to assess and improve their ability to serve children and youth with autism and their families in existing home schools, with support services from community agencies. They needed information about how many students in the county system were diagnosed with autism, how many agencies (school-based or community-based) were actually providing services to children and youth with autism, and how many could serve these individuals in home schools if resources and coordination were made available. An inclusion planning team of representatives from the school and a variety of related service agencies were brought together to discuss the problems and needs. They included elementary, middle, and high school teachers and administrators, school counselors, community-based mental health system staff, early intervention staff, family services personnel, adult service system and rehabilitation staff, private nonprofit vocational training program staff, and business and community college representatives. This group formed several teams which conducted the following activities:

- Identified the size of the population of children and youth with autism.
- Described current school support services and community services available in the home schools, covering early intervention through to postsecondary and adult services.
- Defined new services that needed to be established.
- Conducted information sessions to local board members to inform them of the inclusion goals and implementation issues.

Although the team addressed the continuum of services for children and youth, one of the top priorities for the inclusion initiative was to serve families of younger school children with autism. Over the first 2 years of the initiative, they established an interagency outreach and identification system to identify children with autism and link families with the range of available school and community support services. The agencies and institutions involved in collaboration included schools, public health programs, hospitals, physician referral services, pediatric clinics, community mental health and family services, preschool programs, and a few of the major diagnostic assessment and testing firms in the community. An inclusion coordination agreement was developed to establish a successful "single point of entry" information and referral system for students with autism.

Analysis of the Scenario. It may help to begin by imagining the task of designing and conducting an evaluation for the Hillbrook Valley inclusion initiative. What kinds of questions should be asked about the collaboration among the many school and community professionals, and what are the expected benefits of the services?

- Who wants the evaluation information and who will use it?
- What kind of information is needed?

Think about the key *players* or agencies who are involved in the inclusion collaboration. The next set of questions relate to the different persons or agencies who have a vested interest in the success of the inclusion initiative and service linkages:

- Have inclusion services benefited the children and families for whom they were developed?
- How have the collaborating professionals benefited?
- What do the teachers and administrators need to know about the success of the inclusion initiatives and their perspective roles in that success?
- What questions do teachers want answered by the evaluation?
- Are school administrators interested in evaluation results, and for what purpose?
- What would families of students in inclusive classrooms be interested in knowing?
- How do families feel about the impacts of inclusive services and coordination activities on their children?

The next few questions are related to the kinds of resources that are put into, or invested in, the collaboration to make it work (*inputs*):

- Who is providing funding or resources (materials and equipment) for the inclusion initiative?
- Are there additional training resources to prepare personnel to implement inclusion practices and teams?
- What personnel are assigned to inclusive classrooms, and what related and support personnel are available?
- What other community agencies are contributing resources to achieve the goals of the inclusion initiative—rehabilitation services, employment training programs, social services, community public health and mental health services, and others?

These initial questions may stimulate additional questions about the *implementation and management* of inclusion initiatives (*process*):

- Are there any inclusion evaluation or quality review or monitoring procedures already in place?
- What goals and objectives were included in the original inclusion charter or coordination agreement?
- Are the inclusion practices, policies and procedures reasonable for achieving shared goals, or do they create barriers for collaboration and student achievement?

What questions should be asked about the *impacts or benefits to participating students and their families* for whom this program was designed (*outcomes*)?

- What should be asked about the effects or impacts of inclusion practices on the students and families?
- Have the goals and objectives documented in individualized education programs been accomplished?
- Who benefited from the inclusion initiative?
- How did the target students and families judge the adequacy of the inclusive classrooms and support services?
- Are the original goals, objectives, and vision for the inclusive initiatives being achieved, and how well?
- Did barriers to inclusive practices decrease?

Finally, it is important to think about how to approach the *design* of the evaluation:

- Who should help conduct the evaluation, and who should advise?
- How should data be collected to answer the questions posed above?
- What evaluation tools are available and appropriate?

Keep the Hillbrook scenario in mind while reviewing the purposes and processes for evaluation. Remember, evaluation helps the inclusion planning team determine if and how well inclusive practices are benefiting students, families, and the teaching and learning environment.

What Is Program Evaluation? Program evaluation is the process of determining the effectiveness of any program or initiative. It is particularly important in measuring the success or failure of a program that is designed to improve the education and quality of life for students with special needs. Evaluation is a process by which we collect information about the inclusive services and the inclusion team, in order to

- Find out how much impact the inclusion initiative is having on students, families, teachers, student peers, and the wider school environment.
- Determine if the inclusion team is achieving the goals that it set for the school.
- Determine how valuable the program is (its worth).
- Help in making decisions about the future of the inclusion program.

Evaluation activities help provide feedback about the environment in order to improve the quality of services to students. Because evaluation is closely linked to the decision making process, it is considered successful *if the information it generates becomes part of the inclusion decision-making process within the school.*

Evaluation Defined. Evaluation is a process of assessing a school or agency's performance in terms of agreed-on program objectives and performance indicators (Rossi, Freeman & Lipsay, 1999). Evaluation can also be referred to as a strategy for measuring (1) how well the organization is accomplishing the goals defined in its mission statement and cooperative agreements and (2) to what extent students and families are benefiting from the services and resources. In evaluating inclusive practices, inclusion planners seek answers to questions such as

1. How do we know the inclusion program is helping students?
2. What can we do to improve the inclusion team collaboration and teaching environment to increase the impacts or benefits?
3. How do the students judge the quality, accessibility, and appropriateness of the inclusion supports?
4. How well are the inclusion team members accomplishing the goals and objectives in their cooperative agreements? and in their collaborative teams?

Evaluation, therefore, provides teachers with information about whether inclusive practices and supportive services are actually helping students, families, student peers, and the teaching and learning environment. Evaluation also aids administrators because it provides crucial information for decision making. A coordinated inclusive process should combine individual and team-level evaluation activities to measure its effectiveness and contribute to decision making. *One of the most important decisions we can make about inclusion is whether benefits are accrued by students. How the school personnel answer this question will determine the level of commitment it will make to the future of the inclusion initiative.* Inclusion evaluation is most useful and effective when it takes into consideration the perspectives and judgments of all who are involved in the inclusion initiative—students and families, teachers, student peers, related service personnel, and administrators.

A Basic Vocabulary for Inclusion Evaluation. Evaluation methods can be placed into two basic groups: *formative* and *summative.*

Formative evaluation includes activities that occur during the formation, or early development, of the inclusion initiative and are conducted to answer specific questions about how the inclusive program is operating or how effective it is. How well are services being planned for or coordinated? Are professionals and related service personnel collaborating the way the inclusion planning team originally intended? Formative evaluations are usually conducted during the planning and early implementation phases of an inclusion initiative and often include evaluation of placement decision-making processes, review of inclusive classroom procedures, ongoing program reviews, or periodic individual case reviews. Ongoing, formative evaluation provides useful information to help teachers make adjustments and improvements as inclusive classrooms and services are being formed.

Summative evaluation provides summary information about the *results* of the inclusion practices after they have been established for some time. Summative evaluation is designed to answer questions, such as what results are we getting for students and families and how is the inclusion initiative benefiting all involved? Summative evaluation information involves judgments about the value of different kinds of inclusion practices and is useful for making changes in how services are delivered and managed, how staff are trained, and how school resources are used. A 3-year evaluation of the first group of elementary school children with disabilities placed into inclusive classrooms is an example of summative evaluation.

Both *formative and summative evaluations* are needed in order to conduct a comprehensive inclusion evaluation. (Rossi, Freeman & Lipsey, 1999)

Classifying Evaluation Activities: Inputs, Processes, and Outcomes. Measures of the benefits of inclusion can also be categorized into three groups: inputs, processes and outcomes. Each group refers to different types of evaluation measures.

1. Inputs (the resources put into the program or service)
2. Processes (activities, processes and procedures established to deliver services)
3. Outcomes (what changes or improves as a result of the services).

Inputs. Inputs refer to resources put into, or invested, in the planning and operation of the inclusion initiative. Inputs include resource contributions from the school, district, and other sources in the form of personnel, funds, equipment, transportation, consultation time, and space. Inputs also include the ways in which we design or structure the inclusive classrooms and activities, the selection of students placed into inclusive classrooms, and the types of support services provided. Here are some examples of different types of inputs:

- At the student level, individual students are the primary inputs for the inclusion initiative.
- At the administrative or school level, the collaborating professionals, the related service providers, and the resources they each contribute represent the inputs.
- Inputs also include the inclusion goals and objectives.
- Informal inputs may include family members and others who volunteer to help in the classroom or school.
- Formal inputs include professionals such as teachers, counselors, coordinators, social workers or case workers, administrators, and many others.

Evaluation of inputs includes studies of the demographics and needs of student groups being placed into inclusive classrooms, the variety of resources being devoted to inclusion activities, in-kind contributions to the inclusion effort, staffing arrangements for inclusive classrooms, and use of volunteers.

Processes. Evaluating program processes means examining what the inclusion program does (activities and procedures) to provide inclusive services to students with disabilities. For example, process evaluation provides information about

1. Whether inclusive educational services are being delivered or coordinated in a manner consistent with the original inclusion program goals and objectives.
2. Whether the services are reaching the target student population.
3. Whether students' families are receiving the supports and communication that was provided for in the original inclusion plan.

Process evaluation also includes information on

- The inclusive services and opportunities provided.
- Inclusive service principles that will guide the inclusion team members.
- Activities performed by collaborating professionals.
- Staffing and administrative structure for inclusion coordination.
- Policies, procedures, and guidelines for inclusion implementation.

Process Evaluation Is Important for a Comprehensive Evaluation of Inclusion. Process evaluation is an important part of a comprehensive evaluation because it enables teachers and administrators to monitor and examine the total set of processes for implementing inclusion. Evaluation experts warn that it is easy to get an incomplete picture of a program when evaluators look only at outcomes, yet know little about what students actually received (the processes) while they participated in inclusive classrooms and schools.

Outcomes. Outcomes and benefits refer to that which inclusion implementers hope to see change or improve as a result of the inclusive practices and coordination. Outcome evaluation involves measuring the extent to which inclusive education results in desired achievement and social integration of students with disabilities. It also involves assessing the extent to which the classrooms and teaching practices change to improve education for all students. Outcome evaluation addresses two questions: Are students really benefiting from inclusive education in ways that can be measured, and are there improvements in educational quality and accessibility for all students? Outcomes can be measured at the individual student level and the team or school level.

School and Student Outcomes. *Individual student outcomes* include measures of classroom achievement, social skills progress, and improved functioning in a range of domains. Team- or school-level outcomes include measures of improvements in the way teachers restructure their classrooms or adapt curricula, teaching methods, and materials to accommodate diverse students in the classroom. Such outcomes also include the range of inclusion options and support services provided to students in inclusive settings. Table 26-3 compares examples of student and school-level outcomes.

Summary of Student- and School-Level Outcomes. Both types of outcomes are important for evaluation of inclusion practices. Inclusion practices are designed to directly improve the education of students, and, therefore, evaluations of individual impacts are often the most important measures of the effectiveness of inclusion initiatives. School-level outcomes also positively impact students in less direct ways by improving the overall teaching and learning environment and by improving access to the range of learning opportunities and activities in the school. School outcomes are related to changes and improvements in the school as a whole. Examples of school-level outcomes also include increased capacity of the teachers and principal to project future needs for inclusive placements, increased available support services, improved assessment and identification of students for placement into inclusive classrooms, improved staff training and professional development, and increased capacity of teachers and counselors to coordinate services between the school and the community. Tables 26-4 and 26-5 introduce categories of student- and school-level outcomes and provide examples of measures that can be used in each category.

Follow-Up. Follow-up refers to activities that track the path or disposition of students after they have exited the class, program, or school. It may occur when students leave elementary and transition to middle school, or from middle to high school, or from high school to postsecondary education or employment. Follow-up is designed to answer the following questions:

- What happens to students once they have left the class, program, or school?
- Do students experience long-term benefits or impacts as a result of being served in inclusive classrooms, in terms of the range of functional domains (improved independent living, physical health and mobility, continuing education, social functioning, employment adjustment, family relations, employment, and other domains?

TABLE 26-3. Comparing Student- and School-Level Outcomes at a Glance

Student Level	School Level
• Improved physical status and health. • Improved academic achievement. • Improved family relationships. • Improved attendance in the program. • Gains in job skills. • Increased community service participation. • Reduction in behavior referrals. • Reduction in substance abuse. • Improved peer relationships. • Decrease in program dropout.	• Improved access to inclusive classrooms and extracurricular activities. • Improved assessment of participant needs and support services. • Expansion of support services available in classrooms. • Improved collaboration among interdisciplinary team members and school and community support service providers. • Improved coordination among teachers and support service providers. • Identification of barriers to participation in services. • Follow-up of students.

TABLE 26-4. Student-Level Outcome Measures

Category of Outcome Measure	Examples
1. Family involvement and quality of home life	Improvements in student-parent or student-sibling relationships, family attendance and involvement in interdisciplinary planning for the child, and parent training received, social services interventions (e.g., early intervention, counseling, protective services, foster care), interagency service coordination assistance, reduction of family stress, or general improvement of family functioning.
2. Early childhood education outcomes	Improvement in child's functioning, improvement of health status, reduction of illnesses, visits for follow-up medical care, improvement in mobility or walking, changes in expectations for the child, improved diet, increase in time spent with the child.
3. School-based education training, and supports	Gains in academic skills, and specific occupational skill training, improvement in academic skills, vocational assessment services, received integrated curriculum, types of courses taken, courses taken in integrated or segregated settings, academic and vocational credits taken, paid work participation, wages earned, work experiences, graduation credentials or skill certifications earned, work modifications received, related services received, guidance and counseling services, accommodations or adaptations, assistive technology provided, transportation provided or travel training received, and service coordination support.
4. Supports for transition to independent living, employment, or postsecondary education	Assistance in the transition phase from secondary school, such as assistance in application and entry into postsecondary programs, assessments, service coordination, transfer of responsibility to another agency, types of placements, skill training received, rehabilitation agency participation, assistive technology, guidance and counseling, part time or full time work while in education or job training, social participation, transportation, degrees or skill certificates earned, job placement, community-based training received, on-the-job supports, work adjustment counseling or interventions, employee assistance program participation.
5. Quality of life and adjustment to young adulthood	Adjustment to adult living, such as social participation; marriage and family; community participation; living arrangement and degree of independence; residential setting; continued community-based services and supports; service coordination assistance; church participation; avocational activities; social, recreationaly, and leisure activities; relationships with family and siblings; and citizenship and participation in the political process.
6. Long-range career adjustment and independence	Career advancement and promotion, additional on-the-job training provided by employer, additional certifications or licenses earned on the job, on-the-job supports, career changes, additional work responsibilities assigned, transfers and relocations, continued independent living and self-sufficiency, participation in community affairs and activities, continued participation in social and recreational activities, stability of marriage and family relationships, and continued participation in treatments or therapies needed.

(*Sources:* DeStefano, Heck, Hasazi, & Funey, 1999; Kochhar & Erickson, 1991; Lueking, Fabion & Tilson, 1995)

TABLE 26-5. School-Level Outcome Measure

Category of Outcome Measure	Examples
1. Inclusion collaboration	Collaborative agreements (formal and informal), involvement agencies in collaborative planning for inclusion, student follow-up joint service assessments, and projections of service needs and graduate placements (anticipated services).
2. Interdisciplinary and interagency training and professional development	Interdisciplinary and interagency training activities for school and community-based personnel to help implement inclusion and provide a range of supportive services.
3. Parent outreach and communication	Parent and family training activities, linkages with parent training centers, regular family communications, and invitations to parents to attend demonstrations and student exhibits.
4. Inclusion management	Collecting of data on students placed into inclusive classrooms, the services they need, and planning that occurs; information and referral services; curricular and instructional modifications, test modifications; support services provided; technology adaptations; service monitoring, follow-up and follow-along services; information sharing among teachers and related service professionals; and student emergency management or behavior management service.
5. Interagency system advocacy	Individual and group advocacy to increase services and service responsiveness to consumer or family needs, human rights protection and review activities, and local, state, and national policy advocacy for improved services.
6. Inclusion evaluation	Sharing information with teachers and parents on the effectiveness of the inclusion initiative, participation of teachers in the design of the evaluation, and use of the evaluation information for improvement of inclusive practices.

- Is there a change in the way students perceive the quality and appropriateness of the inclusive services after graduation or exit from the school?
- By examining what happens to students when they leave, can we predict the impact of inclusive services for incoming students?

Examples of Follow-Up Activities. Here are a few examples of follow-up evaluation studies:

- Student and family surveys to obtain the perceptions about the quality, accessibility, and appropriateness of inclusive services.
- Teacher surveys and interviews to obtain their perceptions about the quality and appropriateness of the inclusive services they are providing and the administrative supports that are helpful.
- Interviews with individual students to determine their satisfaction with services.
- Surveys and interviews with students who have left the school to determine whether the benefits to the student have endured over time.
- Contacts to former students to determine if continuing support services were needed.
- Contacts to students who have dropped out of school to assess their attitudes about the inclusive services, about their IEPs, and the communication with students, teachers, and others.
- Six-month follow-up of medically at-risk elementary school children who are placed into inclusive classrooms with teamed teachers.
- One-year follow-up of middle school students using adapted computers in the technology lab.
- Two-year follow-up of middle school program graduates or completers.

- One-year follow-up of families of children with disabilities who were actively involved in IEP planning, training, and counseling.
- Three-year follow-up of high school completers who entered employment.
- Long-range (5-year) follow-up of students who have graduated from high school and have entered two- and four-year colleges.
- Two-year follow-up of youth with severe disabilities who entered the rehabilitation system after high school.

Follow-Up Studies Are Important to Inclusion Evaluation. Follow-up studies involves collecting information on students after they have completed or left the inclusive class or school. They are an important component of inclusion evaluation and serve several very important purposes for the inclusion initiative.

1. They provide a way of finding out if the benefits and achievement of students in inclusive settings endure or remain stable over time.
2. They tell us if the gains that students make in inclusive settings diminish once they leave the program.
3. They tell us if gains made are increased or accelerated once they leave the services.

Services or programs that show good follow-up outcomes (i.e., the students retain over time what they have learned or gained during school participation) are usually judged to be effective.

Effectiveness Measures for Inclusion. The fundamental question in evaluating the effectiveness of an inclusion initiative is: What evidence is there that the program is improving academic and social conditions for students with disabilities? This definition of "improvement" may differ among personnel involved in implementing inclusion. For example, administrators may use standardized measures of effectiveness such as standardized achievement test scores that apply to all students. However, standardized measures alone are usually inadequate to evaluate the full range of contributions an inclusion program can make to the students, classroom, and school as a whole. General education teachers may use progress in learning the general education curriculum material as well as benefits to students without disabilities. Special education teachers may use additional measures such as improved appropriateness of behavior and increased positive social interaction. It is important that the inclusion team members have a clear idea of the kinds of measures of effectiveness they will use to evaluate the inclusion initiative.

Effectiveness measures for inclusion include evaluation measures in the three categories of *inputs, processes,* and *outcomes.* Table 26-6 provides examples of the kinds of measures that can be included in an evaluation.

Determining the Purposes for Evaluation. The purpose for using an evaluation will affect both the design of the evaluation and the way evaluators will report results. Know your purpose. The following provides a summary of the different purposes for which evaluation is conducted.

Purposes for Evaluation

1. **Demonstrating results:** Do you wish to demonstrate positive outcomes for students and families and progress in achieving the goals of the inclusion initiative?
2. **Reevaluation of the inclusion initiatives:** Does the design of the original inclusion initiative need to be modified and do you need information on how and what kinds of changes are needed?
3. **Resource development:** Are the resources still adequate to continue the inclusion initiative and achieve the goals established?
4. **Project replication:** Do you want to reproduce the inclusion model in another school unit or school?
5. **Budget planning:** Are you using evaluation information in annual budget decisions?
6. **Cost effectiveness:** Are you using evaluation information to make major decisions about expansion, continuation, or redistribution of resources for the inclusion initiative?
7. **Needs assessment:** Do you need to reevaluate the priority needs that the inclusion initiative is addressing or expand your needs assessment to other student groups?
8. **Program monitoring:** Are you using evaluation data to monitor the inclusion processes and activities?
9. **Program management:** Are you using evaluation information to assess and revise your management or personnel structure for inclusion?

The evaluation purpose or purposes selected will have implications not only for how the evaluation should be designed, but also how data should be collected and how the information should be reported and shared.

Locating Source Documents to Answer Evaluation Questions. Many documents may already exist within the school and can provide much qualitative and quantitative evaluation information. Box 26-1 provides examples of documents that are rich sources of evaluation information.

BOX 26-1. Documents That Can Provide Evaluation Information

- Student records
- School aggregate records or data collection forms
- Instructional tools
- Orientation materials and documents
- Training materials and documents
- Training feedback surveys
- Policy and procedure manuals
- Student guidelines for participation in inclusive classrooms
- Placement policies and procedures
- Cooperative agreements and mission statements
- Personnel and volunteer records and job descriptions
- Short- and long-range planning documents
- Board meeting agendas, policies, priorities
- State and local educational plans
- State and federal partnership legislation
- Service coordination proposal documents
- Budget documents and annual budget plans
- In-kind services records
- Interdisciplinary team meeting records and actions
- Previous independent evaluation reports of inclusion or monitoring reports
- Previous needs assessments conducted

Action Steps for the Evaluation Process. The following 10 action steps (Figure 26-3) are useful for developing an evaluation plan. These ten steps can be applied whether the evaluator selects one or all of the evaluation components.

Student Participation in Inclusion Evaluation. A comprehensive evaluation of inclusion practices seeks the input of students and families about the effects or outcomes of the inclusion activities. Key "stakeholders" include those who have the greatest "interest" in assuring the quality and continuity of inclusive educational services. Students and families are important for validating the quality of services and service coordination activities. To *validate* means to confirm or substantiate the results or effects of a service or activity. The most important validations are the successes of the individuals for

TABLE 26-6. Effectiveness Measures for Inclusion Coordination

Inclusion Coordination Function	Example Measures
Student information and referral for classroom placement	• Adequacy of the student placement decision-making process. • Increase in the number of students transferred to more inclusive settings. • Number of students enrolled in home schools from more restrictive settings such as hospitals, rehabilitation agencies, institutions, correctional facilities, or residential programs. • Availability of information for parents on inclusion procedures and policies in the school. • Adequacy of documentation of referral information and interdisciplinary team recommendations for the general education classroom.
Review and screening of student needs	• Number of students reviewed and referred for placement. • Adequacy of follow-up on student's adjustment after referral to the general education classroom. • Adequacy and use of support services information directory for teachers and inclusion implementors. • Types of teacher referrals for support services and related service providers and adequacy of the process. • Reduced time lag between referral and entry into inclusive classroom or program after student and parent have been notified and have consented. • Adequate documentation of interdisciplinary team's rationale for decision not to place into the general education classroom.
Evaluation and diagnosis	• Adequacy of procedures for obtaining past academic record information. • Degree to which student evaluation data is used as a basis for determining educational needs. • Timeliness of response to interdisciplinary team's request for student evaluations or assessments. • Comprehensiveness of student evaluation information. • Adequacy with which evaluation process identifies student strengths and needs and provides information to teachers pertinent to educational interventions needed in the classroom. • Adequacy with which medical evaluations and medication needs are communicated to teachers and relevant personnel. • Availability of initial speech/language screening for students who need it. • Availability of initial and annual evaluations of functional skills for students who need them. • Adequacy with which evaluation findings are interpreted to the student and family in understandable terms.
Individual education program planning and development	• Timeliness and adequacy of individualized education program (IEP) development. • Timeliness and adequacy of annual IEP review. • Adequacy of attention to functional skill training goals in the IEP. • Completeness of IEP in addressing short- and long-range goals. • Adequacy of IEP in distinguishing high-priority goals and objectives from those with less priority. • Adequacy with which IEP identifies service barriers and services that are needed by students but not available. • Adequacy of IEP in specifying expected dates for achievement of goals and provision of needed services. • Adequacy of IEP in documenting needed related services and specific dates of provision.
Support service coordination and linking	• Knowledge of teachers and counselors about available support services, related services, and community resource agencies. • Adequacy and regularity of school communications with families. • Student's and family satisfaction with the assigned teacher/service coordinator and adequacy of the service delivery. • Appropriateness of support and related services obtained by teachers/coordinators within and outside the school.
IEP monitoring and follow-along	• Improvements in students' physical status, vision, hearing, mobility, or academic achievement. • Gains in students' levels of adaptive behavior or independent functioning. • Achievement of students' IEP goals within stated time periods. • Completeness and up-to-date status of students' IEPs. • Length of time students have remained in inclusive placements. • Availability of medication and medical or nursing services for students who need it. • Students progress in vocational programs and employment sites. • Adequate documentation of crisis intervention procedures and events. • Regularity of parent–teacher consultations. • Regularity of reporting students' progress using reports cards in a manner similar to reporting for students without disabilities. • Level of family involvement in students' overall programming.

	• Number of students removed from inclusive classrooms and reasons.
	• Adequacy of procedures for advance notice of discontinuations of support services, changes in placement, or intent to remove from the classroom.
Inclusion advocacy and support	• Effectiveness of responses and interventions by teachers and administrators when support services are needed but not provided to students as specified in the IEP.
	• Efforts by teachers and administrators and results of advocacy efforts to develop inclusive services.
Inclusion evaluation and student follow-up	• Adequacy of postschool follow-up activities.
	• Results of postschool outcome evaluations.
	• Number of follow-up interviews conducted.
	• Number of students enrolled in postsecondary training and completion of postsecondary degrees and certifications.
	• Number of students placed in jobs.
	• Types of independent living arrangements of students after graduation.
	• Types of community services sought or accessed by students after graduation.
Inclusion quality factors	• Ratio of students with disabilities to students without disabilities in general education classrooms.
	• Relative consistency of ratio among classrooms (students are equitably placed into classrooms).
	• Qualifications of teachers and special education consultants and specialists.
	• Student satisfaction with placement in inclusive classroom.
	• Family satisfaction with placement and support services provided.
	• Teacher and specialist satisfaction with inclusive practices and resources.
	• Student and family involvement in evaluating inclusion practices.
	• Technical assistance provided to teachers and specialists to implement inclusion.
	• Adequacy of problem-solving and mediation strategies used to avoid disputes and formal due process hearings.

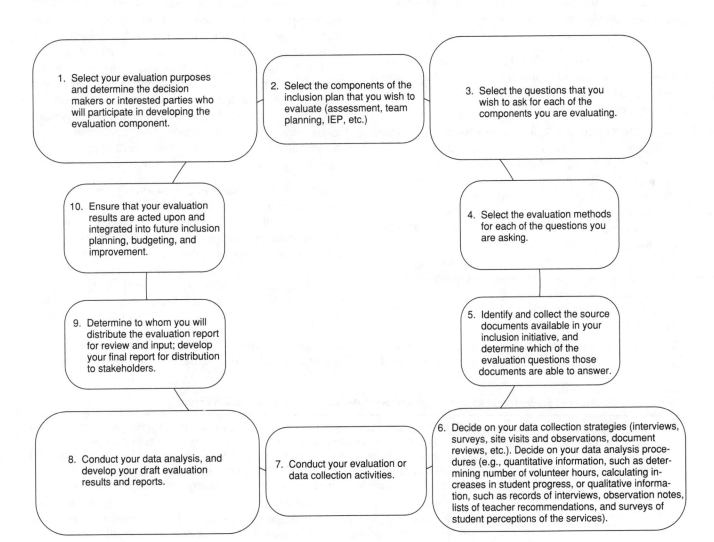

FIGURE 26-3. Ten Action Steps for the Evaluation Process

A comprehensive evaluation of inclusion practices seeks the input of students about the effects or outcomes.

whom services are intended. Table 26-7 provides measures that can be used to solicit student and family input into the quality of inclusion practices and the school environment.

STEP 9. USE EVALUATION RESULTS IN THE IMPROVEMENT PLAN. Evaluation activities help provide feedback on the inclusion initiative in order to improve the quality of services to students. The evaluation information should be used and acted upon in order to improve the inclusion practices and model. Evaluation information will not result in improvements unless there is a *constructive process* for

1. Analyzing and communicating the information in a manner that is understandable and usable by teachers and administrators.
2. Applying the information for change and improvement.

The inclusion improvement process involves identifying the weaknesses, barriers, and gaps in services and de-

veloping a plan of change to restructure services to better meet the needs of students. The steps in utilizing evaluation information for improvement include the following:

1. Analyze the views of multiple stakeholder groups (internal school personnel, administrators, related agency staff, and students) through the evaluation process.
2. Analyze the results of the outcome evaluation of inclusive practices.
3. Identify discrepancies between the actual inclusion outcomes being obtained and the perceptions of key stakeholders (e.g., poor outcomes but positive perceptions by teachers).
4. Share the results of the evaluation analysis with key stakeholder groups and the inclusion planning team.
5. Develop an ongoing dissemination and review process through which stakeholder groups may receive the evaluation results.
6. Solicit direct input from students for the evaluation.
7. Include evaluation results in annual reports of inclusion initiative and collaboration.

Because evaluation is closely linked to the decision-making process, it is considered successful *if the information it generates becomes part of the inclusion decision-making process within the school.* Adjustments are part of the educational process, especially when inclusion efforts are involved. For example, a high school in a suburban area conducted a self-evaluation of the special education program. They identified six goals that needed to be addressed. Consequently, they contacted a local university for technical assistance and support in restructuring and improving their services.

STEP 10. DEVELOP A REWARD SYSTEM AND CELEBRATE SUCCESS. Inclusion planners recognize the need for reward and recognition of all collaborating personnel. Celebrations of individual and program successes will become very important experiences in the lives of those committed to the mission of service coordination. Recognition serves to strengthen commitment and help develop camaraderie and a team spirit. Plans for a reward system should be built into the annual action plan from the start.

Staff Rewards and Celebration of Success. Rewards can include special events, gifts, or tokens given to person-

TABLE 26-7. Measures of Student and Family Perceptions and Satisfaction with the Inclusion Program

Student participation in inclusive classrooms	Satisfaction with (1) education services in inclusive classrooms, (2) school-to-work transition services, (3) postsecondary placement and supports, (4) service coordinator contact, (5) perceptions of service barriers and gaps and service accessibility, (6) IEP goals and content, (7) relationships with teachers and specialists, (8) special education consultant assistance and perceptions of (personal benefits of the placement and barriers to successful participation.
Families of students	Satisfaction with (1) accessibility of materials and equipment in the classroom, (2) IEP service goals and content, (3) relationships between student and teachers, (4) specialist contact and assistance, and perceptions of personal benefits to the student receiving the inclusive services, and perceptions of service barriers and gaps.

nel for the purpose of thanking them for their effort and participation. Reward and celebration also include

- Reminding staff that they are valued contributors.
- Strengthening and ensuring their continued commitment.
- Recognizing individual success stories with participants.
- Encouraging the participation of new staff and volunteers.

There are as many ways to reward people as there are people with imaginations. The list below provides a few common examples of ways to offer rewards and celebrate success.

- Use of local media to make special announcements about new programs or special successes of consumers and families; includes cable TV and radio.
- Newspaper articles about the program or individual teachers or members.
- Articles in educational agency newsletters, business newsletters, annual reports, community agency newsletters, and bulletins.
- Breakfasts, lunches and coffees in which special recognition is made to teachers, students, or parents.
- Plaques for individual achievement and service.
- Certificates for outstanding contributions and performance by teachers.
- A program offering "volunteer or parent of the month" or year, or "most valuable player" awards.
- Pins and buttons with inclusion team logo.
- Dedications of sites or equipment.
- Small gifts or mementos.
- Photograph displays in schools and community agencies.

The Concept of Renewal. The concept of renewal is related to reward but differs because it is directed at teachers and related personnel who have been involved in the inclusion team for some time. Sometimes key staff who helped get the linkages started may need to be reenergized or reminded of the mission of the initiative and the value of their role. Often these key individuals include the very first champions of inclusion who have done more than their fair share in leading and promoting the initiative. They may simply be tired, feeling as though they have reached a plateau. They may have seen many changes and new directions in the relationship and may no longer feel that their role is valued or appreciated. They may feel that their role as initiators and developers has now given way to routine operations, policies, and procedures. In short, they need to renew their sense of commitment, spirit, and purpose with the initiative.

Staff renewal activities are aimed at reenergizing long-term inclusion implementation personnel, reminding them of the mission of the inclusion initiative and the value of their role, and renewing their sense of commitment and purpose. Some of the strategies that can promote this renewal of spirit and dedication in these important and valued individuals include

- Using rewards.
- Conducting special retreats in which key personnel reflect on the mission, goals, successes, and contributions of teachers over the past years in the inclusion initiative, and also envision new directions for the inclusion initiative.
- Developing a video or TV production which chronicles the development of the initiative, its accomplishments, and the contributions of its key players. Such a production should focus on impacts and benefits for consumers and families and on improvements in service coordination effectiveness.
- Making changes in previous roles and granting opportunities for new experiences or responsibilities.
- Offering an individual a more prestigious role in the inclusion team, such as a role in the evaluation, a public relations role, or allowing staff to help other classrooms or schools initiate inclusion practices.

CHAPTER 27

What Should Be Included in a Professional Development Plan?

A well-planned training and professional development program is essential to helping teachers and support personnel prepare to implement inclusion effectively. Professional development can help inclusion implementors overcome doubts and resistance and feel more confident that they can be leaders as well as pioneers in the effort. Inclusion pioneers must have special knowledge to help champion change and transfer the spirit of opportunity to others who will be involved in the inclusion process.

Professional development is vital to the inclusion efforts because it prepares administrators, teachers, and support personnel to understand both the nature and needs of students with disabilities and the strategies and methods of curriculum and instructional adaptations. It prepares teachers for team teaching and support in the general education classroom. Furthermore, it prepares teachers, administrators, and related service personnel to understand their relative roles and responsibilities in the inclusion effort, to work with school-linked agencies, to work with the families of students with disabilities, to implement IEPs in accordance with IDEA, and to evaluate the school's inclusion effort. The inclusion planning team must try to assess the knowledge base of the key personnel who will be affected by the inclusion initiative.

The following sample plans for professional development in Tables 27-1 and 27-2 provide an overview of topics and can be used as a recommended framework for developing content for orienting personnel to the change process for inclusion implementation.

Key personnel in collaborating agencies need a common understanding of the goals of the initiative and individual roles that teachers will play. *This is also essential to the acceptance (adoption) of the new relationships, to fostering a sense of "ownership" of the new initiative and its goals, and to the ultimate success of inclusion.*

WHAT KNOWLEDGE AND SKILL CONTENT SHOULD BE INCLUDED IN STAFF TRAINING AND ORIENTATION? There are several important areas of new knowledge and skills needed by inclusion planners, implementors, and all other personnel who will be involved in achieving the goals of the initiative. These content areas are summarized in Table 27-2 below, which also contains examples of training objectives. These objectives reflect best practices in professional development for inclusion.

These topic areas are suggested as a guide and not a prescription. They are not necessarily inclusive of all of the information or material you may want to cover in orientation and training sessions. Each school will need to develop unique training strategies and materials to meet the needs of its students and teachers.

TABLE 27-1. Professional Development Plan Content: Preparing to Initiate the Change Process for Inclusion

Professional Development Need	Strategies and Content
Teacher training and orientation to the inclusion initiative	Include in teacher training and orientation the following: • The inclusion philosophy, concept, and principles. • The inclusion development process. • The concept of collaborative planning. • The process of change and restructuring to develop inclusive practices and overcome resistance to change. • Strategies for problem-solving. • Key roles and responsibilities of inclusion personnel.
Personnel training in the inclusion change process	Provide special sessions related to the change process. Ensure that cooperating teachers and related personnel are oriented to the principles and processes of inclusion, collaboration, and strategic planning centered on student needs and outcomes.
Promoting teacher leadership in inclusion planning	Provide basic staff training and orientation to new roles, and help teachers understand the broader impacts of the inclusion initiative upon the students and their families, nondisabled students, and the community as a whole. Share with them the expectations that the inclusion team has for its effort and what changes are sought in the school and classroom environment and in student outcomes. Supply teachers strategies for providing peer leadership, training, and mentoring, attitudinal leadership for the initiative.
Promoting professional collaboration	Communicate the goals of the initiative to all personnel in the school, including noninstructional personnel, and to relevant school-linked service agencies. Make sure they are aware of the inclusion goals and are prepared to work together.
Promoting cooperation among school-linked service agencies	Ensure that the relevant school-linked service agencies are prepared to work together. Plan for joint training and orientation seminars with various related staffs, including school, rehabilitation agency, social services, and others.
Promoting constructive change	Ensure that teachers and related personnel are knowledgeable about the change process and their roles in it and that they endorse the shared mission for the inclusion initiatives.

TABLE 27-2. Professional Development Training Content Related to Inclusion (Consistent with IDEA 1997)

Topic	Content
STUDENT-RELATED	
1. Full participation for all students	Addresses the need for accommodation of persons with disabilities in the full range of general and special educational programs available to all students, including academic, vocational education, transition services and job training and placement opportunities, and articulated school-college programs.
2. Related services in general education class	Provides discussion of the range of student support services in general educaton classrooms, including: guidance and counseling, career counseling, peer support and medication services, assistance with application to colleges or postsecondary placement, health services and counseling, and other supportive services.
3. Participation in extracurricular activities	Addresses strategies for the accommodation of persons with disabilities into the full range of extracurricular opportunities generally available, including: student clubs, sports as appropriate, drama and theatrical productions, chorus, debate teams, trade-related clubs, student governance organizations, booster clubs, student fund-raising activities, and other extracurricular opportunities.
4. Participation in technology-related opportunities	Addresses strategies for the accommodation of persons with disabilities into the full range of technology-related opportunities generally available, including: access to libraries, information centers and technology laboratories, school-based weather stations, and accommodations in such centers, adaptations to equipment that may be necessary for use of the technology, and participation in student group activities using technology.
5. Student participation in the IEP process	Provides a rationale for the rights of students and the importance of student participation in his or her own IEP or ITP (individualized transition plan), to the extent possible. Also addresses strategies for supporting students in this effort.
6. Procedures related to student placement	Addresses placement procedures under the 1997 IDEA and rights of students and parents to an "informed" placement, which means having the right to know at least several days in advance about a change of placement. This also should address school's provision of information in advance about the administrative and Interdisciplinary Decision Team rationale for a

TABLE 27-2. *(continued)*

Topic	Content
STUDENT-RELATED	
	decision to place a student into an inclusive classroom and a statement of the expectations of the IDT for the benefits of the placement and expected progress in the classroom within a specified period of time.
7. Students' rights to know about their disability	Addresses the students' rights about their disability and procedures regarding physical, medical, emotional or behavioral problem that might result in the need to take emergency action. There should be a written school policy and the teacher should be trained and knowledgeable of the emergency procedures or actions which should all be in writing.
8. Emergency procedures in the school and classroom	Overview of emergency management and response policies and procedures for the school that guide actions of teachers and other personnel in the event of a behavioral, medical, or natural emergency.
9. Supplemental supports and accommodations in the classroom and school	Overview of supplemental materials, equipment or personnel that are deemed necessary by the IDT for students to benefit from the educational and social program in the classroom, including, but not limited to physical assistive devices or equipment, technology adaptations (computer adaptations), physical adaptations to the classroom, personal or classroom aides, instructional materials, interpreters, recording devices, or other equipment. Other services include guidance and counseling, career counseling, peer support and mediation services, assistance with application to colleges or postsecondary placement, health services, and health counseling, and other supportive services. Includes an introduction to student and parents' rights to be informed in advance about the availability of such supplemental materials and equipment and to have an introduction to or training, if necessary, in the use of such equipment and materials in advance of, or minimally, at the time of, your placement into the classroom.
10. Access to the IEP	Overview of who has rights to access and review the IEP or ITP after placement into the classroom, including the parent and teacher.
11. Problem solving in the inclusive classroom after placement	Explores strategies for implementing an effective, fair and accessible process in which students, teachers or parents may raise issues or concerns at any time about an inclusive placement and progress, and request a consultation or assistance in problem solving or seeking additional support.
12. Professional preparation of personnel	Addresses the need for inclusive classrooms and schools to be staffed by personnel adequately trained in the education and support of students with disabilities. This includes an adequate number and preparation of direct support service and instructional staff to ensure access to the range of educational, career-vocational, technical and technology-related, and transition services.
13. Vocational assessment and education	Provides an introduction to the role and purpose of a comprehensive vocational assessment as part of the transition services required under IDEA.
14. Participation in vocational and school-to-work opportunities	Overview of the rights and importance of participation of youth in career-vocational and school-to-work opportunities that directly addresses the needs of students with disabilities as they prepare for transition to postsecondary settings, employment and independent living.
15. Inclusion in school reform opportunities	Addresses the inclusion of all students in local school improvement and reform initiatives.
16. Inclusion in local, state, and national curriculum standards	Addresses the importance and strategies for preparing all youth, including those with disabilities, to meet local, state and national standards for academic achievement. Also provides an overview of accommodations for students to participate in assessment of progress toward meeting such standards.
PARENT-RELATED	
17. Parent participation in the placement decision process and changes in placement	Examines the right of parents to be informed in advance about their child's placement and to participate in an IEP meeting to discuss the change and to learn about needs and available accommodations. Addresses the importance that parents be provided with information in advance about the Administrative and IDT rationale for a decision to place a child into an inclusive classroom and a statement of the expectations of the IDT for the benefits of the placement and expected progress in the classroom within a specified period of time. This includes procedures for due process and mediation now required under IDEA 1997.

Topic	Content

Topic	Content
18. Informing parents about the child's disability	Addresses procedures for informing parents if their child has been determined to have a physical, medical, emotional or behavioral problem that might result in the need to take an emergency action by teachers or other school personnel, that there is a written school policy on emergency procedures, and that the teacher is trained and knowledgeable about the emergency procedures or action that may be needed.

TEACHER-RELATED

Topic	Content
19. Teachers' expectations about students	Examines teachers' rights to clearly know the expectations about students placed into general education and the content of the IEPs.
20. Technical assistance and support services for teachers	Provides an overview of the resources available for technical assistance and support services to accommodate students with disabilities in (1) the full range of general and special educational programs available to all students, including academic, vocational education, transition services and job training and placement opportunities, and articulated school-college programs; (2) full range of extracurricular opportunities generally available, including: student clubs, sports as appropriate, drama and theatrical productions, chorus, debate teams, trade-related clubs, student governance organizations, booster clubs, student fund-raising activities, and other extracurricular opportunities and (3) the full range of technology-related opportunities generally available, including: access to libraries, information centers and technology laboratories, school-based weather stations, and accommodations in such centers, adaptations to equipment that may be necessary for use of the technology, and participation in student group activities using technology.
21. Informing teachers about related services in general education class	Overview of processes by which teachers will be informed about the range of available student support services in general education classrooms, including: guidance and counseling, career counseling, peer support and medication services, assistance with application to colleges or postsecondary placement, health services and counseling, and other supportive services. Provide information about procedures for referral or access to such services.
22. General education teacher participation in students' IEP meetings	Provides an overview of the IDEA expectations for general education teacher participation in the development of the student's IEP and the importance of their presence and participation in the IEP meetings. This is also important for the placement meeting to discuss and learn about which students will be placed into their classrooms and their needs and available accommodations. This topic should also address the provision of advanced information about the Administrative and IDT rationale for a decision to place a student into the general classroom and a statement of the expectations of the IDT for the benefits of the placement and expected progress of the child in the classroom within a specified period of time.
23. Informing teachers about the nature and extent of disabilities	Introduction to the concept of 'informed' placement from the teacher's perspective. This means providing teachers advanced knowledge about students placed into their classrooms and if they have a significant physical, medical, emotional or behavioral problem that might result in the need to take an emergency action by you. It also means providing teachers with information about the type of emergency procedures or action that may be needed. The IDEA promotes the inclusion of children with chronic health impairments and those dependent on medical technology into the regular classroom. Supportive provisions for these students are essential.
24. Preparation of teachers for emergency procedures	Provides an overview of emergency management policies and procedures for the school which are clearly defined, and prepares teachers for such procedures in order to safely guide their decisions and actions in the event of a behavioral, medical or natural emergency.
25. Constructive problem-solving for teachers	Provides information about effective, fair and accessible procedures by which the teacher may raise issues or concerns at any time about a placement of a student, the student's progress, or the student's behavior and request consultation or assistance in problem-solving or seeking additional support.
26. Planning time	For team teachers, particularly, this addresses the need for common planning time each week and time to develop agreed upon goals for joint students.
27. Vocational teachers and transition planning	Addresses the available support services and accommodations for students in vocational and school-to-work classes or community-based experiences, and provides information for vocational teachers to access such supportive services. Addresses the participation of vocational teachers in the development and implementation of students' individualized transition plans.
28. Assistance to teachers in meeting new standards	Addresses the technical assistance and training services that will be provided to teachers as they work to assist all students, including those with disabilities, to achieve new local, state or national academic standards.

CHAPTER 28

How Can Parent Participation in Inclusion Be Promoted?

ROLE OF FAMILY IN SUCCESSFUL INCLUSION. Over the past century, parents have been among the most powerful advocates in initiating inclusive services for children and youth with special needs. Parents have also stimulated major change in education and human service systems nationally and locally. Many educators and human service professionals believe that the participation of parents and families is the most crucial factor in the success of students with disabilities in inclusive schools. Since family members will vary in the amount and type of involvement they desire, educators should recognize and show respect for family members' level of comfort in working with the school. Likewise, school personnel can have a profound effect on parents and other family members' confidence in developing a true partnership with the school. A lack of family or parent involvement is often a reaction to a perceived lack of support and respect from school personnel in general.

IDEA REINFORCES THE ROLE OF PARENTS AS PARTNERS. The 1990 and 1997 Amendments to IDEA emphasize the role of the family in planning and coordinating services for individuals with disabilities (OSEP, 1997, Wiel, Thomas, Callahan & Carolis, 1992). Specifically, the 1997 Amendments require states and local agencies to improve the ability of professionals and parents to work with youth with disabilities (IDEA, P.L. 105-17). Parents are now given more opportunity to participate in any meetings in which the educational placement of their child is set and to have greater involvement in the evaluation and reevaluation activities. They also are given greater access to their children's records and greater involvement in deliberations over their future. State and local guidelines for coordination of services also must emphasize the role of parents in the decision-making and coordination efforts:

1. Parents must be provided a stronger role in providing evaluation information for purposes of developing the IEP.
2. Reevaluations must occur at least every 3 years.
3. Initial or reevaluation for services, change in placement, or refusal to change a placement must involve notification of and consent of parents.
4. States must ensure public hearings and opportunity for comment before adopting policies/procedures to implement IDEA.
5. Majority of members of the state special education state-level panel that provides input on state-whole implementation of IDEA advisory panel must be individuals with disabilities or parents of children with disabilities.
6. LEA must make available to parents all documents related to the LEA's eligibility for funding under IDEA.
7. The IEP must state how often progress is to be reported to parents and students (at least as often as nondisabled students receive regular report cards).
8. Parents may participate in meetings regarding identification, evaluation, and placement.
9. Parents may include other individuals in the IEP meeting who have knowledge or special expertise about their child and who may examine all records. (Synthesized from the 1997 Amendments to IDEA)

The 1997 IDEA also requires states to establish a mediation system in which parents and schools may voluntarily participate but which may not be used to deny or delay a parent's right to due process.

- Mediation would be conducted by qualified and impartial individuals who would set forth agreements in writing.
- The impartial due process hearing, limitations of conduct of hearings, appeals, safeguards, right to bring civil

action, jurisdiction of the course, and administrative procedures remain the same as they are in current law.

- The Act, however, does set limits on attorney's fees by prohibiting fees for IEP meetings (except if it is convened as a result of an administrative proceeding or judicial action) or for mediation prior to the filing of a due process action.

The 1997 Amendments to IDEA convey two very important messages to parents and service providers:

1. The significance of the parent-family-professional partnership in service delivery and final service outcomes.
2. The importance of including the family unit, as well as the individual, as targets for assistance and support by the schools and human service agencies.

FAMILY DYNAMICS AND PARENTAL INVOLVEMENT. Because families differ in their strengths and needs, school professionals may expect to sometimes experience suspicion, mistrust, and avoidance as they reach out to parents and family members. Awareness and sensitivity of professionals to the pressures, values, and perspectives family members bring to the school-family communication process is the starting point for facilitating productive parental participation. Socioeconomic and cultural differences between families and school personnel can become barriers to full parental participation in their children's school programs. For example, it may be difficult for a family to publicly recognize that their child has a disability, because of the cultural stigma that this may carry. Likewise, low-income families may be struggling to cope with multiple challenges, such as meeting basic life needs of food, shelter, clothing, and safety. Family upheavals, such as divorce or remarriage or chronic problems such as alcoholism, also affect parents' emotional ability to deal with their children's educational needs. One or more of these types of factors may cause parental reticence to participate in school meetings. Some family members may attend a school conference or meeting because they wish to discuss family challenges before focusing on school goals. For these reasons, professionals' sensitivity to families' perceptions and basic needs and an openness to learning more about them is the foundation for successful parental participation in inclusion.

Themes for Participation of Parents and Families. New provisions in special education, health and human services, vocational education services, and disabilities rights legislation have increased the support for children and youth in integrated settings in the schools and community. Several family-related themes are conveyed in the laws:

Parents and Families as Partners. Parents and families are partners with professionals in the service delivery process and must be viewed as collaborators. As collaborators, parents and families accept the relationship of shared responsibility with teachers for educational outcomes. The assumption of parent-professional collaboration fosters a perception that parents and families are *active, not passive* participants in the educational planning process and, as such, should enjoy equal status with professionals in the team decision-making process. Teachers and administrators should emphasize special communication and support to help parents understand and accept their role as partners with teachers and principals.

Responsibility of Parents for Their Children. The parent has the responsibility for the educational progress of the child and for protecting the student's rights to appropriate education under the law. Good communication between teachers and parents is an essential element in inclusive education. When the parents' access to information is diminished, their power as partners with teachers is also diminished.

Parents and Families as Team Members. How schools approach parent participation in the IEP process can greatly affect the quality and degree of parent participation. School personnel can simply follow the letter of the law and send legally correct information to parents to inform them of team meetings, with little or no personal follow-up, or teams can reach out to parents, through person-to-person contact, to make them feel comfortable in participating in team meetings. Although parents and other family members may attend team meetings, they may feel isolated and confused my team procedures. Even though parents have been informed of their rights and have chosen to attend team meetings, they may still feel perplexed and uncomfortable by the due process procedures. If parents are only involved at the point of attending an IEP meeting, their feeling of isolation or marginalization can be exacerbated. Encouraging parental input throughout the school year helps parents participate more fully in school meetings and feel supported by ongoing experiences of interacting with school personnel. This can enhance the relevance of their input, greatly improve the communication process during team meetings, and increase parents' understanding of their role of supporting IEP goals and objectives. Parent and family input should be included in the process for inclusion planning, policy development, evaluation, and planning for training of teachers, parents, and others (Hausslin, 1992).

Parents and Families as Decision Makers. The law recognizes that parents and families have an important role in the decision-making processes regarding the assessments and the educational program of the child. Teachers and administrators must remember that they rely on community support for the development, funding, and continuation of their educational programs and services and that families—as the funders of these services—have a right to know what educational programs are available, who is eligible, how placement decisions are made, and the quality and expected benefits of the programs for the child. Because family involvement is essential, information to parents about the goals and objectives of inclusive classrooms and activities is *best communicated in terms of benefits and outcomes for students and families.*

Parent and Family Training for Advocacy. Training and resources should be provided to assist parents and family members to better support the educational and related goals of the child. Families need to be educated and empowered to acquire, and to assist in the creation of, inclusive services and supports (Fields, 1996; Nesbit, Covert & Schuh, 1992). Parents and guardians need information about available school and community support services. They also need help from teachers and administrators to understand concepts central to inclusive education, such as inclusion, IEP, self-determination, self-advocacy, services coordination, transition, least restrictive environment, and appropriate placement. Parents need to be informed about the legal and human rights of their children to educational services and supports, including rights under IDEA, the Carl D. Perkins Vocational Technical Education Act, the Americans with Disabilities Act, the School-to-Work Opportunities Act, and other job training laws. Teachers can provide informal parent education as part of their parent conferencing activities and annual orientation of parents. Inclusion planners and implementors can develop linkages with college and university special education or teacher education programs to help develop parent training courses or seminars.

Families as Peer Supports. Parents and family members can provide basic support to one another in achieving the educational goals of the child. Teachers and administrators can encourage the organization of support groups, in which experienced parents of children with disabilities help newer parents and provide counseling and support as needed.

Parents as Transition Team Members. Parents should be closely involved and supportive of their adolescent children in the process of preparing for and making the transition from school to work or to postsecondary education. Consulting teachers, special educators, and transition coordinators can be enlisted to provide parent training seminars or to speak at parent orientation sessions and conferences about transition, self-advocacy, and preparation for employment or postsecondary education.

Parent Resources and Supports. Parents need additional information and resources to help support successful inclusion of the child with a disability. Some schools have created resource centers utilizing local, state, or national sources. Others have developed information packets for parents, which are sent home to them before the inclusive placement is made. Some school districts work with

their local or state health department, mental health services, mental retardation services, and other agencies to explore how funds from Medicaid waivers might be used to support parent training efforts. These funds can be used to provide information and training to parents about social security income (SSI) provisions that provide support services and tax deductions to enhance employment training for youths, work trials, and postsecondary education for youth and young adults with disabilities.

Parents as Service Coordinators. Educators and human service professionals now understand the crucial role that families play in helping individuals reach their maximum potential. In response, more current models of service coordination are centering upon family-focused service coordination, in which the service coordinator is given titles such as home visitor, family advocate, family consultant, family service provider, and family development specialist. Though the specific functions that family-centered coordinators play may differ, they all are likely to use family needs assessments and develop a family service plan. The service coordination functions are wedded to family support principles that emphasize family strengths and principles of family empowerment, including a focus on parents as lead decision makers in planning for their sons or daughters. Family-centered service coordinators address family issues such as needs for food and housing, as well as parent literacy and vocational training, parenting skills, mental health issues, family relationships, employment needs, and assistance with accessing public benefits.

The principles of family-centered approaches are also receiving some attention in public schools, as well as in community-based agencies. Educational leaders are realizing that their efforts to improve students' learning and performance are integrally related to the family circumstances and home life. For example, Geer and McWhorter (1990) have found that one reason for the continuing poor outcomes of school-to-work transition programs is the absence of family-focused approaches which promote the students' and families' determination of transition goals and services. Some schools are beginning to affect family circumstances and needs by offering parents special supports. Examples of such supports include basic academic skills classes, language classes, vocational skills training, or employment counseling to parents in the schools in the evening. It is important in the educational arena to understand the difference between strategies that call for "more parent involvement" and strategies that are family-centered, or aimed at promoting family decision making and empowerment.

Many schools are experimenting with "social work" models of family support. For example, a teacher may act as a service coordinator for a "caseload" of students and their families. As a service coordinator, the teacher takes responsibility for contacting and communicating with the families of students in the classroom and may visit the homes of students and their families to conduct consultations or may help to link the student and family with needed support services in the school or community. The inclusive classroom relies on the support and close involvement of each student's family.

Letting Go: Parents Promoting Independence. The parental attitude is a key factor in the ability of a student with disabilities to make the transition to responsible adult life. It is important that parents support the student's efforts to become independent and to achieve a quality of life that promotes the individual's ability to establish and achieve his or her personal goals. It is critical to the transition process that parents learn to release control over the decisions of the young adult's life and transfer the responsibility, as appropriate, for the level of disability (Kochhar & West, 1996).

Strategies for Facilitating Family Involvement. Many strategies have been used by teachers, principals, and human service professionals to strengthen parent and family involvement in the child's development. The following approaches or strategies offer some exemplary practices in promoting parent and family involvement in the provisions of services for the child. Family-centered services are based on the following principles and beliefs:

- The belief in informed choice for the student and his or her family when making educational service-options decisions.
- The principle that the service system needs to help students and their families use available school and community resources.
- The belief that educational services should be coordinated around the life of the student and family, not around the needs of the school.
- Recognition of the ability of the ordinary citizen to teach people skills and to help students participate in community life (adapted from Mount & Zwernik, 1988).

Planning for Parental Involvement. The inclusion planning team may want to commit to developing a program for improving parental involvement in inclusive classrooms and may create a school committee for this purpose. The following sequence of steps could be used to develop such a program:

1. Establish a committee of teachers, support staff, parents, and older students.
2. Assess the current status of home-school relationships and activities fostering parental involvement.
3. Conduct parent surveys and interviews to find out about parents' needs and interests in inclusion practices and supports.
4. Examine a range of programs fostering parental involvement in other schools. Gather ideas that have been successful and could be adopted and adapted for use in the school and community.

Generating Creative Strategies to Improve Parent and Family Involvement. School districts use different strategies to engage parents in the active educational process of their child. Such strategies as special training sessions, volunteering, parents' nights, and open houses (see Table 28-1) are designed to facilitate family involvement in the inclusion of students with disabilities in the regular classroom.

PARENTS/GUARDIANS AND SELF-DETERMINATION. Many children and youth with disabilities have difficulty assuming control of their lives and participating in decisions made each year about their personal educational programs. This situation calls for the help of parents or guardians, family, and professionals together to foster self-determination in the student, through the process of shared decision making. As a self-determined student who is directly involved in informed decision making about his or her education and future also assumes greater responsibility and accountability for the outcomes of those decisions. Students and parents or guardians, therefore, become equal partners and share responsibility both for developing individualized education programs and for the results of those programs.

TABLE 28-1. Engaging Families in the Inclusive School

Strategy	Description
1. Teacher communication with parents	The following strategies are designed to improve the relationship between parents and teachers in inclusive classrooms.
	• Meet with parents in the preparation and planning for integrating the student into the inclusive classroom.
	• Make parent involvement a schoolwide effort.
	• Involve students in encouraging parents to become volunteers in the classroom.
	• Develop homework assignments that involve the whole family.
	• Determine the role the families will play in the progress assessment of their children.
	• Send notes home frequently, even just to say the student had a good day.
	• Focus on encouraging parents, and find out why they may be reluctant to get involved.

continues

TABLE 28-1. *(continued)*

Strategy	Description
	• Hold meetings away from the school to engage parents reluctant to get involved. • Provide child care arrangements for parents when they attend school functions. • Place parent on a parent resource list to receive announcements about the class and school activities, exhibitions, and parent activities. • Invite parents to attend student exhibitions to observe the skills gained by the students. • Honor parents publicly for their participation and support of their sons or daughters. • Invite parents, through interviews and surveys, to help evaluate classroom activities and projects. • Help establish parent support groups.
2. Parent training and supports	The following strategies provide information to parents, teach them how to become advocates for their children, teach them how to enter into partnerships with professionals, and have been very effective for increasing parent involvement: • Apprising parents about rights and resources, such as those under the Social Security Act, IDEA, school-to-work and job training laws. • Providing ongoing parent training and seminars throughout the year. • Engaging parents in the training of other parents. • Using concrete examples and videos when talking about service options and planning. • Helping parents concretely observe the benefits of having participated in service programs, by arranging visits to the programs or observing their sons or daughters once they have graduated and moved on to other levels of service, independent living, employment, etc. • Conducting parent-professional panel discussions and team training. • Developing parent support groups or crisis support teams (Everson, Barcus, Moon & Morton, 1987). • Providing services to parents in convenient locations and at convenient times (e.g., basic skills training, language classes, vocational counseling, and employment assistance).
3. Parents reinforcing skills development	Parents can assist students in social and functional skill development in the home although this may require some preparation and assistance in identifying which skills the school would like to have addressed and practiced. The IEP team can write the specifics in the IEP or simply request the assistance and cooperation of the parents in the home setting. Parents also have many opportunities to provide direct instruction and to help students practice skill development in natural community environments in which the student will ultimately use the skills. For example, math skills (such as estimating, problem solving, counting change) can easily be practiced in the bank, grocery store, or any other retail store.
4. Natural support system	Natural support systems are essential in helping individuals with special needs reach their maximum potential. *Natural support systems* consist of people such as families, friends, neighbors, peer groups, and organizations such as churches, schools, unions, and clubs, which provide support to individuals in need. A social network is essential to help individuals and their families solve problems in daily life, and in periods of crisis. The folk support system has a nourishing and stabilizing effect on the individual during times of change and challenge. The informal support network helps the individual survive by establishing and maintaining nurturing relationships and by rallying to the individual during moments of need. Members of the support system then indirectly also become essential players in the decision making about needed services and program enrollment. Such networks provide self-esteem, value, and dignity in the individual's life, and help reinforce the motivation and achievement of individuals as they participate in services.
5. Personal planning	There are a variety of personal planning strategies that rely on the involvement of families and the informal support network of the individual. Futures planning refers to a long-term planning and problem-solving process that is guided by the individual's and the family's desires and needs. These processes assist a committed group of individuals or families in helping create and support a desirable future for a person with a disability or special need. *Personal futures planning* or *circles of support* planning, consists of a personal profile, a planning meeting, and a futures plan document. The profile contains a record of the person's life including important relationships, places, past events, preferences, future dreams, barriers, and opportunities, it also emphasizes individual gifts, skills, and capabilities. The planning meeting includes the individual, family members, and other key persons in his or her life. The meeting follows several steps in developing the plan:

TABLE 28-1. *(continued)*

Strategy	Description
	a. Review the personal profile;
	b. Review the environment, including the events which are likely to either positively and negatively affect the individual or family (graduation, closing of a program or service, death of a family member, losing a job, etc.)
	c. Create a desirable vision of the future.
	d. Identify obstacles and opportunities.
	e. Identify strategies and make commitments to take specific action steps to implement the vision.
	f. Get started by prioritizing action steps and beginning to work on them.
6. Education and transition planning	Special parent conferences are scheduled to discuss any concerns, ideas, plans, or goals which affect the student's education. Schools provide this opportunity on a routine basis, either quarterly or semiannually. In addition, parents are generally invited to school on an as needed basis. Longer range "life planning" typically begins when the individual is in adolescence and the parents begin to think about the child's separation from the family and life beyond school. Yet, from the very earliest identification of a disability, parents or guardians can be helped to begin to think about "life planning." Gaining autonomy and self-determination skills should begin in the earliest years. Separations from the parent and family begin in the early years, as children move from home to day care, from day care to preschool to elementary school, and then to middle school, high school, and postsecondary life. Each transition and adjustment can be difficult, and the individual may need extra support from family members and professionals. Parents can be better advocates if they can view the educational development of their children with the future in mind rather than simply reacting to present circumstances. Such a view can give parents a more realistic and balanced perspective on the options and choices that need to be made as their children mature.
7. Reduce barriers to the community support services	Individualized education programs should include how the services provided will integrate individuals into the various forms of the folk support system. Efforts should be made by service coordinators to eliminate barriers that prevent individuals and their families from accessing community-based support services.
8. Communicate the value of parent involvement	Communicate to parents at all points in the developmental continuum that they are *needed and valued as contributing members of the educational planning team*. This can be done through written materials that are distributed to parents, special parents' support meetings or education seminars, opportunities for parent volunteer activities, and invitations to service planning meetings. As individuals enter service agencies for assistance, parents often feel that their intense and supportive role is no longer needed and they may begin to feel that their children are now in "other hands." Communication with parents is critical during the major transition from one service agency to another.

ACTION WORK SHEET 1: ASSESSMENT OF READINESS FOR INCLUSION

Activity	How Will You Do This and Who Will Be Responsible	Target Date for Completion
1. Identify the range of local services available in the existing school and service system, in order to identify services that can be coordinated to support a student in inclusive classrooms.		
2. Identify gaps in services and service needs that are not being met within the school and larger system.		
3. Determine the level of "readiness" of teachers from **all** subject areas and of related service professionals in cooperating agencies to form a collaboration for inclusion support in the school. (Who is ready and willing to collaborate and what training will they need?)		
4. Determine the expertise and resources that personnel from each subject discipline and related services bring to the partnership to support inclusion.		
5. Determine the needs of cooperating community agencies (e.g., health profession, speech and hearing, social services, and rehabilitation).		
6. How should teachers and support personnel be prepared for inclusion?		
7. How should the physical environment be changed for inclusion?		
8. What modification in curriculum and instruction should be made, and how can students be accommodated in district and statewide assessments?		
9. How should the IEP and interdisciplinary team process be used?		
10. What classroom supports are needed?		
11. How can students access available technology?		
12. How can students be helped to access and participate in vocational, occupational, and technical education?		
13. How can students participate in extracurricular school activities?		
14. How can students participate in community-based and community service experiences?		

Note: IEP, individualized education program

ACTION WORK SHEET 2: DEFINING A JOINT MISSION AND PHILOSOPHY

Activity	Discuss and Write a Draft Outline for What Each Section Will Include	Target Date for Completion
1. **Statement of context**—A brief introductory paragraph that broadly describes the initiative, how it started, how it addresses current educational needs of students, how it differs from or expands or improves on current methods of promoting inclusion.		
2. **Statement of authority for the initiative**—An introductory section that refers to the legal basis for the initiative (e.g., IDEA, Section 504, and ADA) and lists the local, state, or federal laws or statutes, regulations, or policies that *give authority to this agreement.*		
3. **General statement of philosophy, purpose of the initiative or agreement, and expected benefits and outcomes**—Includes a broad statement of the goals of the initiative and inclusion planning team and the results anticipated for students.		
4. **Broad goals, roles, and responsibilities**—Defines the goals of the initiative and the roles of key planners, implementors, and the cooperating agencies or community agency personnel.		
5. **Discuss and write a draft outline for what this section will include.**		

Note: IDEA, Individuals with Disabilities Education Act of 1997; ADA, Americans with Disabilities Act. Section 504 of the Rehabilitation Act of 1973, which states: Cooperating agencies means any community-based agency which provides support services to assist students with disabilities successfully participate in general education classrooms (e.g., social services, psychological services, occupational and physical therapy, public health services, mental health services, etc.).

Action Work Sheet 3: Strategies for Informing the School Community About a New Inclusion Initiative

Strategy	How Can This Be Accomplished in Your School and Community and Who Will Be Responsible?
1. **Inform parent, student, and consumer organizations,** such as the PTA, parent advocacy groups, and student organizations, about the plans for service coordination. Distribute information and solicit input into the plans and roles of these groups in the development of the collaboration.	
2. **Inform educational leaders and school principals** who have primary responsibility for any new programs or initiatives that will affect instruction or student services. Most school districts and schools establish their educational priorities well in advance (e.g., expansion of special education programs, addition of bilingual program, and improvement of basic skills). *Principals should be among the earliest to be informed of the effort and helped to see how the initiative will aid them in achieving their educational goals and objectives for students.*	
3. **Inform staff and directors of community and adult services agencies.** Because their support is vital to an interagency services coordination initiative (new or renewed), all cooperating (or potential) partners need to know about an intent to collaborate and the process for forming the collaborative arrangement.	
4. **Develop concept papers and rationale statements** to help potential cooperating agencies understand the relationship between the collaborative endeavor and their own individual agency mission, goals, and objectives. All must understand how the new collaboration will help them to achieve their individual agency goals, improve their services and resources, or evaluate their efforts. The mutual benefits to all cooperating agencies must be defined and stressed early in the process.	
5. **Inform relevant teacher unions and educational associations** about new initiatives that involve teaching staff, and help them to understand the potential benefits of collaboration for students and professionals. It might also be helpful to have the county or district educational associations go on record supporting the initiative.	
6. **Conduct local educational reform seminars,** including information about or discussion of the interagency initiative.	
7. **Conduct special seminars** on interagency service coordination and cotraining with members from a variety of agencies and organizations.	
8. **Plan teacher, principal, and parent coffees** to discuss the initiative.	

Action Work Sheet 3: *(continued)*

Strategy	How Can This Be Accomplished in Your School and Community and Who Will Be Responsible?
9. **Conduct highly visible brainstorming sessions** with heads of agency personnel at all levels to discuss inter-agency service coordination.	
10. **Develop informational brochures and materials.**	
11. **Conduct business-education seminars.** Include information about the initiative in these seminars, in Chamber of Commerce meetings, or in Private Industry Council meetings (Job Training Partnership Act).	
12. **Solicit editorials and feature articles** in local newsletters and newspapers.	
13. **Conduct meetings with community leaders** to assist in championing an initiative in interagency service coordination.	
14. **Develop links with local colleges or universities** to develop meetings or seminars related to initiatives or to develop grant proposals.	
15. **Use annual reports of cooperating agencies** including descriptions of interagency initiatives and plans.	

Action Work Sheet 4: Identifying a Collaborative Planning Team

Activity	How Can This Be Accomplished in Your School and Community, and Who Will Be Responsible?
1. Who should be on the inclusion planning team? How will these people be invited to participate?	
2. What incentives should be provided for their time and effort in the planning process?	
3. How should the planning team proceed?	
4. What should be the planning team's purpose?	
5. When and how often should the planning team meet?	
6. What activities should be included in the inclusion process?	
7. When should they take place? Who will be responsible for each activity?	

ACTION WORK SHEET 5: IDENTIFYING PROFESSIONAL DEVELOPMENT NEEDS

Activity	How Can This Be Accomplished in Your School and Community, and Who Will Be Responsible?
1. How can inclusion implementors foster a sense of investment or "ownership" in the initiative?	
2. How should teachers be oriented to the changes that the new collaboration may bring?	
3. What are the overall major professional development needs of the school, and who should receive such training?	
4. Who are possible presenters or trainers for specific topics?	
5. What is the professional development budget, and who is responsible for the expenditures?	
6. Who will be responsible for notifying presenters, participants, and other guests?	
7. How can the teachers share and "celebrate" their successes and honor those who have made important contributions?	

ACTION WORK SHEET 6: DEVELOPING AN ADOPTION PLAN

Activity	How Can This Be Accomplished in Your School and Community, and Who Will Be Responsible?
1. **Establish links with local and state educational agency trainings**—Each local and state educational agency organizes in-service training days for teachers, administrators, and support personnel. Interagency planners should use these existing training activities as vehicles for providing an introduction and orientation to the new inclusion initiative and teacher roles.	
2. **Ensure participation of all cooperating agencies**—Include teachers from all subject disciplines and professionals from all cooperating agencies in the training. This approach increases the likelihood that, over time, action team personnel will come to share a common understanding and vision of the direction of the initiative. The mission statement and inclusion plan should include the schedule for training and staff development.	
3. **Develop inclusion planning materials for training and distribution**—Materials must be developed for use in in-service training for teachers and collaborating personnel. These materials should include specific information about the inclusion goals, strategies, teacher and students, key roles and contact persons, the mission and goals as they relate to inclusion, and new support services that will be offered through the initiative.	

ACTION WORK SHEET 6: *(continued)*

Activity	How Can This Be Accomplished in Your School and Community, and Who Will Be Responsible?
4. **Adopt new educational and human service practices**—Inclusion planners must help key teaching personnel to reassess their teaching practices and adopt new ones. Once the program has been in operation for 1 or 2 years, teachers will need advanced training. Such training also means using the results of the past year of inclusion implementation to renew and strengthen the initiative, identify barriers and weaknesses, and further define and improve its outcomes.	
5. **Evaluate the adoption plan**—Inclusion planners must ensure that adoption plans are evaluated. They must ask if the training is having the desired effect on teachers and the classrooms. Is the training reaching all key school personnel? Is interdisciplinary training occurring? Are the teachers involved in evaluating the adoption plan and the training effort? Are teachers satisfied with the training, and what are their recommendations for improvement? Ongoing evaluation should be included in the inclusion mission statement.	

ACTION WORK SHEET 7: IDENTIFYING TECHNICAL ASSISTANCE RESOURCES

Activity	How Can This Be Accomplished in Your School and Community, and Who Will Be Responsible?
1. **Obtaining outside expertise.** What types of outside expertise or technical support will be needed for the inclusion effort?	
2. **Providing assistance to the school.** What will be the process for providing technical assistance to the school for implementation of inclusion?	
3. **Providing assistance to the classroom teacher.** How will support be provided to classroom teachers involved in the inclusion effort?	
4. **Obtaining assistance with evaluation.** How will technical assistance for evaluation of inclusive practices in the school be obtained?	

ACTION WORK SHEET 8: DEVELOPING A WRITTEN PLAN FOR PHASED-IN INCLUSION

Activity	How Can This Be Accomplished in Your School and Community, and Who Will Be Responsible?
1. **Securing support from administration.** How will commitment and support from administration be secured to meet needs and timelines?	
2. **Identifying students for placement into the general classrooms.** How will students currently in separate classrooms be identified for inclusive classrooms?	
3. **Matching students to teachers and classrooms.** How will classrooms and teachers be selected that will best meet their needs?	
4. **Determining the timetable.** What will be the timetable for a phased-in plan to improve inclusive practices?	
5. **Determining resource needs.** What resources will be needed by students and teachers during inclusion?	
6. **Structuring in planning time.** What schedule will allow teachers (regular and special education) planning time for inclusion?	

ACTION WORK SHEET 9: DEVELOPING A PLAN TO EVALUATE THE INCLUSION INITIATIVE

Activity	How Can This Be Accomplished in Your School and Community, and Who Will Be Responsible?
1. **Deciding on evaluation activities.** What evaluation activities will be included in the plan to improve inclusive practices?	
2. **Organizing for data collection.** What data will be collected and by whom?	
3. **Selecting responsible evaluators.** Who will be responsible for an internal review of inclusion?	
4. **Selecting an external evaluator.** What external consultants can you invite in to conduct an independent evaluation of inclusive practices?	
5. **Determining who will prepare the evaluation report.** Who will synthesize the evaluation data, write a final report, and make recommendations?	

ACTION WORK SHEET 10: DEVELOPING A PLAN TO BASE AN IMPROVEMENT PLAN ON EVALUATION RESULTS

Activity	How Can This Be Accomplished in Your School and Community, and Who Will Be Responsible?
1. **Deciding how to distribute the evaluation report.** How widely, and with whom, will the evaluation report be shared?	
2. **Using the evaluation report.** How will the inclusion development team respond to the evaluators' recommendations?	
3. **Planning for ongoing improvement.** How will the inclusion development team use the evaluation report to craft the next year's activities and continue the improvement of inclusive practices?	

ACTION WORK SHEET 11: DEVELOPING A REWARD SYSTEM TO CELEBRATE SUCCESS

Activity	How Can This Be Accomplished in Your School and Community, and Who Will Be Responsible?
1. What celebration or event should be planned for acknowledging the efforts and successes of inclusion?	
2. Who should be included in the celebration of success?	
3. What and where should the event take place?	
4. What kind of awards, certificates, and incentives will be given and to whom?	
5. Who will develop school and district news releases and other communications?	

Resources

What's in This Resource?

Print and Video Resources

Special education
Assessment
Assistive technology
Behavior
Cultural diversity in special education
Early intervention
Individualized education program
Individualized family service plan
Inclusion
Legal issues in special education
Mediation in special education
Parent resources
School reform
Special education finance
Training
Transition

Organizations

Government agencies
Clearinghouses
Nondisability-specific organizations
Disability-specific organizations

Overview

This module contains a listing of resources of additional information on the many topics relevant to the special education and general education field. This includes: print materials, videos, organizations, and publishers.

Source: Reprinted with permission from the National Information Center for Children and Youth with Disabilities (1997).

Print Materials and Videos

This module provides a listing of print materials and videos, as well as a list of publishers from which these materials can be obtained. (The list of publishers is provided at the very end of the module, following the list of organizations.) The materials are organized by the following subject areas:

- Special education
- Assessment
- Assistive technology
- Behavior
- Cultural diversity in special education
- Early intervention
- Individualized education program
- Individualized family service plan
- Inclusion
- Legal issues in special education
- Mediation in special education
- Parent resources
- School reform
- Special education finance
- Training

List of Organizations

We've also listed many organizations that can provide additional information and assistance on a wide range of subjects. The names, address, telephone numbers, TTY numbers, E-mails, and Web addresses of these organizations are provided, when available. The list is organized in the following way:

- Government agencies
- Clearinghouses
- Nondisability-specific organizations
- Disability-specific organizations

What Does This Sign Mean?

If you see this sign——it means that the resource is a video.

Special Note!

This listing represents resources that have been collected from various sources. Although we have not reviewed these documents for consistency with IDEA 97, we are providing them for your information.

The names of materials and organizations are provided to assist individuals, agencies, and organizations in locating materials of additional information on topics important to the special education field. The mention of trade names, commercial products, or organizations in this section does not imply endorsement by the U.S. Government.

Resources in Special Education

Anderson, W., Chitwood, S., & Hayden, D. (1997). *Negotiating the special education maze: A guide for parents and teachers* (3rd ed.). Bethesda, MD: Woodbine House.

Boundy, K., & Ordover, E. (1996). *Educational rights of children with disabilities: A primer for advocates* (2nd ed.). Cambridge, MA: Center for Law and Education.

Buzzell, J. B. (1996). *School and family partnerships: Case studies for regular and special educators.* Albany, NY: Delmar.

Churton, M. W., Churton-Gingras, & Blair, T. R. (1997). *Teaching children with diverse abilities.* Boston, MA: Allyn & Bacon.

Comforty, J. (Editor). (1994). *Inclusion: Issues for educators* [Videotape]. Lawrence, KS: Learner Managed Designs.

Copenhaver, J. (1995). *Section 504: An educator's primer: What teachers and administrators need to know about implementing accommodations for eligible individuals with disabilities.* Logan, UT: Mountain Plains Regional Resource Center.

Crutchfield, M. (1997). Who's teaching our children with disabilities? *NICHCY News Digest 27,* 1–24. (Available from NICHCY.)

Cutler, B. C. (1993). *You, your child, and "special" education: A guide to making the system work.* Baltimore, MD: Paul H. Brookes.

Giangreco, M. F., Cloninger, C. J., & Iverson, V. S. (1998). *Choosing options and accommodations for children: A guide to planning inclusive education* (2nd ed.). Baltimore, MD: Paul H. Brookes.

Hales, R. M., & Carlson, L. M. (1992). *Issues and trends in special education.* Lexington, KY: Mid-South Regional Resource Center.

Heumann, J. E. (1994, September 16). *Answers to frequently asked questions about the requirements of the Individuals with Disabilities Education Act (IDEA).* Washington, DC: U.S. Department of Education. (Available on the Internet from NICHCY, address: gopher aed.org, or http://www. nichcy.org under "other publications.")

Home, R. L. (1996). The education of children and youth with special needs: What do the laws say? *NICHCY News Digest, 1*(1), 1–16. (Available from NICHCY.)

Jorgenson, C. (Ed.). (1997). *Restructuring high schools for all students: Taking inclusion to the next level.* Baltimore, MD: Paul H. Brookes.

Kerzner, D. L., & Gartner, A. (1997). *Inclusion and school reform: Transforming America's classrooms.* Baltimore, MD: Paul H. Brookes.

Küpper, L. (Ed.). (1993). Questions and answers about the IDEA. *NICHCY News Digest, 3*(2), 1–16. (Available from NICHCY.)

Learning Disabilities Association of America. (1992). *Advocacy manual: A parent's how-to guide for special education services.* Pittsburgh, PA: Author.

Martin, R. (1991). *Parents in the special education process* (a 3-videotape series). Urbana, IL: Baxley Media Group.

National Information Center for Children and Youth with Disabilities. (1994). *Questions often asked about special education services.* Washington, DC: Author.

Olson, J. L., & Platt, J. M. (1995). *Teaching children and adolescents with special needs* (2nd ed.). Upper Saddle River, NJ: Merrill/Prentice Hall.

Orelove, F. P., & Sobsey, D. (1996). *Educating children with multiple disabilities: A transdisciplinary approach* (3rd ed.). Baltimore, MD: Paul H. Brookes.

PACER Center. (1996). *Parents can be the key . . . to an appropriate education for their child with disabilities.* Minneapolis, MN: Author.

Paul, J. L. (1997). *Special education practice: Applying the knowledge, affirming the values, and creating the future.* Belmont, CA: Wadsworth Publishing.

Rainforth, B., York, J., & Macdonald, C. (1997). *Collaborative teams for students with severe disabilities: Integrating therapy and educational services* (2nd ed.). Baltimore, MD: Paul H. Brookes.

Rogers, J. (Ed.). (1994). *Hot topics series: Inclusion: Moving beyond our fears.* Bloomington, IN: Phi Delta Kappa.

Rosenberg, M. S. (1994). *The special education sourcebook: A teacher's guide to programs, materials, and information sources.* Bethesda, MD: Woodbine House.

Rosenberg, M. S., O'Shea, L., & O'Shea, D. J. (1997). *Student teacher to master teacher: A practical guide for educating students with special needs* (2nd ed.). Upper Saddle River, NJ: Prentice Hall.

Smarte, L., & McLane, K. (1994). *How to find answers to your special education questions.* Reston, VA: Council for Exceptional Children.

Smith, D. D. (1997). *Introduction to special education: Teaching in an age of challenge* (3rd ed.). Boston, MA: Allyn & Bacon.

Smith-Davis, J., & Littlejohn, W. R. (1991, Resources updated 1994). Related services for school-aged children with disabilities. *NICHCY News Digest, 1*(2), 1–24. (Available from NICHCY.)

Turnbull, A. P., & Tumbull III, H. R. (1996). *Families, professionals, and exceptionality: A special partnership* (3rd ed.). Upper Saddle River, NJ: Merrill/Prentice Hall.

Turnbull, H. R., III, & Turnbull, A. P. (1997). *Free appropriate public education: The law and children with disabilities* (5th ed.). Denver, CO: Love.

⊗ University of Colorado Health Science Center, School of Nursing. (1993). *Rolling along: Children in wheelchairs at school* [Videotape]. Lawrence, KS: Learner Managed Designs.

⊗ University of Colorado Health Science Center, School of Nursing. (1995). *Safe at school: Planning for children with special needs* [Videotape]. Lawrence, KS: Learner Managed Designs.

Wilson, N. O. (1992). *Optimizing special education: How parents can make a difference.* New York: Insight Books.

Wood, J. W., & Laser, A. M. (1996). *Exceeding the boundaries: Understanding exceptional lives.* Fort Worth, TX: Harcourt Brace College Press.

Ysseldyke, J. E., & Algozzine, B. (1995). *Special education: A practical approach for teachers.* Boston, MA: Houghton Mifflin.

Resources on Assessment

Bognato, S. J., Neisworth, J. T., & Munson, S. M. (1997). *Linking assessment and early intervention: An authentic curriculum-based approach.* Baltimore, MD: Paul H. Brookes.

Choate, J. S. (Ed.). (1997). *Successful inclusive teaching: Proven ways to detect and correct special needs.* Boston, MA: Allyn & Bacon.

Compton, C. (1996). *A guide to 100 tests for special education.* Upper Saddle River, NJ: Merrill/Prentice Hall.

DeStefano, L. (1993). *Effects of standards and assessments on students in special education.* Minneapolis, MN: National Center on Educational Outcomes.

Hart, D. (1994). *Authentic assessment: A handbook for educators.* Reading, MA: Addison-Wesley.

Herman, J. L., Aschbacher, P. R., & Winters, L. (1992). *Practical guide to alternative assessment.* Alexandria, VA: Association for Supervision and Curriculum Development.

Hoy, C., & Gregg, N. (1994). *Assessment: The special educator's role.* Boston, MA: Allyn & Bacon.

King-Sears, M. E., Cummings, C. S., & Hullihen, S. P. (1994). *Curriculum-based assessment in special education.* San Diego, CA: Singular.

Navarette, C., Wilde, J., Nelson, C., Martinez, R., & Hargett, G. (1990). *Informal assessment in educational evaluation: Implications for bilingual education programs.* Washington, DC: National Clearinghouse for Bilingual Education.

Office of Indian Education Programs, Bureau of Indian Affairs. (1993). *Assessment in special education and Section 504: Survival kit.* Washington, DC: Author.

Salvia, J., & Ysseldyke, J. E. (1998). *Assessment.* Boston, MA: Houghton Mifflin.

Taylor, R. L. (1996). *Assessment of exceptional students: Educational and psychological procedures.* Boston, MA: Allyn & Bacon.

Vace, N. A., & Ritter, S. H. (1995). *Assessment of preschool children.* Reston, VA: Council for Exceptional Children. (ERIC Document Reproduction Service No. ED 389 964)

Venn, J. (1993). *Assessment of students with special needs.* Upper Saddle River, NJ: Merrill/Prentice Hall.

Wallace, G., Larsen, S. C., & Elksnin, L. K. (1992). *Educational assessment of learning problems: Testing for teaching.* Boston, MA: Allyn & Bacon.

Wodrich, D. L. (1997). *Children's psychological testing: A guide for nonpsychologists* (3rd ed.). Baltimore, MD: Paul H. Brookes.

Resources in Assistive Technology

Alliance for Technology Access. (1997). *Computer resources for people with disabilities: A guide to exploring today's assistive technology* (2nd ed.). Alameda, CA: Hunter House.

Behrmann, M. M. (1994, November). Assistive technology for students with mild disabilities. *Intervention in School and Clinic, 30*(2), 70–83.

Brett, A., & Provenzo, E. F., Jr. (1995). *Adaptive technology for special human needs.* Albany, NY: State University of New York Press.

Button, C., & Wobschall, R. (1994). The Americans with Disabilities Act and assistive technology. *Journal of Vocational Rehabilitation 4*(3), 196–201.

Center for Developmental Disabilities. (Annual). *Assistive technology information and program referral: A directory of providers.* Columbia, SC: Author.

Galvin, J., & Scherer, M. (1996). *Evaluating, selecting, and using appropriate assistive technology.* Frederick, MD: Aspen.

Higgins, K., & Boone, R. (1997). *Technology for students with learning disabilities: Educational applications.* Austin, TX: Pro-Ed.

Johnson, D. L., Maddux, C. D., Liu, L. (Eds.). (1997). *Using technology in the classroom.* Binghamton, NY: Haworth Press.

Obtaining Resources That Interest You

To help you obtain the resources that interest you, we've listed the addresses and telephone numbers of publishers at the end of this module. The publisher's name generally appears in the final position in the citation—to illustrate, it appears in bold in this sample citation:

Scherer, M. J. (1996). *Living in the state of stuck: How technology impacts the lives of people with disabilities.* Cambridge, MA: **Brookline**.

If you see the word "Author" in the publisher position, this means that the publisher and the author are one and the same. Look at the author's name, find this name in the publishers section, and use the contact information provided.

Lewis, R. B. (1993). *Special education technology: Classroom applications.* Pacific Grove, CA: Brooks/Cole.

Mackenzie, L. (Ed.). (Annual). *Complete directory for people with disabilities: Products, resources, books, and services.* Lakeville, CT: Grey House.

Male, M. (1996). *Technology for inclusion: Meeting the special needs of all students.* Boston, MA: Allyn & Bacon.

Menlove, M. (1996, Spring). A checklist for identifying funding sources for assistive technology. *TEACHING Exceptional Children, 28*(3), 20–24.

National Council on Disability. (1993). *Study on the financing of assistive technology devices and services for individuals with disabilities.* Washington, DC: Author.

National Institute on Disability and Rehabilitation Research. (1995). *Directory of national information sources on disabilities: 1994–95* (6th ed.). Washington, DC: Author.

Parette, Jr., H. P., Hourcade, J. J., & VanBiervliet, A. (1993, Spring). Selection of appropriate technology for children with disabilities. *TEACHING Exceptional Children, 25*(3), 18–23.

Parette, H. P. Jr., Hofmann, A., & VanBiervliet, A. (1994, Spring). The professional's role in obtaining funding for assistive technology for infants and toddlers with disabilities. *TEACHING Exceptional Children, 26*(3), 22–27.

Parette, H. P. Jr., Murdick, N. L., & Gartin, B. C. (1996, Winter). Mini-grant to the rescue! Using community resources to obtain assistive technology devices for children with disabilities. *TEACHING Exceptional Children, 28*(2), 20–23.

Perry, M., & Garber, M. (1993, Winter). Technology helps parents teach their children with developmental delays. *TEACHING Exceptional Children, 25*(2), 8–11.

Ray, J. R., & Warden, M. K. (1995). *Technology, computers, and the special needs learner.* Albany, NY: Delmar.

RESNA. (1992). *Assistive technology and the Individualized Education Program.* Washington, DC: Author.

RESNA. (1995). *Project Reaching Out: Proceedings of the Forum on Human Diversity.* Washington, DC: Author. (This forum was held to discuss critical issues in the delivery of assistive technology devices and services.)

Scherer, M. J. (1996). *Living in the state of stuck: How technology impacts the lives of people with disabilities.* Cambridge, MA: Brookline.

Storeygard, J., Simmons, R., Stumpf, M., & Pavloglou, E. (1993, Fall). Making computers work for students with special needs. *TEACHING Exceptional Children, 26*(1), 22–24.

Resources on Behavior

Ahearn, E. M. (1994). *Discipline and students with disabilities: An analysis of state policies.* Alexandria, VA: National Association of State Directors of Special Education.

Barkley, R. A. (1997). *Defiant children: A clinician's manual for assessment and parent training.* New York: Guilford Press.

☻ Campbell, S. (1995). *Working with hostile and resistant teens* [Videotape]. Lawrence, KS: Learner Managed Designs.

Carr, E. G., Levin, L., McConnachie, G., Carlson, J. I., Kemp, D. C., & Smith, C. E. (1994). *Communication-based intervention for problem behavior.* Baltimore, MD: Paul H. Brookes.

Coleman, M. C. (1995). *Emotional and behavioral disorders: Theory and practice.* Boston, MA: Allyn & Bacon.

Devault, G., Krug, C., Turnbull, A., & Horner, R. (1994). *Why does Samantha act like that? A positive behavioral support story of one family's success.* Lawrence, KS: Beach Center on Families and Disability.

Dornbush, M. P., & Pruitt, S. K. (1995). *Teaching the tiger: A handbook for individuals involved in the education of students with attention deficit disorders, Tourette syndrome or obsessive-compulsive disorder.* Monrovia, CA: Hope Press.

Farrell, P. (Ed.). (1994). *Children with emotional and behavioral difficulties: Strategies for assessment and intervention.* Washington, DC: Falmer Press.

☻ Gallagher, P. A. (1995). *Teaching students with behavior disorders* [Videotape]. Lawrence, KS: Learner Managed Designs.

Gonzalez, P. (1991). *An overview of the standards and policy on the use of time-out as a behavior management strategy.* Alexandria, VA: National Association of State Directors of Special Education.

Hartwig, E., & Ruesch, G. (1994). *Disciplining students with disabilities: A synthesis of critical and emerging issues.* Alexandria, VA: National Association of State Directors of Special Education.

☻ Johns, B. H., & Carr-Garrison, V. G. (Authors), Four Rivers Special Education District Alternative School (Producer), (1994). *Techniques for managing verbally and physically aggressive students* [Videotape]. Lawrence, K5: Learner Managed Designs.

Johns, B. H., Carr, V. G., & Hoots, C. W. (1995). *Reduction of school violence: Alternatives to suspension.* Horsham, PA: LRP.

Jordan, D. D. (1995). *Honorable intentions: A parent's guide to educational planning for children with emotional or behavioral disorders.* Minneapolis, MN: PACER Center. (ERIC Document Reproduction Service No. ED 384 195)

Jordan, D. D. (1996). *A guidebook for parents of children with emotional or behavioral disorders.* Minneapolis, MN: PACER Center.

Kaufman, J. M. (1995). *Issues in educational placement: Students with emotional and behavioral disorders.* Hillsdale, NJ: L. Erlbaum Associates.

Koegel, L. K., Koegel, R. L., & Dunlap, G. (1995). *Positive behavioral support: Including people with difficult behavior in the community.* Baltimore, MD: Paul H. Brookes.

Kohn, A. (1996). *Beyond discipline: From compliance to community.* Alexandria, VA: Association for Supervision and Curriculum Development.

Küpper, L. (Ed.). (1996). Educating students with emotional/behavioral disorders. *NICHCY Bibliography, 10,* 1–12. (Available from NICHCY.)

Küpper, L. (Ed.). (1997, April). Positive behavioral support: A bibliography for schools. *NICHCY Bibliography, 4,* 1–8. (Available from NICHCY.)

Küpper, L. (Ed.). (1997, June). Positive behavioral support: A bibliography for families. *NICHCY Bibliography, 3,* 1–12. (Available from NICHCY.)

Lovett, H. (1996). *Learning to listen: Positive approaches and people with difficult behavior.* Baltimore, MD: Paul H. Brookes.

ERIC Documents

Some of the documents listed in this section are available through the ERIC (Educational Resources Information Center) system. These documents are identified by the "ED" number that follows the citation. If you have access to a university or library that has the ERIC collection on microfiche, you may be able to read and photocopy the document there. If not, you can obtain the document from ERIC Document Reproduction Service (EDRS). Contact information is listed in the publishers list at the back of this module.

National Association of State Directors of Special Education. (1994). *Discipline challenges and opportunities impacting students with disabilities: A policy forum report.* Alexandria, VA: Author.

Riches, V. C., & Dip, B. A. (1996). *Everyday social interaction: A program for people with disabilities.* Baltimore, MD: Paul H. Brookes.

Rivera, D. P., & Smith, D. D. (1996). *Teaching students with learning and behavior problems* (3rd ed.). Boston, MA: Allyn & Bacon.

Rosenberg, M. S. (1996). *Educating students with behavior disorders* (2nd ed.). Boston, MA: Allyn & Bacon.

Ruesch, G. M. (1995, April). Gun-Free Schools Act and the Jeffords Amendment: Disciplining gun-toting students with disabilities [Special issue]. *SARRC Reports.* (Available from the South Atlantic Regional Resource Center.)

Sprick, R., Sprick, M., & Garrison, M. (1993). *Interventions: Collaborative planning for students at risk. A procedural manual.* Longmont, CO: Sopris West.

⊛ University of Colorado Health Science Center, School of Nursing. (1994). *Understanding and managing behavior of young children. Part I: Understanding challenging behavior in school and child care settings; Part II: Managing challenging behavior in school and child care settings* [Videotape series]. Lawrence, KS: Learner Managed Designs.

⊛ University of Colorado Health Science Center, School of Nursing. (1996). *Why do we behave that way?* [Videotape for classmates of children and youth with behavior problems.] Lawrence, KS: Learner Managed Designs.

Wagner, C. (Ed.). (1993). *National directory of organizations serving parents of children and youth with emotional and behavioral disorders.* Portland, OR: Research and Training Center on Family Support and Children's Mental Health.

⊛ Weatherly, J. J., & Weatherly, C. L. (1995). *Videotape #3: Discipline* [Videotape]. Horsham, PA: LRP.

West, M. D., Rayfield, R. G., Clements, C., Unger, D., & Thorton, T. (1994). An illustration of positive behavioral support in the workplace for individuals with severe mental retardation. *Journal of Vocational Rehabilitation, 4*(4), 265–271.

Zionts, P. (Ed.). (1997). *Inclusion strategies for students with learning and behavior problems: Perspectives, experiences, and best practices.* Austin, TX: Pro-Ed.

Resources on Cultural Diversity in Special Education

Anderson, M., & Goldberg, P. (1991). *Cultural competence in screening and assessment: Implications for services to young children with special needs ages birth through five.* Minneapolis, MN: PACER Center.

Artiles, A. J., & Zamora-Duran, G. (1997). *Reducing disproportionate representation of culturally diverse students in special and gifted education.* Reston, VA: Council for Exceptional Children.

Boca, L., & Cervantes, H. (1991). *Bilingual special education* (ERIC Digest #E496). Washington, DC: Office of Educational Research and Improvement. (ERIC Document Reproduction Service No. ED 333 618)

Brockenbrough, K. (1991). *Preparing personnel for pluralism.* Chapel Hill, NC: National Early Childhood Technical Assistance System (NEC*TAS).

Duran, E. (1996). *Teaching students with moderate/severe disabilities, including autism: Strategies for second language learners in inclusive settings* (2nd ed.). Springfield, IL: Charles C Thomas.

Gonzalez, V., Brusa-Vega, & Yawkey, T. (1997). *Assessment and instruction of culturally and linguistically diverse students with or at-risk of learning problems: From research to practice.* Boston, MA: Allyn & Bacon.

Grossman, H. (1994). *Special education in a diverse society.* Boston, MA: Allyn & Bacon.

Hamayan, E. V., & Damico, J. S. (1991). *Limiting bias in the assessment of bilingual students.* Austin, TX: Pro-Ed.

Harry, B. (1994). *Disproportionate representation of minority students in special education: Theories and recommendations.* Alexandria, VA: Project FORUM, National Association of State Directors of Special Education.

Harry, B. (1996). *A teacher's handbook for cultural diversity, families, and the special education system: Communication and empowerment.* New York: Teachers College Press.

Kamhi, A. G., Pollock, K. E., & Harris, J. L. (1996). *Communication development and disorders in African-American children: Research, assessment, and intervention.* Baltimore, MD: Paul H. Brookes.

Luft, P. (1995, July). *Addressing minority overrepresentation in special education: Cultural barriers to special education.* Paper presented at the Annual International Convention of the Council for Exceptional Children, Indianapolis, IN. (ERIC Document Reproduction Service No. ED 385 093)

Lynch, E. W., & Hanson, M. J. (1998). *Developing cross-cultural competence: A guide for working with young children and their families* (2nd ed.). Baltimore, MD: Paul H. Brookes.

National Association of State Directors of Special Education. (1995). *Disproportionate representation of culturally and linguistically diverse students in special education: A comprehensive examination.* Alexandria, VA: Author. (ERIC Document Reproduction Service No. ED 374 637)

National Association of State Directors of Special Education. (1996). *Strategies that address the disproportionate representation of culturally and linguistically diverse students in special education: Case studies of selected states and school districts.* Alexandria, VA: Author.

Tabors, P. O. (1997). *One child, two languages: A guide for preschool educators of children learning English as a second language.* Baltimore, MD: Paul H. Brookes.

Winzer, M. A. (1997). *Special education in multicultural contexts.* Upper Saddle River, NJ: Merrill/Prentice Hall.

Resources in Early Intervention

Bagnato, S. J., Neisworth, J. T., & Munson, S. M. (1997). *Linking assessment and early intervention: An authentic curriculum-based approach.* Baltimore, MD: Paul H. Brookes.

Beckman, P. J. (1996). *Strategies for working with families of young children with disabilities.* Baltimore, MD: Paul H. Brookes.

Bowe, F. G. (1995). *Birth to five: Early childhood special education.* New York: Delmar.

Bricker, D. (Ed.). (1993). *Assessment, evaluation, and programming system for infants and children: Volume 1: Measurement—birth to three.* Baltimore, MD: Paul H. Brookes.

Bricker, D. (Ed.). (1993). *Assessment, evaluation, and programming system for infants and children: Volume 2: Curriculum—birth to three.* Baltimore, MD: Paul H. Brookes.

Bricker, D. (Ed.). (1996). *Assessment, evaluation, and programming system for infants and children, Volume 3: Measurement—three to six.* Baltimore, MD: Paul H. Brookes.

Bricker, D. (Ed.). (1996). *Assessment, evaluation, and programming system for infants and children, Volume 4: Curriculum—three to six.* Baltimore, MD: Paul H. Brookes.

Bricker, D., & Cripe, J. (1992). *Activity-based approach to early education.* Baltimore, MD: Paul H. Brookes.

Briggs, M. H. (1996). *Building early intervention teams: Working together for children and families.* Frederick, MD: Aspen.

Cantor, R. F., & Cantor, J. A. (1995). *Parents' guide to special needs schooling: Early intervention years.* Westport, CT: Auburn House.

Chandler, P. A. (1994). *A place for me: Including children with special needs in early care and education settings.* Washington, DC: National Association for the Education of Young Children.

Coleman, J. G. (1994). *Early intervention dictionary: A multidisciplinary guide to terminology.* Bethesda, MD: Woodbine House.

Danaher, J. (1995). *Preschool special education eligibility classifications and criteria.* Chapel Hill, NC: National Early Childhood Technical Assistance System (NEC*TAS).

Guralnick, M. J. (1996). *Effectiveness of early intervention.* Baltimore, MD: Paul H. Brookes.

Hanson, M. J., & Lynch, E. W. (1995). *Early intervention: Implementing child and family services for infants and toddlers who are at risk and disabled* (2nd ed.). Austin, TX: Pro-Ed.

Harrington, R. G. (1995). *Developmental assessment and intervention: Birth to six years old* [Audiotape]. Lawrence, KS: Learner Managed Designs.

Howard, V. F. (1996). *Very young children with special needs: A formative approach for the 21st century.* Upper Saddle River, NJ: Merrill/Prentice Hall.

Johnson, L. J., Gallagher, R. J., LaMontagne, M. J., Jordan, J. B., & Gallagher, J. J. (Eds.). (1994). *Meeting early intervention challenges: Issues from birth to three.* Baltimore, MD: Paul H. Brookes.

Linder, T. W. (1993). *Transdisciplinary play-based assessment: A functional approach to working with young children.* Baltimore, MD: Paul H. Brookes.

Linder, T. W. (1993). *Transdisciplinary play-based intervention: Guidelines for developing a meaningful curriculum for young children.* Baltimore, MD: Paul H. Brookes.

⊛ Linder, T. W. (Producer), & Newman, R. S. (Director). (1995). *And you thought they were just playing: Transdisciplinary play-based assessment* [Videotape]. Baltimore, MD: Paul H. Brookes.

⊛ Linder, T. W. (Producer), & Walker, M. (Director). (1996). *Observing Kassandra: A transdisciplinary play-based assessment for a child with severe disabilities* [a companion training tape to *And you thought they were just playing,* above]. Baltimore, MD: Paul H. Brookes.

McWilliam, P. J., & Bailey, D. B. (1993). *Working together with children and families: Case studies in early intervention.* Baltimore, MD: Paul H. Brookes.

McWilliam, R. A. (Ed.). (1996). *Rethinking pull-out services in early intervention: A professional resource.* Baltimore, MD: Paul H. Brookes.

Shackelford, J. (1997). *State ICC overview: Policies, practices, and programs of state interagency coordinating councils.* Chapel Hill, NC: National Early Childhood Technical Assistance System (NEC*TAS).

Winton, P. J., McCollum, J. A., & Catlett, C. (1997). *Reforming personnel preparation in early intervention: Issues, models, and practical strategies.* Baltimore, MD: Paul H. Brookes.

Resources on Inclusion

Aefsky, F. (1995). *Inclusion confusion: A guide to educating students with exceptional needs.* Thousand Oaks, CA: Corwin Press.

Anderson, P. L. (1997). *Case studies for inclusive schools.* Austin, TX: Pro-Ed.

Beninghof, A. M., & Singer, A. L. T. (1995). *Ideas for inclusion: The school administrator's guide.* Longmont, CO: Sopris West.

Biklen, D. (1992). *Schooling without labels: Parents, educators, and inclusive education.* Philadelphia, PA: Temple University Press.

Blenk, K., & Landau Fine, D. (1995). *Making school inclusion work: A guide to everyday practices.* Cambridge, MA: Brookline.

Falvey, M. A. (1995). *Inclusive and heterogeneous schooling: Assessment, curriculum, and instruction.* Baltimore, MD: Paul H. Brookes.

Friend, M. P., & Bursuck, W. D. (1998). *Including students with special needs: A practical guide for classroom teachers* (2nd ed.). Boston, MA: Allyn & Bacon.

Giangreco, M. F., Cloninger, C. J. & Iverson, V. S. (1998). *Choosing options and accomodations for children: A guide to planning inclusive education* (2nd ed.). Baltimore, MD: Paul H. Brookes.

Hammeken, P. A. (1995). *Inclusion: 450 strategies for success: A practical guide for all educators who teach students with disabilities.* Minnetonka, MN: Peytral.

Hammeken, P. A. (1996). *Inclusion: An essential guide for the paraprofessional: A practical reference tool for all paraprofessionals working in inclusionary settings.* Minnetonka, MN: Peytral.

Hewit, J. S., & Whittier, K. S. (1997). *Teaching methods for today's schools: Collaboration and inclusion.* Boston, MA: Allyn & Bacon.

King-Sears, M. E., & Carpenter, S. L. (Eds.). (1996). Inclusion: Promising practices in schools. *Remedial and Special Education, 17*(4).

Kochhar, C. A., West, L. L., & Taymans, J. M. (1995). *Handbook for successful inclusion.* Gaithersburg, MD: Aspen.

Lewis, R. B., & Doorlag, D. D. (1994). *Teaching special students in the mainstream* (4th ed.). Upper Saddle River, NJ: Merrill/Prentice Hall.

Manus, R. M. (1990). *The skillful teacher's handbook: Effectively teaching regular and special education students.* Springfield, IL: Charles C. Thomas.

McTaggart, N., & Burt, E. (1994). *Inclusionary education for students with disabilities: Keeping the promise.* Washington, DC: National Council on Disability.

Moore, L. (1997). *Inclusion: Strategies for working with young children: Resource guide for teachers, child care providers, and parents.* Minnetonka, MN: Peytral.

National Education Association. (1993). *Integrating students with special needs: Policies and practices that work.* Washington, DC: Author.

National Education Association. (1994). *Toward inclusive classrooms.* Washington, DC: Author.

⊛ Phi Delta Kappa. (1995). *Facing inclusion together through collaboration and coteaching* [Videotape]. Bloomington, IN: Author.

Power-deFur, L. A., & Orelove, F. P. (Eds.). (1996). *Inclusive education: Practical implementation of the least restrictive environment.* Gaithersburg, MD: Aspen.

Rief, S. F., & Heimburge, J. A. (1996). *How to reach & teach all students in the inclusive classroom: Ready-to-use strategies, lessons, and activities for teaching students with diverse learning needs.* West Nyack, NY: Center for Applied Research in Education.

Rogers, J. (Ed.). (1994). *Hot topics series: Inclusion: Moving beyond our fears.* Bloomington, IN: Phi Delta Kappa.

Salend, S. J. (1997). *Effective mainstreaming: Creating inclusive classrooms* (3rd ed.). Upper Saddle River, NJ: Merrill/Prentice Hall.

Siegel, L. M. (1995). *Least restrictive environment: The paradox of inclusion.* Horsham, PA: LRP.

Stainback, S., & Stainback, W. (1991). *Curriculum considerations in inclusive classrooms: Facilitating learning for all students.* Baltimore, MD: Paul H. Brookes.

Stainback, S., & Stainback, W. (1996). *Inclusion: A guide for educators.* Baltimore, MD: Paul H. Brookes.

Tiegerman-Faber, E. (1997). *Collaborative decision making: The pathway to inclusion.* Upper Saddle River, NJ: Merrill.

Tilton, L. (1996). *Inclusion: A fresh look: Practical strategies to help all students succeed.* Shorewood, MN: Cavington Cave Publications.

Vaughn, S. R., Bos, C. S., & Schumm, J. (1996). *Teaching mainstreamed, diverse, and at-risk students in the general education classroom.* Boston, MA: Allyn & Bacon.

Waldron, K. A. (1995). *Introduction to special education: The inclusive classroom.* Albany, NY: Delmar.

Wood, J. W. (1997). *Adapting instruction to accommodate students in inclusive settings* (3rd ed.). Upper Saddle River, NJ: Merrill/Prentice Hall.

York-Barr, J. (Ed.). (1996). *Creating inclusive school communities: A staff development series for general and special educators.* Baltimore, MD: Paul H. Brookes.

York-Barr, J. (Ed.). (1996). Inclusion: Conceptual foundations [Special issue]. *Remedial and Special Education, 17*(3).

Resources on the Individualized Education Program

Arena, J. (1989). *How to write an IEP* (Rev. ed.). Novato, CA: Academic Therapy.

Ebenstein, B. (1995). IEP strategies. *Exceptional Parent, 25*(4), 62–65.

Guzzo, P., & Guzzo, B. (1991). Scott's IEP includes technology: One family's journey to obtain assistive technology for their son. *Exceptional Parent, 21*(8), 12–14.

Jacuso, Y. C. (1994). *Training special education teachers to write appropriate goals and short-term objectives for individualized education plans.* Miami, FL: Southeastern University. (ERIC Document Reproduction Service No. ED 374 597)

Küpper, L. (1996). Helping students develop their IEPs. *NICHY Technical Assistance Guide, 2,* 1–24. (ERIC Document Reproduction Service No. ED 391 335) (Available from NICHCY.)

Love, L. (1995). *Developing and including transition services in the IEP.* Phoenix, AZ: Arizona State Department of Education, Division of Special Education. (ERIC Document Reproduction Service No. ED 380 964)

McGahee-Kovac, M. (1996). A student's guide to the IEP. *A Student's Guide, 1,* 1–12. (ERIC Document Reproduction Service No. ED 391 336) (Available from NICHCY.)

McLaughlin, M. J., & Warren, S. H. (1995). *Individual educational programs: Issues and options for change.* Alexandria, VA: National Association of State Directors of Special Education.

Peters, M. T. (1990). Someone's missing: The student as an overlooked participant in the IEP process. *Preventing School Failure, 34*(4), 32–36.

Rodger, S. (1995). Individual education plans revisited: A review of the literature. *International Journal of Disability, Development and Education, 42*(3), 221–39.

School, B. A., & Cooper, A. (1997). *The IEP primer and the individualized program: Preschool through postsecondary transition.* Novato, CA: Academic Therapy.

Schrag, J. (1997). *The IEP: Benefits, challenges, and future directions*. Alexandria, VA: Project FORUM, National Association of State Directors of Special Education. (ERIC Document Reproduction Service No. ED 399 734)

Siegel, L. (1997). *The complete IEP guide: How to advocate for your special education child*. San Francisco, CA: Nolo Press.

Wandry, D., & Repetto, J. (1993). Transition services in the IEP. *NICHCY Transition Summary, V*(1), 1–28. (Available from NICHCY.)

West, L. (1992). *Integrating transition planning into the IEP process*. Reston, VA: Council for Exceptional Children.

Resources on the Individualized Family Service Plan

Beach Center on Families and Disability. (1994). *Get a family-friendly IFSP* (Fact Sheet 11). Lawrence, KS: Author.

Beach Center on Families and Disability. (1995). *Family-friendly IFSP research package* (Product No. 21). Lawrence, KS: Author.

Beach Center on Families and Disability. (1997). *Parent handbook for individualized family service plans* (Product No. 51). Lawrence, KS: Author.

Chandler, L. K., Fowler, S. A., Hadden, S., & Stahurski, L. (1995). *Planning your child's transition to preschool: A step-by-step guide for families*. Champaign, IL: University of Illinois Children's Research Center Press.

✺ Cripe, J. J., (Producer), & Crabtree, J. (Director). (1995). *A family's guide to the individualized family service plan* [video and booklet]. Baltimore, MD: Paul H. Brookes.

DeFosset, S., Rasbold, R., Battigelli, S., Ament, N., & Rooney, R. (1996). *Including young children with disabilities in community settings: A resource pocket*. Chapel Hill, NC: National Early Childhood Technical Assistance System (NEC*TAS).

Donegan, M., Fink, D. B., Fowler, S. A., & Wischnowski, M. W. (1994). *Entering a new preschool: How service providers and families can ease the transitions of children turning three who have special needs*. Champaign, IL: University of Illinois Children's Research Center Press.

Fink, D. B., Borjia, E., & Fowler, S. A. (1993). *Interagency agreements: Improving the transition process for young children with special needs and their families*. Champaign, IL: University of Illinois Children's Research Center Press.

Hadden, S., Fowler, S. A., Fink, D. B., & Wischnowski, M. W. (1995). *Writing an interagency agreement on transition: A practical guide*. Champaign, IL: University of Illinois Children's Research Center Press.

Hurth, J. L., & Goff, P. E. (1996). *Assuring the family's role on the early intervention team: Explaining rights and safeguards*. Chapel Hill, NC: National Early Childhood Technical Assistance System (NEC*TAS).

Johnson, B. H., McGonigel, M. J., & Kaufmann, R. K. (1991). *Guidelines and recommended practices for the Individualized Family Service Plan* (2nd ed.). Bethesda, MD: Association for the Care of Children's Health (ACCH).

Küpper, L. (Ed.). (1994). *A parent's guide to accessing programs for infants, toddlers, and preschoolers with disabilities*. Washington, DC: NICHCY.

McGonigel, M., Kaufmann, R., & Johnson, B. (Eds.). (1992). *Guidelines and recommended practices for the individualized family service plan (IFSP)*. Bethesda, MD: Association for the Care of Children's Health (ACCH). (ERIC Document Reproduction Service No. ED 336 907)

National Early Childhood Technical Assistance System (NEC*TAS). (1995). *Helping our nation's infants and toddlers with disabilities and their families: A briefing paper on Part H of the Individuals with Disabilities Education Act, 1986–1995*. Chapel Hill, NC: Author.

Trohanis, P. L. (1995). Progress in providing services to young children with special needs and their families: An overview to and update on implementing the Individuals with Disabilities Education Act. *NEC*TAS Notes*, Number 7, 1–20. (Available from NEC*TAS.)

Resources on Legal Issues in Special Education

Arnold, J. B. (1995). Attorney's fees in special education cases under the Individuals with Disabilities Education Act. *West's Education Law Quarterly, 4*(4), 604–612.

Garfinkel, L. (1995). *Legal issues in transitioning students*. Horsham, PA: LRP.

Gom, S. (1997). *What do I do when . . . the answer book on special education law* (2nd ed.). Horsham, PA: LRP.

Latham, P., & Latham, P. (1993). *Learning disabilities and the law*. Washington, DC: JKL Communications.

Osborne, A. G. (1995). Statutes of limitation for filing a lawsuit under the Individuals with Disabilities Education Act. *West's Education Law Quarterly, 5*(3), 377–388.

Osborne, A. G. (1996). *Legal issues in special education*. Boston, MA: Allyn & Bacon.

Pitasky, V. (1997). *How to challenge attorneys' fees in special education cases*. Horsham, PA: LRP.

Rothstein, L. F. (1995). *Special education law*. (2nd ed.). Redding, MA: Longman.

Underwood, J., & Mead, J. F. (1995). *Legal aspects of special education and pupil services*. Boston, MA: Allyn & Bacon.

✺ Weatherly, C. L., & Weatherly, J. J. (1995). *Special law for special people*. Horsham, PA: LRP. (A series of 10 training videos on special education law.)

Resources on Mediation in Special Education

Ahearn, E. M. (1994b). *Mediation and due process procedures in special education: An analysis of state policies. Final report*. Alexandria, VA: Project FORUM, National Association of State Directors of Special Education.

Goldberg, S. S., & Huefner, D. S. (1995). Dispute resolution in special education: An introduction to litigation alternatives. *West's Education Low Quarterly 4*(3), 534–542.

Hayden, P. S., & Blythe, T. (1995). *Survey of state mediation systems*. Lexington, KY: Mid-South Regional Resource Center.

Schrag, J. (1996). *Mediation and other alternative dispute resolution procedures in special education*. Alexandria, VA: National Association of State Directors of Special Education.

Schrag, J. (1996). *Mediation in special education: A resource manual for mediators*. Alexandria, VA: National Association of State Directors of Special Education.

Schumack, S., & Stewart, A. (1995). *When parents and educators do not agree: Using mediation to resolve conflicts about special education.* Cambridge, MA: Center for Law and Education. (ERIC Document Reproduction Service No. ED 387 990)

Whelan, R. J., & Smith, R. (Producers). (1996). *Mediation in special education* [Videotape]. Lawrence, KS: Learner Managed Designs.

Resources for Parents

Algozzine, B., & Ysseldyke, J. (Eds.). (1995). *Tactics for improving parenting skills.* Longmont, CO: Sopris West.

Ambler, L. (1996, June). Respite care. *NICHCY Briefing Paper,* 1–8. (Available from NICHCY.)

Baker, B. L., & Brightman, A. J. (1997). *Steps to independence: Teaching everyday skills to children with special needs* (3rd ed.). Baltimore, MD: Paul H. Brookes.

Beach Center on Families and Disability. (1996). *Parent to parent: Annotated bibliography and literature review* (Product No. 3P). Lawrence, KS: Author.

Beach Center on Families and Disability. (1997). *Resources for families and people who work with families* (Product No. Y4). Lawrence, KS: Author.

Callahan, C. R. (1990). *Since Owen: A parent-to-parent guide for care of the disabled child.* Baltimore, MD: Johns Hopkins University Press.

Cantor, J. A., & Cantor, J. A. (1995). *Parent's guide to special needs schooling: Early intervention years.* Westport, CT: Greenwood.

Capper, L. (1995). *That's my child: Strategies for parents of children with disabilities.* Washington, DC: Child Welfare League of America.

Cernoch, J. (1996). Respite care. *NICHCY Briefing Paper,* 1–8. (Available from NICHCY.)

Conroy, M. K. (Ed.). (1996, August). Paying the medical bills (Rev. ed.). *NICHCY Briefing Paper,* 1–18. (Available from NICHCY.)

✪ Cripe, J. J. (Producer), & Crabtree, J. (Director). (1995). *A family's guide to the individualized family service plan* [Videotape]. Baltimore, MD: Paul H. Brookes.

Des Jardins, C. (1993). *How to get services by being assertive.* Chicago, IL: Family Resource Center on Disabilities.

Ferguson, S., & Ripley, S. (1991). Special education and related services: Communicating through letter writing. *Parent's Guide, II*(1), 1–20. (Available from NICHCY.)

Fuller, M. L. & Olson, G. (Eds.). (1998). *Homeschool relations: Working successfully with parents and families.* Boston, MA: Allyn & Bacon.

Gibbs, B., & Springer, A. (1995). *Early use of total communication: An introductory guide for parents.* Baltimore, MD: Paul H. Brookes.

Küpper, L. (Ed.). (1994, August). *A parent's guide to accessing programs for infants, toddlers, and preschoolers with disabilities.* Washington, DC: NICHCY.

Küpper, L. (Ed.). (1994). Bibliography for Families: Assessing children for the presence of a disability. *NICHCY Bibliography, 2* 1–4. (Available from NICHCY.)

Küpper, L. (Ed.). (1994). Planning a move: Mapping your strategy. *NICHCY Parent's guide, 1*(3), 1–11. (Available from NICHCY.)

Küpper, L. (Ed.). (1996, August). *A parent's guide to accessing the ERIC resource collection* (Rev. ed.). Washington, DC: NICHCY.

Küpper, L. (Ed.). (1997, February). Parenting a child with special needs: A guide to reading and resources (2nd ed.). *NICHCY News Digest, 20,* 1-28. (Available from NICHCY.)

Lobato, D. J. (1990). *Brothers, sisters, and special needs: Information and activities for helping young siblings of children with chronic illnesses and developmental disabilities.* Baltimore, MD: Paul H. Brookes.

Marsh, J. D. B. (Ed.). (1995). *From the heart: On being the mother of a child with special needs.* Bethesda, MD: Woodbine House.

Meyer, D. J. (Ed.). (1995). *Uncommon fathers: Reflections on raising a child with a disability.* Bethesda, MD: Woodbine House.

Miller, N. B. (1993). *Nobody's perfect: Living and growing with children who have special needs.* Baltimore, MD: Paul H. Brookes.

Moore, L. O. (1996). *Inclusion, a practical guide for parents: Tools to enhance your child's success in learning.* Minnetonka, MN: Peytral.

PACER Center. (1996). *A guide for parents to the individualized education program (IEP).* Minneapolis, MN: Author. (ERIC Document Reproduction Service No. ED 394 237)

PACER Center. (1996). *Parents can be the key . . . to an appropriate education for their child with disabilities.* Minneapolis, MN: Author.

Pierangelo, R., & Jacoby, R. C. (1996). *Parents' complete special education guide: Tips, techniques, and materials for helping your child succeed in school and life.* Upper Saddle River, NJ: Prentice Hall.

Pueschel, S., Scola, P. S., Weidenman, L., & Bernier, J. (1997). *The special child: A sourcebook for parents and children with developmental disabilities* (2nd ed.). Baltimore, MD: Paul H. Brookes.

Rebhorn, T., & Takemoto, C. (1995). *Unlocking the door: A parent's guide to supported inclusive education.* Fairfax, VA: Parent Educational Advocacy Training Center.

Ripley, S. (1990). *A parent's guide to doctors, disabilities, and the family.* McLean, VA: NICHCY.

Ripley, S. (1993). *A parent's guide to accessing parent groups.* McLean, VA: NICHCY.

Resources for Rehabilitation. (1996). *Resources for people with disabilities and chronic conditions* (3rd ed.). Lexington, MA: Author.

Rosenfeld, L. R. (1994). *Your child and health care: A "dollars & sense" guide for families with special needs.* Baltimore, MD: Paul H. Brookes.

Russell, M., & Grant, A. E. (1994). *The life planning workbook: A hands-on guide to help parents provide for the future security and happiness of their child with a disability after their death.* Evanston, IL: American Publishing.

Schwartz, S., & Miller, J. E. H. (1996). *The new language of toys: Teaching communication skills to children with special needs: A guide for parents and teachers* (2nd ed.). Bethesda, MD: Woodbine House.

Senisi, E. B. (1998). *Just kids.* New York: Dutton Children's Books.

Social Security Administration. (1997). *Social Security: Benefits for children with disabilities* (SSA Publication No. 05-10026). Baltimore, MD: Author.

Social Security Administration. (1997). *Definition of a disability for children: Fact sheet.* (SSA Publication 05-11053.) Baltimore, MD: Author.

Sullivan, T. (1996). *Special parent, special child: Parents of children with disabilities share their trials, triumphs, and hard-won wisdom.* East Rutherford, NJ: Putnam.

Sweeney, W. (1997). *The special-needs reading list: An annotated guide to the best publications for parents and professionals.* Bethesda, MD: Woodbine House.

Tovray, S., & Wilson-Portuondo, M. (1995). *Helping your special needs child: A practical and reassuring resource guide.* Rocklin, CA: Prima.

Waterman, B. B. (1994). Accessing children for the presence of a disability. *NICHCY News Digest, 4*(1), 1-28.

Resources on School Reform

Berres, M. S., Ferguson, D., Knoblock, P., & Woods, C. (Eds.). (1996). *Creating tomorrow's schools today: Stories of inclusion, change, and renewal.* New York: Teachers College Press.

Consortium for Policy Research in Education. (1996). *Public policy and school reform: A research summary.* San Francisco, CA: Jossey-Bass.

Elliott, J. L., & Thurlow, M. L. (1997). *Opening the door to educational reform: Understanding standards.* Minneapolis, MN: National Center for Educational Outcomes (NCEO) and Parents Engaged in Education Reform (PEER) Project.

Elmore, R. F. (Ed.). (1990). *Restructuring schools: The next generation of education reform.* San Francisco, CA: Jossey-Bass.

Fuhman, S. H. (Ed.). (1993). *Designing coherent education policy: Improving the system.* San Francisco, CA: Jossey-Bass.

Fullen, M. (1993). *Change forces: Probing the depths of educational reform.* Bristol, PA: Falmer Press.

Goor, M. B. (1995). *Leadership for special education administration: A case-based approach.* Fort Worth, TX: Harcourt Brace College Press.

Jorgenson, C. (Ed.). (1997). *Restructuring high schools for all students: Taking inclusion to the next level.* Baltimore, MD: Paul H. Brookes.

Kerzner, D. L., & Gartner, A. (1997). *Inclusion and school reform: Transforming America's classrooms.* Baltimore, MD: Paul H. Brookes.

Meyen, E. L., & Skrtic, T. M. (Eds.). (1995). *Special education and student disability: An introduction: Traditional, emerging, and alternative perspectives.* Denver, CO: Love.

Olsen, K. (1994). Have we made progress in fifteen years of evaluating the effectiveness of special education programs? *Special Services in the Schools, 9*(2), 21-37.

Paul, J. L., Rosselli, H., & Evans, D. (Eds.). (1994). *Integrating school restructuring and special education reform.* Fort Worth, TX: Harcourt Brace College Press.

Sailor, W., & Skrtic, T. M. (Eds.). (1996). School/community partnerships and educational reform [Special issue]. *Remedial and Special Education, 17*(3).

Villa, R., Thousand, J., Stainback, W., & Stainback, S. (1992). *Restructuring for caring and effective education: An administrative guide to creating heterogeneous schools.* Baltimore, MD: Paul H. Brookes.

Woods, C. (Ed.). (1996). *Creating tomorrow's schools today: Stories of inclusion, change, and renewal.* New York: Teachers College Press.

Resources on Special Education Finance

Duenas, I. E. (1993). *Center for Special Education Finance: Topical and annotated bibliographies: A user's guide.* Palto Alto, CA: Center for Special Education Finance.

Kreb, R. A. (1994). *Third party payment for funding special education and related services* (2nd ed.). Horsham, PA: LRP.

O'Reilly, F. E. (1995). *State special education funding formulas and the use of separate placements for students with disabilities: Exploring linkages.* Palo Alto, CA: Center for Special Education Finance.

Parrish, T. B. (1996). *Special education finance: Past, present, and future.* Palo Alto, CA: Center for Special Education Finance.

Parrish, T. B., O'Reilly, F., Duenas, I. E., & Wolman, J. (1997). *State special education finance systems, 1994-95.* Palo Alto, CA: Center for Special Education Finance.

Verstegem, D. A. (1994). *Fiscal provisions of the Individuals with Disabilities Education Act: Historical overview.* Palo Alto, CA: Center for Special Education Finance.

Verstegem, D. A. (1995). *Consolidated special education funding and services: A federal perspective.* Palo Alto, CA: Center for Special Education Finance, American Institutes for Research.

Verstegem, D. A., & Parrish, T. B. (1993). *Fiscal provisions of the Individuals with Disabilities Education Act: Policy issues and alternatives.* Palo Alto, CA: Center for Special Education Finance.

Resources on Training Adults

Apps, J. W. (1991). *Mastering the teaching of adults.* Malabar, FL: Krieger.

Charner, I. (1995). *How to facilitate groups.* Washington, DC: National School to Work Institute.

Silberman, M. L., & Lawson, K. (1995). *101 ways to make training more active.* New York: Pfeiffer & Co.

Silberman, M. L. (1996). *Active learning: 101 strategies to teach any subject.* Boston, MA: Allyn & Bacon.

Vella, J. (1995). *Training through dialogue: Promoting effective learning and change with adults.* San Francisco, CA: Jossey-Bass.

Resources on Transition

Anderson, A. G., & Asselin, S. B. (1996). Factors affecting the school-to-community transition of students with disabilities. *Journal for Vocational Special Needs Education,* 18(2), 63-68.

Colley, D., & Gingerich, J. (1996). *Vocational rehabilitation services: A consumer guide for postsecondary students.* Washington, DC: HEATH.

Greene, G., & Albright, L. Best practices in transition services: Do they exist? *Career Development for Exceptional Individuals,* 18(1), 1-2.

Martin, J. E., & Marshall, L. H. (1995). ChoiceMaker: A comprehensive self-determination transition program. *Intervention in School and Clinic,* 30(3), 147-56.

Sands, D. J. (1995). Live-in training experience (LITE). A transition program for youth with disabilities. *TEACHING Exceptional Children,* 27(2), 19-23.

Sitlington, P. L. (1996). *Assess for success: Handbook on transition assessment.* Reston, VA: Council for Exceptional Children.

Storms, J., DeStefano, L., & O'Leary, E. (1996). *Individuals with Disabilities Education Act: Transition requirements: A guide for states, districts, schools, and families.* Eugene, OR: Western Regional Resource Center.

Tilson, G. P. (1996). The employer partnership in transition for youth with disabilities. *Journal for Vocational Special Needs Education,* 18(3), 88-92.

Wandry, D., & Repetto, J. (1993). Transition services in the IEP. *NICHCY Transition Summary,* V(1), 1-28. (Available from NICHCY.)

Wehmeyer, M. L., & Ward, M. (1995). The spirit of the IDEA mandate: Student involvement in transition planning. *Journal for Vocational Special Needs Education,* 17(3), 108-11.

Wehmeyer, M. L., & Lawrence, M. (1995). Whose future is it anyway? Promoting student involvement in transition planning. *Career Development for Exceptional Individuals,* 18(2), 69-83.

West, L. (1992). *Integrating transition planning into the IEP process.* Reston, VA: Council for Exceptional Children.

Organizations

Government Agencies

Administration on Developmental Disabilities, U.S. Department of Health and Human Services, 200 Independence Avenue SW, Room 329-D, Washington, DC 20201. Telephone: (202) 690-6590; (202) 690-6415 (TTY).

Americans with Disabilities Act Disability and Business Technical Assistance Centers (DBTACs). Telephone: (800) 949-4232 (V/TTY). Callers are automatically routed to the DBTAC in their region.

Communications and Information Services (formerly the Clearinghouse on Disability Information), Office of Special Education and Rehabilitative Services (OSERS), Room 3132, Switzer Building, 330 C Street SW, Washington, DC 20202-2524. Telephone: (202) 205-8241 (V/TTY).
URL: http://www.ed.gov

Head Start Bureau, Administration on Children, Youth and Families, U.S. Department of Health & Human Services, P.O. Box 1182, Washington, DC 20013. Telephone: (202) 205-8579.

National Council on Disability (NCD), 1331 F Street NW, 10th Floor, Washington, DC 20004-1107. Telephone: (202) 272-2004; (202) 267-3232 (TTY).
E-mail: mquigley@ncd.gov
URL: http://www.ncd.gov

National Institute on Disability and Rehabilitation Research (NIDRR), 330 C Street SW, Room 3036, Washington, DC 20202. Telephone: (202) 205-8134 (V); (202) 205-9433 (TTY).
URL: http://www.ed.gov/officer/OSERS/NICRR/nidrr.html

Office of Indian Education Programs (OIEP), Bureau of Indian Affairs (BIA), 1849 C Street, NW, MS-3512-MIB-OIE-23, Washington, DC 20240. Telephone: (202) 208-3596 (V).

Office of Minority Health Resource Center (OMH-RC), Office of Minority Health, Public Health Service, U.S. Department of Health and Human Services, P.O. Box 37337, Washington, DC 20013-7337. Telephone: (800) 444-6472 (V); (301) 587-9704 (V); (301) 589-0951 (TTY).
E-mail: info@omhrc.gov
URL: http://www.omhrc.gov

Office of Special Education Programs, U.S. Department of Education 330 C Street, SW, Switzer Building, Washington, DC 20202. Telephone: (202) 205-5507; (202) 205-9754 (TTY).

President's Committee on Employment of People with Disabilities (PCEPD), 1331 F Street, NW, Suite 300, Washington, DC 20004. Telephone: (202) 376-6200 (V); (202) 376-6205 (TTY).
E-mail: info@pcepd.gov
URL: http://www.pcepd.gov

Social Security Administration (SSA), Department of Health and Human Services, Baltimore, MD 21235. Telephone: (800) 772-1213 (V); (800) 325-0778 (TTY). For publications, contact Communications Office at (410) 965-0921.
URL: http://www.ssa.gov

Clearinghouses

Clearinghouse for Immigrant Education (CHIME), 100 Boylston Street, Suite 737, Boston, MA 02116. Telephone: (800) 441-7192 (V); (617) 357-8507 (V).
E-mail: ncasmfe@aol.com

DB-LINK (National Clearinghouse on Children Who Are Deaf-Blind), 345 North Monmouth Avenue, Monmouth, OR 97361. Telephone: (800) 438-9376; (800) 854-7013 (TTY).
E-mail: dblink@tr.wosc.osshe.edu
URL: http://www.tr.wosc.osshe.edu/dblink

ERIC Clearinghouse on Disabilities and Gifted Education, Council for Exceptional Children, 1920 Association Drive, Reston, VA 20191. Telephone: (800) 328-0272 (V); (703) 264-9449 (TTY).
E-mail: ericec@cec.sped.org
URL: http://www.cec.sped.org/ericec.htm

HEATH Resource Center (HEATH is the national clearinghouse on postsecondary education for individuals with disabilities), One Dupont Circle, Suite 800, Washington, DC 20036-1193. Telephone: (202) 939-9320 (V/TTY). E-mail: heath@ace.nche.edu URL: http://ace-infoserver.nche.edu/Programs/HEATH/ home.html Gopher: gopher://bobcat-ace-nche.edu

National Arthritis and Musculoskeletal and Skin Diseases Information Clearinghouse, 1 AMS Circle, Bethesda, MD 20892-3675. Telephone: (301) 495-4484 (V); (301) 565-2966 (TTY) URL: http://www.nih.gov/niams

National Clearinghouse for Bilingual Education (NCBE), 1118 22nd Street, NW, Washington, DC 20037. Telephone: (202) 467-0867 (V). Fax requests to: (800) 531-9347. E-mail: askncbe@ncbe.gwu.edu URL: http://www.ncbe.gwu.edu

National Clearinghouse for ESL Literacy Education (NCLE), Center for Applied Linguistics, 1118 22nd Street, NW, Washington, DC 20037. Telephone: (202) 429-9292, ext. 200 (V) E-mail: ncle@cal.org URL: http://www.cal.org/NCLE

National Clearinghouse for Professions in Special Education, Council for Special Education, 1920 Association Drive, Reston, VA 22091. Telephone: (703) 264-9476 (V); (800) 641-7824; (703) 264-9446 (TTY). E-mail: NCPSE@cec.sped.org URL: http://www.cec.sped.org/ncpse.htm

National Clearinghouse on Family Support and Children's Mental Health, Portland State University, P.O. Box 751, Portland, OR 97207-0751. Telephone: (800) 628-1696 (V); (503) 725-4165 (TTY).

National Health Information Center (NHIC), P.O. Box 37266, Washington, DC 20013-7366. Telephone: (800) 336-4797. E-mail: nhicinfo@health.org URL: http://nhic-nt.health.org

National Information Center for Children and Youth with Disabilities (NICHCY), P.O. Box 1492, Washington, DC 20013. Telephone: (800) 695-0285 (V/TTY). E-mail: NICHCY@aed.org URL: http://www.nichcy.org Gopher: gopher aed.org

National Information Center on Deafness, Gallaudet University, 800 Florida Avenue, NE, Washington, DC 20002. Telephone: (202) 651-5051(V); (202) 651-5052 (TTY). E-mail: ncid@gallaudaux.gallaudet.edu URL: http://www.gallaudet.edu/~ncid

National Rehabilitation Information Center (NARIC), 8455 Colesville Road, Suite 935, Silver Spring, MD 20910. Telephone: (800) 346-2742; (800) 227-0216 (V/TTY); (301) 588-9284 (V/TTY in MD). URL: http://www.naric.com/naric

Nondisability-Specific Organizations

Activating Children Through Technology (ACTT), Western Illinois University, Macomb Projects, 28 Horrabin Hall, Macomb, IL 61455. Telephone: (309) 298-1634 (V). E-mail: TL-Carley@wiu.edu URL: http://www.ecnet.net/users/mimacp/wiu

---

The Regional Resource and Federal Center Network

Federal Resource Center for Special Education, Academy for Educational Development, 1875 Connecticut Avenue NW, Suite 900, Washington, DC 20009. Telephone: (202) 884-8215; (202) 884-8200 (TTY) E-mail: trc@aed.org URL: http://www.dssc.org/frc/

Serving Region 1:
Northeast Regional Resource Center (NERRC), Trinity College of Vermont, McAuley Hall, 208 Colchester Avenue, Burlington, VT 05401-1496. Telephone: (802) 658-5036; (802) 860-1428 (TTY) E-mail: NERRC@aol.com URL: http://interact.uoregon.edu/WRRC/NERRC/index.htm

Serving Region 2:
Mid-South Regional Resource Center-(MSRRC), Human Development Institute, University of Kentucky, 126 Mineral Industries Building, Lexington, KY 40506-0051. Telephone: (606) 257-4921; (606) 257-2903 (TTY). E-mail: MSRRC@ihdi.ihdi.uky.edu URL: http://www.lhdl.uky.edu/projects/MSRRC/index.html

Serving Region 3:
South Atlantic Regional Resource Center (SARRC), Florida Atlantic University, 1236 North University Drive, Plantation, FL 33322. Telephone: (954) 473-6106.

E-mail: SARRC@acc.fau.edu URL: http://www.fau.edu/divdept/SARRC/

Serving Region 4:
Great Lakes Area Regional Resource Center (GLARRC), Center for Special Needs Populations, Ohio State University, 700 Ackerman Road, Suite 440, Columbus, OH 43202. Telephone: (614) 447-0844; (614) 447-8776 (TTY) E-mail: marshall.76@asu.edu URL: http://www.csnp.ohio-state.edu/glarrc.htm

Serving Region 5:
Mountain Plains Regional Resource Center (MPRRC), Utah State University, 1780 North Research Parkway, Suite 112, Logan, UT 84341. Telephone: (801) 752-0238; (801) 753-9750 (TTY) E-mail: cope@cc.usu.edu URL: http://www.usu.edu/~mprrc

Serving Region 6:
Western Regional Resource Center (WRRC), 1268 University of Oregon, Eugene, OR 97403-1268. Telephone: (541) 346-5641; (541) 346-0367 (TTY). E-mail: richard_zeller@ccmail.uoregon.edu/wrrc/wrrc.html URL: http://interact.uoregon.edu/wrrc/wrrc.html

Alliance for Technology Access, 2175 East Francisco Boulevard, Suite L, San Rafael, CA 94901. Telephone: (415) 455-4575. E-mail: atafta@aol.com URL: http://marin.org/npo/ata/

American Council on Rural Special Education (ACRES), Department of Special Education University of Utah, Milton Bennian Hall, Room 221, Salt Lake City, UT 84112. Telephone: (801) 585-5659. E-mail: acres@gsu.utah.edu

American Speech-Language-Hearing Association (ASHA), 10801 Rockville Pike, Rockville, MD 20852. Telephone: (800) 638-8255; (301) 897-5700 (V/TTY). E-mail: webmaster@asha.org URL: http://www2.asha.org/asha/

ARCH National Resource Center for Respite and Crisis Care Services, Chapel Hill Training-Outreach Project, 800 Eastowne Drive, Suite 105, Chapel Hill, NC 27514. Telephone: (800) 473-1727 (V); (919) 490-5577 (V); (800) 773-5433 (National Respite Locator Service). E-mail: HN4735@connectinc.com URL: http://chtop.com/archbroc.htm

Assistive Technology Funding and Systems Change Project of the United Cerebral Palsy Associations (UCPA), 1660 L Street, NW, Suite 700, Washington, DC 20036. Telephone: (800) 827-0093 (V); (800) 833-8272 (TTY). E-mail: ATFSCP@aol.com URL: http://homepage.interaccess.com/~taad/atfscp.html

Association for the Care of Children's Health, 7910 Woodmont Avenue, Suite 300, Bethesda, MD 20814-3015. Telephone: (800) 808-2224, ext. 327 (orders); (301) 654-6549. E-mail: acch@clark.net URL: http://www.acch.org

Association for Supervision and Curriculum Development, 1250 North Pitt Street, Alexandria, VA 22314. Telephone: (703) 549-9110. E-mail: member@ascd.org URL: http://www.ascd.org

Center of Minority Research in Special Education (COMRISE), The University of Virginia, Curry School of Education, 405 Emmet Street, Charlottesville, VA 22903-2495. Telephone: (804) 924-1022 (V); (804) 982-HEAR (TTY). URL: http://curry.edschool.virginia.edu/go/comrise

Center to Link School Districts with Technology, Educational Media and Materials, Education Development Center, Inc., 55 Chapel Street, Newton, MA 02158-1060. Telephone: (617) 969-7100, ext. 2424 (V); (617) 969-4529 (TTY). E-mail: arlener@edc.org URL: http://www.edc.org/FSC/NCIP/

Children's Defense Fund, 25 E Street, NW, Washington, DC 20001. Telephone: (202) 628-8787 (V). E-mail: cdinfo@childrensdefense.org URL: http://www.childrensdefense.org

Consortium on Inclusive Schooling Practices (CISP), Allegheny University of the Health Sciences, Child and Family Studies Program, One Allegheny Center, Suite 510, Pittsburgh, PA 15212. Telephone: (412) 359-1600. E-mail: mcnutt@pgh.auhs.edu URL: http://WWW.pgh.auhs.edu/CFSP/brochure/obtcons.htm

Council of Administrators of Special Education, 615 16th Street, NW, Albuquerque, NM 87104. Telephone: (505) 243-7622 (V). E-mail: thomason@apsicc.aps.edu

Council on Quality and Leadership in Supports for People with Disabilities, 100 West Road, Suite 406, Towson, MD 21204. Telephone: (410) 583-0060 (V). E-mail: council@accredcouncil.org URL: http://www.thecouncil.org

Disability Rights Education and Defense Fund, 2212 Sixth Street, Berkeley, CA 94710. Telephone: (510) 644-2555 (V); (510) 644-2629 (TTY). E-mail: dredica@aol.com

Disability Statistics Rehabilitation, Research and Training Center, Institute for Health and Aging, Box 0646, Laurel Heights, UCSF, San Francisco, CA 94143-0646. Telephone: (415) 502-5210 (V); (415) 502-5217 (TTY). E-mail: information_specialist@quickmail.ucsf.edu URL: http://dsc.ucsf.edu

Early Intervention Research Institute, Center for Persons with Disabilities, Utah State University, Logan, UT 84322-6580. Telephone: (801) 797-1172 or (800) 887-1699. URL: http://www.usu.edu

Family Resource Center on Disabilities, 20 East Jackson Boulevard, Room 900, Chicago, IL 60604. Telephone: (800) 952-4199 (V/TTY, toll-free in IL only); (312) 939-3513 (V); (312) 939-3519 (TTY).

Family Village (a global community of disability-related resources), Waisman Center, University of Wisconsin-Madison, 1500 Highland Avenue, Madison, WI 53705-2280. URL: http://www.familyvillage.wisc.edu/

Family Voices, P.O. Box 769, Algodones, NM 87001. Telephone: (505) 867-2368. E-mail: famy01rw@wonder.em.cdc.gov URL: http://www.ichp.ufl.edu/MCH-NetLink/FamilyVoices/

Federation of Children with Special Needs, 95 Berkeley Street, Suite 104, Boston, MA 02116. Telephone: (617) 482-2915 (V/TTY); (800) 331-0688 (V, toll-free in MA only). E-mail: fscninfo@fcsn.org URL: http://www.fcsn.org

National Association of State Directors of Special Education, 1800 Diagonal Road, Suite 320, Alexandria, VA 22314. Telephone: (703) 519-3800 (V); (703) 519-7008 (TTY). E-mail: specialed@nasde.org URL: http://www.lrp.com/lrpnet/inasdse.htm

National Center for Youth with Disabilities, University of Minnesota, General Pediatrics and Adolescent Health, Box 721, 420 Delaware Street, SE, Minneapolis, MN 55455-0392. Telephone: (612) 626-2825 (V); (612) 624-3939 (TTY). E-mail: ncyd@gold.tc.umn.edu URL: http://www.peds.umn.edu/Centers/ncyd

National Center on Educational Outcomes (NCEO), University of Minnesota, 350 Elliott Hall, 75 East River Road, Minneapolis, MN 55455. Telephone: (612) 626-1530 (V); (612) 624-4848 (TTY). E-mail: scott027@maroon.tc.umn.edu URL: http://www.coled.umn.edu/NCEO

National Center to Improve Practice (NCIP), Education Development Center, Inc., 55 Chapel Street, Newton, MA 02158-1060. Telephone: (617) 969-7100, ext. 2387 (V); (617) 969-4529 (TTY). E-mail: ncip@edc.org
URL: http://www.edc.org/FSC/NCIP/

National Center to Improve the Tools of Educators (NCITE), College of Education, University of Oregon, 805 Lincoln, Eugene, OR 97401. Telephone: (503) 683-7543.
E-mail: Douglas_Camine@ccmail.uoregon.edu
URL: http://darkwing.uoregon.edu/~ncite/

National Coalition for Parent Involvement in Education (NCPIE), 1201 16th Street, NW, Box 39, Washington, DC 20036. Telephone: (202) 822-8405, ext. 53.
E-mail: ferguson@iel.org
URL: http://www.ncpie.org

National Coalition of Title I Chapter I Parents, 1541 14th Street, NW, Washington, DC 20005. Telephone: (202) 547-9286.
URL: http://www.nctic 1p.com

National Council of La Raza (NCLR), 1111 19th Street, NW, Suite 1000, Washington, DC 20036. Telephone: (202) 785-1670.
URL: http://www.nclr.org

National Early Childhood Technical Assistance System (NEC*TAS), University of North Carolina at Chapel Hill, 500 NationsBank Plaza, 137 East Franklin Street, Chapel Hill, NC 27514. Telephone: (919) 962-2001 (V); (919) 966-4041 (TTY).
E-mail: trohanis.nectas@mhs.unc.edu
URL: http://www.nectas.unc.edu/

National Education Association (NEA), Room 710, Section BT, 1201 16th Street, NW, Washington, DC 20036-3290. Telephone: (202) 833-4000 (main number); (800) 229-4200 (professional library).
URL: http://www.nea.org

National Institute for Urban School Improvement, Resources for Inclusionary Practices 1444 Wazee Street, Suite 135, Denver, CO 80202-1326. Telephone: (303) 620-4074.
E-mail: Elizabeth_Kozleski@ceo.cudenver.edu

National Parent Network on Disabilities, 1200 G Street, NW, Washington, DC 20005. Telephone: (703) 684-6763.
E-mail: npnd@cs.com
URL: http://www.npnd.org

National Resource Center for Paraprofessionals in Education and Related Services (NRC), 25 West 43rd Street, Room 620N, New York, NY 10036. Telephone: (212) 642-2948.

National Technical Assistance Center for Children's Mental Health, Georgetown University Child Development Center, 3307 M Street, NW, Suite 401, Washington, DC 20007. Telephone: (202) 687-5000.
E-mail: gucdc@medlib.georgetown.edu
URL: http://www.dml.georgetown.edu/depts/pediatrics/gucdc

National Transition Alliance for Youth with Disabilities, Transition Research Institute at the University of Illinois, 51 Gerty Drive, Champaign, IL 61820. Telephone: (217) 333-2325 (V/TTY). E-mail: leachlyn@ux1.cso.uiuc.edu
URL: http://www.dssc.org/nta/

National Transition Network (NTN), Institute on Community Integration, University of Minnesota, 430 Wulling Hall, 86 Pleasant Street, SE, Minneapolis, MN 55455. Telephone: (612) 626-8200.
E-mail: uyxx002@maroon.tc.umn.edu
URL: http://www.ici.coled.umn.edu/ntn/

Networking System for Training Education Personnel (NSTEP), National Association of State Directors of Special Education, 1800 Diagonal Road, Suite 320, Alexandria, VA 22314. Telephone: (703) 519-3800; (703) 519-7008 (TTY).
E-mail: karlm@nasdse.org

Office of Student Services, National Center for Research in Vocational Education, University of Illinois Site, 345 Education Building, 1310 South 6th Street, Champaign, IL 61820. Telephone: (217) 333-0807 (V).
E-mail: L-iliff@uiuc.edu
URL: http://ncrve-oss.ed.uiuc.edu

PACER Center, 4826 Chicago Avenue South, Minneapolis, MN 55417-1098. Telephone: (612) 827-2966; (612) 827-7770 (TTY); (800) 537-2737 (V/TTY in MN only).
E-mail: taalliance@pacer.org
URL: http://www.taalliance.org

Parents Engaged in Education Reform (PEER) Project, Federation for Children with Special Needs, 95 Berkeley Street, Suite 104, Boston, MA 02116. Telephone: (617) 482-2915
E-mail: peer@fcsn.org
URL: http://www.fcsn.org/peer

Technical Alliance for Parent Centers (The Alliance)

Alliance Coordinating Office
PACER Center, 4826 Chicago Avenue South, Minneapolis, MN 55417-1098. Telephone: (612) 827-2966 (V); (612) 827-7770 (TTY).
E-mail: taalliance@pacer.org
URL: http://www.taalliance.org

Midwest Regional Center
PACER Center, 4826 Chicago Avenue South, Minneapolis, MN 55417. Telephone: (612) 827-2966 (V/TTY); in MN only, (800)-537-2737 (V/TTY).

Northeast Regional Center
Parent Information Center, P.O. Box 2405, Concord, NH 03302-2405. Telephone: (603) 224-7005 (V).
E-mail:picnh@aol.com

South Regional Center
Partners Resource Network, 1090 Longfellow Drive, Suite B, Beaumont, TX 77706-4819. Telephone: (409) 898-4684 (V). E-mail: TXPRN@juno.com

West Regional Center
Matrix Parent Network and Resource Center, 555 Northgate Drive, San Rafael, CA 94903. Telephone: (415) 499-3877 (V). E-mail: matrix@marin.k12.ca.us

Phi Delta Kappa International, P.O. Box 789, Bloomington, IN 47402-0789. Telephone: (800) 766-1156.
E-mail: cpd@pdkintl.org
URL: http://www.pdkintl.org

Project ACTION, 700 13th Street, NW, Suite 200, Washington, DC 20005. Telephone: (800) 659-6428 (V/TTY).
E-mail: projaction@aol.com
URL: http://www.projectaction.org

Project FORUM, National Association of State Directors of Special Education, 1800 Diagonal Road, Suite 320, Alexandria VA 22314. Telephone: (703) 519-3800; (703) 519-7008 (TTY). E-mail: eaheam@nasdse.org

Research and Training Center on Family Support and Children's Mental Health, Portland State University, P.O. Box 751, Portland, OR 97207-0751. Telephone: (800) 628-1696; (503) 725-4040 (V); (503) 725-4165 (TTY).
E-mail: stepheb@rri.pdx.edu
URL: http://www.adm.pdx.edu/user/rri/rtc

RESNA, 1700 North Moore Street, Suite 1540, Arlington, VA 22209-1903. Telephone: (540) 542-6686 (V); (540) 524-6639 (TTY).
URL: http://www.resna.org/resna/reshome.htm

Resources in Special Education (RiSE), 9738 Lincoln Village Drive, Sacramento, CA 95827. Telephone: (916) 228-2422 (V). E-mail: megsch@sac-co.k12.ca.us

Rural Institute on Disabilities, 52 Carbin Hall, The University of Montana, Missoula, MT 59812. Telephone: (406) 243-5467 (V/TTY); (800) 732-0323 (V, for information Service).
E-mail: muarid@selway.umt.edu
URL: http://www.ruralinstitute.umt.edu

Technical Assistance Center for Elementary and Middle Schools, American Institutes for Research, 1000 Thomas Jefferson Street, NW, Suite 400, Washington DC 20007. Telephone: (202) 944-5300. E-mail: jhamilton@air-dc.org
URL: http://www/air-dc/org

Technical Assistance in Data Analysis, Evaluation, and Report Preparation, Westat, Inc., 1500 Research Boulevard, Rockville, MD 20850. Telephone: (301) 738-3668.
E-mail: Brauenm1@westat.com

Technology, Educational Media, and Materials Program, Chesapeake Institute, 1000 Thomas Jefferson Street, NW, Suite 400, Washington, DC 20007. Telephone: (202) 342-5600.
E-mail: DOsher@air-dc.org

Transition Research Institute at Illinois, 51 Gerty Drive, Champaign, IL 61820. Telephone: (217) 333-2325 (V/TTY).
URL: http://www.ed.uiuc.edu/coe/sped/tri/institute.html

Zero to Three/National Center for Infants, Toddlers and Families, 734 15th Street, NW, Suite 1000, Washington, DC 20005-1036. Telephone: (202) 638-1144; (800) 899-4301 (Publications).

Disability-Specific Organizations

Alexander Graham Bell Association for the Deaf, 3417 Volta Place, NW, Washington, DC 20007. Telephone: (202) 337-5220 (V/TTY). E-mail: agbell2@aol.com
URL: http://www.agbell.org

Alliance of Genetic Support Groups, 35 Wisconsin Circle, Suite 440, Chevy Chase, MD 20815. Telephone: (800) 336-4363; (301) 652-5553. E-mail: alliance@capaccess.org
URL: http://medhlp.netusa.net/WWW/agsg.htm

American Speech-Language-Hearing Association (ASHA), 10801 Rockville Pike, Rockville, MD 20852. Telephone: (800) 638-8255; (301) 897-5700 (V/TTY).
E-mail: webmaster@asha.org
URL: http://www2.asha.org/asha/

American Foundation for the Blind (AFB), 11 Penn Plaza, Suite 300, New York, NY 10001. Telephone: (800) 232-5463; (212) 502-7600 (V); (212) 502-7662 (TTY).
E-mail: afbinfo@afb.org
URL: http://www.afb.org/afb

Anorexia Nervosa and Related Eating Disorders, Inc., P.O. Box 5102, Eugene, OR 97405. Telephone: (541) 344-1144.
URL: http://www.anred.com

Aplastic Anemia Foundation of America, Inc., P.O. Box 613, Annapolis, MD 21404. Telephone: (800) 747-2820; (410) 867-0242. E-mail: aafacenter@aol.com
URL: http://www.teleport.com/nonprofit/aafa

The Arc (formerly the Association for Retarded Citizens of the US), 500 E. Border Street, Suite 300, Arlington, TX 76010. Telephone: (800) 433-5255; (817) 261-6003 (V); (817) 277-0553 (TTY). E-mail: thearc@metronet.com
URL: http://thearc.org/

Association for Persons with Severe Handicaps (TASH), 29 West Susquehanna Avenue, Suite 210, Baltimore, MD 21204. Telephone: (410) 828-8274 (V); (410) 828-1306 (TTY).
E-mail: info@tash.org
URL: http://www.tash.org

Attention Deficit Disorder Association (ADDA), P.O. Box 972, Mentor, OH 44061. Telephone: (216) 350-9595; (800) 487-2282 (to request information packet).
E-mail: NATLADDA@aol.com
URL: http://www.add.org

Autism Society of America, 7910 Woodmont Avenue, Suite 650, Bethesda, MD 20814-3015. Telephone: (800) 3-AUTISM; (301) 657-0881 (V).
URL: http://www.autism-society.org

Brain Injury Association (formerly the National Head Injury Foundation), 1776 Massachusetts Avenue, NW., Suite 100, Washington, DC 20036. Telephone: (202) 296-6443.
URL: http://www.biausa.org

Center for Developmental Disabilities, Department of Pediatrics, School of Medicine, University of South Carolina, Columbia, 5C 29208. Telephone: (803) 935-5270.

Center for Effective Collaboration and Practice (Improving Services for Children and Youth with Emotional and Behavioral Problems), 1000 Thomas Jefferson Street, NW, Suite 400, Washington, DC 20007. Telephone: (202) 944-5389. E-mail: center@air-dc.org
URL: http://www.air-dc/cecp/cecp.html

Children and Adults with Attention Deficit Disorders (CH.A.D.D.), 499 NW 70th Avenue, Suite 101, Plantation, FL 33317. Telephone: (954) 587-3700; (800) 233-4050 (to request information packet).
URL: http://www.chadd.org

Epilepsy Foundation of America (EFA), 4351 Garden City Drive, 5th Floor, Landover, MD 20785-4941. Telephone: (800) 332-1000; (301) 459-3700. E-mail: postmaster@efa.org URL: http://www.efa.org

Hydrocephalus Association, 870 Market Street, #955, San Francisco, CA 94102. Telephone: (415) 732-7040. E-mail: hydroassoc@aol.com URL: http://neurosurgery.mgh.harvard.edu/ha/

International Dyslexia Association (formerly the Orton Dyslexia Society), Chester Building, #382, 8600 LaSalle Road, Baltimore, MD 21286-2044. Telephone: (800) 222-3123; (410) 296-0232. E-mail: info@ads.org URL: http://www.ods.org

International Resource Center for Down Syndrome, Keith Building, 1621 Euclid Avenue, Suite 514, Cleveland, OH 44115. Telephone: (216) 621-5858; (800) 899-3039 (toll-free in OH only). E-mail: hf854@cleveland.freenet.edu

International Rett Syndrome Association, 9121 Piscataway Road, Suite 2B, Clinton, MD 20735-2561. Telephone: (800) 818-7388; (301) 856-3334. E-mail: irsa@paltech.com URL: http://www2.paltech.com/irsa/irsa.htm

Learning Disabilities Association of America (LDA), 4156 Library Road, Pittsburgh, PA 15234. Telephone: (412) 341-1515; (412) 341-8077. E-mail: ldanatl@usaar.net URL: http://www.ldanatl.org

March of Dimes Birth Defects Foundation, 1275 Mamaroneck Avenue, White Plains, NY 10605. Telephone: (914) 428-7100. E-mail: resourcecenter@modimes.org URL: http://www.modimes.org

Muscular Dystrophy Association (MDA), 3300 East Sunrise Drive, Tucson, AZ 85718. Telephone: (800) 572-1717; (520) 529-2000. E-mail: mda@mdausa.org URL: http://www.mdausa.org

National Alliance for the Mentally Ill (NAMI), 200 North Glebe Rd., Suite 1015, Arlington, VA 22203-3754. Telephone: (800) 950-NAMI; (703) 524-7600. E-mail: namiofc@aol.com URL: http://www.nami.org

National Center for Learning Disabilities (NCLD), 381 Park Avenue South, Suite 1401, New York, NY 10016. Telephone: (212) 545-7510; (888) 575-7373. URL: http://www.ncld.org

National Down Syndrome Congress, 1605 Chantilly Drive, Suite 250, Atlanta, GA 30324. Telephone: (800) 232-6372; (404) 633-1555. E-mail: ndsc@charitiesusa.com URL: http://www.carol.net/~ndsc/

National Down Syndrome Society, 666 Broadway, New York, NY 10012-2317. Telephone: (800) 221–4602. URL: http://ndss.org

National Easter Seal Society, Inc., 230 West Monroe Street, Suite 1800, Chicago, IL 60606. Telephone: (800) 221-6827; (312) 726-6200 (V); (312) 726-4258 (TTY). E-mail: nessinfo@seals.com URL: http://www.seals.com

National Fragile X Foundation, 1441 York Street, Suite 303, Denver, CO 80206. Telephone: (800) 688-8765; (303) 333-6155. E-mail: natlfx@aol.com

National Library Services for the Blind & Physically Handicapped, The Library of Congress, Washington, DC 20542. Telephone: (800) 424-8567; (202) 707-5100 (V); (800) 424-9100 (TTY, English); (800) 345-8901 (TTY, Spanish). E-mail: nls@loc.gov URL: http://www.loc.gov/nls

National Mental Health Association, 1021 Prince Street, Alexandria, VA 22314-2971. Telephone: (800) 969-6642; (703) 684-7722. E-mail: nmhainfo@aol.com URL: http://www.nmha.org

National Neurofibromatosis Foundation, 95 Pine Street, 16th Floor, New York, NY 10005. Telephone: (800) 323-7938; (212) 344-NNFF. E-mail: NNFF@aol.com URL: http://www.nf.org

National Organization for Rare Disorders (NORD), 100 Route 37, P.O. Box 8923, New Fairfield, CT 06812-8923. Telephone: (800) 999-6673; (203) 746-6518 (V); (203) 746-6927 (TTY). E-mail: orphan@nord-rdb.com URL: http://www.nord-rdb.com/~orphan

National Scoliosis Foundation, 5 Cabot Place, Stoughton, MA 02072. Telephone: (800) 673-6922; (617) 341-6333. E-mail: scoliosis@aol.com

National Sleep Foundation, 729 15th Street, NW, 4th Floor, Washington, DC 20005. Telephone: (202) 347-3471. E-mail: natsleep@erols.com URL: http://www.sleepfoundation.org

National Spinal Cord Injury Association, 8300 Colesville Road, Suite 551, Silver Spring, MD 20910. Telephone: (800) 962-9629; (301) 588-6959. E-mail: nscia2@aol.com URL: http://www.spinalcord.org

National Tuberous Sclerosis Association, 8181 Professional Place, Suite 110, Landover, MD 20785-2226. Telephone: (800) 225-6872; (301) 459-9888. E-mail: ntsa@aol.com URL: http://www.ntsa.org/

Neurofibromatosis, Inc., 8855 Annapolis Road, Suite 110, Lanham, MD 20706-2924. Telephone: (800) 942-6825. E-mail: NFinc@gnn.com

Orton Dyslexia Society, see International Dyslexia Association

Osteogenesis Imperfecta Foundation, 804 Diamond Avenue, Suite 210, Gaithersburg, MD 20878. Telephone: (800) 981-BONE. E-mail: bonelink@aol.com URL: http://users.aol.com/bonelink

Recording for the Blind and Dyslexic, The Anne T. Macdonald Center, 20 Roszel Road, Princeton, NJ 08540. Telephone: (800) 221-4792; (609) 452-0606. URL: http://www.rfbd.org

Research and Training Center for Children's Mental Health, Portland State University, P.O. Box 751, Portland, OR 97207-0751. Telephone: (800) 628-1696; (503) 725-4040 (V); (503) 725-4165 (TTY). E-mail: stepheb@rri.pdx.edu URL: http://WWW-adm.pdx.edu/user/rri/ric

Spina Bifida Association of America, 4590 MacArthur Boulevard, NW, Suite 250, Washington, DC 20007-4226. Telephone: (800) 621-3141; (202) 944-3285. E-mail: spinabifda@aol.com URL: http://www.infohiway.com/spinabifida

United Cerebral Palsy Associations, Inc, 1660 L Street, NW, Suite 700, Washington, DC 20036. Telephone: (202) 776-0406; (800) 872-5827. E-mail: ucpnatl@ucpa.org URL: http://www.ucpa.org

Publishers

Aspen, P.O. Box 990, Frederick, MD 21705. Telephone: (800) 638-8437.

Association for the Care of Children's Health, 7910 Woodmont Avenue, Suite 300, Bethesda, MD 20814-3015. Telephone: (800) 808-2224, ext. 327 (orders); (301) 654-6549.

Association for Supervision and Curriculum Development, 1250 North Pitt Street, Alexandria, VA 22314. Telephone: (800) 933-2723.

Auburn House: Contact Greenwood Publishing, 88 Post Road West, Box 5007, Westport, CT 06881. Telephone: (800) 225-5800; (203) 226-3571.

Baxley Media Group, 110 West Main Street, Urbana, IL 61801. Telephone: (217) 384-4838.

Beach Center on Families and Disability, University of Kansas, 3111 Haworth Hall, Lawrence, KS 66045. Telephone: (913) 864-7600.

Brookline, P.O. Box 1047, Cambridge, MA 02238. Telephone: (800) 666-2665.

Brooks/Cole, see Wadsworth.

Center for Applied Research in Education, see Allyn & Bacon.

Center for Developmental Disabilities, Department of Pediatrics, School of Medicine, University of South Carolina, Columbia, SC 29208. Telephone: (803) 935-5270.

Center for Law and Education, 1875 Connecticut Avenue, NW, Suite 510, Washington, DC 20009. Telephone: (202) 462-7688.

Center for Special Education Finance (CSEF), American Institutes for Research, 1791 Arastradero Road, P.O. Box 1113, Palo Alto, CA 94302. Telephone: (650) 493-3550, ext. 240.

Charles C. Thomas Publishers, 2600 S. First Street, Springfield, IL 62794-9265. Telephone: (800) 258-8980 (orders); (217) 789-8980.

Child Welfare League of America, 9590 Junction Drive, Annapolis Junction, MD 20701-2019. Telephone: (800) 407-6273.

Corwin Press, 2455 Teller Road, Thousand Oaks, CA 91320. Telephone: (805) 499-9734.

Council for Exceptional Children, 1920 Association Drive, Reston, VA 20191. Telephone: (800) CEC-READ (information); (888) CEC-SPED (orders).

Covington Cove Publications, 5620 Covington Road, Shorewood, MN 55331. Telephone: (888) 218-3224.

Delmar: Contact ITP, P.O. Box 6904, Florence, KY 41022. Telephone: (800) 347-7707; (606) 525-2230.

Dutton Children's Books, 375 Hudson Street, New York, NY 10014. Telephone: (212) 366-2000.

ERIC Document Reproduction Service (EDRS), CBIS Federal, Inc., 7420 Fullerton Road, Suite 110, Springfield, VA 22153-2852. Telephone: (800) 443-3742; (703) 440-1400.

Falmer Press: Contact Taylor and Francis, 1900 Frost Road, Suite 101, Bristol, PA 19007-1598. Telephone: (800) 821-8312.

Family Resource Center on Disabilities, 20 East Jackson Boulevard, Room 900, Chicago, IL 60604. Telephone: (800) 952-4199 (V/TTY; toll-free in IL only); (312) 939-3513 (V).

Greenwood Publishing, 88 Post Road West, Box 5007, Westport, CT 06881. Telephone: (800) 225-5800; (203) 226-3571.

Grey House Publishing, Pocket Knife Square, Lakeville, CT 06039. Telephone: (800) 562-2139.

Guildford Press, 72 Spring Street, New York, NY 10012. Telephone: (800) 365-7006.

Harcourt Brace College Press, Division of Harcourt Brace Publishers, 6277 Sea Harbor Drive, Orlando, FL 32887. Telephone: (800) 782-4479.

Haworth Press, 10 Alice Street, Binghamton, NY 13904. Telephone: (800) 429-6784.

HEATH Resource Center, One Dupont Circle, Suite 800, Washington, DC 20036-1193. Telephone: (202) 939-9320 (V/TTY).

Hope Press, P.O. Box 188, Duarte, CA 91009. Telephone: (800) 321-4039.

Houghton Mifflin, 181 Ballard Vale Street, Wilmington, MA 01887-7050. Telephone: (800) 225-1464.

Hunter House, P.O. Box 2914, Alameda, CA 94501. Telephone: (800) 266-5592.

Insight Books, Division of Plenum Press, 233 Spring Street, New York, NY 10013. Telephone: (800) 221-9369

JKL Communications, P.O. Box 40157, Washington, DC 20016. Telephone: (202) 223-5097.

Johns Hopkins University Press, Hampden Station, Baltimore, MD 21211. Telephone: (800) 537-5487.

Jossey-Bass, 350 Sansome Street, 5th Floor, San Francisco, CA 94104-1310. Telephone: (800) 274-4434.

Krieger, P.O. Box 9542, Melbourne, FL 32902. Telephone: (407) 724-9542.

Learner Managed Designs, Inc., P.O. Box 747, Lawrence, KS 66044. Telephone: (785) 842-9088 or (800) 467-1644.

Learning Disabilities Association of America (LDA), 4156 Library Road, Pittsburgh, PA 15234. Telephone: (412) 341-1515; (412) 341-8077.

L. Erlbaum, 365 Broadway, Hillsdale, NJ 07642. Telephone: (201) 666–4110. Orders only to: (800) 926-6579.

Longman, see Addison-Wesley.

Love Publishing, P.O. Box 22353, Denver, CO 80222. Telephone: (303) 757-2579.

LRP, Inc., 747 Dresher Road, P.O. Box 980, Horsham, PA 19044-0980. Telephone: (800) 341-7874, extension 275.

Merrill, see Prentice Hall.

Mid-South Regional Resource Center (MSRRC), Human Development Institute, University of Kentucky, 126 Mineral Industries Building, Lexington, KY 40506-0051. Telephone: (606) 257-4921 (V); (606) 257-2903 (TTY)

Mills & Sanderson Publishers: for books by Nancy Wilson, contact Nancy Wilson, 135 Lake Terrace Drive, Monroe Falls, OH 44262. Telephone: (330) 686-0805. URL: http://www.bright.net/—srwilson/index.html

---

Obtaining Journal Articles

Articles in professional journals may be found at your local college or university library, or you may be able to obtain copies directly from the journal's publishers. Some journal publishers may make copies of articles available through duplication services. Three common services are listed below; all three accept requests on-line.

University Microfilms International (UMI), 300 North Zeeb Road, P.O. Box 1346, Ann Arbor, MI 48106-1346. Telephone: (800) 248-0360. URL: http://wwwlib.umi.com/infostore

Copyright Clearance Center, 222 Rosewood Drive, Danvers, MA 01923. Telephone: (508) 750-8400. URL: http://www.copyright.com/

Uncover Web, 3801 East Florida Avenue, Suite 200, Denver, CO 80210. Telephone: (303) 758-3030, ext. 1523. URL: http://uncweb.carl.org

---

Mountain Plains Regional Resource Center (MPRRC-UTAH), Utah State University, 1780 North Research Parkway, Suite 112, Logan, UT 84341-9620. Telephone: (801) 752-0238. (801) 753-9750 (TTY).

National Association for the Education of Young Children (NAEYC), 1509 16th Street, NW, Washington, DC 20036-1426. Telephone: (202) 232-8777; (800) 424-2460.

National Association of State Directors of Special Education, 1800 Diagonal Road, Suite 320, Alexandria, VA 22314. Telephone: (703) 519-3800 (V); (703) 519-7008 (TTY).

National Center on Educational Outcomes (NCEO), University of Minnesota, 350 Elliott Hall, 75 East River Road, Minneapolis, MN 55455. Telephone: (612) 626-1530 (V); (612) 624-4848 (TTY).

National Clearinghouse for Bilingual Education (NCBE), 1118 22nd Street, NW, Washington, DC 20037. Telephone: (202) 467-0867 (V). Fax requests to: (800) 531-9347.

National Council on Disability (NCD), 1331 F Street, NW, 10th Floor, Washington, DC 20004-1107. Telephone: (202) 272-2004; (202) 267-3232 (TTY).

National Early Childhood Technical Assistance System (NEC*TAS), University of North Carolina at Chapel Hill, 500 NationsBank Plaza, 137 East Franklin Street, Chapel Hill, NC 27514. Telephone: (919) 962-2001 (V); (919) 966-4041 (TTY).

National Education Association (NEA), Room 710, Section BT, 1201 16th Street, NW, Washington, DC 20036-3290. Telephone: (202) 833-4000 (main number); (800) 229-4200 (professional library).

National Information Center for Children and Youth with Disabilities (NICHCY), P.O. Box 1492, Washington, DC 20013. Telephone: (800) 695-0285 (V/TTY).

Nolo Press, 950 Parker Street, Berkeley, CA 94710. Telephone: (510) 549-1976.

Office of Indian Education Programs (OIEP), Bureau of Indian Affairs (BIA), 1849 C Street, NW, MS-3512-MIB-OIE-23, Washington, DC 20240. Telephone: (202) 208-3596 (V).

PACER Center, 4826 Chicago Avenue South, Minneapolis, MN 55417-1098. Telephone: (612) 827-2966 (V/TTY); (800) 537-2237 (V/TTY, in MN only).

Parent Educational Advocacy Training Center (PEATC), 10340 Democracy Lane, Suite 206, Fairfax, VA 22030. Telephone: (703) 691-7826.

Paul H. Brookes Publishing Company, P.O. Box 10624, Baltimore, MD 21285-0624. Telephone: (800) 638-3775.

Penguin Putnam Publishing Group, Attention: Mail Order, 390 Murray Hill Parkway, East Rutherford, NJ 07073. Telephone: (800) 631-8571.

Peytral Publishing, P.O. Box 1162, Minnetanka, MN 55345. Telephone: (612) 949-8707.

Pfeiffer & Co., see Jossey-Bass.

Phi Delta Kappa International, P.O. Box 789, Bloomington, IN 47402-0789. Telephone: (800) 766-1156

Prentice Hall, 111 10th Street, Des Moines, IA 50395. Telephone: (800) 947-7700.

Prima Publishing, P.O. Box 1260, Rocklin, CA 95677. Telephone: (800) 632-8676.

Pro-Ed, 8700 Shoal Creek Boulevard, Austin, TX 78758. Telephone: (512) 451-3246.

Putnam Publishing, see Penguin Putnam Publishing Group.

Resources for Rehabilitation, 33 Bedford Street, Suite 19A, Lexington, MA 02173. Telephone: (617) 862-6455.

RESNA, 1700 North Moore Street, Suite 1540, Arlington, VA 22209-1903. Telephone: (540) 542-6686 (V); (540) 524-6639 (TTY).

Singular Publishing, 401 West A Street, Suite 325, San Diego, CA 92101. Telephone: (800) 521-8545; (619) 238-6777.

Social Security Administration (SSA), Department of Health and Human Services, Baltimore, MD 21235. Contact the Communications Office, (410) 965-0921.

Sopris West, 4093 Specialty Place, Longmont, CO 80504. Telephone: (800) 547-6747; (303) 651-2829.

South Atlantic Regional Resource Center (SARRC), Florida Atlantic University, 1236 North University Drive, Plantation, FL 33322. Telephone: (954) 473-6106.

State University of New York Press, State University Plaza, Albany, NY 12246. Telephone: (518) 472-5000.

Teachers College Press, P.O. Box 20, Williston, VT 05495. Telephone: (800) 488-2665.

Temple University Press, 1601 N. Broad Street, Philadelphia, PA 19122-4919. (215) 707-2000; (800) 447-1656 (orders).

University of Illinois Children's Research Center Press: Contact IRHD Publications, 61 Children's Research Center, 51 Gerty Drive, Champaign, IL 61820. Telephone: (217) 333-4123.

Wadsworth: Contact ITP Distribution Center, Customer Service, 7625 Empire Drive, Florence, KY 41042. Telephone: (800) 354-9706.

Woodbine House, 6510 Bells Mill Road, Bethesda, MD 20817. Telephone: (800) 843-7323; (301) 897-3570.

Bibliography

Academy for Educational Development. (1993). *School reform and youth transition*. Washington, DC: Academy for Educational Development.

Affleck, J., Edgar, E., Levine, P., & Kortering, L. (1990). Post-school status of students classified as mildly mentally retarded, learning disabled, or non-handicapped: Does it get better with time? *Education and Training in Mental Retardation, 25,* 315–324.

American Federation of Teachers. (1999, March 19). Public comment at the *IDEAs That Work* teleconference, Galludet College, Washington DC.

American Vocational Association. (1994, October 10). Clinton signs vocational education appropriations. *Vocational Education Weekly,* p. 4.

American Vocational Association. (1998). *AVA official guide to the Perkins Act of 1998,* Alexandria, VA.: Author.

American Youth Policy Forum. (1993). *Improving the transition from school to work in the United States.* New York: Author.

Americans With Disabilities Act of 1990, 42 U.S.C.A. §12101 et seq. (West 1993).

Appling, R. N. (1998). *The School-to-Work Opportunities Act.* (Congressional Research Service No. 98-541). Washington, DC: Penny Hill Press.

Appling, R. N. (1998). *Vocational education: Overview of the Carl D. Perkins Vocational and Applied Technology Education Act.* (Congressional Research Service No. 97-283EPW). Washington, DC: Renny Hill Press.

Asche, M. (1993). *The impact of educational reform on vocational education.* Berkeley, CA: National Center for Research in Vocational Education.

Association for Supervision and Curriculum Development. (1990). *Public schools of choice* (Issues Analysis Series No. 90-33927). Alexandria, VA: Author.

Association for Supervision and Curriculum Development. (1998). *Changing school culture through staff development.* Alexandria, VA: Author.

Baer, R., Simmons, T., & Flexer, R. (1997). Transition practice and policy compliance in Ohio: A survey of secondary special educators. *Career Development for Exceptional Individuals, 19*(1), 61–72.

Barlow, M. (1990). Historical background of vocational education. In A. Paulter, Jr., (Ed.), *Vocational education in the 1990s: Major issues* (pp. 5–24). Ann Arbor, MI: Prakken.

Bates, P., Bronkema, J., Ames, T., & Hess, C. (1992). State level interagency planning models. In F. Rusch, L. Destefano, J. Chadsey-Rusch, L. A. Phelps, & E. Szymanski (Eds.), *Transition from school to adult life: Models, linkages and policy.* Sycamore, IL: Sycamore Publishing.

Bates, P., Suter, C., & Poelvoorde, R. (1986). *Illinois Transition Plan: Final report.* Chicago: Governor's Planning Council on Developmental Disabilities.

Behrman, R. (Ed.). (1992). School-linked services. *The Future of Children, 2*(1), 4–18.

Behrmann, M. (1984). *Handbook of microcomputers in special education.* San Diego: College-Hill.

Benz, M., & Kochhar, C. (1996). School-to-Work Opportunities Act: A position statement. *Development for Exceptional Individuals, 19*(1), 31–48.

Benz, M. R., & Lindstrom, L. (1997). *Building collaborative school-to-work transition programs: Strategies for special needs youth.* Austin, TX: Pro-Ed.

Benz, M. R., Lindstrom, L., & Halpern, A. S. (1995). Mobilizing local communities to improve transition services. *Career Development for Exceptional Individuals, 19*(1), 133–144.

Benz, M. R., Yovanoff, P., & Doren, B. (1997). Building school-to-work programs for all students: What components predict success for students with and without disabilities. *Exceptional Children, 64*(2), 69–83.

Bernhardt, V., & Higgins, P. (1992). *Framework for school change.* San Francisco: Pacific Telesis Foundation.

Biklen, D. (Ed.). (1985). *Achieving the complete school: Strategies for effective mainstreaming.* New York: Teachers College Press.

Biklen, D. (1992). Typing to talk: Facilitated communication. *American Journal of Speech Language Pathology, 1*(2), 15–17.

Board of Education of Hendrick Hudson Central School District v. Rowley. 458 U.S. 176, 103 S. Ct. 3034. (1982). 73 L.Ed. 2d 690, 5 Ed. Law Rep. 34, p. 3.

Board of Education v. Rowley, 458 U.S. 176 (1982).

Bonnadonna v. Cooperman, 619 F. Supp, 401, 28 Ed. Law Rep. 430 (D. N.J. 1985).

Braun v. Board of Education, 347 U.S. 483, 74 S. Ct. 686, 98 L. Ed. 873 (1954).

Brown v. Board of Education of Topeka, Kansas, 347 U.S. 483 (1954).

Bruno, R., Johnson, C., & Gilliard, J. (1994). A comparison of reform in special education in England and in Kentucky, USA. *Instructional Journal of Special Education, 9*(1), 53–64.

Bryson, J. M. (1988). *Strategic planning for public and non-profit organizations.* San Francisco: Jossey-Bass.

Bussey, K., & Bandura, A. (1992). Self-regulation mechanisms governing gender development. *Child Development, 63,* 1236–1250.

Carkhuff, R. R. (1993). *The art of helping VII* (7th ed.). Amherst, MA: Human Resource Development.

Carl D. Perkins Vocational and Applied Technology Education Act of 1990. Pub. L. No. 101–392.

Carl D. Perkins Vocational and Technical Education Act Amendments of 1998. Pub. L. No. 105–800.

Carnegie Forum on Education and the Economy. (1986). *A nation prepared: Teachers for the 21st Century.* New York: Carnegie Corporation.

Carnegie Foundation for the Advancement of Teaching. (1999). Web site: www.carnegiefoundation.org/history.html.

Carnine, D., & Kameenui, E. (1990). The general education initiative and children with special needs: A false dilemma in the face of true problems. *Journal of Learning Disabilities, 23,* 141–44.

Cashman, J. (1998). Design and plausibility in school to work systems developed to serve all students, with implications for individuals with disabilities. Unpublished doctoral dissertation.

Center for Policy Options. (1992). *Issues and options in restructing and special education programs.* College Park: University of Maryland.

Center for the Study of Social Policy. (1991). *Kids count data book: State profiles for child well-being.* Washington, DC: Author.

Cetron, M., & Gayle, M. (1991). *Educational renaissance: Our schools at the turn of the twenty-first century.* New York: St. Martin's.

Chalmers, L., & Faliede, E. (1996). Successful inclusion of students with mild/moderate disabilities in rural school settings. *Teaching Exceptional Children, 29*(1), 22–25.

Chubb, J. E., & Moe, T. M. (1990). *Politics, markets, and American schools.* Washington, DC: The Brookings Institution.

Churchill, A., Lashman, R., Gibbs, L., & Carlson, H. (1995). *Key STW system components: The initial eight STWOA grantees.* Paper compiled for the National School-to-Work Office, Washington, DC.

Clark, C. R., & Bott, D. A. (1991). Issues in implementing the Adaptive Learning Environments Model. *Teacher Education and Special Education, 14*(1), 26–39.

Clark, G., & Kolstoe, O. (1995). *Career development and transition education for adolescents with disabilities* (3rd ed.). Boston: Allyn & Bacon.

Cobb, B., & Johnson, D. (1997). The statewide systems change initiative as a federal policy mechanism for promoting educational reform. *Career Development for Exceptional Individuals, 20*(2), 179–190.

Convention on the Rights of the Child in the United Nations. (1990). *Human rights the rights of the child* (Fact Sheet No. 10, Articles 2/1 and 23). See also *The Declaration of the rights of the child,* adopted by the U.N. General Assembly on 20 November 1959 and recognized in the *Universal Declaration of Human Rights.* New York: United Nations.

Cornett, L. M. (1995). Lessons for 10 years of teacher improvement reforms. *Educational Leadership, 52*(5).

Council of Chief State School Officers. (1998). *What every special educator should know about the changing social policy landscape and efforts to ensure student success.* Alexandria, VA: Author.

Council of Chief State School Officers (CCSSO). (1991). *Families in school: State strategies and policies to improve family involvement in education. A four-state case study.* Washington, DC: Author.

Council for Children with Behavioral Disorders. (1997). Position statement on inclusion. Reston, VA: The Council for Exceptional Children.

The Council for Exceptional Children. (1993). *Federal outcomes for exceptional children.* Reston, VA: Author.

The Council for Exceptional Children. (1997). *Position paper on delivery of services to students with disabilities.* Reston, VA: Council of Administrators of Special Education.

The Council for Exceptional Children. (1994). *Issues in the implementation of IDEA.* Reston, VA: Author.

The Council for Exceptional Children. (1995). CEC launches drive to protect IDEA, special education funding. *CEC Today, 1*(10), 1–2.

Crain-Thoreson, C., McLendon-Magruson, D., & Lippman, M. (1987). Windows on comprehension: Reading comprehension processes as revealed by two read-aloud procedures. *Journal of Educational Psychology, 89*(4), 69–82.

Cuban, L. (1988). You're on the right track. *Phi Delta Kappan, 70*(3), 571–573.

Dalheim, M. (Ed.). (1994). *Toward inclusive classrooms.* Washington, DC: National Education Association.

Darling-Hammond, L. (1994). Performance-based assessment with education equality. *Harvard Educational Review, 64*(1), 5–30.

Data Research Inc. (1997). *Statues, regulations, and case law protecting individuals with disabilities.* Rosemont, MT: Author.

DeStefano, L., Hasazi, S., & Trach, J. (1997). Issues in the evaluation of a multi-state federal systems change initiative. *Career Development for Exceptional Individuals, 20*(2), 123–140.

DeStefano, L., Heck, D., Hasazi, S., & Furney, K. (1999). Enhancing the implementation of the transition requirements of IDEA: A report on the policy forum on transition. *Career Development for Exceptional Children, 22*(1), 89–99.

Developmental Disabilities Act of 1984, 42 U.S.C., 6001 *et. seq.*

Developmentally Disabled Assistance and Bill of Rights Act of 1975, 42 U.S.C., 6001 *et. seq.*

Division for Early Childhood. (1996). *Position statement on inclusion.* Reston, VA: The Council for Exceptional Children.

Dodd, A. W. (1999). *How parents and students can enrich the work of a community of learners.* Alexandria, VA: National Association of Secondary School Principals.

Dover, W. (1994). *The inclusion facilitator.* Manhattan, KS: Master Teacher.

Dunivant, N. (1986). The relationship between learning disabilities and juvenile delinquency: Current state of knowledge. *Remedial and Special Education 7*(3), 18–26.

Dunn, W. (1994). *Public policy analysis: An introduction.* Upper Saddle River, NJ: Prentice Hall.

Edgar, E. (1991). Providing ongoing support and making appropriate placements: An alternative to transition planning for mildly handicapped students. *Preventing School Failure, 35*(2), 36–39.

Education for All Handicapped Children Act, 20 U.S.C. 1400 *et. seq.*

Education Goals Panel. (1993). *Summary of the National Education Summit.* Washington, DC: Author.

Educational Testing Service. (1992). *Beyond the school doors: The literacy needs of job seekers served by the U.S. Department of Labor.* Princeton, NJ: Author.

Epstein, S. (1995). Learning in the right places. *Journal of Learning Sciences, 4*(3), 281 to 319.

Erickson, M., & Kochhar, C. (1991). *Evaluating business–education partnerships: Simple to complex.* Alexandria, VA: National Association of Partners in Education.

Erickson, R. (1997). *Accountability, standards, and assessment.* Washington, DC: Federal Resource Center.

Evans, D. (1993). Restructuring special education services. *Teacher Education and Special Education, 19,* 137–145.

Evans, K., & King, J. (1994). Research on outcomes-based education: What we know and don't know. *Educational Leadership, 51*(6), 18–22.

Evans, S. (1995, March 18). Able-bodied students deal with disabilities. *The Washington Post,* p. B1.

Everson, J. M., Barcus, M., Moon, M. S., & Horton, W. (1987). *Achieving outcome: A guide to interagency training in transition and supported employment.* Richmond: Virginia Commonwealth University, Project Transition into Employment.

Fabian, E., Luecking, R., & Tilson, G. (1994). *A working relationship—The job development specialist's guide to successful partnerships with business.* Baltimore: Brookes.

The Fair Labor Standards Act, Publ. L. No. 99–486.

Fedoruk, G. (1989). Kindergarten screening for first grade learning problems: The conceptual inadequacy of a child-deficit model. *Childhood Education, 66,* 40–42.

Feichner, S., & Apolloni, T. (1990). *Career vocational education for special populations IMPACT plan: An approach for planning school improvement.* Sonoma: Sonoma State University, California Institute on Human Services.

Field, S., & Hoffman, A. (1994). Development of a model for self-determination. *Career Development for Exceptional Individuals, 17,* 159–170.

Field, S., Martin, J., Miller, R., Ward, M., & Wehmeyer, M. (1998). *A practical guide for teaching self-determination.* Reston, VA: The Council for Exceptional Children, Division on Career Development and Transition.

Fiske, K. J., & Todd, S. S. (1994). *Classroom strategies for assessing limited English proficient students in vocational programs: A resource handbook.* Chevy Chase, MD: Crosspaths Management Systems.

Fitzpatrick, K. A. (1991). Restructuring to achieve outcomes of significance for all students. *Educational Leadership, 48*(8), 49–65.

Fraser, B., Hubbard, S., Chaner, L., & Weinbauer, A. (1993). *School reform and youth transition: Literature review and annotated bibliography.* Washington, DC: Academy for Education Development, National Institute for Work and Learning.

Frazier, K. (1993). The state of American education. *Rethinking Schools, 8*(2), 16–17.

Friend, M., & Bursuck, W. (1999). *Including students with special needs: A practical guide for classroom teachers* (2nd ed.). Needham Heights, MA: Allyn & Bacon.

Friend, M., & Cook, L. (1996). *Interactions: Collaboration skills for school professionals* (2nd ed.). White Plains, NY: Longman.

Fuchs, D., & Fuchs, L. S. (1986). Effects of systematic formative evaluation: A meta-analysis. *Exceptional Children, 53,* 199–208.

Fuchs, D., & Fuchs, L. S. (1994). Inclusive schools and the radicalization of special education reform. *Exceptional Children, 60,* 294–309.

Gardner, H. (1983, 1992). *Frames of mind: The theory of multiple intelligences.* New York: Basic Books.

Gardner, S. (1992). Key issues in developing school-linked, integrated services. *The Future of Children (Annual report), 2*(1), 6–18.

Gartner, A., & Lipsky, D. K. (1990). Students as instructional agents. In S. Stainback & W. Stainback (Eds.), *Support systems for educating all students in the mainstream* (pp. 81–94). Baltimore: Brookes.

Gartner, A., & Lipsky, D. K. (1992). Beyond special education: Toward a quality system for all students. *Harvard Educational Review* Reprint series no. 23, 123–157.

Gerald, D. (1997). High school graduates. In D. Gerald & W. Hussar (Eds.), *Projections of education statistics to 2007* (pp. 49–52). Washington, DC: National Center for Educational Statistics.

Gerhard, R. J., Dorgan, R. E., & Miles, R. G. (1981). *The balanced service system: A model of personal and social integration.* Clinton, OK: Responsive Systems.

Gerry, M. H., & McWhorter, C. M. (1990). A comprehensive analysis of federal statutes and programs for persons with severe disabilities. In L. H., Meyer, C. A. Pack, & L. Brown (Eds.), *Critical issues in the lives of people with severe disabilities* (pp. 495–527). Baltimore: Brookes.

Golby, M., & Gulliver, J. R. (1985). Whose remedies, whose ills? A critical review of remedial education. In C. J. Smith (Ed.), *New directions in remedial education* (pp. 7–19). London: Falmer.

Goodlad, J. I. (1991). Better teachers for our nation's schools. *Educational Leadership. 48*(8), 9–11.

Gordon, E. (1973). Broadening the concept of career education, In McClure, D. & Buan, E. (Eds.), *Essays on career education*. Portland, OR: Northwest Regional Educational Laboratory.

Gordon, H. (1999). *History and growth of vocational education in America*. Needham Heights, MA: Allyn & Bacon.

Guy, B., Goldberg, M., McDonald, S., & Flom, R. (1997). Parental participation in transition systems change. *Career Development for Exceptional Individuals, 20*(2), 165–178.

Guy, B., & Johnson, D. (1997). Career development for exceptional individuals: Topical issue systems change in transition. *Career Development for Exceptional Individuals. 20*(2), 107–108.

Guy, B., & Schriner, K. (1997). Systems in transition: Are we there yet? *Career Development for Exceptional Individuals, 20*(2), 141–164.

Hallahan, D. P., & Kaufman, J. M. (1997. *Exceptional children: Introduction to special education* (6th ed.). Needham Heights, MA: Allyn & Bacon.

Halloran, W., & Simon, M. (1995). The transition service requirement. A federal perspective on issues, implications and challenges. *Journal of Vocational Special Needs Education, 17*(3), 94–98.

Halpern, A. (1987a). Transition: A look at the foundations. *Exceptional Children, 51,* 463.

Halpern, A. (1987b). Characteristics of quality programs. In C. S. Warger and B. B. Weiner (Eds.), *Secondary special education: A guide to promising public school programs* (pp. 25–55). Reston, VA: The Council for Exceptional Children.

Halpern, A. (1994). The transition of youth with disabilities to adult life: A position statement of the Division on Career Development and Transition, the Council for Exceptional Children. *Career Development for Exceptional Individuals, 17,* 115–124.

Halpern, R. (1990). Community based interventions. In S. J. Meisels & J. P. Sharkoff (Eds.), *Handbook for early childhood intervention* (pp. 469–498). Cambridge, England: Cambridge University Press.

Hammond, L. (1994). *The current status of teaching and teacher development in the U.S.* Washington, DC: National Commission on Teaching and America's Future.

Hansen, S. (1993). Career development trends and issues in the U.S. *Journal of Career Development, 20*(1) 7–24.

Hardman, M., Drew, C., & Egan, M. (1999). *Human exceptionality: Society, school, and family* (6th ed.). Needham Heights, MA: Allyn & Bacon.

Harris, K. C. (1991). An expanded view on consultation competencies for educators serving culturally and linguistically diverse exceptional children. *Teacher Education and Special Education. 14*(1), 49–63.

Hehir, Y. T., & Latus, T. (Eds.). (1992). Special education at the century's end: Evolution of theory and practice. *Harvard Educational Review* (Reprint series no. 23).

Henderson, A. T. (1987). *The evidence continues to grow: Parent involvement improves student achievement.* Columbia, MD: National Center for Citizens in Education.

Herman, J. L., Aschbacher, P. R., & Winters, L. (1992). *A practical guide to alternative assessment.* Alexandria, VA: Association for Supervision and Curriculum Development.

Higher Education Act of 1965, Publ. L. No. 89–329.

Hoachlander, G. (1998). Taking responsibility for academic achievement: A new standard for vocational education. *Centerwork, 9*(4).

Hodgkinson, H. (1991). Reform versus reality. *Phi Delta Kappan, 73*(1), 8–16.

Honig v. Doe 108 S. Ct. 592 (1988).

Hoover, J. J., & Collier, C. (1991a). Teacher preparation for educating culturally and linguistically diverse exceptional learners: Overview of topical issue. *Teacher Education and Special Education, 14*(1), 69–83.

Hoover, J. J., & Collier, C. (1991b). Meeting the needs of culturally and linguistically diverse exceptional learners: Prereferral to mainstreaming. *Teacher Education and Special Education, 14*(1), 89–99.

Horne, R. (1996 December). Transition from school to work. *The Alliance Newsletter,* pp. 1–2.

Hoyt, K. (1991). Education reform and relationship between the private sector and education: A call for integration. *Phi Delta Kappan, 72*(8), 364–372.

Hoyt, K. (1995). *Career education: A vital component in the transition of youth from schooling to employment.* 〈http://members.mint.net/lifework/hoytl〉 National Career Development Web site, Columbus, Ohio.

H. R. Rep. No. 101-544. 101st Congress, 4th Session (1990).

H. R. Rep. No. 1953. 105th Congress, 1st Session (1998).

Hueman, J. & Hehir, T. (1999, September 19). Initial disciplinary guidance related to the removal of children with disabilities from their current educational placement (Memorandum no. OSEP97-7). Washington, DC: U.S. Department of Education, Office of Special Education and Rehabilitative Services.

Hughes-Booker, A. (1994). *A survey of teachers in the District of Columbia Public Schools on the changing nature of seriously emotionally disturbed youth.* Unpublished doctoral dissertation, George Washington University.

Improving America's Schools Act of 1994 (ESEA), 20 U.S.C. §6301 (1994).

Individuals with Disabilities Education Act. Final Rules and Regulations. (1999, March 12). *Federal Register, 64*(48), 12239–12742.

Individuals with Disabilities Education Act Amendments of 1997, Publ. L. No. 105–17.

Janney, R., & Meyer, L. (1990). *Child centered educational consultation to assist schools in serving students with disabilities and severe behavior problems in integrated settings.* Syracuse, New York: Syracuse University, Division of Special Education and Rehabilitation.

Janney, R., Snell, M. E., Beers, M. K., & Raynes, M. (1995). Integrating students with moderate and severe disabilities into general education classes. *Exceptional Children, 61,* 425–439.

Job Training Reform Act of 1993, Publ. L. No. 102–367.

Johnson, A., Johnson, J., & DeMatta, R. (1991). Predictive exploration of the educational-failure paradigm. *Canadian Journal of Special Education, 7,* 164–180.

Johnson, D., & Guy, B. (1997). Implications of the lessons learned from a state systems change initiative on transition for youth with disabilities. *Career Development for Exceptional Individuals, 20*(2), 191–200.

Johnson, D., & Halloran, W. (1997). The federal legislative context and goals of the state systems change initiative on transition for youth with disabilities. *Career Development for Exceptional Individuals, 20*(2), 109–122.

Johnson, D., & Johnson, R. (1978). Many teachers wonder . . . Will the special-needs child ever really belong? *Instructor, 87,* 152–154.

Joint Task Force for the Management of Children with Special Needs of the AFT, CFC, NASM, and MSA. (1990). *Guidelines for the delineation of roles and responsibilities for the safe delivery of specialized health care in educational settings.* Reston, VA: The Council for Exceptional Children.

Jones, L. T. (1991). *Strategies for involving parents in their children's education.* Bloomington, IN: Phi Delta Kappa Educational Foundation.

Kagan, S. L. (1991). *Collaboration in action: Reshaping services to young children and their families.* Unpublished manuscript, Yale University, The Bush Center in Child Development and Social Policy, New Haven, CT.

Kauffman, J. M. (1993). How we might achieve the radical reform of special education. *Exceptional Children, 60,* 6–16.

Kauffman, J. M., & Hallahan, D. P. (1993). Toward a comprehensive service delivery system. In J. J. Goodlad & T. C. Lovett (Eds.), *Integrating general and special education.* Upper Saddle River, NJ: Merrill/Prentice Hall.

Kiernan, W., & Schalock, R. (1989). *Economics, industry and disability.* Baltimore: Brookes.

Kinkead, L. (1995). Trials and tribulations of a first year team teacher. In J. M. Taymans (Ed.), *Cases in urban teaching* (pp. 23–29). Washington, DC: George Washington University.

Klein, S., Medrich, E., & Perez-Ferriero, V. (1996). *Fitting the pieces: Education reform that works.* Washington, DC: U.S. Department of Education, Office of Educational Research and Improvement.

Kochhar, C. (1987). Development of an evaluation model for case management services to developmentally disabled persons in community-based settings. *Dissertation Abstracts International.* (University Microfilms No. 87–25, 264).

Kochhar, C. (1995a). Future directions in federal legislation affecting transition services for individuals with special needs. *Journal of Vocational Special Needs Education, 17*(3), 85–94.

Kochhar, C. A. (1995b). How well do school-to-work plans promote full participation for all students? In J. Gugerty (Ed.), *Tech Prep Advocate: Preparing Students with Disabilities for the Workplace.* Madison: University of Wisconsin, Center on Education and Work.

Kochhar, C. (1995c). *Training for interagency, interdisciplinary service coordination: An instructional modules series.* Des Moines: Iowa State Department of Education and the Mountain Plains Regional Resource Center, Drake University.

Kochhar, C. (1997). Capital Capsule: Policy directions for youth development under the new administration and congress. *Journal of Vocational Special Needs Education, 18*(2), 86–91.

Kochhar, C. (1998). *Literature synthesis on alternative schools and programs for violent, chronically disruptive, and delinquent youth. Hamilton Fish Institute on School and Community Violence.* Washington, DC: The George Washington University, Institute for Educational Policy Studies.

Kochhar, C. (1999). *Participation of youth with disabilities in the Carl D. Perkins Vocational and Applied Technology Education Act Amendments of 1998. Journal of Vocational Special Needs Education.*

Kochhar, C., & Erickson, M. (1993). *Partnerships for the 21st century: Developing business–education partnerships for school improvement.* Gaithersburg, MD: Aspen.

Kochhar, C., & Leconte, P. (1997). Slouching toward full participation in the work of the nation: States' responsibility for career-vocational education. *Journal of Vocational Special Needs Education, 19*(3), 103–116.

Kochhar, C., Leconte, P., & Ianacone, R. (1987). *Frontiers in employment training: Relating the Job Training Partnership Act to vocational education for persons with handicaps.* Washington, DC: The George Washington University.

Kochhar, C., & West, L. (1995). Future directions for federal legislation affecting transition services for individuals with special needs. *Journal of Vocational Special Needs Education, 17*(3), 83–93.

Kochhar, C., & West, L. (1996). *Handbook for successful inclusion.* Rockville, MD: Aspen.

Kohler, P. (1997). *A conceptual model of effective transition practiced.* Champaign, IL: University of Illinois, Transition Research Institute.

Kohler, P., Field, S., Izzo, M., & Johnson, J. (1998). *Transition from school to life: Workshop series for educators and transition service providers.* Chicago: University of Illinois, Transition Research Institute.

Kornblau, B. (1992). Preparing adolescents to enter the work force: The effects of the Americans with Disabilities Act. *WORK: A Journal of Prevention, Assessment & Rehabilitation, 2*(2), 15–19.

Kuhn, T. (1973). *The structure of scientific revolutions.* Chicago. University of Chicago Press.

Kupper, L. (1997). *The Individuals with Disabilities Education Act Amendments of 1997: Curriculum.* Washington, DC: National Information Center for Children and Youth with Disabilities.

Kvaraceus, W. (1963). Alienated youth here and abroad. *Phi Delta Kappan, 45*(2), 5–12.

Leconte, P. (1992). Back to basics: Fundamentals of vocational assessment. *Vocational Assessment and Evaluation Bulletin.* Washington, DC: The George Washington University.

Leconte, P. (1994a). *A perspective on vocational appraisal: Beliefs, practices, and paradigms.* Unpublished doctoral dissertation, The George Washington University.

Leconte, P. (1994b). Vocational appraisal services: Evolution from multidisciplinary origins and applications to interdisciplinary practices. *Vocational Evaluation and Work Adjustment Bulletin, 27*(4), 119–127.

Leone, P. E., Rutherford, R. B., & Nelson, C. M. (1991a). Juvenile corrections and the exceptional students. *ERIC Digest,* (No. E508), 2–3. (ERIC Document Reproduction Service No. 340 153)

Leone, P. E., Rutherford, R. B., & Nelson, C. M. (1991b). *Special education in juvenile corrections. Working with behavioral disorders.* (CEC Mini-Library). Reston, VA: The Council for Exceptional Children. (ERIC Document Reproduction Service No. 333 654).

Levine, E. (1994). *Annotated bibliography: Nine Issues of inclusion.* Washington, DC: National Education Association.

Levine, I. S., & Fleming, M. (1985). *Human resource development: Issues in case management.* (Human Resources Development Monograph). College Park: University of Maryland, Center for Rehabilitation and Manpower Services.

Lieberman, L. M. (1988). *Preserving special education, for those who need it.* Newtonville, MA: GloWorm.

Lieberman, L. M. (1990). RFI: Reunited . . . again. *Exceptional Children, 56,* 561–562.

Lipsky, D., & Gartner, A. (Eds.). (1989). *Beyond separate education: Quality education for all.* Baltimore: Brookes.

Lipsky, D., & Gartner, A. (1996). Inclusion, school restructuring, and the remaking of American society. *Harvard Educational Review, 66,* 762–796.

Lunenburg, F., & Ornstein, A. (1991). *Educational administration: Concepts and practices.* Belmont, CA: Wadsworth.

Lynch, J. (1995). *Provision for children with special education needs in the Asia Region.* (World Bank Technical Paper No. 261). Washington, DC: Asia Technical Department, Population and Human Resources Division, The World Bank.

Macmillan, D. (1991). *Hidden youth: Dropouts from special education.* Reston, VA: The Council for Exceptional Children.

Madaus, G. (1994). A technological and historical consideration of equity issues associated with proposals to change the nation's testing policy. *Harvard Educational Review, 64,* 26–95.

Malouf, D., & Schiller, E. (1995). Practice and research in special education. *Exceptional Children, 61,* 414–424.

Marsh, C., & Willis, G. (1999). *Curriculum: Alternative approaches, ongoing issues.* Upper Saddle River, NJ: Prentice Hall.

Martin, J., & Kohler, P. (1998). *Transition from school to life.* Chicago: Transition Research Institute, University of Illinois.

Martin, J. E., & Marshall, L. H. (1995). Choicemaker: A comprehensive self-determination transition program. *Intervention in School and Clinic, 3,* 30.

Marzano, R. (1994). Glances from the field about outcomes-based performance assessments. *Educational Leaderships, 51*(6), 44–50.

Marzano, R., Pickering, D., & McTighe, J. (1993). *Assessing student outcomes: Performance assessment using the dimensions of learning model.* Alexandria, VA: Association for Supervision and Curriculum Development.

McCoy, K. M. (1995). *Teaching special learners in the general education classroom: Methods and techniques* (2nd ed., pp. 13–30). Denver: Love.

McDaniel, L. (1992). Transition programs in correctional institutions. In F. Rusch, et al. (Eds.), *Transition from school to adult life: Models, linkages and policy* (pp. 425–442). Sycamore, IL: Sycamore Publishing.

McGilchrist, B. (1995, June 30). Change from top to toe: Creating the conditions for school improvement. In D. Hopkins, L. Stoll, K. Myers, J. Myers, J. Learmonth, & H. Durman (Eds.), Schools make a difference. *Times Educational Supplement.* p. 4122, 19.

McLaughlin, M., & Warren, S. (1992). *Issues and options in restructuring schools in special educational programs.* College Park: University of Maryland, Center for Policy Options in Special Education.

McLeskey, J., & Waldron, N. (1996). Responses to questions teachers and administrators frequently ask about inclusive school programs. *Phi Delta Kappan, 78,* 150–156.

McWorter, A. (1986). Mandate for quality: Examining the use of public authority to redesign mental retardation service systems. In *Changing the system: An analysis of New Brunswick's approach, 3.* Downsview, Ontario: New Brunswick Institute for Health Management.

Meers, G. (1993). On their own: Preparing disabled students for independent living and productive careers. *Vocational Education Journal, 68*(8), 30–31.

Meyen, E., & Skrtic, T. (1995). *Special education and student disability: Traditional, emerging, and alternative perspectives.* Denver: Love.

Michaels, C. (1994). *Transition strategies for persons with learning disabilities.* San Diego: Singular.

Miller, W. (1995, January 9). Test beds for school improvement. *Industry Week.* pp. 11–12.

Mills y. Board of Education of the District of Columbia. 348 F. Supp. 866 D.D.C. (1972).

Minow, M. (1996). Children's studies: A proposal. *Ohio State Law Journal, 57,* 511–575.

Mount, B., & Zwernik, K. (1988). *It's never too early; it's never too late: A booklet about personal futures planning.* Minneapolis: Metropolitan Council.

National Academy of Education. (1993). *The Trial State Assessment: Prospects and realities. The third report of the National Academy of Education Panel on the evaluation of the NAEP 1992 Trial State Assessment.* Palo Alto, CA: Stanford University.

National Alliance of Business. (1987). *The fourth R: Workforce readiness. A guide to business–education partnerships.* Washington, DC: Author.

National Association of Elementary School Principals. (1999). *An educators guide to school-wide reform.* Alexandria, VA: Author.

National Association of State Boards of Education. (1992). *Winners all: A call for inclusive school.* Alexandria, VA: Author.

National Association of State Directors of Special Education. (1993). *Critical information needs of state directors of special education.* Alexandria, VA: Author.

National Center for Education Statistics. (1997). Dropout rates in the United States: 1995. In *The condition of education 1996.* Washington, DC: U.S. Department of Education.

National Center for Educational Outcomes. (1994a). *Making decisions about the inclusion of students with disabilities in large-scale assessments—A report on a working conference to develop guidelines on inclusion and accommodations.* St. Paul: University of Minnesota, College of Education.

National Center for Educational Outcomes. (1994b). *Recommendations for making decisions about the participation of students with disabilities in statewide assessment programs—A report on a working conference to develop guidelines for statewide assessments and students with disabilities.* St. Paul: University of Minnesota, College of Education.

National Commission on Children. (1991). *Beyond rhetoric: A new American agenda for children and families.* Washington, DC: U.S. Government Printing Office.

National Commission on Employment Policy, 1981. *Youth Transition.* Washington, DC: Author.

National Community Service Act of 1990, 42 U.S.C. §12501.

National Council on Disability. (1993). *Serving the nation's students with disabilities: Progress and prospects: A report to the President and Congress of the United States.* Washington, DC: Author.

National Council on Disability. (1996). *Improving the implementation of the Individuals with Disabilities Education Act: Making schools work for all of America's children.* Washington, DC: Author.

National Criminal Justice Association. (1997, October). Juvenile boot camps. *Juvenile Justice Reform Initiatives in the States, 1994–1996.* Program Report [On-line]. Available: http://www.ncjrs.org/ojjdp/reform/ch2_g.html

National Education Association. (1994). *Toward inclusive classrooms.* West Haven, CT: National Education Association.

National Education Association. (1996). *American education statistics at a glance* [On-line]. Available: http://nea/org/society/96edstat.htm

National Education Goals Panel. (1993). *Handbook for local goals reports: Building a community of learners.* Washington, DC: Author.

National Education Goals Panel. (1994). *National education goals report: Building a nation of learners.* Washington, DC: U.S. Government Printing Office.

National Governors Association. (1996). *Summary of the Nebraska Mandate Management Initiative: A community-based process using risk assessment, cost-benefit analysis and common-sense government.* Washington, DC: Author.

National Information Center for Children and Youth with Disabilities. (1993). Including special education in the school community. *News Digest, 2*(2), 3.

National Joint Committee on Learning Disabilities. (1992). School reform: Opportunities for excellence and equity for individuals with learning disabilities. *Journal of Learning Disabilities, 25,* 276–280.

National Joint Committee on Learning Disabilities. (1994). Learning disabilities: Issues of definition, a position paper of the National Joint Committee on Learning Disabilities. In *Collective perspectives on issues affecting learning disabilities: Position papers and statements* (pp. 8–13). Austin, TX: Pro-Ed.

National Organization on Disability. (1994). *N.O.D. survey of Americans with Disabilities.* Washington, DC: Author.

National Research Council. (1993). *Losing generations: Adolescents in high risk settings.* Washington, DC: National Academy Press. Write to: 2101 Constitution Avenue, N.W., Box 285, Washington, DC, or call (800) 624-6242 or 202-334-3313.

National School Boards Association. (1995). *A survey of public education in the nation's urban school districts* (No. 056135). Alexandria, VA: Author.

National Service Trust Act of 1993, Publ. L. No. 103–82.

Neubert, D. A. (1994). Vocational evaluation and assessment in vocational-technical education: Barriers and facilitators to interdisciplinary services. *Vocational Evaluation and Work Adjustment Bulletin, 27*(4), 149–153.

The New American School Development Corporation. (1991). *Designs for a new generation of American schools. Request for proposals.* Arlington, VA: Author.

Nirje, B. (1976). The normalization principle. In R. B. Kugel & A. Shearer (Eds.), *Changing patterns in residential services for the mentally retarded* (Rev. ed., pp. 35–48). Washington, DC: President's Committee on Mental Retardation.

Nisbet, J., Covert, S., & Schuh, M. (1992). Family involvement in the transition from school to adult life. In F. Rusch, L. Destephano, J. Chadsay-Rusch, L. Phelps, C. E. Scymanski (Eds.), *Transition from school to adult life: Models, linkages and policy* (pp. 407–424). Sycamore, IL: Sycamore Publishing.

Oakes, J., & Lipton, M. (1992). Detracking schools: Early lessons from the field. *Phi Delta Kappan, 73,* 448–454.

Oberti v. Board of Education of the Borough of Clementon School District (C.A. 91-2818. D.N.J. 1992).

O'Brien, R. (1992). *Building supportive communities for youth: Local approaches to enhancing community youth services and supports.* Washington DC: Academy for Educational Development.

O'Brien, R. (1992). *Building supportive communities for youth: Local approaches to enhancing community youth services and supports.* Washington, DC: Academy for Educational Development.

O'Neil, J. (1995). On lasting school reform: A conversation with Ted Sizer. *Educational Leadership, 52*(5), 4–9.

Ortize, A., & Ramirez, B. (1988). *Schools and culturally diverse exceptional students.* Reston, VA: The Council for Exceptional Children.

Osborne, A. G. Jr. (1988). *Complete legal guide to special education services.* West Nyack, NY: Baker.

Osborne, A. G. Jr. (1992). Legal standards for appropriate education in the post-Rowley era. *Exceptional Children, 58,* 488–494.

Parese, S. (1998). *Study of the development of mentor relationships among Black youth in an alternative educational setting.* Unpublished doctoral dissertation.

Patton, J., & Blalock, G. (1996). *Transition and students with learning disabilities.* Austin, TX: Pro-Ed.

Pennsylvania Association for Retarded Citizens v. Commonwealth of Pennsylvania, 343 F. Supp. 279 (E.D. Pa., 1972).

Perrone, V. (Ed.). (1991). *Expanding student assessment.* Alexandria, VA: Association for Supervision and Curriculum Development.

Phelan, P., Dadison, A., & Yu, H. (1998). *Adolescents' worlds: Negotiating family, peers, and school.* New York: Teachers College Press.

Pisces Full Inclusion Project: *What inclusion is and what it is not.* (1994). Baltimore: Maryland State Department of Education.

Pullin, D. (1994). Learning to work: The impact of clinic and assessment standards in education opportunity. *Harvard Educational Review, 64*(1), 31–54.

Putnam, J. (1993). *Cooperative learning and strategies for inclusion: Celebrating diversity in the classroom.* Baltimore: Brookes.

Racino, J. A. (1992). Living in the community: Independence, support, and transition. In F. Rusch, L. Phelps, & E. Szymanski (Eds.), *Transition from school to adult life: Models, linkages, and policy* (pp. 131–152). Sycamore, IL: Sycamore Publishing.

Rawls, J. (1971). *A theory of justice.* Cambridge, MA: Harvard University Press; Sycamore, IL: Sycamore Publishing.

Raywid, M. (1991). Is there a case for choice? *Educational Leadership, 48*(4), 48–54.

Raywid, M. (1994). Synthesis of research: Alternative schools: The state of the art. *Educational Leadership, 52*(1), 26–30.

Rehabilitation Act Amendments of 1992, 19 U.S.C. §794.

Reich, R. (1991). *The work of nations: Preparing ourselves for 21th century capitalism.* New York: Knopf.

Report to the House Committee on Education and Labor on P. L. 101–476. (H. R. Rep. No. 101–544, 10). 101st Congress, First session, 1990.

Resnick, L. (1990). Literacy in school and out. *Dedalus, 119,* 169–190.

Reynolds, M. (1988). Reactions to the JLD special series on the regular education initiative. *Journal of Learning Disabilities, 21,* 352–356.

Reynolds, M. C., Wang, M. C., & Walberg, H. J. (1992). The knowledge base for special and general education. *Remedial and Special Education, 13*(5), 6–10.

Riffle, A., & Smith-Davis, J. (1991). *Planned change for personnel development: Strategic planning and the CSPD.* Lexington: Mid-South Regional Resource Center, University of Kentucky.

Rigden, D. (1992). *Business and the schools: Guide to effective programs.* New York: Council for Aid to Education.

Riley, R. (1995, June 20). *Testimony Before the House Subcommittee on Early Childhood, Youth and Families on the reauthorization of the Individuals with Disabilities Education Act (IDEA).*

Rojewski, J. (1992). Key components of model transition services for students with learning disabilities. *Learning Disability Quarterly, 15,* 135–150.

Rossi, P., Freeman, H., & Lipsey, M. (1999). *Evaluation: A systematic approach* (6th ed.). Thousand Oaks, CA: Sage.

Rothstein, L. (1995). *Special education law* (2nd ed.). White Plains, NY: Longman.

Rousseau, J. J. (1911). *Emile.* Boston: Tuttle.

Rowley v. Hendrick Hudson School District, 458 U.S. 176 (1982).

Rusch, F., DeStefano, L., Chadsey-Rusch, J., Phelps, L., & Szymanski, E. (1992). *Transition from school to adult life: Models, linkages, and policy.* Sycamore, Il: Sycamore Publishing.

S-1 v. Turlington, 635 F. 2d 342 (5th Cir. 1981).

Sage, D., & Burello, L. (1994). *Leadership in education reform: An administration's guide to changes in special education.* Baltimore: Brookes.

Sailor, W. (1991). Special education in the restricted school. *Remedial and Special Education, 12*(6), 8–22.

Sailor, W., Anderson, J., Halvorsen, A., Doering, K., Filler, J., & Goetz, L. (1989). *The comprehensive local school: Regular education for all students with disabilities.* Baltimore: Brookes.

Salisbury, C. L., Palombaro, M. M., & Hollowood, T. M. (1993). On the nature and change of an inclusive elementary school. *Journal of the Association for Persons with Severe Handicaps, 18,* 75–84.

Salvia, J., & Ysseldyke, J. (1988). *Assessment in special and remedial education* (4th ed.). Boston: Houghton-Miffin.

Sarason, S., & Doris, J. (1978). Mainstreaming: Dilemmas, opposition, opportunities. In M. C. Reynolds (Ed.), *Future of education for exceptional students: Emerging structures* (pp. 11 to 27). Reston, VA: The Council for Exceptional Children.

Sawyer, R. J., Mclaughlin, M. J., & Winglee, M. (1992). *Is integration of students with disabilities happening? An analysis of national data trends over time.* Rockville, MD: Westat.

Schalock, R. L. (1983). *Services for developmentally disabled adults: Development, implementation, and evaluation.* Baltimore: University Park Press.

Schalock, R. L., Harper, R. S., & Genung, T. (1989). Community integration of mentally retarded adults: Community placement and program success. *American Journal of Mental Deficiency, 85,* 478–488.

Scharff, D., & Hill, J. (1976). *Between two worlds: Aspects of the transition from school to work.* London: Careers Consultants.

Schattman, R., & Benay, J. (1992). Inclusive practices transform special education in the 1990s. *School Administration, 49*(2), 8–12.

Schmidt, M., & Harriman, N. (1998). *Teaching strategies for inclusive classrooms: Schools, students, strategies, and success.* New York: Harcourt Brace.

School-to-Work Opportunities Act of 1994, Publ. L. No. 103–239. (1985)

Separate and unequal: How special education programs are cheating our children and costing taxpayers billions each year. (1993, December 13). *U.S. News and World Report,* pp. 10–15.

Shapiro, H. (1990). Society, ideology, and the reform of special education: A study of the limits of educational change. *Educational Theory, 30*(3), 46–59.

Sherer, M. (1994). On schools where students want to be. *Educational Leadership, 52*(1), 26–40.

Shriner, J., Yesseldyke, J., Thinlaw, M., & Honetschlager, D. (1994). "All means all": Including students with disabilities. *Educational Leadership, 51*(6), 38–42.

Simon, M., Cobb, B., Halloran, W., Norman, M., & Bourexis, P. (1994). *Meeting the needs of youth with disabilities: Handbook for implementing community-based vocational education programs according to the Fair Labor Standards Act.* Washington, DC: U.S. Department of Education, Office of Special Education and Rehabilitative Services.

Simpson, R., & Sasso, G. (1992). Full inclusion of students with autism in general education settings: Values versus science. *Focus on Autistic Behavior, 7*(3), 1–13.

Singer, J. D., & Butler, J. A. (1987). The Education for All Handicapped Children Act: Schools as agents of school reform. *Harvard Educational Review, 57*(2), 27–35.

Sitlington, P. (1992). *Iowa follow-up study for youth with disabilities.* Des Moines: Iowa Department of Education.

Sitlington, P. L., Neubert, D. A., Begin, W., Lombard, R. C., & Leconte, P. J. (1996). *Assess for success: Handbook on transition assessment.* Reston, VA: The Council for Exceptional Children.

Sizer, T. (1991a). *No pain, no gain. Educational Leadership, 48*(8), 49–55.

Sizer, T. (1992). *Horace's school.* New York: Houghton-Mifflin.

Skrtic, T. (1988). An organizational analysis of special education reform. *Counterpoint, 8*(2), 15–19.

Skrtic, T. (1991a). *Behind special education: A critical analysis of professional knowledge and school organization.* Denver: Love.

Skrtic T. (1991b). The special education paradox: Equity as the way to excellence. *Harvard Educational Review. 61*(2), 148–206.

Smith, D. (1998). *Introduction to special education* (3rd ed.). Needham Heights, MA: Allyn & Bacon.

Smith, D., & Lukasson, R. (1992). *Introduction to special education.* Needham Heights, MA: Allyn & Bacon.

Smith, F., Lombard, R., Neubert, D., Leconte, P., Rothenbacher, C., & Sitlington, P. (1994). The position statement of the interdisciplinary council on vocational evaluation and assessment. *Journal for Vocational Special Needs Education, 17*(1), 41–42.

Smith, T., Polloway, E., Patton, J., & Dowdy, C. (1995). *Teaching children with special needs in inclusive settings.* Needham Heights, MA: Allyn & Bacon.

Smith-Davis, J. (1990). Exceptional children in tomorrow's schools. In E. Meyen (Ed.), *Exceptional children in today's schools* (pp. 101–121). Denver: Love.

Smith-Davis, J., & Smith, D. (1994). *Data concerning representation by United States racial/ethnic groups in public schools, the teaching force, higher education, and preservice teacher education, with a focus on education of students with disabilities.* Albuquerque: University of New Mexico, Alliance 2000 Project.

Spring, J. (1988). *Conflicts of interest: Politics of American education.* White Plains, NY: Longman.

Stainback, S., Stainback, W., & Forrest, M. (1989). *Educating all students in the mainstream of regular education.* Baltimore: Brookes.

Stainback, W., & Stainback, S. (1992). *Controversial issues in confronting special education: Divergent perspectives.* Needham Heights, MA: Allyn & Bacon.

The status of education. (1993, March). *Education USA,* pp. 1–2.

Stuart v. Nappi, 443 F. Supp. 1235 (D. Conn. 1978).

Sutherland, J. (1973). *A general systems philosophy for the social and behavioral sciences.* New York: Braziller.

Taylor, J. A., & Vineberg, R. (1978). Evaluation of indirect services to schools. In C. C. Attkisson, W. A. Hargreaves, & M. J. Horowitz (Eds.), *Evaluation of human service programs* (pp. 445–461). New York: Academic Press.

Taylor, S. (1988). Caught in the continuum: A critical analysis of the principle of least restrictive environment. *Journal of the Association for Persons with Severe Handicaps, 13,* 41–53.

Taylor, S. J., McCord, W., Giambetti, A., Searl, S., Mlinarcik, S., Atkinson, T., & Licher, S. (1981). *Title XIX and deinstitutionalization: The issue for the 80s.* Syracuse, NY: Syracuse University, Center on Human Policy.

Taymans, J. M. (1995). *Cases in urban teaching.* Washington DC: The George Washington University.

Taymans, J. M., Culbertson, D., Thomas, J., Duran, R., & Jacobs, J. (1991). *Challenges in developing transition services for adolescents and young adults with learning disabilities.* (Final report submitted to the U.S. Department of Education). Washington DC: The George Washington University.

Taymans, J. M., & deFur, S. H. (1994). Pre-service and in-service professional development for school-to-adult life transition. In *School-to-work transition for youths with disabilities: A Consensus Validation Conference Resource Paper.* Washington, DC: National Institute on Disability and Rehabilitation Research.

Technology-Related Assistance for Individuals with Disabilities Act of 1988, 34 CFR, Part 300, 300.6.

Thagard, P. (1992). *Contraceptual revolutions.* Princeton, NJ: Princeton University Press.

Travis, J. (1995). Alienation from learning: School effects on students. *Journal for a Just and Caring Education, 1,* 434–448.

Turnbull, A. P., Turnbull, H. R., Shank, M., & Leal, D (1995). *Exceptional lives: Special education in today's schools.* Upper Saddle River, NJ: Merrill/Prentice Hall.

Turnbull, H. R. (Ed.). (1991). *The least restrictive alternative: Principles and practice.* Washington, DC: The American Association on Mental Deficiency.

Turnbull, H. R. (1994). *Free appropriate public education: The law and children with disabilities* (4th ed.). Denver: Love.

Turnbull, H. R., & Turnbull, A. P. (1989). *Free appropriate public education: Law and implementation.* Denver: Love.

Turnbull, J., Barber, P., & Garlow, J. (1991). A policy analysis of family support for families with members with disabilities. *Kansas Law Review, 39,* 739–782.

Underwood, J., & Mead, J. *Legal aspects of special education and pupil services.* Needham Heights, MA: Allyn & Bacon.

United Nations. (1960). Declaration of the rights of the child. In *Yearbook of the United Nations 1959.* (pp. 192–199). New York: United Nations, Office of the Public Information.

United Nations. (1983). *World program of action concerning disabled persons.* New York: United Nation, Division for Economic and Social Information.

United Nations Center for Human Rights. (1988). The International Bill of Human Rights. *Human Rights* (Fact Sheet No. 2, pp. 21, 23). Geneva: United Nations.

United Nations Center for Human Rights (1990). The Rights of the Child. *Human Rights* (Fact Sheet No. 10, pp. 21, 23). Geneva, United Nations.

United Nations Educational, Scientific and Cultural Organization, & Ministry of Education, and Science, Spain. (1993). *Education for all: Status and trends.* Paris: UNESCO.

United Nations Educational, Scientific and Cultural Organization, & Ministry of Education and Science, Spain. (1994). *The Salamanca Statement and framework for action on special needs education.* Paris: UNESCO.

U.S. Congress, House of Representatives. *Conference Report to the Senate Committee on Labor and Human Resources on the reauthorization of the Individuals with Disabilities Education Act.* (1997).

U.S. Department of Education. (1991). *Combining school and work: Options in high school and two-year colleges.* Washington, DC: Office of Vocational and Adult Education.

U.S. Department of Education. (1992a). *Learning a living, Part 1.* Washington, DC: The Secretary's Commission on Achieving Necessary Skills. (Order No. 029-000-00439-1).

U.S. Department of Education. (1992b). *What work requires of schools: A SCANS report for AMERICA 2000.* Washington, DC: The Secretary's Commission on Achieving Necessary Skills. (Order No. 029-000—433-1)

U.S. Department of Education. (1993a). *Fifteenth annual report to Congress on implementation of the Individuals with Disabilities Education Act.* Washington, DC: Office of Special Education Programs.

U.S. Department of Education. (1993b). *National agenda to achieving better results for children with disabilities.* Washington, DC: Consumers Corporation.

U.S. Department of Education. (1994a). *The educational progress of Black students: Findings from the Conditions of Education,* National Center for Education Statistics (NCES No. 95-765). Pittsburgh, PA: Office of the Superintendent of Documents.

U.S. Department of Education. (1994b). *Goals 2000: Getting communities started.* Washington, DC: Office of the Secretary of Education.

U.S. Department of Education (1994c). *High school students ten years after "A Nation At Risk." Findings from the Conditions of Education* (NCES No. 95-764). Washington, DC: National Center for Education Statistics, Office of Educational Research and Improvement.

U.S. Department of Education. (1994d). *Sixteenth annual report to Congress on implementation of the Individuals with Disabilities Education Act.* Washington, DC: Office of Special Education Programs.

U.S. Department of Education. (1996a). *Eighteenth annual report to Congress on implementation of the Individuals with Disabilities Education Act.* Washington, DC: Office of Special Education Programs.

U.S. Department of Education. (1996b). *Proceedings of the Conference on Inclusion Guidelines and Accommodations for Limited English Proficient Students in the National Assessment of Educational Progress, 2*(1) (NCES No. 96-894). Washington, D.C.: National Center for Education Statistics, Office of Educational Research and Improvement.

U.S. Department of Education, National Center for Education Statistics. (1997b). Urban schools: The challenge of location and poverty. In Schools and staffing survey: 1997–98 (pp. 13-19). (NCES No. 96-864). Washington, DC: Author.

U.S. Department of Education, National Commission on Excellence in Education. (1983). *A nation at risk.* Washington, DC: U.S. Government Printing Office.

U.S. Department of Education, Office of Educational Research and Improvement. (1994). *National Assessment of Educational Progress.* Washington, DC: U.S. Government Printing Office.

U.S. Department of Education, Office of Special Education Programs (1992). *Report to Congress on implementation of the Individuals with Disabilities Education Act.* Washington, DC: Author.

U.S. Department of Education, Office of Special Education Programs. (1994). *National agenda for achieving better results for children and youth with disabilities.* Washington, DC: Cosmos Corporation.

U.S. Department of Education, Office of Special Education Programs. (1997a). *Individuals with Disabilities Education Act Amendments of 1997.* Washington, DC: National Information Center for Children and Youth with Disabilities.

U.S. Department of Education, Office of Special Education Programs. (1997b, September 19). *Memorandum to the Chief State School Officers.* Washington, DC: Author.

U.S. Department of Education, Office of Vocational and Adult Education. (1994, January). *National Assessment of Vocational Education, Interim report to Congress.* Washington, DC: Author.

U.S. Department of Health, Education and Welfare. (1976). *Final report of service integration for deinstitutionalization.* Washington, DC: U.S. Government Printing Office.

United States Department of Justice. (1995a). Challenges activities program areas—challenge activity H. *Office of Juvenile Justice and Delinquency Prevention* [On-line serial]. Available: http://www.ncjrs.org/txtfiles/chalproh.txt

United States Department of Justice. (1995b). *Juvenile offenders and victims: A focus on violence,* Washington, DC: Office of Juvenile Justice and Delinquency Prevention.

U.S. Department of Labor. (1993). *Finding one's way: Career guidance for disadvantaged youth.* Washington, DC: U.S. Government Printing Office.

U.S. Department of Labor, Commission on Skills of the American Workplace. (1990). *America's choice: High skills and low wages.* Washington, DC: U.S. Government Printing Office.

U.S. General Accounting Office. (1989). *Vocational education: Opportunity to prepare for the future* (GAO/HRD-89-55). Washington, DC: U.S. Government Printing Office.

U.S. General Accounting Office. (1993). *System-wide education reform: Federal leadership could facilitate district level efforts* (GAO/HRD-93-97). Washington, DC: U.S. Government Printing Office.

U.S. General Accounting Office. (1994a). *Multiple training programs* (GAO/HEHS-94-193). Washington, DC: U.S. Government Printing Office.

U.S. General Accounting Office. (1994b). *Transition from school: Linking education and worksite training* (GAO/HRD-91-105). Washington, DC: U.S. Government Printing Office.

U.S. General Accounting Office. (1994c). *Occupational skills standards: Experience shows industry involvement to be key* (GAO/HEHS-94-194). Washington, DC: U.S. Government Printing Office.

Van Der Doelen, F. (1998). The "give and take" of packaging of policy instruments: Optimizing legitimacy and effectiveness. In M.L. Bemelmans-Videc, R. Rist, E. Vedung (Eds.), *Carrots, sticks and sermons: Policy instruments and their evaluation.* New Brunswick, NJ: Transaction.

Violent Crime Control and Law Enforcement Act of 1994 (establishes many programs for at risk youth and high crime communities), U.S. Congress. To obtain from the U.S. Senate, write: Senate Documents.

Virginia Department of Education. (1998). *Special Education State Improvement Grant.* Richmond: Author.

Von Bertalanffy, L. (1968). *General system theory: Foundations, development, associations.* New York: Braziller.

Wagner, M. (1989a). *The school programs and school performance of secondary school students classified as learning disabled: Findings from the National Longitudinal Transition Study of Special Education Students.* Menlo Park, CA: SRI International.

Wagner, M. (1989b). *The transition experiences of youth with disabilities: A report from the National Longitudinal Transition Study.* Menlo Park, CA. SRI International.

Wagner, M. (1990). *Report from the National Longitudinal Transition Study.* San Francisco: SRI International.

Wagner, M. (1993). *Summary findings from the National Longitudinal Transition Study.* San Francisco, CA: SRA International.

Wagner, M. (1994). *Summary findings of the National Longitudinal Transition Study.* San Francisco: SRI International.

Wagner, M., & Blackorby, J. (1996). Transition from high school to work or College: How special education students fare. *The Future of Children: Special Education for Students with Disabilities, 6*(1), 103–120.

Wagner, M., Blackorby, J., Cameto, R., & Newman, L. (1994). *What makes a difference? Influences on postschool outcomes of youth with disabilities.* Menlo Park, CA: SRI International.

Wagner, M., Newman, L., D'Amico, R., Jay, E. D., Butler-Nalin, P., Marder, C., & Cox, R. (1991). *Youth with disabilities: How are they doing?* Menlo Park, Cal. SRI International.

Waldron, K. (1996). *Introduction to special education: The inclusive classroom.* Albany, NY: Delmar.

Wall, J. T., & Moriarty, J. B. (1977). The caseload profile: An alternative to weighted disclosures. *Rehabilitation Literature, 38,* 285–291.

Walther-Thomas, C., Korinek, L., McLaughlin, V., & Williams, B. (2000). *Collaboration for inclusive education: Developing successful programs.* Needham Heights, MA: Allyn & Bacon.

Wang, M., & Birch, J. (1984). Comparison of a full-time mainstreaming program and a resource room approach. *Exceptional Children, 51,* 33–40.

Ward, M., & Halloran, W. (1993). Transitions. *OSERS news in print, 6*(1), Washington, DC: U.S. Department of Education, Office of Special Education Programs.

Wehman, P. (1990). *Competitive employment: New horizons for severely disabled individuals.* Baltimore: Brookes.

Wehman, P. H., Kregel, J., Barcus, J. M., & Schalock, R. L. (1986). Vocational transition for students with developmental disabilities. In W. E. Kiernan & L. Stark (Eds.). *Pathways to employment for adults with developmental disabilities* (pp. 113–127). Baltimore: Brookes.

Wehmeyer, W., & Ward, M. (1995). The spirit of the IDEA mandate: Student involvement in transition planning. In L. West & C. Kochhar (Eds.), Emerging transition legislation for the 21st century [Special issue]. *Journal of Vocational Special Needs Education, 17*(3), 43–51.

Weil, M., Thomas, C., Callahan, J., & Carolis, G. (1992). *Service integration and coordination at the family/client level: Is case management the answer?* Washington DC: Family Impact Seminar, The AAMFT Research and Education Foundation.

West, J. (1991). *The Americans with Disabilities Act: From policy to practice.* New York: Milbank Memorial Foundation.

West, L. (1991). *Dropout prevention strategies for at-risk youth.* Gaithersburg, MD: Aspen.

West, L., Corbey, S., Boyer-Stephens, A., Jones, B., Miller, B., & Sarkees-Wircenski, M. (1991). *Integrating transition planning in the IEP process.* Reston, VA: The Council for Exceptional Children, Division on Career Development.

West, L., & Kochhar, C. (Eds). (1995). Emerging transition legislation for the 21st century [Special issue]. *Journal of Vocational Special Needs Education, 17*(3).

West, L., Taymans, J., Corbey, S., & Dodge, L. (1994). National survey of state transition coordinators. *Capital Connection, 2*(2), 4–5.

Will, M. (1983a). Transition: Linking disabled youth to a productive future. *OSERS News in Print, 1*(1), 1, 5.

Will, M. (1983b). *A shared responsibility for educating all children.* Washington, DC: U.S. Department of Education, Office of Special Education Programs.

Will, M. C. (1991). Educating children with learning problems: A shared responsibility. *Exceptional Children, 52,* 411–415.

William T. Grant Foundation. (1988). *The forgotten half: Pathways to success for America's youth and young families* (Final report). Washington, DC: Author.

Wixson, K. K., & Lipson, M. Y. (1986). Reading disability research: An interactionist perspective. *Review of Educational Research, 56,* 111–136.

Wolfensberger, W. (1983). *Reflections on the status of citizen advocacy.* Downsview, Ontario: National Institute on Mental Retardation.

Wolfensberger, W. (Ed.). (1978). *The principle of normalization in human services.* Toronto: National Institute on Mental Retardation.

Wolfensberger, W., & Thomas, S. (1983). *Program analysis of service systems' implementation of normalization goals.* Downsview, Ontario: National Institute on Mental Retardation.

The Workforce Investment Act of 1998, Publ. L. No. 105–220.

The World Bank. (1995). *Provision for children with special education needs in the Asia Region* (Technical Paper No. 261). Washington, DC: Asia Technical Department, Population and Human Resources Division.

World Health Organization. (1980). *International classification of impairments, disabilities, and handicaps: A manual of classification relating to the consequences of disease.* New York: United Nations.

Wvor v. Zitnay, No. 75-80-SD (Maine, 1978).

Ysseldyke, J., & Erickson, R. (1997, Winter). How are you doing? *RRFC LINKS.* pp. 5–7.

Ysseldyke, J., & Thurlaw, M. (1993). *Self-study guide to the development of education outcomes with educators.* Minneapolis. National Center on Educational Outcomes, University of Minnesota.

Ysseldyke, J., Thurlaw, M., and Gilman, S. (1993a). *Education outcomes and indicators for early childhood (age 3).* Minneapolis: University of Minnesota, National Center on Educational Outcomes.

Ysseldyke, J., Thurlaw, M., & Gilman, C. (1993b). *Education outcomes and indicators for early childhood (age 6).* Minneapolis: University of Minnesota, National Center on Educational Outcomes.

Ysseldyke, J., Thurlaw, M., & Gilman, C. (1993c). *Education outcomes and indicators for individuals at the post-school level.* Minneapolis: University of Minnesota, National Center on Educational Outcomes.

Ysseldyke, J., Thurlaw, M., & Gilman, C. (1993d). *Education outcomes and indicators for students completing school.* Minneapolis: University of Minnesota, National Center on Educational Outcomes.

Zionts, P. (1997). *Inclusion strategies for students with learning and behavior problems: Perspectives, experiences and best practices.* Austin, TX: Pro-Ed.

Index

Note: Letters f and t following page numbers indicate figures and tables, respectively.